D0805666

AN INTRODUCTION TO
MENNONITE
history

AN INTRODUCTION TO MENNONITE HISTORY

A Popular History of the Anabaptists
and the Mennonites

Third Edition

Cornelius J. Dyck

HERALD PRESS
Scottdale, Pennsylvania
Waterloo, Ontario

Library of Congress Cataloging in Publication Data
An introduction to Mennonite history : a popular history of the
    Anabaptists and the Mennonites / [edited by] Cornelius J. Dyck.—
    3rd ed.
        p.   cm.
    Includes bibliographical references and index.
    ISBN 9-8361-3620-9
    1. Mennonites—History. 2. Anbaptists—History. I. Dyck, Cornelius J.
    BX8115.I57   1993
    289.7'09-dc20   93-9203

PHOTO CREDITS: The majority of the photographs in this book and all
cover photos are from the Anabaptist Heritage Collection of Jan Gleysteen,
Scottdale, Pennsylvania.

Exceptions are as follows: p. 120, Alan Kreider; 239 (top), Harold Lambert;
281, 285 from Center for M. B. Studies in Canada; 289, 298 (J. Nurmi), from
Mennonite Brethren Herald; 291 (bottom, Bob La Mar), 295 (Don Isaac),
from *The Christian Leader;* 345 (Harold Weaver), 351, 376 (bottom, Harold
Weaver), 381 (both by Ken Anderson Films), from Mennonite Board of
Missions; 349 (Luke Beidler), 372 (both by Daniel Wenger), 374 (Mahlon
Hess), from Eastern Mennonite Board of Missions; 362 (top, T. B. Ediger),
364 (bottom, T. B. Ediger), 369 (bottom, John Zook), from Commission for
Overseas Missions; 376 (top), Blair Seitz; and 424, from Mennonite Central
Committee.

Maps on pages 320, 323, 326, 347, 360, 385, 395, and 421 are by Harriet Miller
(artist) and Richard Beyler (researcher), from *The Mennonite Encyclopedia,*
volume 5 (Herald Press, 1991), and used by permission.

To order or request information, please call
1-800-759-4447 (individuals) 1-800-245-7894 (trade).
Website: www.mph.org

FORWARD THROUGH THE AGES

Forward through the ages, in unbroken line,
Move the faithful spirits, at the call divine;
Gifts in diff'ring measure, hearts of one accord,
Manifold the service, one the sure reward.

Forward through the ages, in unbroken line,
Move the faithful spirits, at the call divine.

Wider grows the kingdom, reign of love and light;
For it we must labor, till our faith is sight;
Prophets have proclaimed it, martyrs testified,
Poets sung its glory, heroes for it died.

Not alone we conquer, not alone we fall;
In each loss or triumph, lose or triumph all.
Bound by God's far purpose, in one living whole,
Move we on together, to the shining goal.

—*Frederick L. Hosmer, 1908*

98352

Contents

List of Maps and Charts

Abbreviations

AIMM   Africa Inter-Mennonite Mission (Formerly CIM)
CPS   Civilian Public Service
CRR   Classics of the Radical Reformation series
EMEK   European Mennonite Evangelism Committee
HPC   Historic Peace Churches (Brethren, Friends, Mennonites)
IMO   International Mennonite Organization (Europe)
IMPC   International Mennonite Peace Committee
MCC   Mennonite Central Committee
MCSFI Mennonite Christian Service Fellowship of India
ME   *The Mennonite Encyclopedia*, 5 volumes
MEA   Mennonite Experience in America series
MEDA   Mennonite Economic Development Associates
MQR   *Mennonite Quarterly Review*
MWC   Mennonite World Conference
SEDA   Service for the Development of Agriculture (Zaire)
SMO   Swiss Mennonite Organization for Relief work

Preface

THIS IS A HISTORY of Anabaptist-Mennonite life and thought from the sixteenth century to the present, written particularly for young adults. The progress of scholarly studies of Anabaptism and the growing unity among Mennonites around the world seems to call for a book which describes in simple terms who the Mennonites are in relation to their sixteenth-century ancestors as well as in relation to each other. This book is intended to introduce students, church study groups, and others to the basic historical and doctrinal developments through nearly 500 years of Anabaptist and Mennonite efforts to be the faithful church.

The preparation of the manuscript for the original volume published in 1967, as well as for the second edition in 1981, and now this third edition, has been a project of the Institute of Mennonite Studies, which is a research agency of the Associated Mennonite Biblical Seminaries (AMBS) of Elkhart, Indiana. During the mid-1960s it seemed to the editor that Mennonites could and should write their history together. He therefore submittted a proposed outline and work schedule to some of his colleagues, together with an invitation to submit rough drafts of specific chapters to him for reworking into a homogeneous manuscript.

When final agreement had been reached the chapters of the original volume were submitted to the editor in preliminary form to allow him maximum freedom in achieving a relative uniformity of style. In the previous and present revision process the editor was granted authorization by the writers to undertake any revisions he considered necessary. The original writers were not involved in the revision process except in the reading of certain sections of the new manuscript. Appreciation is expressed here for this fraternal act of trust and cooperation.

The revisions made in the present volume include a necessary restatement of recent historiography in Anabaptist studies. Some new material has been added. The present chapters were originally drafted by the following persons: John H. Yoder, 3; John S. Oyer, 4; Walter Klaassen, 5; William E. Keeney, 6 and 7.

Major changes were made originally, then again in 1981 and now in chapters 9, by Ernst Crous, and 10, by Frank H. Epp, both now deceased. Chapters 11 and 12 are now largely the work of the editor with some indebtedness to J. C. Wenger, particularly in chapter 12. The remaining chapters are largely the work of the editor, except for part of 15, originally drafted by Frank C. Peters, and parts of 18 and 20, originally drafted by Walter Klaassen and William E. Keeney respectively. The editor, of course, continues to remain responsible for any errors of fact or interpretation or omission.

Appreciation is expressed to the following for reading a rough draft and providing counsel on the following chapters: Roelf and Juliette Kuitse on chapters 9 and 20, Walter W. Sawatsky and Peter J. Dyck on chapter 10, Richard A. Kauffman and J. Howard Kauffman on chapter 12, Abe Dueck on chapter 15, Gerald Mumaw and Daniel S. Schipani on chapter 17, and Harriett Miller for maps originally prepared for *Mennonite Encyclopedia V*. A special word of appreciation is due J. Kevin Miller for his skillful computer work, and surely to editor Michael A. King, with whom it is always a pleasure to work, and also to Paul M. Schrock of Herald Press for continuing encouragement and moral support.

Teachers, students and all users of this edition will note that a special effort has been made to locate the endnotes with each chapter for easy reference and that *Other Resources* have been listed as well for those wishing to pursue issues arising from the reading of a given chapter. In view of this method, it has not seemed necessary to add a final end bibliography which would, in any case, need to be brief and incomplete. Bibliographical volumes are available in most libraries for those seeking further information.

—*Cornelius J. Dyck*
Elkhart, Indiana

AN INTRODUCTION TO
MENNONITE history

1

The Church Before the Reformation

THE REFORMATION was a sixteenth-century movement in Europe to reform the church. Sometimes October 31, 1517, is given as the date of its beginning. On that day Martin Luther posted ninety-five statements about the church for discussion at Wittenberg University in Germany. The problems which brought about the Reformation were spiritual, social, economic, and political in origin and combined to bring about important changes in the life and thought of the Western world.

At the center of this movement was a desire to reform the church. All through the Middle Ages the voices of councils, clergy, kings, and lay people had been calling for an end to the corruption of the institutional church. By the year 1500, many proposals for reform had been heard, but there was little agreement about how these might be carried out.

All reformers, however, seemed to agree that reformation meant a return of the church to its first-century apostolic purity. In this sense the Reformation was a backward-looking movement. Somewhere along the way the church had fallen and needed to return to a virtue it had once possessed. A brief look at the church before the Reformation will help us to understand more fully the events of the early sixteenth century and their influence upon us.

Persecution: Soon after Pentecost the church which Jesus Christ had founded suffered persecution. The baptism with water and by the Spirit was often followed by the baptism of blood—martyrdom. Hated by the Jews and suspected by the Romans as "enemies of the human race" (Tacitus), suffering became part of the new life in Christ for his disciples (Heb. 11:37-38). But "the blood of martyrs is seed" (Tertullian). By mid-second century the *Epistle to Diognetus* reminded the persecutors that they were fighting a losing battle: "Do you not see that the more of them are punished, the more do others increase? These things do not seem to come from a human power; they are a mighty act of God; they are proofs of his presence."

The church had indeed spread incredibly, from Rome to Asia Minor and India, from Europe to North Africa. It included men and women of many different cultural backgrounds. Some of its leading teachers and writers, like Tertullian, Cyprian, Augustine, and others, were North Africans. Some of its major leaders, as in Montanism, which tried to restore a declining emphasis upon the Holy Spirit, were women. But the church was also adapting to its environment and being changed by it. There were still occasional persecutions in the third and early fourth centuries, but political leaders found many Christians increasingly cooperative and congenial. By A.D. 173 army life had become so attractive and Christianity so much a part of society that young Christian men began enlisting in the Roman legions. Increasingly, becoming a Christian came to be the acceptable thing to do.

Constantine: This trend toward the total acceptance of Christians into society received dramatic reinforcement when Constantine became emperor of Rome early in the fourth century. Christians were now the royal favorites while non-Christians were soon persecuted. Sunday was decreed a public day of rest and worship, combining a pagan celebration with the Christian desire to celebrate the resurrection of Jesus as Christ and to distinguish themselves from the Sabbath-keeping Jews. As emperor, Constantine wrote letters of instruction to the clergy, though he himself was not a baptized Christian, and enforced the discipline of the church with the power of the state. He called the clergy together at state expense to consider basic issues of the faith and sometimes chaired their meetings personally.

Why he did all this is not clear. He needed an appealing state religion to unify the empire, and he may himself have been attracted to the Christian faith. Whatever the reasons, from that time on church and state went hand in hand. Though they were to quarrel often in the centuries to come, no one seriously questioned this *Constantinian synthesis* for over 1,000 years. A Christian society into which all persons were born as citizens, and baptized in infancy as Christians, seemed to be the fulfillment of God's plan for humankind.

The church now faced the enormous task of making society Christian and absorbing into its life the masses of people who had become members without knowing it. This already hopeless undertaking was doomed to certain failure soon after it began by the infiltration into the Roman Empire, and therefore into the church, of thousands upon thousands of Goths, Vandals, and other tribes from the North. By A.D. 500 all of Italy was under the rule of their king Theodoric (d. 526). Much of Northern Europe was ruled by Clovis (d. 511), who became a Christian because, like Constantine, he believed that God had given him victory in battle. Externally the church prospered. Some of the old glory of the disintegrating Roman Empire came to be associated with the papacy. As spiritual successors of the apostle Peter, and political successors in Rome of the emperors who had moved to Constantinople, the bishops (popes) of Rome soon became the most powerful men in Europe.

A double standard: There were those, of course, who protested against this secularization of the church. Hermits arose to live in lonely and desert places, torturing their bodies to liberate the spirit for communion with God. Monks banded together to build monasteries in which they could escape the sin and temptation of a wicked world by giving themselves to prayer and fasting. Similarly, convents were built for nuns. But instead of leading to a general repentance, the lives of these few stimulated the developing double moral standard whereby the excess merit which these saints were assumed to possess was transferred to those who seemed unable to or did not want to live a godly life. Soon lay people were not expected to live on the same moral and spiritual level as saints or clergy.

Attempts at reform: There were many persons who tried to renew the life of the church in these centuries and with some success. Protestant preoccupation with the Reformation of the sixteenth century has tended to overlook these movements. Among the reformers was Benedict of Nursia (d. ca. 547) whose spiritual concern led to the founding of the Benedictine Order, a renewal movement which has continued to this day. His *Rule* gave guidance to the worship and work of monasteries and convents. Early in the seventh century Gregory the Great prepared new forms of worship and sent missionaries to England, which led to a return missionary program from England to the continent under Boniface in the eighth century. One of the greatest forces of reform was Charlemagne (d. 814). With the help of the Benedictine adviser, Alcuin of York (d. 804), clergy training was undertaken, preaching encouraged, church discipline initiated, mutual aid encouraged, monasteries reformed, and a vast network of schools established in much of what is now known as Western Europe.

Other reform movements came upon the scene. In the tenth century the monastic reforms of Cluny touched most of the monasteries of Europe, and in the eleventh priests were forbidden to marry in order, among other reasons, to prevent them from being a hereditary caste with inherited power and wealth. In the twelfth and thirteenth centuries the Franciscans, Dominicans, and other priestly orders arose to teach, preach, and serve among the people. And in the thirteenth century Innocent III convened a council to reform the church, while Thomas Aquinas hammered out a theological system which attempted to pull together all the traditions of the church into a meaningful faith.

Yet none of these reforms turned the church decisively in a new direction. By the ninth century, for example, almost one half of the land in Europe was under the control of the church. It became ever more difficult for the church to limit itself to spiritual affairs while leaving secular things to the authorities of the state. By the twelfth century the authority of the church was almost universal. Princes and statesmen, bankers and scholars were subject to its will. As the moon shines only by the reflected light of the sun, so the glory and power of the state is only a reflection of the greater glory and power of the church, it was said.

The Crusades: But the very "success" of the church became its undoing. In 1096 Pope Urban II launched the Crusades to recover the Holy Land from the Muslims. The sword became the missionary instrument of the church. All who went to fight were assured full remission of the penalties for their sins, and tens of thousands went in repeated waves until the thirteenth century. There was even a Children's Crusade in 1212. The wealthy, and those who could not go, were able to buy indulgences granting the same re-

For more than twelve centuries the church was the dominant power in Western Europe. **The cathedral complex of Bamberg** recalls the day when the church owned 50 percent of the land and employed 15 percent of the population.

mission of sins as those who went received, a development which was to become the direct cause of Luther's protest in 1517.

The Crusades brutalized the life of the church. In 1208 Pope Innocent III declared a Crusade in Europe itself against the Cathari of France. When a Crusader asked how he might know the heretical Cathari from true believers, he was told to kill them all, for the Lord would know his own and would sort them out at the pearly gates.

The Sacramental System: At the heart of church life was the sacramental system which had grown up around the teaching of Jesus and the early church. There were now seven sacraments: baptism, confirmation, penance, the mass (Lord's Supper), marriage, ordination, and extreme unction. In each of these the ritual itself became more important than faith and obedience. It was believed that water baptism saved the infant from hell and that in the mass the bread and wine became the actual flesh and blood of Christ (transubstantiation). Extreme unction became the last rite to prepare for death, instead of a prayer for healing, as taught in James 5:14-15. The spiritual had become almost entirely objective and mechanical. But the sacraments were necessary for the functioning of society, a tradition, ritual or structure without which things would have fallen apart, the glue which held Christendom together. Sacraments meant unity, community, life and hope.

Late medieval piety: There were, obviously, also people who had a deep personal faith. There were faithful, dedicated priests. There were skeptics who didn't care about faith, but most people relied on this sacramental system for their salvation. Plagues, wars, and fear of death made people long for a guaranteed escape from hell. Helping the sacramental routine were woodcuts on religious themes which people unable to read could hang on the wall as aids in prayer. There were also Bibles for those who could read and their number increased rapidly with Gutenberg's invention of movable type. More popular, however, were the relics of saints and pilgrimages to shrines. In 1509, Frederick the Wise, Prince of Saxony and Luther's protector, had 5,005 relic items on display. The viewing of each was said to give one hundred days' remission from purgatory. A grand total reduction of 500,000 years of purgatory could be obtained at Wittenberg.

Great trust was placed in the help of saints. They aided the sinners' access to God. None were called on more often than Mary, for whom veneration increased enormously in the twelfth and following centuries. Folk piety had to have a sinless Mary to intercede for them with the sinless Christ. Mary was considered the second Eve—as the disobedience of the first Eve had made the coming of Christ necessary, so the obedience of the second Eve (Mary) had made it possible (cf: 1 Cor. 15:22). The devil and his seduction became a dominant theme in literature, art, and conversation. He was a real competitor with God for the soul of the sinner. Some people, of course, did not care but many were afraid. Many believed that the end of the world was near, and God seemed far away; they longed for a personal rather than an institutional church relationship to God.

Preparing the Way

The Reformation did not come unannounced. The influence of the Crusades and of the Renaissance, the rise of nationalism and its clash with the international papal church, the corruption of the clergy and the church, the growing restlessness of the common people all became signs that a major storm was about to break.

Not least among these signs were men and movements which

helped to prepare the way for the spiritual renewal which the Reformation was to bring. Consciously or unconsciously the reformers of the sixteenth century stood on the shoulders of these men and movements. We think, for example, of Francis of Assisi (d. 1226), who recaptured in his own life what it means to be a disciple of Christ. We think also of Girolamo Savonarola, who was hanged in Florence in 1498, because of his powerful preaching and growing popularity. And there were many others!

Among these others were three men and two groups of men whose thought and work were particularly important in preparing the way for the Reformation. The men were Peter Waldo, John Wyclif, and John Hus; the groups of men were the mystics and the humanists. Waldo, Wyclif, and Hus were men of conviction. They were also men of action. The mystics and the humanists were not activist reformers, but their spiritual and intellectual leadership prepared the way for the men of action and created the kind of climate in the minds of the people which made reform possible.

Peter Waldo (d. ca. 1218): In 1176, the song of a minstrel stirred a deep longing in the heart of Waldo, a rich merchant of Lyon, France. Upon asking a theologian for the best way to God, he was quoted Matthew 19:21: "If you would be perfect, go, sell what you possess and give to the poor, and you will have treasure in heaven; and come, follow me." A new life began for Waldo with this verse. He sold his property, resolving to be as poor as Jesus and the apostles had been. He left enough money to support his wife and family. Then he began to study the New Testament, memorizing favorite passages, and reciting them to whoever would listen, also sharing his own interpretation of the passage.

He was soon joined by others. The group eventually became known as Waldensians, calling themselves the *Poor in Spirit*, and asked the Third Lateran Council in 1179 for permission to preach as lay persons. This was denied, but they felt compelled by God to continue nevertheless. Severe persecution followed for almost 700 years; relative freedom was granted them in Italy, where the largest groups came to live, only in 1848.

At the heart of the Waldensian reform movement was a love for the Scriptures and a desire to put into practice in their own lives what they read in them. They studied the Bible together in small group meetings. In their writings the Word of God is called

One objectionable feature of the medieval church was **the selling of indulgences** —the pardon of one's sins in return for specific sums of money. The practice was questioned by thinking Christians, but the church took no action on their concerns, since the system provided a steady source of revenue. The wild claims made by Johannes Tetzel, shown here, led to Luther's break with Rome.

. . . salvation for the soul of the poor, a tonic for the weak, food for the hungry, teaching for the true, comfort unto the chastened, the cessation of slander and the acquisition of virtue.

Even as they who are assailed by the enemy flee to a strong tower so do the assailed saints betake themselves to the Holy Scripture. There they find weapons against heresies, armor against the assaults of the devil, the assaults of the flesh, the glory of the world.[1]

Because they placed special emphasis on the New Testament and obedience to the words of Jesus recorded in Matthew 5, 6, and 7, they became known as the Sermon on the Mount people. And, because they were convinced that the Scriptures held the answer to people's problems, they traveled all over Europe two by two, preaching, witnessing, and suffering for the sake of Christ. The neglect of the Scriptures in Roman Catholicism was to them a certain sign that the church had fallen from the faith.

The Waldensians were not Protestants before the Reformation, but Christians who took the Word of God seriously. They rejected the mass, purgatory, and participation in warfare as unbiblical, but continued to practice infant baptism. They believed that all Christians, whether men or women, were called to witness to their faith by living it and preaching it. So effective were they in this lay witnessing that long before the Reformation a Roman Catholic leader wrote, "One third of Christendom if not more has attended illicit Waldensian conventicles [meetings] and is at heart Waldensian."[2] Numerous attempts to link the Anabaptists historically with the Waldensians have failed, but through them the spiritual soil was being prepared for the events of the sixteenth century.

John Wyclif (d. 1384): A man who prepared the way for Martin Luther and other reformers much more than the Waldensians was John Wyclif, the "Morning Star of the Reformation." Wyclif, a professor at Oxford University, became a reformer only in the last decade of his life. He had long believed that the church should be poor as were the apostles and that Christ had given it authority over spiritual matters only. When he met representatives of the pope at Bruges in 1374 and found that they did not agree with him, he gave up all hope of reform through councils and clergy.

On his return to England he called upon the king to reform the church, by force, if necessary. At the same time, however, he urged that the Scriptures be made available to all people as the only certain ground for reform. "Holy Scripture is the highest authority for

Peter Waldo (twelfth century), a rich merchant in Lyon, France, sold his business to finance the translation and distribution of the Scriptures. His followers became known as Waldensians. **John Hus** (ca. 1369-1415) initiated a reform in Czechoslovakia. The Council of Constance decreed his burning at the stake. The invention of printing by **Johann Gutenberg** (ca. 1400-1468) was a major factor in spreading the concerns for church renewal among the people. This prepared the way for **Martin Luther** (1483-1546) who initiated the Reformation by posting the ninety-five theses on October 31, 1517.

every Christian and the standard of faith and of all human perfection," he said.[3] Because his hope for reform rested in a recovery of the Word of God by the people, he trained persons to memorize Scripture and recite it as they traveled. These "poor preachers" or "Lollards," as they were called, were really traveling evangelists in England.

In the meantime, Wyclif's own biblical studies led him to reject the pope as necessary for the church. The church, he said, is made up of those whom God elects for salvation. He also rejected the papal interpretation of the Lord's Supper as being the actual flesh and blood of Christ, saying that the bread and wine are symbols or signs of the work and grace of Christ. He considered indulgences, which were taken to forgive sin, to be the work of the devil, and taught that priests should marry. The work of the clergy is acceptable before God, he said, only if they themselves lead holy lives; those who did not should be removed from office by the state.

Because he had powerful protectors among the nobles, who wanted him to succeed for their own personal interests, Wyclif died a natural death. Later, his bones were dug up, burned and cast on the River Swift. His books were also burned. Nevertheless, like the Waldensians, he had pioneered in the recovery of the authority of the Scriptures over the life of the church. Later, in 1572, a picture was painted in Bohemia showing Wyclif striking a spark, Hus kindling the coals with it, and Luther holding up the flaming torch. A monument to the Reformation in Worms, Germany, shows Luther surrounded by four men: Waldo, Wyclif, Hus, and Savonarola.

John Hus (d. 1415). As a professor at the university of Prague he became a major leader of the reform movement in Bohemia. In this he was guided by the writings of Wyclif, but he placed less reliance on the reforming ability of the state, and developed a deeper understanding of the nature of the church. With Wyclif he urged the study of the Scriptures by the people and argued from them without rejecting tradition as strongly as Wyclif did.

His preaching and reform proposals were extremely popular. Because he attacked the papacy, the corruption of the clergy, and other problems of the church—especially the sale of indulgences—he lost the support of the bishops and of King Wenceslas. He went into hiding with friends in the country and continued his reform writing. During this period he wrote his treatise on the church. The church, he said, is not where the pope is, but where two or three are gathered in the name of Christ. Similarly it is not the pope but the

Holy Spirit who gives unity to the church. Nor does the pope have any power to include or exclude people from heaven. This power of the keys is held by the believing church under the guidance of the Holy Spirit and consists in preaching, witnessing, counseling, church discipline, and the Lord's Supper.

Because he was accused of heresy and rejected the authority of the pope, Hus repeatedly declared his desire to defend his views before a general council of the church. When such a council convened at Constance to end the schism in the church, and he was asked to appear before it, he went. Though his friends warned him of the dangers to his life, he said:

> I confide altogether in my Saviour. I trust that he will accord me his Holy Spirit to fortify me in his truth, so that I may face with courage temptations, prison, and if necessary a cruel death.[4]

Emperor Sigismund issued a safe-conduct guarantee for him, but after his arrival in Constance he spent most of his time in prison. Instead of presenting his teachings to the council fathers, they put him on trial for his life as a heretic. Pope John 23 pressed for his condemnation. His fate was sealed. From his prison he wrote:

> It is better to die well than to live ill. One should not flinch before the sentence of death. To finish the present life in grace is to go away from pain and misery. He who fears death loses the joy of life. Above all else truth triumphs. He conquers who dies, because no adversity can hurt the one over whom iniquity holds no sway.[5]

He was given one last chance to recant, which he refused. Then they put a paper crown on his head with three demons drawn on it and the words, "We commit your soul to the devil," after which they took him outside of the city and burned him to ashes. The date was July 6, 1415.

So effectively had John Hus prepared the way for the Reformation that 105 years later Martin Luther said, "We are all Hussites without knowing it." During that 100 years, however, bloody Hussite wars devastated the land as his followers struggled for religious and political independence. A crusade was eventually launched against them. Most of them finally made their peace with Roman Catholicism, but some continued separately as the Bohemian Brethren, known today as the Moravians. One of their great early leaders was Peter Chelcicki (active 1420-60), who taught many of the principles the Anabaptists were to emphasize a century later.[6]

The Mystics: Influencing the thought and work of these reformers, and of the entire Middle Ages, were the mystics—men and women who cultivated an inner, personal religion and practiced the presence of God. The mystics sought union with God. Personal, firsthand experience was for them the final authority in matters of faith. The church with its priests, sacraments, and traditions was not rejected. All of its rites and ceremonies could, in fact, help the mystics in their spiritual pilgrimage, but they were not really necessary. God could be known best, they believed, through self-denial, contemplation, and spiritual insight. The key to the knowledge of God was love.

There were almost as many kinds of mysticism in the Middle Ages as there were mystics. In Bernard of Clairvaux (d. 1153), we find a man of orthodox Catholic theology who could lose himself completely in the love of God, yet who was also one of the most active church reformers of all time. Hugh (d. 1141) of St. Victor near Paris was much more intellectual by inclination, yet his mysticism is apparent, for example, in his description of the three levels of faith. On the lowest level Christians believe what the church teaches because the church says it is true; on the second level they believe because reason says it makes sense. On the highest level Christians believe because inner experience has taught them that what the church and reason have already said is true.

Of importance in the development of Luther's thought were the German mystics Master Eckhart (d. 1327) and John Tauler (d. 1361), as well as an anonymous book called *A German Theology.* Luther was not a mystic, but the writings of these men and the *German Theology* mirrored the longing for God which he himself felt and which drove him unrelentingly to find a gracious God. These mystics wanted to remain faithful to the church, but longed for it to be reformed, and believed this could only come about through a deeper commitment to the inner voice and work of the Spirit. Their utter abandonment to the will of God is reflected in Luther's later willingness to face any threat regardless of the personal consequences for himself.

In the Netherlands mysticism was particularly at home among the Brethren of the Common Life, the most famous of whom was possibly Thomas à Kempis (d. 1471), who is believed to have been the author of *The Imitation of Christ.* In contrast to many earlier mystics, the Brethren were serious and able students of the Bible. They tended to take its message literally and personally, as a result of which following in the footsteps of Jesus became their highest goal. This piety came to be known as the *devotio moderna* or new devotion. During the fifteenth century the Brethren established many schools which soon gained an excellent reputation for piety and learning. Both Erasmus and Luther studied under the Brethren, but neither seemed to enjoy the experience. Still, the influence of the schools was clearly evident in the later work of both.

The Humanists: Humanism was the life and spirit of the Renaissance, the fourteenth- and fifteenth-century recovery of the ancient culture of Greece and Rome. Humanism was this-worldly calling on people to shift their gaze from heaven to the earth around them. It rejected many of the irrational superstitions and customs of the age. It expressed itself in a flowering of the arts and sciences—the poetry of Dante (d. 1321) and Petrarch (d. 1374), the sculpture of Donatello (d. 1466), the architecture of Alberti (d. 1472), the painting of da Vinci (d. 1519) and Michelangelo (d. 1564), and a multitude of other creative masters. Humanism was inspired by a new spirit of freedom and inquiry.

The humanists north of the Alps generally had a stronger religious concern than those in Italy, giving themselves more to biblical studies than to classical sources. As Christian humanists they were also concerned with the problems of the church, though they did not usually participate in action programs of reform. Their tools were a pen, a critical intellect, satire, humor, and thorough scholarship. Humanist circles could be found in most of the major universities and cities; they were respected, hated, feared, and loved. In these circles and throughout Europe, no one was more respected than Desiderius Erasmus (d. 1536), the "prince of the humanists." As a young man Luther almost worshiped Erasmus, writing to him, "Where is he in whom Erasmus does not control the inner thoughts, does not teach, does not rule. . . ?" But by 1524 he called him a babbler and a skeptic and felt he was undercutting the Reformation.

Erasmus and Luther had many things in common. Both deplored the corruption of the clergy and the papacy; both emphasized the central place Scripture should have in the life of the church; both taught the importance of Christ for the believer. Nevertheless, the two men were very different. Erasmus was scholarly and polite; Luther could be vulgar and dogmatic. Luther came to be a reformer because of his personal search for faith. Erasmus had more of a detached scholar's interest in Reformation issues. There were also basic differences in understanding the faith. Luther saw salvation primarily as grace, Erasmus primarily as imitating Christ, though both stressed the importance of faith. Luther held all people to be miserable sinners, while Erasmus, together with all humanists, stressed their fundamental goodness. Luther might be described as crying, "Back to the Bible," while Erasmus might have asked, "What is the Bible?" (Bainton).

In all of this Erasmus represented the best in humanism. The Reformation would not have been possible without the humanists' recovery of the Scriptures and of biblical scholarship. Their sharp pens goaded the church to act where the actions of the reformers often caused a reaction. The humanists added spiritual depth to the church by stressing the inward and personal dimension of faith, where the reformers were often forced to quarrel over doctrine or external church issues. Yet all of the major reformers had a humanist education and were scholars in their own right. Luther wrote much more than Erasmus, but at a given point each of the reformers became deeply and personally involved in the life and problems of the church.

The Lutheran Reformation

The Lutheran Reformation centered in Wittenberg, Germany, where Martin Luther was professor of theology at the university from 1512 until his death in 1546. His road to becoming a theologian, prophet, and reformer had been a stormy one because of his own inner struggles of faith. He had learned that Christians must love God and do good works in order to be saved, but he could not love God—he was afraid of him—and he was constantly seeing himself as a sinner. All the well-meant counsel of friends did not change this. God was angry with him, he said, and would send him straight to hell if he should die.

In desperation he finally became a monk, as he later said, "against the wishes of my father, of my mother, of God, and of the devil." Yet his doubts continued, though he fasted and prayed more than other monks. His studies led him deep into the Scriptures and he became an effective and popular teacher at the university. It was while lecturing on the Book of Galatians and then Romans that the final breakthrough came for him. One day, while studying in his little tower room, he discovered a new meaning in the words of the apostle Paul in Romans 1:17, "He who through faith is righteous shall live." God is not angry with sinners; he loves them, not because of what they do for God, but because of what God does for them in Christ. They are justified by faith in Christ, not by good works. After discovering this Luther could finally say, "Now I felt myself newborn and in Paradise. All the Holy Scriptures looked different to me. . . ."

This experience of the grace of God was at the heart of Luther's movement. He now became an extremely busy man, preaching, writing, counseling, and traveling. He was summoned to Rome to be tried for heresy, but he remembered the fate of Hus and did not go. Consequently he was excommunicated and later placed under the ban of the empire, meaning that anyone could kill him as a heretic, but he was a man of the people and they loved him. He defended his faith before Emperor Charles and had to flee for safety to Wartburg castle, where he translated the Greek New Testament into German because he wanted every German, including every simple plowboy, to be able to read the Bible. Later he translated the Old Testament also. After his return to Wittenberg under the protection of Duke Frederick the Wise, he sent teachers and ministers to the churches to help the clergy. He wrote catechisms for use in the churches and many hymns, including "A Mighty Fortress Is Our God."

Opposition to Luther's work did not come only from Rome. Among his own friends were those who disagreed with him, as we saw in Erasmus. Another critic was Andreas Karlstadt (d. 1541), Luther's colleague, who has been called the father of Anabaptism.[7] He urged Luther to give more attention in his preaching to the importance of following Jesus in life, since many people took the Reformation emphasis on grace to mean that works were not important. He rejected the swearing of oaths, and instead of the sacramental interpretation of the Lord's Supper, he began to celebrate it as a memorial service of what Christ had done on the cross. He forbade others to call him doctor, saying that all are equal in the church of Christ.

Thomas Müntzer (d. 1525), a spiritualist whom we will meet in the following chapters, demanded reforms which went much further than those of Karlstadt. He had become a pastor at Luther's suggestion, and was an able speaker, but his program for social reform soon seemed revolutionary to Luther and the princes. When this brought him into conflict with them, he began holding meetings in homes. Persons from the lower classes of society felt particularly attracted to his messages about equality, freedom and anti-clericalism.

Among those attending his meetings were three men who came to be known as the Zwickau prophets. Zwickau was the name of their hometown, and the prophet role was ascribed to them because they had moved from Bible study to spiritual visions which they freely shared with others. In 1521, they went to Wittenberg to show the Lutheran reformers that they must rely more on the Holy Spirit. Some of the Wittenberg men, including Karlstadt, were impressed by them, but when Luther heard of their work he returned quickly from his hiding place in the Wartburg and sent them scurrying. Following this incident Müntzer was reported to have said that he would not trust Luther even if he had swallowed a dozen Bibles, to which Luther replied that he would not trust Müntzer either, even if he had swallowed the Holy Spirit, feathers and all.

Gradually Müntzer succeeded in gaining a large following among the peasants, who saw in him a man who could lead them against the oppression of the nobles. He organized many of them into an armed force, using a red cross and unsheathed sword as banner emblems. Soon armed uprisings were occurring as the peasants took justice into their own hands. In doing this they thought they were simply helping to fulfill the divine plan for society as they understood it from the preaching of Luther. A military showdown came on May 15, 1525, at Frankenhausen where thousands of peasants were killed by the well-armed nobles. Müntzer himself was captured, tortured, and executed several days later. These events are known as the Peasants' Revolt.

Karlstadt, the Zwickau prophets, and the Peasants' Revolt helped close Luther's mind to the Anabaptists when they appeared in 1525. He lumped together as fanatics all those who felt that his Reformation had not gone far enough. One of his favorite terms for them was *Schwärmer*, meaning a person driven by irrational impulses and emotions rather than by common sense.

The Anabaptists actually rejoiced at the work Luther had done but saw it as a halfway reformation. They did not find the Bible teaching his sacramental understanding of the Lord's Supper nor baptism as having saving power, but they were particularly disappointed in his definition of the church as being where the Word of God was preached and the sacraments rightly administered. To them the church, according to the New Testament, should consist of believers only. By their free decision they would bind them-selves to witness and to discipline as the body of Christ. While Lu-ther had brought many changes and had, above all, restored the gospel as grace, they felt that he had left unchanged the really basic problem of the church which had come when Constantine merged it with the state.

It will be noted in the following chapter that Ulrich Zwingli also relied on the state to reform the church. Because of this the Swiss Brethren were finally forced out of the church to go their own way. Their intention was not to begin a separate movement. The persons and movements which prepared the way for the Ref-ormation, therefore, also helped to prepare the way for Anabap-tism. Anabaptism cannot be understood without seeing its devel-opment in relation to these movements. The history of Anabaptism is part of the universal history of the church through the ages. The history of the Christian church begins with Christ, not in the six-teenth century!

Endnotes

1. Quoted in Leonard Verduin, *The Reformers and Their Stepchildren*. Grand Rapids, Mich.: Eerdmans, 1964, p. 143, note 1.

2. Quoted in ibid., p. 173.

3. Quoted in Matthew Spinka (ed.) *Advocates of Reform*, Vol. XIV, *The Library of Christian Classics*. Philadelphia, Pa.: Westminster Press, 1953, p. 26.

4. Quoted in Elgin S. Moyer, *Great Leaders of the Christian Church*. Chicago, Ill.: Moody Press, 1951, p. 296.

5. Quoted in Harry E. Fosdick, *Great Voices of the Reformation*. New York, N.Y.: Modern Library, 1952, p. 41.

6. Jarold Knox Zeman, *The Anabaptists and the Czech Brethren in Moravia 1526-1628*. The Hague, Neth.: Mouton, 1969.

7. Calvin Augustine Pater, *Karlstadt as the Father of the Baptist Movements*. To-ronto, Ont.: University of Toronto Press, 1984.

Other Resources: ME 5:749-753. Bruce L. Shelley, *Church History in Plain Language*. Dallas, Tex.: Word Publishing, 1982, pp. 179-273. Howard Clark Kee, Emily Albu Hanawalt, et al., *Christianity. A Social and Cultural History*. New York, N.Y.: Macmillan, 1991, pp. 145-360. Jaroslav Pelikan, *The Growth of Medieval Theology (600-1300)* Chicago, Ill.: The University of Chicago Press, 1978.

2

Anabaptist Origins

ANABAPTISM was a sixteenth-century church reform movement with
roots in religious, social, economic, and political conditions in most
of Western Europe. It drew upon the work of the Protestant Reformers, biblical studies made possible by humanism, social unrest,
exploitation of the masses, anticlericalism, and a deep unfulfilled
spiritual longing among the people, most of whom believed that
the end of the world was near. The date of the first adult (believers)
baptism was January 21, 1525, in Zurich, certainly a landmark date,
but only one of numerous earlier and later impulses that came to be
known collectively as *Anabaptism* (*ana*, meaning "again," plus "to
baptize," yielded "Anabaptist"). Yet the Zurich event gave the
movement its name because there persons who had been baptized
as infants were "re-baptized," according to their opponents.

An event of long-range significance occurred in 1927 when
Harold S. Bender of Goshen College in Indiana published the first
issue of what was called *The Mennonite Quarterly Review* (MQR),
which he edited until his death in 1962. Among his many helpers
was Robert Friedmann (d. 1970), an Austrian Jew who had been
working on Austrian Anabaptism since 1923. Friends, including
Bender, helped Friedmann escape the holocaust by coming to
Goshen in 1939. There he was baptized and joined the Mennonite
church, all the while being very productive in Anabaptist research

and writing, particularly on the Hutterian Brethren. After Bender's significant address on "The Anabaptist Vision" in 1943,[1] he, Friedmann, Guy F. Hershberger, J. C. Wenger and others, including non-Mennonite scholars, gradually became known as the "Bender School," or the "Goshen School" of Anabaptist interpretation. MQR became the primary vehicle for new and growing scholarly studies in Anabaptism.

The "Bender School" was revisionist, seeking to change the largely negative 400-year view of Anabaptism, based primarily on the polemical works of their enemies, by telling the story as they found it in the original documents of the sixteenth century. A whole new, and generally favorable, interpretation gradually emerged, aided by a growing number of Anabaptist sources volumes already being published in Germany and the Netherlands. But Bender was also a churchman and had another goal: to make Anabaptism a new third way between the polarizing influences of theological liberalism and fundamentalism (see ME 5:318-320, 518-520) among Mennonites in North America from the 1920s to the 1940s. The newly available documents, and Bender's theological values, meant eventually that a rather careful grid developed for who was in the Anabaptist family and who was not; Denck, Hut and Hubmaier, for example, were definitely out, as were many others, including the whole Münster affair. There was to be no connection whatever with the Peasants' War of 1525.

Eventually the picture of Anabaptism as exclusively a peaceful, Bible-centered group wanting only to complete the Reformation was almost too good to be true. Its effect on Mennonites was also negative ultimately because none of the heroes of the past seemed to have "feet of clay"; who could match the martyrs? In taking the sixteenth-century "vision" to have been "reality" then and now, Mennonites, while generally grateful for their heritage and the present identity it implied, still somehow found the vision uncomfortable and unattainable. They were hard pressed to build congregations "without spot or wrinkle" (Eph. 5:27), as Menno Simons had taught. Yet the "Bender School" had been successful. Aside from its continuing historical legacy it did achieve its two implicit goals, that is, Anabaptism was thoroughly rehabilitated and legitimated among scholars, and it became a major challenge (option) for twentieth-century Mennonites and others. These were major achievements.

More contextualized new interpretations began to appear in

In 1522 **Ulrich Zwingli** (1484-1531), pastor of the Grossmünster in Zurich, broke with Rome, but was immediately reinstated under the authority of Zurich's city council. **Christopher Froschauer**, pioneer printer in Zürich, took an active part in church reform. In 1529 he completed a beautifully executed German Bible, several years ahead of Luther. His Bible was long a favorite with Anabaptists.

large numbers in the 1960s and 1970s through the writings of Mennonite and non-Mennonite scholars. Partly through a new interest in social history in general, greater attention was given to social, economic, and political factors in the rise of Anabaptism also. Further studies showed the wide diversity of thought and practice among early Anabaptists, which called for new criteria about the identity of the movement. Obviously many who were outside needed to be admitted into the "family." This raised other questions about different, multiple origins and influences. One scholar made an excellent case for Karlstadt (Luther's erstwhile colleague) as the father of Anabaptism, though others had already hinted at it earlier. In view of this pluralism in what had earlier appeared to be a fairly homogeneous movement, some scholars despaired prematurely about identifying any common core of Anabaptist values. There seemed to be only an endless variety of separatist groups and individuals, making the writing of Anabaptist history, not to speak of a common or normative theology, almost impossible. All of this work was again revisionist, just as that of the "Bender School" had been earlier.

This is, of course, the nature of scholarship, to use new evidence and apply new concepts while welcoming challenge and new interpretations. Yet the new approach also represented a shift in methodology from theological and intellectual inquiry (history of ideas) to a focus on socio-political, economic and cultural history. In historical studies these approaches may be separated for particular investigations, but ultimately they cannot be separated into one-cause paradigms or explanations; all are needed for a comprehensive and accurate story, lest we end up like the fable of the five blind men trying to describe an elephant.

We turn now to a brief description of the origins of the major streams which made up the sixteenth-century Anabaptist family: the Swiss, South and Central German, Communitarian-Moravian, and Dutch Anabaptism. Common and unique causes will emerge in the process, which will be addressed more fully in the discussion about a common core of beliefs and values in chapter 8. It will become clear that Anabaptism represented much more, but not less, than an attempt to "complete the Reformation," as has sometimes been stated in the past. The nature of this volume prevents extensive footnoting, but references will be given at the end. (See ME 5:378-382.)

Zurich and the Grebel Circle

Huldreich [Ulrich] Zwingli began his ministry in Zurich, Switzerland on January 1, 1519 by preaching daily from the Gospel of Matthew. He would read a few verses in Greek or Latin, translate them into Swiss German and interpret them. He was an excellent preacher whom one listener described as holding him suspended from the ceiling by his hair. He had grown up in a loving home and used homey illustrations. The familiar line in Psalm 23 became (roughly) "He pastures me on a green Alp." In applying the gospel he taught, for example, that the taking of interest was unchristian, that Swiss mothers should not simply bear sons in order to send them as hired soldiers (mercenaries) across Europe to fight the wars of other people, and that the church must suffer: "I believe that, as the church came into existence by blood, so it can be renewed only by blood, not otherwise. Never will the world be a friend to Christ." By 1522 it became clear that no bishop of Rome could tolerate his views, so he resigned, only to be reappointed immediately by the city council, to which he now became responsible. In Germany the princes were taking similar action with Luther and his helpers.

Among Zwingli's admirers and followers was a group of young university-trained men like Conrad Grebel, Felix Mantz and others. How, these now wondered, would Zwingli move to bring about the kind of reform in the church which they had talked about with him: a change in the liturgy, abolition of the mass and of dietary laws, the removal of images, and many similar issues? It soon became clear that the customary procedure of convening a public discussion which the city council would moderate and for which Zwingli would help provide the agenda was to be the procedure. Several key debates (disputations) were held in 1523. For the one in January Zwingli had prepared 67 theses he was willing to defend. The Catholic bishop, key universities and others were invited. When the time came no one really rose to challenge Zwingli; the Catholic bishop considered the meeting illegal. The result was that the council instructed Zwingli to continue his work. People were to become familiar with the gospel.

At the second debate in October of 1523 Zwingli proposed, among other things, that the mass be replaced with the Lord's Supper, as Jesus had instituted it, but the council feared that the people were not ready for such a radical step and demurred. Zwingli agreed to wait, while still believing that the mass was wrong, but Grebel, Mantz and others in that group felt he had betrayed their cause by letting the council decide on what they saw as a nonpolitical spiritual issue. The issue must have occupied them in their Bible study group. The mass was abolished eighteen months later, but the group no longer trusted Zwingli to carry out a thorough biblical reform. They accused him of "false forbearance" (waiting till everybody would be ready to change).

Meanwhile reforms were moving faster in the village churches surrounding Zurich, though they were responsible to the city and had to pay taxes (tithes) to it, which they resented. There priests turned reforming pastors or proto-Anabaptists were not only discouraging the payment of taxes and demanding greater local autonomy in church affairs, but as a result of their Bible studies and the influence of others, were also not baptizing infants under the dynamic guidance of Wilhelm Reublin, formerly of Basel and now at Witikon near Zurich. He also took the lead among former priests by marrying in April of 1523. In Zollikon, Hans Brötli acted similarly in reform and marriage. Both men were members of the Grebel-Mantz circle.

In 1524 repeated attempts by this circle to dialogue with

Zwingli on issues of reform, especially infant baptism, proved fruitless, though Zwingli had earlier shown some openness to abolishing infant baptism. Zwingli also would have nothing to do with the Grebel circle's secret proposal to bring about reform by working to elect a "godfearing" council which would hasten reform, obviously a political strategy. Consequently Mantz wrote to the council itself asking for them to initiate dialogue on the baptism question. The council did indeed issue a call to a debate for January 17, 1525, but it was already clear that their minds were made up against any change in practice. At that non-debate the council forbade the Bible study meetings and gave Reublin and Brötli, as non-citizens, eight days to leave the Zurich area. It is believed that this action precipitated the first believers' baptism event on January 21, at which Reublin, and possibly Brötli, were baptized along with others.[2] Both then crossed the border into Germany.

Preceding the January events letters had been sent by the Grebel circle in September 1524 to Luther, Karlstadt and Thomas Müntzer.[3] Luther asked a student (Hegenwald) to reply. Karlstadt visited Zurich personally, but no reply was received from Müntzer. He may not have received it. Grebel and Mantz found funds to help Karlstadt publish six treatises on the Lord's Supper while he waited in Zurich. There was thus ample time for discussion. It seems likely that Grebel and Mantz found support in Karlstadt against infant baptism, which the latter had already abandoned in Germany in 1523, though he did not rebaptize those who had received infant baptism. He gave Mantz a treatise on baptism for publication which, however, Mantz was unable to get printed. In their September letter to Müntzer, Grebel and Mantz also commented favorably on his (Müntzer's) views of baptism and elaborated on their own understanding, including the importance of discipline according to the Rule of Christ in Matthew 18:15-18 which, it appears, they may also have learned from Karlstadt. In their letter they also admonished Müntzer about his inclination to violence when they stated that "the gospel and its adherents are not to be protected by the sword." Müntzer is usually seen as the primary ideological force behind the Peasants' War of 1525, though interpretations on his role are also changing.

Finally, returning to the exiled Reublin and Brötli, we find them at the Swiss-German border in the Klettgau-Hallau-Waldshut-Schaffhausen region where peasant unrest was rife. They were joined there by Grebel and Mantz. Müntzer had just spent eight weeks in that area. We do not know whether he had contact with them there. As in the Zurich hinterland, the peasants here too began to withhold their taxes and demanded greater autonomy, including the right to call their own clergy. They rejected images in the churches. Reublin was again baptizing many as he had done in Waldshut. Most of the adults in Hallau seem to have been baptized by him and Brötli. The role of Hubmaier at this time is not clear, except that he did help the peasants articulate their grievances which took form in the "Twelve Articles." He was clearly in close dialogue with Zwingli and the Grebel circle. Eventually military force was used ruthlessly against the peasant uprisings, a prelude to the final reckoning at Franckenhausen in May 1525, where thousands of peasants perished.

We note then, that the Grebel circle, particularly Reublin and Brötli, were deeply involved in the turbulence of events both in the Zurich area and at Hallau-Schaffhausen-Waldshut. Their activities had religious, but also economic and socio-political implications. Many people were nominally won to a kind of proto-Anabaptism, which they abandoned when events changed the balance of power. It would appear that Reublin, Brötli, Grebel, and Mantz may have had in mind trying again in the Klettgau area what they had failed to achieve in Zurich, that is, a non-separatist territorial church based on a New Testament order going beyond Zwingli. We do not know. If so, they were clearly not sectarian separatists at that time. Adult baptism itself would not have needed to be a separatist sign unless it were so labeled. Is that what the 1527 Schleitheim conference then achieved? [4]

Was the February 1527 conference at Schleitheim on the Swiss-German border the *real* beginning of Anabaptism, as Haas has suggested? Yes and no. Yes, if we think of Anabaptism as a more or less orderly and homogeneous movement for which the articles of Schleitheim provide the charter; no, if we acknowledge that Anabaptism, like most other movements, did not suddenly appear full-orbed and mature but had many growing pains, was initially amorphous, and was heterogeneous in its origins, life and thought also after Schleitheim. Yet Schleitheim, particularly the seven articles agreed upon, were and remain of landmark importance for Anabaptism and for Mennonites. We note that they soon received broad circulation, being found on many persons captured as well as in their homes. Zwingli and Calvin both felt it important to write a refutation of them. [5]

The **city of Zurich** today with the river Limmat in the foreground and Lake Zurich and the Alps to the south. The twin-spired Grossmünster is Zurich's major landmark. The **Neustadtgasse** stands immediately behind the Grossmünster. Somewhere on this street, in the house of Felix Mantz, the first Anapabtist baptisms took place.

Yet, while the full extent of the influence of Schleitheim cannot easily be measured, we do not find reliance on the articles among the other streams of Anabaptism. It seems most unlikely that what happened in Zurich and at Schleitheim did not, in some way, influence at least South German and Austrian-Moravian Anabaptism. The Schleitheim articles must have been in circulation in Strasbourg and thus accessible to Denck, Hoffman, Marpeck and others. Did they deliberately ignore them? Was there an ideological gap needing to be bridged between parallel movements? Travelers, including Anabaptist refugees, came and went in Strasbourg and would have known of them. Michael Sattler, primary author of the articles, had himself made a strong impact in the city earlier. Menno surely could have benefited from them in his apologetic writings, but does not seem to have known them. How then, if at all, were the other movements dependent upon the Swiss events? We know that the articles first appeared in Dutch in 1560.[6]

The story of Swiss origins is not complete without Michael Sattler. As prior of St. Peter's Benedictine monastery he had ample contact with the peasants and was sympathetic to their grievances. He was aware of increasing violence between the powerful and the poor, finally coming face-to-face with his own growing social and spiritual convictions. He left the monastery for an uncertain future. Today we know much more about him than we did in the 1970s. He strikes us as a powerful role model, irenic in his dialogue with the Reformers in Strasbourg, yet firm and, ultimately, separatist. His unusually cruel martyrdom on May 20, 1527, and that of his wife, Marguerita, a few days later, drew public protests from the populace, which held them in high regard, as well as from prominent non-Anabaptists.[7]

South and Central German Anabaptism

Thomas Müntzer, the revolutionary, was not an Anabaptist; and the friendly September 1524 letter of the Grebel circle to him did not make him one any more than did Luther's arguments. His influence upon them, however, as the September letter shows, was considerable—through his writings, bold preaching against political and ecclesial authorities and, not least, through personal contact with Hans Hut, as also possibly Hubmaier, and others. Thus, while Swiss Brethren influence on the origins of South German and Austrian Anabaptism cannot be denied—through Sattler and others in

Strasbourg, Hubmaier in Augsburg and other places, Marpeck, and the Grebel circle as indicated—a strong influence came from Müntzer via Hans Hut. The influence of Denck on Hut, whom he baptized in Augsburg, on Pentecost eve, 1526, is also evident in helping Hut mute his fiery apocalyptic message. Did Hut, at his baptism, give up everything Müntzer had taught him? Probably not. Whether Müntzer, in turn, really influenced Denck requires further evidence. Denck was a very independent thinker. While many of their mystically inspired statements sound parallel, it is more likely due to their common roots in the same medieval mystical tradition than to dependence.

Müntzer was deeply influenced by medieval mysticism as he found it in the *Theologia Deutsch* (German Theology), Johannes Tauler [d. 1361], and Meister Eckhart [d. 1327]. How did this influence South German Anabaptism through the work of Hut? We find an emphasis on the nearness of God in and through creation. The three mystical stages of purgation, illumination, and finally union with God meant suffering as purification, inner enlightenment through the living Word, and finally deification—becoming more Christlike through union with him and following him. The indwelling of Christ in the soul led to less emphasis on sin and greater emphasis on becoming like him through suffering. In contrast to Luther and Zwingli, sin lay more in doing than in being, thus laying a basis for discipleship. Hut's "Gospel of all Creatures" (Rom. 8:19-23) meant that the gospel was preached through all creation, including animals and birds; the Scriptures as the written Word were only one channel of divine revelation and, without the power of the Spirit within the human heart, right understanding would be impossible. Müntzer's violent apocalyptic was transformed into a more modest and non-violent missionary zeal which made Hut the most dynamic evangelist of Anabaptism. The driving force was the immanent end of the age. Here is an important influence on the origin and nature of South German Anabaptism. Hut died of asphyxiation in his cell, while unconscious from torture, in 1527.[8]

But there was also influence from Hans Denck. Denck has, perhaps, been studied more than any other Anabaptist but he still remains enigmatic. Does an overarching emphasis on the love of God make him a universalist? Since God is only good he would be against himself if he created evil; sin is negative good which people bring upon themselves. God works through his Word, the Scriptures, but especially through the unwritten inner Word, which is the divine Spirit. These thoughts again indicate the influence of medieval mysticism but were likely arrived at independently, though he knew Müntzer.

Their basic concerns were very different. Denck reacted against Luther's dogmatism, perhaps with encouragement from Karlstadt. Though Denck knew Hubmaier and Grebel from his 1525 visit to the large Anabaptist congregation in St. Gall, and may have been baptized by the former later in Augsburg, Denck's views do not reflect the Swiss movement. Was he one of the false brethren against which Schleitheim was aimed, a spiritualizer and mystic? Sattler and he would have had ample opportunity for dialogue in Strasbourg during the fall of 1526. It is hard to visualize South German Anabaptism without Denck the theologian, the evangelist, the first translater of the minor prophets from Hebrew into German, with Ludwig Haetzer and in consultation with Jewish scholars. More will be said about Denck in chapter 4.[9]

We mention only one more formative source, Pilgram Marpeck, among many others, including the Reformed pastor Martin Bucer in Strasbourg, who was persuasive and effective in winning Anabaptists away from their commitment. A well-educated and rather well-to-do city engineer in Rattenburg, Austria, Marpeck suddenly resigned and left for Strasbourg early in 1528. His story will be told in chapter 5, a man and movement arising out of South German-Austrian Anabaptism with theological emphases supplementary to, rather than a product of the Swiss legacy, rounding out Anabaptism yet being closer to Luther and Zwingli than we have seen thus far except, perhaps, in Hubmaier.

Communitarian-Moravian Anabaptism

In the preceding pages we have described Anabaptist origins by geographic regions in Switzerland, South-Central German, and now Moravian contexts, to which the Dutch movement will be added later. In terms of social and economic practice, however, communal Anabaptism was so unique, and pervasive to the present, that separate identity should be given to the Hutterian Brethren. True, their initial origin, as described in chapter 4, goes back to Nikolsburg and the Hut-Hubmaier debate of May 1527. Yet their genesis lies in a particular understanding of the meaning of community rooted in an actual situation of dire necessity, and in a unique biblical interpretation which dared to identify all others as inadequate or even unfaithful.

Most Anabaptists believed in sharing their possessions with the needy. Menno wrote numerous memorable passages affirming this practice, as did others. They practiced it, often at great cost. The socio-economic threat of Anabaptism to society at large, as the authorities saw it, can be seen in the records of interrogations, which almost always asked whether it was not true that they advocated holding everything in common, even wives. This was partly the legacy of Münster, but these questions were also asked before 1535. Unless they were communitarian Anabaptists, they always answered no, adding however, that the earth was the Lord's and that he called them to help the needy out of love.

In communitarian Anabaptism we have a different typology: a more separatist view of church-world relationships, a fairly legalistic view of congregational membership and of community, a rigid canonizing of specific passages in Acts describing early church life, a different vision of individual identity and need, a thoroughly functional view of material things, perhaps even marriage, and a more hierarchical view of authority. And yet withal a more appealing missionary witness, perhaps because of the relative security of community. It is amazing that, while members of the communities came from many different backgrounds—Tirol, Austria, Palatinate, Switzerland—the discipline rules and structure (*Ordnung*) of the community was rigorous enough to unify them more than other groups in the Anabaptist family—though initially the communitarian groups also suffered divisions. Thus a difference in degree became a real difference in kind. (No Slavic members were received into the community, as far as we know, though non-community children, including those of nobility, attended Hutterian schools.)

Thus, when we speak of Anabaptist origins, we must go beyond geography, or the nexus of converging events, or even the charisma of given leaders, though these are all important, to the existential and ideological roots of a movement. While historians tend to see the initial impetus for this movement in the real need of people moving from Nikolsburg to Austerlitz thirty miles away on a cold winter day, the *Chronicle* reports a theological point of origin in 1528: under Jakob Wiedemann's leadership,

"They took counsel together in the Lord because of their immediate need and distress and appointed servants for temporal affairs: . . . These men then spread out a cloak in front of the people, and each one laid his possessions on it with a willing heart—without being forced—so that the needy might be supported in accordance with the teaching of the prophets and apostles. Isa. 23:18; Acts 2:44-45; 4:34-35; 5:1-11." (p. 81).

For 1529 the *Chronicle* reports that: "Wolfgang Brandhuber faithfully held and taught Christian community: in the church no one should be the steward of his own purse . . . and everything should be held in common to serve God's glory. . . ." (p. 61). With community as the core value—*gelassenheit*-yieldedness, surrender, trust—a unique movement had arisen in large part out of Hut's millenial vision turned earthward in egalitarian communalism.

Dutch Anabaptism

A common saying among Dutch scholars is that the Reformation in the Lowlands was born out of the soul of its own people; a second one is that the Dutch Reformation has no "Made in Germany" stamp on it. There is truth in both statements, yet both can be challenged if the totality of influences is meant. Nevertheless, there are many events which are indeed unique to the Netherlands.

The Dutch Mennonite historian W. J. Kühler was prominent in tracing Dutch Anabaptism back through folk piety to the Brothers of the Common Life, Sacramentarianism, and Erasmus. While the Brothers of the Common Life showed many of the characteristics of later Anabaptism, and they seem in many ways to have been parallel movements, the most that can be said is that they helped to prepare the way. No direct historical link has been established. Sacramentarians, on the other hand, often did appear to be Anabaptist before 1530 as, for example, the martyr Weynken in 1527[10] and the proto-Anabaptist David Joris. Many of their Bible study conventicles later became Anabaptist core groups. Perhaps an earlier date than 1530 should be set for the beginnings of Anabaptism in the Netherlands. Yet we need more evidence for this than anticlericalism.[11]

Kühler was convinced that Erasmus was the father of Dutch Anabaptism though he never formally left the Catholic Church. This thesis has been argued cogently by Kenneth Davis, who not only sees significant Erasmian emphases in Anabaptism, coming via Denck, Hubmaier and others, but that even when the Anabaptists borrow from Luther and Zwingli, these Reformers too took it first from Erasmus. Davis concludes that "almost the whole essential and distinctive core of the Anabaptist synthesis is contained in Erasmus' pre-1525 religious writings. . . ." [12] It may be more correct to attribute common Erasmian and Anabaptist values to common roots in Dutch culture with its spiritual milieu and reformatory concerns.

Did Erasmus have "copious direct and indirect contact with many of the founding leaders of Anabaptism," as Davis states? This awaits further documentation. Still, in 1986 Cornelis Augustijn of the Free University of Amsterdam, not a Mennonite, asked the question "Is it apparent from Menno Simons' writings that he has been significantly influenced by Erasmus?" and came to the conclusion that "the basic structure of Menno Simons' theology manifestly derives from Erasmus." Augustijn identifies three areas: emphasis on the way of salvation, material-spiritual dualism, and criticism of the old church as "a religion of the material" (unspiritual).[13] We know, for example, that both Menno and Dirk Philips quote him, but infrequently and not on decisive issues. We await further studies while affirming what has been done. Meanwhile, as with the antisacramentalists, Erasmus' writings and spirit, directly and indirectly, helped prepare the soil in which Anabaptist seeds were to grow, though most early Dutch Anabaptists would not have known this.

We turn to Melchior Hoffman (chapter 6), hence Strasbourg, to look for further origins. He came to Emden from Strasbourg in 1530 with an apocalyptic message of the endtime, encouraged by the visions of Ursula and Lienhard Jost that the kingdom would come soon in Strasbourg. His message found a ready response in Emden and he baptized many. It seems probable that the poverty of the people, brought about by floods, poor harvests, near starvation, wars which interrupted shipping, and other factors gave a desperate people hope in Anabaptism as the resolution of problems in the endtime. From Emden Hoffman's emissaries scattered across the land, particularly into the Netherlands. They were known as *Melchiorites*.

Hoffman's message was one of peace, but not tranquillity or *gelassenheit*. No weapons were needed. At Christ's return he himself would arm the faithful to help him destroy the godless, yet his fiery message was incendiary. Thus while Hoffman returned to Strasbourg to await the *return*, some of his disciples were carried away into violence by their zeal. Though Dutch city authorities were frequently sympathetic to the new movement, the radicalism of Hoffman's disciples eventually led to some executions in Amsterdam and elsewhere. The end result was the debacle of Münster 1534-1535, an episode which continues to live in infamy.

It was this event which finally ended Menno's eleven-year struggle of faith under the papacy and led him to accept the call to leadership in the Anabaptist movement in 1536. He was joined in his task by Dirk Philips, a former Franciscan monk of the area in Friesland, and later by others. Menno was not the founder of the "Mennonites" even in the Netherlands. Others like David Joris and Obbe Philips would have priority. Yet in a time of severe crisis he gave wise and vigorous leadership to a movement at the point of disintegration. In 1545 Countess Anna of East Friesland allowed peaceful Anabaptists, whom she named *Menists* after Menno, to live in her territory, but not the more unpredictable Jorists and others. Eventually all were known as Menists or Mennonists, even though the Dutch themselves came to be known as *Doopsgezinde* i.e. baptism-minded, not wanting to be named after any person.

The early Menno was a Melchiorite, but not apocalyptic or violent. He called the leaders in Münster brothers, but only for a short time. While he was still a priest he had become known as an "evangelical preacher" for denouncing the violence of many reformist revolutionaries. His rejection of the Münster radicals was soon total. Yet he held to the heavenly flesh Christology of Hoffman, an ancient Valentinian doctrine believing that a sinless Christ had to be born without human contact, passing through Mary as sunlight passes through a glass of water. This led to unfounded charges of docetism, i.e., that there had not really been a *human* Jesus. Menno placed great stress on the importance of: conversion (regeneration), the congregation, discipleship and discipline (a church without "spot or wrinkle," Eph. 5:27). He believed that the faithful church would always be a suffering church.

There is evidence that by 1534 some Dutch Anabaptists had followed the trade routes East to Hamburg, Danzig (Gdansk) and Königsberg. They were widely appreciated for their skills in draining marshes and river deltas. Menno spent some weeks in the Danzig area in 1549 and Dirk Philips served there as elder for a number of years until shortly before his death in 1568. Obbe Philips, brother of Dirk, who left Anabaptism in the late 1530s disillusioned by Münster and related events, probably lived in the Rostock area, but his Confession was found in the records of the Mennonite congregation in Heubuden, West Prussia.

This, then, is a brief sketch of the changes which new sources, scholars, and methodologies have brought to our present understanding of Anabaptist origins. John S. Oyer's and Rodney J. Sawatsky's articles and bibliographies in ME 5:378-382 and 382-384 respectively, will serve as a useful supplement and guide to further studies. The theological implications of these changes will be discussed further in chapter 8.

Endnotes

1. Given as President of the American Society of Church History and reprinted many times; see *Church History* (March 1944), 13:3-24, also MQR (April 1944) 18:67-88.

2. The story of these earliest beginnings is told more fully by Fritz Blanke in *Brothers in Christ*. Scottdale, Pa.: Herald Press, 1961, and in Leland Harder, ed., *The Sources of Swiss Anabaptism*. Scottdale, Pa.: Herald Press, 1985, 68F, pp. 341-342. See also John H. Yoder in "The Turning Point in the Zwinglian Reformation," MQR (April 1958), 32:128-140.

3. Harder, *Swiss Anabaptism*, pp. 284-92. Cf: George H. Williams and Angel M. Mergal, ed., *Spiritual and Anabaptist Writers*. Philadelphia, Pa.: The Westminster Press, 1957, pp. 71-85.

4. James M. Stayer, "Reublin And Brötli: The Revolutionary Beginnings of Swiss Anabaptism," in Marc Lienhard, *The Origins and Characteristics of Anabaptism*. The Hague, Neth.: Martinus Nijhoff, 1977, pp. 83-102. Idem, *The German Peasants' War and Anabaptist Community of Goods*. Montreal, Que.: McGill-Queen's University Press, 1991, pp. 61-92. Martin Haas, "The Path of the Anabaptists into Separation. . ." in James M. Stayer and Werner O. Packull, *The Anabaptists and Thomas Müntzer*. Toronto, Ont.: Kendall/Hunt Publishing Co., 1980, pp. 72-84. Calvin A. Pater, *Karlstadt as the Father of the Baptist Movements*. Toronto, Ont.: University of Toronto Press, 1984, pp. 117-169. ME 5:481-482.

5. Harder, Zwingli's "Elenchus" in *Swiss Anabaptism*, pp. 475-505. B. W. Farley, trans./ed., John Calvin, *Treatises Against the Anabaptists and the Libertines*. Grand Rapids, Mich.: Baker Book House, 1982, pp. 36-118.

6. S. Cramer en F. Pijper, *Bibliotheca Reformatoria Neerlandica*. V. s'Gravenhage, Neth.: Martinus Nijhoff, 1909, pp. 583ff. Editor Cramer's comment that there was "not a single trait of the *Brotherly Union*, but we find it again in the later Mennonite brotherhood. . ." (p. 594) does not specify which brotherhood, i.e., Dutch or other.

7. C. Arnold Snyder, *The Life and Thought of Michael Sattler*. Scottdale, Pa.: Herald Press, 1984. Idem, "The Monastic Origins of Swiss Anabaptist Sectarianism," MQR (January 1983), 57:5-26. John H. Yoder, trans./ed., *The Legacy of Michael Sattler*. Scottdale, Pa.: Herald Press, 1973. For the articles see Yoder, pp. 34-43.

8. Gottfried Seebass, "Müntzer's Erbe. Werk, Leben und Theologie des Hans Hut," unpublished Habilitationsschrift, U. of Erlangen, 1972, 2 vols. Werner O. Packull, "Gottfried Seebass on Hans Hut: A Discussion," MQR (January 1975), 49:57-67. Werner O. Packull, *Mysticism and the Early South German-Austrian Anabaptist Movement, 1525-1531*. Scottdale, Pa.: Herald Press, 1977.

9. Clarence Bauman, translator-editor. *The Spiritual Legacy of Hans Denck*. Leiden, Neth.: E. J. Brill, 1991. E. J. Furcha, *Selected Writings of Hans Denck, 1500-1527*. Lewiston, Pa.: Edwin Mellen Press, 1989.

10. T. J. van Braght, *Martyrs Mirror*. Scottdale, Pa.: Herald Press, 1950, pp. 422-424.

11. Gary K. Waite, *David Joris and Dutch Anabaptism, 1524-1543.* Toronto, Ont.: Wilfred Laurier University Press, 1990, chapters 1 and 2.

12. W. J. Kühler, *Geschiedenis der Nederlandsche Doopsgezinden in de Zestiende Eeuw.* Haarlem, Neth.: H. D. Tjeenk Willink & Zoon, 1961, chapter 2. This view is also strongly defended by Kenneth Davis, *Anabaptism and Asceticism.* Scottdale, Pa.: Herald Press, 1974, chapter 5. See also Irvin B. Horst, *Erasmus, the Anabaptists and the Problem of Religious Unity.* Haarlem, Neth.: H. D. Tjeenk Willink en Zoon, 1967. Dale R. Schrag, "Erasmian Origins of Anabaptist Pacifism." M.A. thesis, Wichita State University, 1984.

13. Cornelis Augustijn, "Erasmus and Menno Simons," MQR (October 1986), 60:497-508.

Other Resources: J. Denny Weaver, *Becoming Anabaptist.* Scottdale, Pa.: Herald Press, 1987. Werner O. Packull, *Mysticism and the Early South German-Austrian Anabaptist Movement, 1525-1531.* Scottdale, Pa.: Herald Press, 1977. J. K. Zeman, *The Anabaptists and the Czech Brethren in Moravia, 1526-1628.* The Hague, Neth.: Mouton, 1969. Hans-Jürgen Goertz, *Profiles of Radical Reformers.* Scottdale, Pa.: Herald Press, 1982. Contact any MCC or conference office for audiovisual resources.

3

Swiss Anabaptism

THE JANUARY 21 baptismal meeting had already taken place under the threat of persecution. Members of this group were soon called Anabaptists or *re-baptizers,* though they themselves preferred simply to be called *brethren.* Instead of trying to resist the decree of the Council against them, the Brethren now made plans for sharing their newfound convictions with others. The first church meeting became a missionary meeting. Each of the persons who had to leave the city of Zurich returned to some place where they were known and could expect people to listen to them. For some, especially the tradesmen, this meant going northeast to St. Gall, northwest to Basel, or southwest to Bern—cities in which the stirrings of the Reformation had already begun to be felt. For others it meant taking refuge in rural areas where the repressive measures of the city government would be enforced less severely. Thus Hans Brötli and Wilhelm Reublin went northward into the area between Zurich, Waldshut, and Schaffhausen. Others went eastward into Appenzell, and west into the area ruled jointly by Zurich and Bern and, therefore, not rigidly controlled by either. In the course of the spring and summer of 1525, small groups of sympathizers were established in most of these places.

Hubmaier at Waldshut

Situated on the north side of the Rhine, just 32 kilometers from Zurich, was the small town of Waldshut. It was an Austrian possession under the rule of the still solidly Catholic Holy Roman Empire. Its nearness to Schaffhausen and Zurich, however, had nevertheless brought it into close contact with religious developments in the Swiss cities. This contact was increased significantly by the arrival of Balthasar Hubmaier in Waldshut in 1521. As a south German priest and doctor of theology, he was well known for his popular preaching in Regensburg and his service at the University of Ingolstadt. While he showed no special sympathies for the young Reformation movement upon his arrival, he soon became a close friend and co-worker of Ulrich Zwingli in Zurich. In 1523 his sympathies for the Reformation cause were so outspoken that Waldshut itself became suspect in the eyes of the Austrian government.

Though he considered Zwingli both his friend and colleague, Hubmaier was less his disciple and intellectually more independent than were the younger men in Zurich. Nevertheless, he shared Zwingli's low opinion of infant baptism in 1523-1524, and his concern for a pure church order according to the Bible. He was left out of the late 1524 discussions in Zurich which led to the January 18, 1525, decision of the council and the baptismal meeting of the Brethren. Hubmaier considered himself a friend of Zwingli's, but rejected infant baptism. In the spring of 1525 Wilhelm Reublin, while preaching in the countryside east of Waldshut, also began to convince some members of Hubmaier's church in the city itself, and several received baptism. In the Easter season, Hubmaier and most of the members of his congregation were baptized upon their profession of faith. This was the first time that an organized church joined the Anabaptist cause. It was a political as well as a religious act. The Austrian authorities feared, perhaps with some reason, that Hubmaier and the city government might scheme to take Waldshut out of the Empire and annex it to the Swiss cantons. In any case, no Protestants or Anabaptists could be tolerated for the sake of political unity. Waldshut, however, was prepared to defend itself with the full support of most of its citizens, including Hubmaier.

In the following months Hubmaier produced a flood of literature on baptism and the church. Most of his pamphlets, however, were not printed until later. The first and most complete statement of early Anabaptism on the question of baptism, called *On the Christian Baptism of Believers*, was written by Hubmaier. It was written after Zwingli had refused to answer his letter inviting the reformer to a debate with Hubmaier on the subject. It is an analysis of the major biblical texts on baptism as taught and practiced by John the Baptist, by Christ, and by the apostles. He concluded that everywhere baptism followed after some kind of preaching or instruction, and after faith in the message heard had been expressed. The book does not deal with rebaptism, since he considered the infant baptism of the Roman Catholic Church not to be baptism by biblical standards. The simplicity, clear biblical basis, and blunt statement of the case make this sixty-eight-page booklet a classic.[1] In later writings Hubmaier further elaborated his conviction, drawing upon statements from church fathers and theologians of all ages to support his position. He answered the anti-Anabaptist writings of Zwingli and Oeclampadius, the state-church pastor in Basel, and drafted orders of worship in keeping with his vision of the committed, disciplined church of believers.

In December Waldshut was seized by the Austrian forces of the empire and recatholicized. Hubmaier managed to escape.

The Brethren in St. Gall

In these early days the cause of the Reformation in St. Gall was carried by two laymen: the weaver Hans Kessler and the humanist scholar and medical doctor Joachim von Watt (Vadian). Both of these men, though not theologians but self-educated in matters of faith, led in Bible studies and encouraged renewal in the absence of strong clerical leadership. Late in 1523 their movement was strengthened with the coming of Lorenz Hochrütiner, who had been banished from Zurich under the charge of having removed images from churches. The Bible reading movement in St. Gall had experienced tension even before they heard of the first baptisms in Zurich. Whereas Watt and Kessler favored a slow evolution within the church, Hochrütiner and Wolfgang Uolimann were calling for a more radical rejection of all traditions, even refusing to use the church building which had been offered to them for Bible reading meetings by the city authorities.

It was, therefore, no surprise that a division took place in St. Gall when news of the Zurich baptisms reached the Bible reading group. For a time it seemed that the more aggressive Anabaptist party was the stronger. It had weighty friends, if not actual baptized members, on the city council. On Palm Sunday, 1525, Conrad

Grebel himself was present when a group of persons numbering perhaps 200 publicly paraded down to the Sitter River for a mass baptism.

The movement was even more successful in some of the rural areas surrounding St. Gall, especially in the small canton of Appenzell, where the villages had a high degree of autonomy. Here it was possible for a whole village, being both a political and ecclesiastical unit at the same time, to vote to expel a Roman Catholic priest or even a Zwinglian preacher, and replace him with an Anabaptist. There was certainly an element of political and economic interest involved in this development. Since Anabaptism was opposed to the legal requirements of the tithe and to the support of ministers through compulsory taxation, there were those who saw in the movement the possibility of economic relief and even revolutionary social changes favoring the peasants.

It was also for this reason that the developing sympathy for Anabaptism in St. Gall and Appenzell called forth such a strong reaction from the authorities. Hans Krüsi, the most active leader in the villages, was seized at night by the troops of the bishop of St. Gall and taken to Lucerne where he was executed. After a public debate the council of St. Gall imposed fines on those who persisted in their Anabaptist commitment. The effect of these measures was that those whose enthusiasm had been superficial quickly returned to the official church, while the convictions of those who were committed to the movement became stronger.

For decades the Anabaptists of St. Gall were marked by an especially radical emphasis. It is reported that some of them refused to use medicine when the city was struck by a plague in 1530. They were also stricter about Christian simplicity of dress and about nonresistance than were other Anabaptists. Still others, especially among those who had first belonged to the movement and then withdrawn from it under pressure, seemed to have justified various kinds of misbehavior on religious grounds. They either claimed that the true believer was free from the law, or that they had received special visions and revelations.

Suffering Comes to the Believers

Persecution began even before the first baptism in Zurich since the threat of banishment was announced on January 18, 1525. The first imprisonment of Anabaptists in Zurich was in early February. Prisons, fines, and sometimes torture were standard procedure for prisoners. Release from prison came only when the prisoner would promise to forsake the Anabaptist meetings. By March 1526 life imprisonment sentences were being imposed. Wherever Anabaptism became known similar measures were initiated.

The first death penalties were inflicted on Anabaptists by the governments of Roman Catholic cantons, who executed them simply as Protestants, rather than specifically as Anabaptists. Thus Hippolytus (popularly called Bolt) Eberle, who had apparently joined the fellowship at St. Gall in April or May 1525, was executed just a few weeks later in his home canton of Schwyz. He is also known as the first Protestant martyr, since the authorities of the canton did not distinguish between Protestant and Anabaptist heresy. The first death penalty at the hands of a Protestant government was the drowning of Felix Mantz in the Limmat River in Zurich on January 5, 1527. The official grounds for these extreme measures included more than the simple offense of baptizing, being baptized, or attending Anabaptist meetings. The authorities held that the real reason for execution was either sedition, i.e., a refusal to obey the government injunction not to baptize, or perjury, i.e., returning to Anabaptism after having promised to forsake it. Thus a religious offense was transformed into a civil one.

By early 1527 the Zurich Anabaptist movement was severely threatened with disintegration. Of the original leadership circle, Conrad Grebel had died of illness, and Felix Mantz had been executed. George Blaurock had escaped execution only because he was not a citizen of Zurich and was not able to return. Other leaders were widely scattered, facing dangers and problems for which they were not prepared.

Under the mounting pressure of persecution the movement was threatened on two sides from within. On the one hand was a widening circle of those who were sympathetic with the Anabaptist message, especially its criticism of the abuses in the established churches, but who excused themselves from the high cost of full and open identification with the movement. Perhaps this caution was covered with an argument to the effect that true faith is spiritual and not bound by outward forms. Thus they could give inner assent to Anabaptist teaching without suffering for it. On the other side were those whom the pressure of persecution and religious enthusiasm could push into emotional moral excesses in the name of special revelation or heroic faithfulness.

Consolidation

It was in response to these needs that a group of Anabaptist leaders met in the village of Schleitheim near the Swiss-German border later in February of 1527. We cannot tell how the meeting was called nor how long it continued. Tradition tells us that Michael Sattler was the author of its conclusions. George Blaurock could have been there. We may assume that Wilhelm Reublin, who was working closely with Sattler at that time, attended. But little as we know of the organization and attendance, it is still no exaggeration to say that it was this meeting, and the conclusions which it reached, which fixed the identity and saved the life of the young movement. The meeting provided continuity with the legacy of Grebel, Mantz, and Hubmaier, but a new dimension was also added through Sattler, who came fresh out of the Freiburg Benedictine monastery and its support of peasant grievances against church and state.

This was not a representative meeting to which delegates came each to vote for the position of their supporters, and whose conclusions represented a minimum to which they could all agree without changing their minds. The persons who gathered at Schleitheim came together in disagreement and confusion, testifying later that during the meeting the Holy Spirit had led them to agreement and common convictions.[2]

> ... we ... make known ... unto all that love God, that ... we have been united ... and (praise and glory be to God alone) uncontradicted by all the brothers, completely at peace. Herein we have sensed the unity of the Father and of our common Christ as present with us in their Spirit. For the Lord is a Lord of peace and not of quarreling. ...

The first result of this common conviction was the recognition that the Anabaptists were not in spiritual unity with those who had a different understanding of "spiritual liberty." To some at that time "spiritual liberty" meant the freedom of fanaticism and licentiousness; to others the freedom of the conformists to continue in the state church with its sacraments, civil oaths, and the bearing of arms. In their meeting at Schleitheim the Brethren rejected both of these alternatives:

> A very great offense has been introduced by some false brothers among us, whereby several have turned away from the faith, thinking

to practice and observe the freedom of the Spirit and of Christ. But such have fallen short of the truth and (to their own condemnation) are given over to the lasciviousness and license of the flesh. They have esteemed that faith and love may do and permit everything and that nothing can harm nor condemn them, since they are "believers." Note well, you members of God in Christ Jesus, that faith in the heavenly Father through Jesus Christ is not thus formed. . . .

In the first three articles substantial agreement was recorded on the meaning of church membership, being defined in their understanding of baptism, the ban, and the Lord's Supper. *Baptism* is only for those who

have been taught repentance and the amendment of life and [who] believe truly that their sins are taken away through Christ, and to all those who desire to walk in the resurrection of Jesus Christ and be buried with him in death, so that they might rise with him; to all those who with such an understanding themselves desire and request it from us. . . .

Obviously no child could "walk in the resurrection," but only those who had counted the cost. And these had to take the initiative in asking for baptism. Baptism was a covenant not only with God, but also with the congregation, whereby the members pledged to help each other in the life of obedience through admonition and, if necessary, the *ban*. The *Lord's Supper* was to be a celebration only of those who were in full unity with the fellowship: "Whoever had not been called by one God to one faith, to one baptism, to one Spirit, to one body, with all the children of God's church cannot be made one bread with them. . . ."

The fourth article defined the principle of separation from the world of darkness and unbelief in specific terms appropriate to the situation, yet at the same time must be seen as a protestantization of Sattler's monastic background.[3]

. . . everything which has not been united with our God in Christ is nothing but an abomination which we should shun. By this are meant all popish and repopish works and idolatry, gatherings, church attendance, winehouses, guarantees and commitments of unbelief, and other things of the kind, which the world regards highly, and yet which are carnal or flatly counter to the command of God. . . .

The fifth article provided for local church leadership more

clearly than had been done before stating that "the shepherd in the church of God shall be someone according to the rule of Paul, who has a completely good testimony among those outside the faith." The faithful are encouraged to support the shepherd according to his need, and if he is taken from them, either through persecution or through being sent on a missionary assignment, he is to be replaced immediately: "Should this shepherd be driven away or taken home to the Lord through the cross, that very hour another shall be ordained in his place. . . ."

In the last two articles of agreement, the relation of a Christian to the state is dealt with through a discussion of "the sword" and the swearing of oaths. Both articles are longer than the preceding five and enter into considerable detail of argument. The special emphasis given to these themes likely indicates both that they were subjects concerning which Anabaptists were especially criticized and threatened by the official churches, and that they were issues concerning which it was less clear to some of the members what position they should really take and how to explain it. The argument is based on a radical simplicity in following the words and example of Jesus, but this simplicity does not avoid the challenge of detailed argument with the opposing positions. It became clear that those who belong to Christ can neither resort to violence to achieve their objectives, nor swear by the name of God to confirm their own good intentions.

The Schleitheim meeting saved the Swiss movement in at least two ways. The very fact that this meeting took place successfully and was able to define the position against both conformists and fanatics made them an organized body able to meet their problems and survive instead of degenerating into a mere flurry of radical enthusiasm. On the level of doctrine, the positon defined here was simple, biblical, complete, and consistent enough that a simple Christian could understand it, testify to it, and suffer for it. The seven articles of agreement are sometimes referred to as the *Schleitheim Confession of Faith* (1527), the first such confession among the Anabaptists. It is closer to the intention of those who were present, however, to call it a *brotherly understanding* as they themselves did.

As indicated earlier, it is believed that Michael Sattler was the primary drafter of this statement of the faith. Soon after the meeting he was arrested together with thirteen other Anabaptists and subjected to a merciless interrogation and tortured. When he was given the possibility of hiring an attorney to aid in his defense, he de-

In response to violent opposition from without and differences of opinion from within, the Swiss Brethren met at Schleitheim in February 1527 to draw up the seven articles of the **Brotherly Agreement.**

clined on the ground that this was not a legal matter but simply a defense of the faith which he, as a believer, must always be ready and willing to do himself. Nine charges were filed against him, including the charge that "he has forsaken the (Benedictine) order and has married a wife," as well as the charge that he intended to overthrow both the Roman Catholic Church and the civil order. Sattler responded briefly to each of these charges, concluding with the statement:

> Therefore, you servants of God, in case you might not have heard or read the Word of God, would you send for the most learned (men) and for the godly books of the Bible, in whatever they might be, and let them discuss the same with us in the Word of God. If they show us with Holy Scripture that we are in error and wrong, we will gladly retract and recant, and will gladly suffer condemnation and the punishment for our offense. But if we cannot be proved in error, I hope to God that you will repent and let yourselves be taught.

The response given by the authorities was that the "hangman will debate with you," and the sentence of death was confirmed.

Because of his great popularity with the people, a heavy guard had to be set around the prison to prevent a revolt in his behalf. On the day of execution his tongue was cut out, he was torn seven times with red-hot irons, and eventually burned. We know very little about Sattler's wife, Marguerita. However, his close companion Wilhelm Reublin wrote:

> On Wednesday Michael's wife was taken out on the waters of the Neckar. She could not be turned away from her faith by any human grace or words. In great joy and strong faith she accepted and suffered death. God be praised! Thus she was drowned.

Heinrich Hug, one of the chroniclers of these events, concluded his account with the words, "It was a miserable affair, they died for their conviction." Four others were executed with the sword, but the agony of those days is seen in even sharper focus with Reublin's further report that:

> The other women and men all recanted at Rottenburg and abjured with two fingers laid in a Bible, and swore an oath: that the blood and flesh of Jesus Christ are in the sacrament of the altar, etc., further that infant baptism is right, etc. And that they hold and believe what the Roman church has established, and that it is correct. . . .

In one sense these developments were a fulfillment of the early Zwinglian vision, but they went further. While Swiss Anabaptism was forced into separation by persecution, the Schleitheim articles provided the necessary justification for separatism. The expectations of church and state could not be brought into harmony with the new identity emerging as Anabaptist.

Endnotes

1. H. Wayne Pipkin and John H. Yoder, eds. *Balthasar Hubmaier. Theologian of Anabaptism.* Scottdale, Pa.: Herald Press, 1989, pp. 95ff., 166ff., 245ff., 275ff.

2. The quotations of the Schleitheim meeting and of the trial and martyrdom are taken from the translation prepared by John H. Yoder in *The Legacy of Michael Sattler.* Scottdale, Pa.: Herald Press, 1973, pp. 34ff.

3. C. Arnold Snyder, *The Life and Thought of Michael Sattler.* Scottdale, Pa.: Herald Press, 1984. Idem, "The Monastic Origins of Swiss Anabaptist Sectarianism," MQR (January 1983), 57:5-26, in which Snyder states: "There is ample textual evidence that the explicit sectarianism of Schleitheim derives from Michael Sattler," pp. 9-10.

Other Resources: Leland Harder, ed. *The Sources of Swiss Anabaptism.* Scottdale, Pa.: Herald Press, 1985. Martin Haas, "The Path of the Anabaptists into Separation . . ." in James M. Stayer and Werner O. Packull, trans./eds. *The Anabaptists and Thomas*

Muntzer. Toronto, Ont.: Kendall/Hunt Publishing Co., 1980, pp. 72ff. Charles Nienkirchen, "Reviewing the Case for a Non-Separatist Ecclesiology in Early Swiss Anabaptism," MQR (July, 1982), 56:227ff; James M. Stayer, "The Separatist Church of the Majority," MQR (April 1983), 57:151ff. Contact any MCC or conference office for audiovisual resources.

4

Central German and Moravian Anabaptism

THE PEOPLE of Europe were excited beyond self-control by the burn-ing issues of the Reformation. Anabaptism was born in that atmo-sphere and shared in it. As Anabaptist ideas spread among the Ger-man and Dutch-speaking people of Europe, they were developed by a variety of leaders and took a variety of forms. It now becomes our task to examine several of the new leaders who arrived on the scene somewhat independent of each other and added their own characteristic touches to the work of the Spirit in the lives of the people of Europe.

One of the most kindly spirits among the early Anabaptist leaders was Hans Denck (d. 1527). Born in Bavaria and educated at the University of Ingolstadt, he applied his humanist training to the work of editing and proofreading in two of the better presses in Ba-sel. Here he became a friend of the reformer Johannes Oecolampa-dius. Here too he must have absorbed some of the fresh Reforma-tion teaching. Upon the recommendation of Oecolampadius, the city of Nürnberg engaged Denck as principal of its St. Sebald school in September of 1523.

Nürnberg witnessed its share of religious controversy during the course of the next year, and Denck became thoroughly in-

volved in it. Both Müntzer and Karlstadt, who were becoming increasingly dissatisfied with the Lutheran Reformation, visited the
city and left pamphlets to be printed there. The Lutheran pastor,
who was trying to introduce the Reformation gradually, was disturbed by the growing radicalism. At his urging the city council
asked three suspect artists to appear before it in defense of their
view of the Lord's Supper. It was believed that they denied the official church teaching of the real, physical presence of the body and
blood of Christ in the bread and wine of the Supper.

In January 1525, Denck himself was called before the city
council because he had associated with one of the artists. The town
fathers were especially eager to make certain that the schoolmaster
did not dabble in heresy. In a series of meetings through the month
Denck's views on a variety of religious topics were examined by the
council. It seemed to the town fathers that Denck was hedging in
his responses to their questions and unwilling to give a clear and
direct answer.

Their suspicions seemed confirmed in his reply to their question about the Lord's Supper. While not denying directly the physical presence of Christ in the bread and wine, he stressed that the
primary question was really whether the person who ate the bread
and drank the wine had a living, personal faith. This answer was
obviously not satisfactory and on January 21, 1525—the day on
which the first baptism occurred in Zurich—Denck was banished
from the city for life, threatened with death if he came within fifteen
kilometers of the city limits. His property was confiscated, the
council said, to provide for his wife and children.

Denck spent most of the year 1525 wandering around Germany. He may have been in Mühlhausen with Müntzer, and he visited
with the Swiss Brethren and the Zwinglians in St. Gall. In the autumn of the year he turned his steps to Augsburg where he was
able to secure a teaching position again. Within a year, however,
the Lutheran pastor there began to attack Denck's religious views
and, being unable to reach agreement with him in a series of meetings, Denck abruptly left town in November 1526. It may be that
during his Augsburg residence he had been persuaded by
Balthasar Hubmaier to accept believer's baptism.[1] There is no evidence that he formed an Anabaptist congregation, but he was undoubtedly responsible for the development of interest in Anabaptism on the part of many. A congregation was established in
Augsburg after he left. Among his Augsburg activities was also the

baptism of the most vigorous of Anabaptist missioners, Hans Hut.

From Augsburg Denck went to Strasbourg, a city with more religious freedom than existed elsewhere, and one in which a number of Anabaptists found refuge from persecution. Within a month, however, he was deeply involved in religious arguments, not only with Capito and Bucer, the leaders of the Reformation there, but also with Michael Sattler. On Christmas Day, 1526, he left Strasbourg to wander down the Rhine, discussing his faith with the local Lutheran pastors in the towns to which he came and, when possible, speaking to the people. He even tried to convert some Jews, but without success. By February 1527 he was in Worms, where he joined Ludwig Hätzer in producing a German translation of the Old Testament prophets. At the same time he was so busy discussing his faith with others that the leaders of the Reformation in both Strasbourg and Basel became alarmed. Consequently the Elector of the Palatinate took firm measures against the Worms radicals, and Denck was on the march again.

In August of 1527 he returned to Augsburg where the Anabaptist congregation had meanwhile become established. Here he met with Hans Hut, whom he had baptized earlier, and possibly several others in religious discussion. This meeting has sometimes been called the *Martyrs' Synod* because some of its members met their death soon afterward. Discussion apparently centered around the role of the "last times" in their evangelistic preaching. Hut agreed not to give undue emphasis in his missionary preaching to the early return of Christ and to the last judgment, both truths in which he believed devoutly.

In September Denck was in Ulm, and from there he went to Basel. He was weary beyond measure with the life of a fugitive, and wrote to the Basel reformer Oecolampadius begging for permission to settle in that city. Oecolampadius wanted some form of written word from Denck that would indicate a renunciation of his Anabaptist views, and Denck provided a statement of belief which Oecolampadius published two years later. But it was not a recantation, as the reformer claimed it to be. Denck had not changed his basic position. He had been pained by the sharpness of disagreement between the major reformers and the Anabaptists and wanted to find some way of reconciliation. He remained in Basel until his death from the plague in November 1527, at the age of 27.

In his faith, Denck was influenced by medieval mysticism, which he got in part from the anonymous book known as the

German Theology and in part from Müntzer and Karlstadt. Because of this he believed that God reveals himself to the inner man in a reflective, nonrational way, as well as in the Scriptures. He disliked the Lutheran reliance on Scripture alone as revelation because Scripture by itself, unaided by the Spirit, leads to a dead legalism. The reader of Scripture, Denck believed, needs the presence of that same Spirit who inspired its authors in order to understand it. It is likely that this was also the reason for his disagreement with the Swiss Brethren. Denck was deeply interested in the inner life, life in the Spirit.

Denck also was overwhelmed by the love of God. He praised this love of God so much, wrote a critic in 1525, that he seemed to suggest that all people, even the devil, would eventually be saved. Whether he actually taught that cannot be determined from his writings, but it is clear that the love of God forms the very core of his faith.[2] Yet human free will and responsibility were also central to his theology.

He was attracted to Anabaptism by the emphasis on discipleship. "No one may truly know Christ," he said, "except one follows him in life. And no one can follow him, except he first know him." He deplored the absence of moral improvement in the lives of most of the new Protestants. This emphasis on moral living led him to join Anabaptism, but he had difficulty fitting into their church life. Dogmatic statements and emphasis upon minor details of the faith distressed him. He was a man born in the wrong century. The early sixteenth century did not know religious pluralism and delighted in dogmatic statements of a most binding and restrictive sort. Because he could not bring himself to agree with statements of dogma, he was accused by the reformers, and one suspects also by the Anabaptists, of hedging, of never committing himself.

Hans Hut

Of all the traveling missioners who visited south Germany and Austria, Hans Hut stands out because of his wide influence. Hut was born and raised in southern Thuringia. For a time he served as sexton in the village of Bibra but soon developed a trade in books to supplement his income as a bookbinder. The pursuit of this trade took him to many parts of Germany, where he became familiar with Lutheran doctrine and promoted it after a fashion through the sale of tracts and pamphlets.

But Hut also encountered more radical ideas. At his trial in 1527 he said that he had first heard attacks against the practice of infant baptism from three men whom he met in his travels. Stirred by this encounter, he studied the Scriptures on the issue and even consulted the Lutheran theologians in Wittenberg, but he remained dissatisfied with the practice. Indeed, he refused to have his newborn child baptized, sometime early in 1524. When the lords of Bibra heard of this they ordered a public debate, the result of which was that those who did not accept infant baptism were told to leave the region.

This event was a turning point in Hut's life. Leaving Bibra with his wife and five children, he began a life of wandering which ended only with his capture and death in Augsburg in 1527. He appeared at the Battle of Frankenhausen which crushed the Peasants' Revolt in 1525, after having heard some of Müntzer's sermons to the peasants. Though he was captured first by the peasants and then by the lords, he was released unharmed. Müntzer perished after the battle, but his vision of the imminent return of the Lord made a profound impression on Hut. For over a year he wandered about Germany, preaching on baptism, the Lord's Supper, and the end times until he came to Augsburg in May 1526. Here Hans Denck and a friend talked to him about the earnest Christian lives of those who had received believers baptism. After lengthy persuasion, he accepted baptism himself by Denck on May 26.

For the remainder of his short life Hut went from village to town in Franconia, Bavaria, Austria, and Moravia, preaching and baptizing. On coming to a town he would begin speaking in any available place with the words, " 'Go into all the world and preach the gospel to the whole creation. He who believes and is baptized will be saved' (Mark 16:15-16) and this is the baptism—to endure anxiety, want, sorrow, and all tribulations in patience." He preached wherever people were—in isolated farmhouses, or in forests, or in homes of workers in the towns. His fiery sermons made an appeal in part because they conveyed his own burning conviction of the imminent destruction of Europe at the hands of the Turks. His critics said he was actually preaching revolution, but he denied this at his trial. He won many to the Anabaptist movement; one historian has declared that he won more converts during the two years of his ministry than all of the other Anabaptist missioners together.

Hut was captured in Augsburg in August 1527, tried, tortured severely, and killed accidentally in his cell. Some claimed that he tried to escape by lighting a fire in his cell intending to call it to the attention of the guards and grab their keys, but that he became asphyxiated in the process. His son declared that a lighted candle, placed by his pallet of straw by the guards when they brought him back unconscious from torture, ignited the straw and killed him. In any event his corpse was carried to the judgment hall and tied to the executioner's cart. The dead body was sentenced to death by burning and was recommitted to the flames on December 7.

Hut's teaching had several characteristic features which set it off from that of the Swiss Brethren. In the first place, he was much more fascinated with Christ's second coming than they were. He was reported to have specified the exact time of Christ's visitation to be during Pentecost of 1528. Some even said he had counseled his listeners to prepare to destroy the godless after a dramatic battle in which the Turks would crush the flower of European chivalry near Nürnberg. Hut denied these charges, and we have seen that Denck helped him to modify his emphasis on the second coming. Hut was not the only preacher of Reformation times who stressed the second coming of Christ. Many devout people in those days believed that God was about to bring an end to human history with a decisive divine act.

A second distinctive feature of Hut's teaching, as found especially in the writings and court testimonies of some of his followers, was his mysticism. This mysticism, which he learned from Müntzer and the late medieval mystics, is found in an emphasis on personal suffering as the mark of the Christian who truly follows Christ. The Christian must suffer as Christ suffered, and this suffering becomes, in part, a means whereby the Christian is saved from the hell of this world. It is to the last part that the Swiss Brethren would have objected. No Anabaptist denied the fact of suffering for the true Christian, but some would deny that suffering played a role in salvation. By suffering, moreover, Hut did not mean only physical suffering but also mental anguish over sin and separation from God.

A third distinctive feature was Hut's emphasis on the "Gospel of all Creatures." In it he drew both on medieval mysticism and natural theology, saying that a true knowledge of God can be had through all of his creation (Rom. 1:20), and is preached to every creature (Col. 1:23; Mark 16:15), or better, in and through all creation. Creation itself is suffering and longs for deliverance (Rom.

8:19-23). The Genesis 9:8-17 covenant account included "every living creature."[3]

A fourth feature was his baptismal theology and practice. Hut was given to "baptizing" (sealing) the elect by making a T (from the Greek *thau*, or *tav*, the last letter in the Hebrew alphabet) or the sign of the cross on the forehead of believers, usually with two moist fingers or the thumb. This was, of course, an eschatological sign opposed to the sign of the antichrist according to Revelation 13:16-17, signifying that the baptized were among the 144,00 elect. But at times he also baptized by pouring.[4]

Finally, among other features of Hut's teaching was an emphasis on the sharing of material goods. There ran through his messages, at least as his listeners interpreted them, a note of rebuke to the owner of material goods who did not share these goods with others. He made the sharing of goods more central than some Anabaptists did.

Central German Anabaptism

Anabaptism in Central Germany began with the evangelizing of Hut. Hut preached and baptized in his native Thuringia in 1526, but he also founded a congregation in the city of Königsberg. When the authorities discovered this movement, some of the new members were executed in February 1527, while others managed to escape with Hut to Austria and beyond. Some also fled north, so that despite persecution, a flourishing movement arose within three years in both Saxony and Hesse. The most vigorous Anabaptist congregation, which furnished leadership and inspiration to the movement elsewhere and thus became a center, was in the small village of Sorga, a few miles east of the town of Hersfeld. Here Melchior Rink was the acknowledged leader of the movement.

Rink appeared as chaplain at Hersfeld in 1523. He and a colleague developed an interest in Reformation teachings and began to preach them openly; their sermons included denunciations of the sins of the local Franciscan monks. The anger of the monks and the rebellious, unsettled mood of the people who heard Rink and his colleague prompted the political authorities to expel both of them. Rink found a pastorate in a village south of Eisenach, aided and probably supervised by Jacob Strauss, a Reformation leader with Lutheran inclinations. Strauss influenced Rink toward a more radical position on baptism, including rejection of infant baptism,

The St. Sebald church and school in Nürnberg. Hans Denck was rector of the school until his expulsion from the city in 1525. **Balthasar Hubmaier,** a Catholic priest from Waldshut on the Rhine, and most of his congregation joined the Anabaptists at Eastertime 1525. Hubmaier died a martyr three years later. The **Grossgeschichtsbuch** (Great Chronicle) of the Hutterians is a major source of their early history. The handwritten original is found in South Dakota.

on Christian communal attitudes on possessions, and on the prominent role of the congregation in basic church polity. In all of these matters Strauss, and Rink after him, took sharp issue with the Lutheran theologians. In effect Strauss launched Rink on his radical Reformation career. Rink was also influenced by Müntzer and like Hut followed him into the Peasants' War in 1525, emerging unscathed in body but changed in spirit. He fled south to the Palatinate, where he met Denck and came under his influence.

By 1528 Rink was back in the neighborhood of Hersfeld, attacking infant baptism in his sermons and winning converts to the Anabaptist cause. Hearing of his activities Landgrave Philip of Hesse summoned him to give an account for preaching the Anabaptist doctrines which had been expressly forbidden by law. Philip gave Rink three choices: to renounce his views publicly, to leave the area, or to submit to a theological examination by the theological faculty of the University of Marburg. Rink chose the latter and was, as expected, found guilty but refused to go into exile as commanded. Consequently he was arrested in 1529 and imprisoned for two years, released in 1531, rearrested in November of that year, and sentenced to life imprisonment. He died in prison near the scene of his labors, sometime in the 1550s.

Others succeeded Rink as leaders in Central Germany, including Fritz Erbe, whose imprisonment for sixteen years became a symbol of Lutheran persecution and Anabaptist patience in suffering. No one, however, had the same fiery zeal for believers baptism that Rink had shown and by the 1540s continuing persecution, flight, and recantations led to a sharp decline in the movement in this area.

To the west of Rink's center at Sorga, within the heart of Landgrave Philip's land, Hesse, a flourishing movement of Anabaptists was to be found in the 1530s. Able leaders came up the Rhine from the north and courageous missioners from the Moravian Anabaptists, later called Hutterian Brethren, visited them. When persecution became too severe some, in turn, went to Moravia. Philip preferred exile to execution as punishment for the Anabaptists, arguing that if all heretics were to be killed he would need to include Jews and Catholics also. Most of the contemporary princes in Germany thought him too mild in his treatment of the Anabaptists, and the movement in Hesse was indeed vigorous. When a group of them, perhaps as many as twelve, were jailed at one place for well over a year, they were able to make a hole in the wall large enough to escape, but most of them remained in order not to alarm the authorities. Those who were at large did not flee, but continued their evangelizing, one of them converting and baptizing thirty persons while he was supposedly in jail.

But for all their zeal the Hessian Anabaptist leaders, who were linked more to the Melchiorites of the north than to the Central German movement, finally gave up and returned to the state (Lutheran) church. In 1538 Philip arranged for a debate between four of them and Martin Bucer, the reformer of Strasbourg. Bucer persuaded them that the evil of separation from the one body of Christ, the true church, was greater than the evil of immoral living among the people in the state church. But they had made their point that the Christian must lead a clean and pure life. As a result the state church in Hesse decided to excommunicate those people who did not live morally as Christians should, a victory of sorts for the former Anabaptists.[5]

The Hutterian Brethren

Anabaptism spread from Switzerland and Bavaria into the Austrian lands and the Tirol. Late in 1527 Leonhard Schiemer and Hans Schlaffer were spreading Anabaptist doctrine in the Inn Valley, where Schiemer was caught and executed in January 1528. Both missioners reflected the teachings and evangelical zeal of Hans Hut, by whom they had been baptized and instructed. These men and others worked from Rattenberg and Schwaz east into Upper and Lower Austria, and south into the Tirol. Blaurock of the Zurich circle baptized converts and established congregations south of the Brenner Pass in the Tirol. It was here that he was finally caught, tortured, and burned at the stake in September 1529. Other leaders were Georg Zaunring and eventually Jacob Hutter.

The Austrian authorities were especially harsh in their treatment of Anabaptists. Within the old Austrian holdings the Archduke Ferdinand held a firmer control over his feudal noble vassals than in the Tirol. But in all regions he struck at the Anabaptists with fury, issuing mandates to the local authorities to ferret them out and destroy them. He appointed special officials to judge those who were caught. He organized bands of *Täuferjäger*, Anabaptist hunters, whose task it was to find them among the people. The punishment was always the same: death. Even the Anabaptist who recanted under torture was to be killed, though the form of execution was the more merciful beheading rather than the crueler burning.

It was this severity of persecution that gave rise to a flow of refugees into Moravia, which became a promised land for the Anabaptists in the early decades of the movement. Moravia also came under the political control of Ferdinand, in 1526, but the Moravian nobles had a tradition of relative freedom from control by their political overlord. Thus they were not inclined to look with favor on Ferdinand's attempts to bring them under his control on the Anabaptist question or on any other issue. Ferdinand was able to enforce his will in Anabaptist matters in Moravia only very slowly. For a period of several decades it became a haven in Europe for the persecuted flocks. Austrian refugees fleeing to Moravia made up a large share of the Hutterian communities after the early 1530s.

Hubmaier was one of these refugees who welcomed the relative peace and quiet of the Moravian lands. After unhappy experiences with Zwingli and the other Zurichers, including imprisonment and a forced recantation, he was only too happy to settle down in Nikolsburg (Mikulov), where we find him early in the summer of 1526. There the lords of Liechtenstein, particularly Leonhard, gave protection to the Anabaptists. Nikolsburg had a Lutheran congregation among its German-speaking people and with the aid of the refugees, Hubmaier set himself to the task of converting it into an Anabaptist one. Most of the Anabaptists tried by the courts in Tirol in 1528 and 1529 indicated that they either had been baptized in Nikolsburg or had lived there for some period of time. By late spring of 1527 Nikolsburg was a major center, numbering perhaps as many as 12,000 Anabaptists.

At this juncture the fiery evangelist Hans Hut entered the town. Even before his coming the Anabaptists had grown restless with conflicting opinions on several major issues including the Christian's attitude toward the use of force in political affairs. Hut helped to bring the issues to a head. One of the most pressing issues was that of the war tax. It was brought on by the somewhat feverish preparations of the Austrian political leaders and some Germans to fight the Turks. Should a Christian pay war tax? Hubmaier had always sided with the major reformers on letting the state regulate religious affairs. Consequently he was interested in winning political leaders to his cause in whose lands he and his fellow Anabaptists could find refuge. When those political rulers faced the necessity of levying a war tax, it naturally had to be paid. Hut was far less willing than Hubmaier to support political rulers in any shape or form, but especially when they asked for money to outfit their armies against the Turks. Hut believed that the Turks were being used by God to destroy the political rulers of Europe. Of course the Christian could not pay war tax.

There were other, more important, issues in the Nikolsburg Disputation of May 1527. Hubmaier countered Hut's view of special divine revelations in visions or dreams, as against the more sober view of revelation by Scripture alone. Hubmaier also rejected Hut's prediction on the imminent second coming of Christ; apparently Denck and others had not been successful in inducing Hut to cease promoting his views. Hubmaier did not dispute what seemed to him the fact of the return of Christ, relatively soon; he merely had a different set of calculations on the time of that return. Hut challenged Hubmaier's interpretation of the role of the Christian magistrate in the work of the Lord in view of Christ's imminent return.

Hut also joined the band, made up largely of refugees who insisted on a sharing of material goods in the form of Christian communalism. No one owned private property in their group. On the other hand, Hubmaier, with his noble backing, felt that the lords of Liechtenstein were generous enough in providing a place of refuge for the Anabaptists without going to the extreme of renouncing title to all their lands and property, if those lords became Anabaptists. Finally, Hut's special form of nonresistance to the Turkish menace (not a biblicist pacifism, it should be noted again) seemed dangerously irresponsible to Leonhard von Liechtenstein, who thereupon imprisoned him. The imprisonment, as well as various brief accounts about the Disputation, tell us that the issues on which there was disagreement were numerous, and that the Disputation itself was acrimonious. A friend helped Hut to escape. But the community remained divided into the Hubmaier group called *Schwertler* (swordbearers) and the Hut group called *Stäbler* (staff bearers).

Neither of the two opponents lived long after the debate. Hut was caught in Augsburg in August and died the following December. Hubmaier was arrested a few months after the debate, and his noble protectors proved either unwilling or unable to defend him. Archduke Ferdinand of Austria had been elected Margrave of Moravia in October 1526, after the former Margrave, Louis of Hungary, had been killed in the war against the Turks at Mohacs.

Ferdinand was as determined to repress the Anabaptists in his newly acquired territory as he was in his hereditary Austrian lands. He demanded the life of Hubmaier, against whom he had an old grudge: Hubmaier had been one of the leaders of the revolt of Waldshut against the Austrian overlord.

The circumstances of Hubmaier's capture are not known. For the last several months in 1527 until March 1528, Hubmaier was held prisoner in the Kreuzenstein castle. He went through a series of trials or examinations, with the customary use of torture. He also carried on a lengthy conversation with at least one Catholic theologian, an old university colleague and friend, Johannes Faber. Hubmaier could give more ground to a Catholic than most Anabaptists could, on such issues as the authority of the state and the place of works within salvation, but he could not reach agreement with Faber on believers baptism and on the nature of the Lord's Supper. He decided, therefore, to write an account of his faith to be presented to Ferdinand in an attempt to gain mercy from the archduke and composed his *Rechenschaft seines Glaubens,* but mercy was not granted. He was condemned to death both for heresy and for treason and burned at the stake on March 10, 1528, before a large crowd of people. The executioner rubbed gunpowder into his hair and beard as an act of mercy: it would explode and bring quick death. Elsbeth [Hügline], his wife, who faithfully urged him to keep up his courage, refused to recant and was drowned in the Danube three days later.

With the death of their spiritual leader the *Schwertler* group faded away. Not so the *Stäbler.* Before the Nikolsburg Disputation a number of them had withdrawn from fellowship with the former. Now, in the spring of 1528, Leonhard of Liechtenstein felt he could no longer tolerate religious differences among them and ordered those *Stäbler* who had broken fellowship with the others to leave. Approximately two hundred adults prepared to leave with their families. Outside of Nikolsburg they spread a coat on the ground and "each one laid his possessions on it with a willing heart—without being forced—so that the needy might be supported. . . ." [6] They travelled to Austerlitz, where the lords of Kaunitz took them in and gave them a place to live and work. Under their leaders Jacob Widemann and Philip Weber, they increased in number through the addition of refugees.

The years from 1529 to the coming of Jacob Hutter in 1533 were, nevertheless, difficult for this Austerlitz group. Frequent tensions arose because they had not yet developed a thoroughgoing Christian community of goods. The initial action at Nikolsburg had been aimed primarily at meeting an immediate need on the part of those who had nothing at all, but there had also been in it the eschatological urging spirit of Hans Hut. He had received a vision of dramatic events to occur in the spring of 1528 and some *Stäbler* consequently believed it useless to own any property after that time of Christ's return. While their first sharing had been in emergency, they soon moved to sharing both the things they consumed and the work of production as a community. Eventually they were to move to where the community owned everything and gave each person their tasks to perform as well as their food, clothing and housing.

In the fully developed idea of community of goods, from the mid-1530s to the present, the single most important factor was that of love. The Hutterian Brethren considered their expression of Christian love to be the only true one. There could be no Christian love among believers who did not renounce private possessions. Along with sharing because of need, biblical texts soon supported the practice and were, in fact, the bedrock for the initial action. Failure to join in community of goods called into question the very salvation of the individual.

In mid-seventeenth century their great leader Andreas Ehrenpreis wrote: "If Christian love to the neighbor cannot achieve as much as community in things temporal, in assistance and counsel, then the blood of Christ does not cleanse a person from sin." [7] The Hutterian communities also used a reference from the second century *Didache* about the Lord's Supper: just as a grain of wheat and a single grape lose their own identities and are crushed to form the loaf of bread and the wine, so also each member must be completely absorbed as a part of the larger unity of the community. This conviction cut at natural human selfishness and demanded of each member a yieldedness of self, a surrender, which they called *Gelassenheit*. No true discipleship, no true following after Christ, was possible without it.

The problems which had arisen from a lack of experience in communal living were eventually solved under the vigorous leadership of Jacob Hutter. Hutter, which means hat-maker, came from the Tirol in 1529 to investigate the Moravian lands as a possible place of refuge for Anabaptists in Tirol. Hutter himself returned to the Tirol to continue his evangelical work, but was appealed to by the Brethren in Moravia on several occasions to settle differences of opinion among them. Problems arose between the original Auster-litz group and those who had moved to Auspitz. Continued friction among some leaders and mismanagement of the resources of the community compelled him to remain for two years. By 1535 affairs were in order through his vigorous leadership, but several of the former leaders, dissatisfied with his decisions and probably jealous of his popularity with the majority of the members, left Auspitz for other regions.

In that year all the Anabaptists in Moravia faced renewed per-secution under the prodding of Archduke Ferdinand of Austria. The communities centering at Auspitz, which had grown larger through the addition of countless refugees from the Tirol and else-where, were broken up; their inhabitants were reduced to wander-ing about under the open skies, and finally to settling in smaller groups on those estates whose lords were willing to wink at Fer-dinand's commands. But in the meantime it seems that the brother-hood urged Hutter to leave them because the civil authorities placed such a high priority on the capture of this leader. He re-turned to the Tirol in the hope that persecution would have de-clined there but within a few months he and his wife were sur-prised at night in the home of a friend. Tried in December, he was publicly burned at the stake on February 25, 1536. The measure of his influence on the Brethren in Moravia is evidenced by their re-ferring to themselves henceforth as the *Hutterische Brüder*, from which we derive the English name Hutterian Brethren. The name and fate of his wife is not known.

The "Golden Period"

After Hutter's departure the Brethren were led by a succession of very able men, including Hans Amon (d. 1542), Peter Rideman (d. 1556), Peter Walpot (d. 1578), Klaus Braidl (d. 1611) and An-dreas Ehrenpreis (d. 1662). The communities thrived, for precisely when the Anabaptists elsewhere in Europe faced fresh and vigor-ous efforts of the Catholic Counter Reformation, efforts aimed at complete suppression, the Brethren in Moravia experienced a re-markable degree of freedom. From approximately 1555 to 1595 the Brethren flourished; they referred to a part of this period as their "Golden Period." [8] They sent out a succession of missioners to many parts of Europe; most of these paid for their activities with their lives, but they did so with the courage that was in itself a most attractive feature of Anabaptism, helping to win converts. The Brethren added to their number, through converts and through an almost constant stream of refugees from other parts of Europe. New colonies were founded, both in Moravia and beyond the eastern borders into Slovakia, then a part of Hungary. Perhaps they had as many as one hundred communities, totaling from 20,000 to 30,000 members.

This was also a period of vigorous literary activity. Braitmichel began the *GeschichtBuch* (Chronicle) which his successors carried on to 1665.[9] The Brethren were careful to keep records of letters to and from the brotherhood and of tracts written by and against them. Their organizational skills, developed to the highest degree by the demands of the community life which they practiced, were apparent in the fact that they could organize original materials into a historical account far in advance of their own times in terms of the method used.

What was the organizational pattern of their colonies? The entire brotherhood was under the direction of one bishop *(Vorsteher)*. Each colony *(Bruderhof)* had one or more preachers *(Diener des Wrotes)* and several men who managed the economic affairs, including the farming *(Diener der Notdurft)*. Each colony consisted of a series of whitewashed houses grouped around a central courtyard. Here the members, numbering usually several hundred, lived and performed their various tasks, bound less by family ties than by ties of the entire colony. The continuous performance of the same kinds of tasks by the members developed in them an efficiency of operation that made their colonies so economically successful that neighboring peasants complained of unfair competition. The *Chronicle* itself reports:

> Think of the ingenious works of a clock, where one piece helps another to make it go, so that it serves its purpose. Or think of the bees, those useful little insects working together in their hive . . . until their noble work of making sweet honey is done, not only for their own needs but enough to share with man.[10]

Their very efficiency led to tales among the neighboring outsiders about their enormous wealth. Later monetary fines imposed on them by the civil authorities indicate that they were wealthy, but persecution and the rigor of their self-imposed discipline kept them from an economic and spiritual laxity which such comparative wealth often produces.

In the course of time the Brethren wrote a large number of rules and regulations, governing how they lived together and how they practiced certain crafts. The most famous of these was formulated in 1651 during the rule of Andreas Ehrenpreis; this *Gemeinde-Ordnungen* is still in use today. The Brethren excelled in the exercise of certain crafts: the making of ceramics, cutlery, carriages, certain kinds of beds, and clocks. Medicinal skills were developed to such an extent that Hutterian physicians and surgeons were sometimes called to the courts of nobles to practice their arts. Any income which a visiting brother gained from his outside employment was to be turned over to the community. Even the occasional coin found on the roadside was to go into this treasury.

Family life was not emphasized in the colony. Children left their parents for the communal nursery-kindergarten at the age of two or three. Here they were under the care of women attendants and teachers. They were taught proper cleanliness, how to pray, and how to conduct themselves. From the kindergarten they passed to the elementary school, arranged in what we could call a boarding-school fashion. Children from outside the colony, including some from the families of nobles, were accepted and trained in the Hutterian elementary schools. The quality of the education was high, as evidenced by the later writings of the schools' graduates. Penmanship and spelling were excellent, and knowledge of the Bible together with certain elements of logic used in debate was very high.

By the time young adults reached their early twenties, they became candidates for baptism. The ceremony itself was performed after they had undergone a period of instruction; it was based on the candidate's solemn promise to be faithful to God and to the brotherhood. The young people also married while in their early twenties. Romance was not the basis for choice of marriage partners. The elders brought together all the unmarried people of both sexes and suggested two or three possible males to each girl, one of whom she had to choose. The wedding ceremony followed the assembly by a few days, allowing no time for courtship. Marriage was viewed as one of several human relations which God had commanded humans to enter. The Christian did so, as the Hutterians had it, reluctantly and with no thought for their own pleasure. Marriage was entered into because the Lord had commanded his children to marry in order to multiply.

Extermination

The relative peace of the "Golden Period" came to an end late in the 1590s. It was inevitable that persecution would break out against people whom most Europeans thought of as heretical. Cardinal Franz von Dietrichstein led the renewed persecution while, at the same time, keeping Balthasar Goller, a Hutterian physician, in his employ until the latter's death in 1619. A campaign of vilification was pressed against them by the Austrian government. In this campaign they were aided by two priests who knew them well and by two former Hutterians who were urged to show their orthodoxy by denouncing their former brethren. The wealth of the communities came under frequent attack, and financial demands for help against the Turks were pressed upon them. In 1605 the Turks plundered the colonies and carried off not only material goods but also women and children. One Hutterian wandered in Turkish lands for three years trying to locate and ransom some of his fellow believers, but he had little success and died in the attempt. The events of the Turkish War from 1593 to 1606, and the persecution of their own Austrian government shook these Moravian communities to the core.

The Thirty Years' War (1618-48) was another calamity which struck them. With the Roman Catholic forces victorious in the early part of the war, pressure against the Brethren became even more severe. In 1622 they were forced to retreat to their colonies in Slovakia, then under the rule of Hungary, with the loss of their land, buildings, and most of their possessions. With these migrations and the loss of spiritual leadership much of the earlier life went out of them. But in this hour of need another leader of exceptional ability arose to guide them: Andreas Ehrenpreis, who ruled as bishop from 1639 to his death in 1662. Ehrenpreis' greatest contributions were a fresh ordering of the organizational pattern and the direction of a spiritual renewal among them. During this period also began the practice of recording sermons that were preached which, together with the *Gemeinde-Ordnungen* of 1651, are much used today by the Hutterians in Canada and the United States.

After the death of Ehrenpreis a new decline set in. Late in the seventeenth century they abandoned their earlier form of communal living in favor of forms which gave a larger role to private property and initiative. They appealed to the Dutch Mennonites for financial help on several occasions and apparently received some. The internal decay and loss of discipline were too great, however, and in the eighteenth century most of them surrendered to the pressure of the Jesuits coupled with the threat of force by the Austrian government. One of their colonies, far to the southeast in Transylvania, revived in spirit and in numbers by Lutherans who accepted the Hutterian faith in the 1750s, decided to migrate eastward into Ukraine in 1767. A few families from Slovakia followed them in 1782-83 under the leadership of Jacob Walter, just a few years before Mennonites from Prussia began to settle there. The remaining colonies in the old regions turned Roman Catholic.

Despite the internal decay among the Brethren, the Jesuits did not have an easy time converting them. Many tactics were used to this end. They sent the spiritual leaders among the males to monasteries, where most of them finally gave in or died. Catholic services were held in the colonies, and the remaining brothers and sisters were forced to attend. Children were taken from the colonies and brought up by dedicated Catholics. For a time in the 1750s and 1760s the Hutterians became nominal Catholics, but met secretly to practice their old faith. By the late eighteenth century it appears that their resistance was completely overcome. They were given the nickname *Habaner* by the peasants, and their descendants still occupied some of the old Slovakian colonies until World War II. But the distinctive faith and practice was lost in these regions; it was carried to Ukraine, and from there again to Canada and the United States in the 1870s.

Endnotes

1. There is no certain evidence that Hubmaier baptized Denck, but it is assumed the latter would not have baptized Hans Hut on Pentecost eve, 1526, if he had not himself first been baptized. This is of significance for the influence of Swiss Anabaptism on the South German movement. But Denck had also spent time in St. Gall earlier in 1525 and would have known Anabaptism from there. For the thesis against Denck's baptism in Augsburg, and against Swiss influence in South Germany, see Werner O. Packull, "Denck's Alleged Baptism By Hubmaier," MQR (October 1973), 47:327-338.

2. William Klassen, "Was Hans Denck a Universalist?" MQR (April 1965), 39:152-154. See also Clarence Bauman, *The Spiritual Legacy of Hans Denck*. Leiden, Neth.: E. J. Brill, 1991, especially pp. 7-47.

3. Gordon Rupp, *Patterns of Reformation*. Philadelphia, Pa.: Fortress Press, 1969, 325-399.

4. Werner O. Packull, "The Sign of Thau . . ." MQR (October 1987), 61:363-374.

5. For a transcript of a debate see Franklin H. Littell, ed. *Reformation Studies*. Richmond, Va.: John Knox Press, 1962, pp. 145-167.

6. *The Chronicle of the Hutterian Brethren*. Volume I. Rifton, N.Y.: Plough Publishing House, 1987, p. 81.

7. Andreas Ehrenpreis, *Ein Sendbrief* . . . 1652. Scottdale, Pa.: Mennonite Publishing House, 1920, p. 49.

8. Leonard Gross, *The Golden Years of the Hutterites*. Scottdale, Pa.: Herald Press, 1980. ME 5:406-409.

9. *Chronicle*, 1987.

10. Ibid., p. 406.

Other Resources: Werner O. Packull, *Mysticism and the Early South German-Austrian Anabaptist Movement 1525-1531*. Scottdale, Pa.: Herald Press, 1977. Robert Friedmann, *Hutterite Studies*. Goshen, Ind.: Mennonite Historical Society, 1961. Merrill Mow, *Torches Rekindled. The Bruderhof's Struggle for Renewal*. Rifton, N.Y.: Plough Publishing House, 1989. John A. Hostetler, *Hutterite Society*. Baltimore, Md.: Johns Hopkins University Press, 1974. James M. Stayer, *The German Peasants' War and Anabaptist Community of Goods*. Montreal, Que.: McGill-Queen's University Press, 1991, especially pp. 139-159. Wes Harrison, "The Role of Women in Anabaptist Thought and Practice: The Hutterite Experience of the Sixteenth and Seventeenth Centuries," *Sixteenth Century Journal*. (Spring, 1992), 23:49-69. Contact any MCC or conference office for audiovisual resources.

5

South German Anabaptism

THE RECORDS of the ancient imperial city of Strasbourg on the Rhine reveal that on September 19, 1528, an Austrian civil engineer by the name of Pilgram Marpeck became a citizen of that city. He had come to Strasbourg because his life was in danger in his ancestral home of Rattenberg, located in the beautiful valley of the Inn River in Austria. The events of his life leading up to September 1528 can be reconstructed from the sixteenth-century records of Rattenberg and neighboring cities, as well as from some comments Marpeck himself made several years later.

The date of his birth is not known, and the only fragment of information we have about his early life is that, as he himself tells us, he was raised by God-fearing parents in the Roman Catholic faith. To judge from his later social prominence and technical ability he must have enjoyed a good education, most likely in the Rattenberg Latin School. In the year 1520 he became a member of the miners' guild of Rattenberg and was occupied with transporting copper ore from the mines of the city of Kitzbühel, some miles to the east of Rattenberg. Several years later his name appears on the roster of the city council of Rattenberg. As a trusted civic official he was appointed to the post of mining magistrate. This involved legal jurisdiction over the extensive mining operations in the lower Inn Valley. His salary was 65 pounds with a three-pound allowance for the proper dress on official occasions.

Marpeck was moderately wealthy. He was able to make a large loan to the city in 1525, and is known to have owned several houses. He and his wife undertook to pay for the education of three orphan children, which reflects his wealth as well as his sense of social responsibility. Because of his wealth and social standing Marpeck moved freely in the circles of the nobility. His lifelong friendship with Countess Helene von Freyberg, whose castle was near Kitzbühel, reflected this.

Life apparently flowed along pleasantly for the Marpecks for several years after 1525. Pilgram was a member of the inner council of the city, business was thriving, and it appeared that the Marpeck tradition of social standing and responsibility would continue. But it was not to be. The next entry in the Rattenberg records announces that Pilgram Marpeck had been dismissed from his office as mining magistrate but without stating a reason. It was most likely because, as a public official, he refused to aid in the detection and capture of Anabaptists. The date is January 28, 1528, two weeks after Leonhard Schiemer had been executed! Sometime during the next eight months he left his wealth, home, and station, never to return. His property, valued at 3,500 guilders, was confiscated by the city.

What made a fugitive out of so solid and respected a citizen as Pilgram Marpeck? Only something more compelling than wealth, position, and social prominence could have brought about such a change. Although all direct evidence is lacking, the reason was clearly that Marpeck had become an Anabaptist. As seen in the preceding chapter, it was dangerous to be an Anabaptist in Austria in 1528. On August 20, 1527, Ferdinand I of Austria issued a mandate against all "sectarians and heretics." He would tolerate no beliefs within his domain that were contrary to those held by the church of Rome. Everywhere Anabaptists were caught and imprisoned and many executed. We know that an Anabaptist congregation existed in Rattenberg late in 1527, because on November 25 Leonhard Schiemer was arrested after serving as elder of the congregation for only one day. He was beheaded on January 14, 1528. Another notable Anabaptist preacher, Hans Schlaffer, was caught near Rattenberg on December 5, 1527, and executed on February 4, 1528. Marpeck must have known of these two martyrs and particularly the letters Schiemer wrote to the Rattenberg congregation during his imprisonment. If Marpeck was an Anabaptist at the time, he would have been a member of that congregation.

It is likely that Marpeck and his family were among the many Anabaptist refugees who left their homes for places of safety, for to remain meant almost certain death. This was especially true after April 1, 1528, when an even harsher mandate was issued by Ferdinand against Anabaptists. The Marpecks decided upon Strasbourg as their destination. That city had a reputation for tolerance toward Anabaptists and was one of the few such places in all of Europe.

Strasbourg

Strasbourg was an unusually important European city of the sixteenth century. It was the link between the Netherlands and Italy, between Paris and Vienna, and its location on the junction of two important routes of commerce contributed much to its prosperity. But along those same highways came men with ideas, traveling voluntarily in search of a better hearing or forced to flee by persecution. The range and diversity of the ideas held by the people who either traveled through or settled down in Strasbourg is truly astonishing.

But Strasbourg was not only a popular and exciting place for overnight stops on the way to some other place. Like a magnet it drew people who, because of some point of view usually connected with Christian belief, were unwanted elsewhere. As a result of political revolts in the thirteenth and fourteenth centuries, the city had become independent of its ruler who, as was so often the case, was both prince and bishop at the same time. A democratic form of government was developed with a complicated system of councils and elected officials representing the two main social groups, the nobility and the commoners. The main center of power lay with the twenty guilds, which were unions of craftsmen.

Wherever the bishops of the church of Rome were in full control they dealt decisively with any dissenters. For many centuries church law had insisted on the death penalty for denial of any church doctrine or for rebaptism. But in Strasbourg the bishop had little power and could therefore not significantly interfere in religious matters. Strasbourg's tolerant attitude to difference of opinion and moderation in punishing offenders had a long tradition. "He who would be hanged anywhere is simply driven from Strassburg by flogging" was a saying of the day.

When the Reformation began and its main ideas flooded the

Strasbourg, located at the junction of numerous trade routes and rivers, derived its name from the Roman strataburgum—city of roads. Truly cosmopolitan, it also became a marketplace for new ideas such as Anabaptism. The engineer Pilgram Marpeck arrived in Strasbourg in the fall of 1528. Employed by the city he built the **channel dams on the Kinzig,** but was eventually relieved of his job and exiled because of his preaching activities.

countries of Europe in the form of pamphlets and tracts, Strasbourg was quickly in the middle of things. Because of its reputation for toleration it became a center for printing and distribution of all kinds of Reformation literature. Naturally the citizens did not remain unaffected by what was happening. The insistence of Martin Luther that a person is acceptable to God only through faith and never through the works prescribed by the church of Rome found welcome ears in a city that had already in its own way challenged the big church. When Luther's ninety-five theses arrived in Strasbourg in 1518, copies were nailed to the doors of every church and parsonage in the city.

In the same year Matthew Zell came to Strasbourg to serve as pastor of the cathedral parish. He was won for the Reformation and began soon after to express his newly won convictions. By 1523 he supported the use of German instead of Latin in church worship and rejected the Roman practice of giving only the bread to the people at communion. When he was denied the use of the cathedral pulpit by the authorities of the Roman church, the powerful guilds came to his aid and built for him a wooden platform from which he preached to congregations numbering as many as 3,000 people.

Support was so strongly on the side of reform that the government of Strasbourg issued a mandate at the end of 1523 authorizing evangelical preaching. When Zell was excommunicated in 1524 for having married, the government kept him in office. By August 1524 the city authorities took over the responsibility for nominating, installing, and paying the pastors of the seven churches in the city in a manner similar to that of Zurich under Zwingli. In May 1523 Martin Bucer arrived in the city and, because of his talent for leadership and his energy, soon became the chief reformer of Strasbourg.

Anabaptists began coming to Strasbourg early in 1526 although Balthasar Hubmaier had his book on baptism published there in July 1525. Among the first to arrive were Michael Sattler and Wilhelm Reublin, both belonging to the Swiss Brethren. In November 1526 Hans Denck arrived from Augsburg and had a public debate with the Strasbourg ministers. Denck was ordered out of the city and the council decreed that no more public debates between the ministers and dissenters should be held without the express permission of the council. Several more prominent Anabaptists, as well as other sorts of Reformation dissenters, came to Strasbourg in 1526-27.

Matthew Zell exhibited a truly Christian spirit toward the Anabaptists and completely rejected the notion that anyone should be persecuted for their faith. He regarded most of the Anabaptists as true Christians who ought to be commended, not coerced. He publicly stated that he was not in agreement with the oppressive measures proposed by Bucer and city officials. Wolfgang Capito, another of the Strasbourg reformers, found himself drawn to the Anabapists, especially to Michael Sattler. Although he held some views in common with them, he nevertheless agreed that those Anabaptists who stubbornly insisted on their schismatic views were to be punished. It was due mainly to Zell and Capito that Strasbourg was the "City of Hope" for the persecuted Anabaptists.

Martin Bucer, the chief reformer, also had friendly feelings for Anabaptists at the beginning, due chiefly to his friendship with Michael Sattler, but when the Anabaptists insisted on forming their own fellowship, his attitude toward them became one of total opposition. Although he strongly advocated that Anabaptists be turned from their beliefs by persuasion, he did not hesitate to use violence if they showed no inclination to change. On July 27, 1527, a severe mandate was issued prohibiting all citizens from giving assistance and shelter to Anabaptists. It was put into effect immediately, but the tradition of tolerance in Strasbourg made it impossible to win the struggle with the Anabaptists. Even with the expulsion in 1534 of Leopold Scharnschlager, a strong leader and associate of Pilgram Marpeck, organized congregational life continued, although not as strongly as before. The tradition of tolerance made possible Anabaptist conferences in Strasbourg in 1554, 1556, 1557, 1568, 1592, and 1607.[1]

Marpeck and Anabaptism

After that digression into the history of the city of Strasbourg and its attitude towards the Anabaptists, we return now to the story of Pilgram Marpeck. It is clear that he came to the city in order to join and work in the Anabaptist brotherhood. A notation from October 22, 1528, read: ". . . Pilgram Marpeck from Rattenberg in the Inn Valley, a citizen, with his wife, in whose house the meetings of the Anabaptists took place. . . ." He apparently gained immediate employment in the city, perhaps as a member of the gardeners' guild. And it was not long before his engineering talents were discovered, for he was soon employed by the city as engineer.

Across the Rhine to the east of Strasbourg lies the Black Forest. In 1528 as today it contained vast stands of silver fir on the higher elevations of the mountains and beech, birch, and oak lower down in the valleys. But the forests were at least twenty-five to thirty kilometers from Strasbourg and the transport of logs over mountainous roads was a laborious, slow, and inefficient affair. It was to solve this economic problem that Marpeck was hired by the city.

His task was to bring the timber from the mountains into Strasbourg by water. The Kinzig River divides the Black Forest into its northern and southern sections and flows into the Rhine near Strasbourg. This river had been used for generations to float logs into Strasbourg, but its usefulness was limited to the springtime when the water ran high due to the thawing snow up in the mountains. Marpeck's assignment was to make possible the use of the river at least for the duration of the summer and autumn. This he accomplished by constructing a system of dams, behind which water was conserved in the spring. When the timbers were ready to float, a gate in the dam was opened, releasing enough water to float the logs down. In addition to the dams he constructed a series of special spillways primarily to bypass the many rock obstructions and rapids on the Kinzig. He did similar work on the Murg River further to the north and on several small streams flowing into the Rhine from the Vosges Mountains to the west. This engineering accomplishment added much to the economic welfare of the city. It was undoubtedly Marpeck's usefulness to the city which made his stay possible, even though he was known as an Anabapist leader from the beginning. Evidently his work had lasting significance, for generations later the timber brought down from the Black Florest was still known as "Pilgramwood."

Martin Bucer and Wolfgang Capito were the most influential Protestant leaders in Strasbourg while Marpeck lived there. Capito regarded him highly and seems to have been chiefly responsible for his extended stay. It was Bucer who was determined to get rid of him. His attitude was prompted primarily by Marpeck's public and penetrating criticism of church affairs in Strasbourg, for which Bucer bore the main responsibility. Nor is it altogether surprising that he should have resented and feared Marpeck, for Marpeck was a strong and forthright leader. His theological writings reveal a man of high intelligence, especially when we remember that he was a layman with no formal theological training. Although his writings tend to be wordy and repetitious, they reveal the mind of a man who had struggled effectively with some of the basic religious questions of his day. Evidently he had read much and listened carefully. Even though the Strasbourg clergy found his presence highly disturbing, they gave him the testimony that "he had many splendid gifts from God and in many respects manifested a vigorous good zeal." Bucer himself agreed that, although he was a "stiffnecked heretic," he and his wife exhibited a "fine, blameless behavior."

But Marpeck was not content to be the quiet leader of the Anabaptist church in Strasbourg. He felt compelled to speak to other Christians about his understanding of the Christian faith. Since Bucer and his fellow ministers were so influential in the city he spoke to them. In fact, during a discussion with Bucer in December of 1531 Marpeck said that the opportunity for such discussion with other Christians was the reason for his coming to Strasbourg. But this conviction about the necessity to witness to his fellow Christians finally led to his expulsion from the city.

He was known as an Anabaptist leader from the beginning of his stay, but because of his professional skill he had been left unmolested. By 1531, however, Bucer began to get impatient, for Marpeck was influencing not only the common people but also some of higher standing. Bucer's letters to his friends revealed his growing feeling that he could no longer tolerate his presence. Late in 1531 Bucer therefore managed to have Marpeck arrested and put in prison. But his success was of short duration, for Marpeck was released unconditionally, in part due to Capito's intercession, and likely because the city needed his skilled services.

This experience did not discourage Marpeck. In fact, it seems to have prompted his next step, which was a request to the council for a public debate with the ministers. He evidently felt that a public hearing would aid a true understanding of the Christian faith. The council, however, remembering the public debate with Hans Denck five years earlier, denied the request, and instead arranged for a private discussion between Marpeck and Bucer before the council and other city officials. The public was excluded, very likely because the council feared that the simple logic of the Anabaptist leader would turn the public against the established order in the city. Capito had left Strasbourg for an extended vacation on the insistence of Bucer.

Thus the stage was set for the contest. Actually it was no contest because it was like a baseball game in which the manager of one team is the umpire. Under such conditions the outcome was predictable. The council decided on December 18 that unless Marpeck abandoned his opinions and his efforts to "overthrow infant baptism" he was to be banished from the city. He was also warned that if he returned, his reception would be such that he would soon wish he had stayed away.

Marpeck responded calmly and without anger or excitement to this shattering announcement. He said that he could not promise never to return since God might lead him back. He also requested four weeks of grace so that he could settle the sale of his property and some financial matters relating to his employment with the city. During this time he wrote a long confession of faith which fills about thirty-five printed pages. To this Bucer wrote an equally long reply, point by point. These documents, as well as the minutes of the debate of December 9, clearly reveal the two main points of difference between Christians of the Anabaptist and Reformed faiths in Strasbourg in 1531: baptism and the relationship of the church to the civic government.[2]

The Interpretation of Scripture

We begin with Bucer because his interpretation of Scripture and the position derived from it was accepted as the official view of the city of Strasbourg. This was the interpretation Marpeck criticized and against which we must see and understand Marpeck's own interpretation. Bucer believed that the Old and New Testaments formed an indivisible unity, with the Old Testament having practically the same authority for the Christian as the New. God made a covenant with Abraham in which he graciously and freely pledged himself to be the God of Abraham's descendants. This same covenant extended through both Old and New Testaments and on into the present day. Since the coming of Jesus that covenant is better understood. People understand better what God has done and what he wants them to do, but the original covenant has in no basic way been changed or canceled by the coming of Jesus.

For Bucer, this understanding of the Bible led to a number of important consequences. First, baptism in the Christian church was regarded as the equivalent of circumcision in the Hebrew community. As circumcision was the sign that a person was included in the covenant, so baptism was also the sign of the same covenant. It is the sign that God is gracious and merciful, and desires to be gracious to this particular child. Faith is not connected with baptism, for both sin and salvation begin before there is any faith. Each child is a sinner, having inherited evil from Adam, and because she needs God's grace and forgiveness, she must also have the sacrament of baptism.

The second consequence of Bucer's understanding of the Bible was that although not all the people in the city of Strasbourg were obedient followers of Christ, yet they must all be in the church even as all the Hebrews were included in the Old Testament covenant. God, said Bucer, was the only one who could decide who was a Christian and who was not; humans cannot make such decisions. In fact, Bucer held to the idea of special election which really means that God has in his mysterious wisdom appointed some persons to salvation and some to damnation. No one knows what God's choice is with respect to any person. Thus we cannot decide who belongs to the church because even a thoroughly evil person may be elected to salvation. It was assumed that in due course God would draw such a person to himself. To say that such a person is not in the church is to put oneself in the place of God.

A third consequence had to do with the relationship of the church and the civil government which in Strasbourg was the city council. Bucer held that God has two kinds of servants. The first preach the Word of God and tell people what is right and what is wrong like the prophets and priests in the Old Testament. The second, like the Old Testament kings, are responsible to see that everyone does what is right and to punish those who do not. This meant that all who opposed the work of the ministers whether by evil living or by contradicting their ideas would be punished. An example of how this works was the petition of Bucer and his fellow ministers to the council in December of 1531 to punish those who contradicted and despised their teachings.

There can be little doubt that Marpeck was among those at whom this petition was aimed. Bucer insisted that it was a Christian's duty to bear the sword of a magistrate since only the Christian truly knew what God wanted people to do. He also believed in the support of the council for the sake of those who did not have a sufficiently strong will to do what was right; such weak persons would be helped to do the right by the threat and use of force. Church and government were thus thoroughly intertwined, and there was some confusion about the responsibility of each. The outcome of such an arrangement was often that the decisions in the life of the church were governed by political and social considerations rather than by the Bible.

The fourth consequence of Bucer's understanding of the Bible was that since Christians had a fuller understanding of God's will than the Old Testament Hebrews, most of the rules and regulations of the Old Testament were no longer binding. The Hebrews needed such external observances as sacrifice and food laws because of their lack of understanding, but in the Christian church only faith and love are required. For the situation in Strasbourg this meant simply that there was no definite order in church life. Everyone was assumed to be a member of the church regardless of what they did or whether they wanted to be in the church or not.

We now turn to Marpeck's understanding of the Bible and his views of baptism and the relationship of the church to the civic government that flowed from it. The Old and New Testments formed a unity for him, but of a different kind than the unity which Bucer found. Marpeck said that Old and New Testaments stand to each other in a relationship of promise and fulfillment, just as today, for example, the pledge of marriage in the engagement and the marriage itself are inseparable, but still quite clearly distinguishable. One is introductory to the other.

When Jesus came, the old order was replaced by a new one. The old is no longer authoritative because the new covenant in Christ is of a different nature than the old covenant made with Abraham. The same gracious God gave both covenants, but the old covenant was characterized by a complex system of rules and regulations because, although people wanted to do God's will, they neither clearly understood it nor did they have the strength to do it. It was, said Marpeck, a covenant of slavery.

The new covenant, however, is characterized by freedom. No system of regulations is necessary because the people that accept it both know God's will and are free and able to do it because God gives them the strength. Briefly then Marpeck held that under the old covenant people were forced to do right and under the new they are free to do right. From this view followed four important consequences.

First, he believed that God wants all persons to obey him freely, without compulsion, and that it is possible for every person to obey God if they so choose. Thus Marpeck completely rejected Bucer's doctrine of election; God wants every person to be saved. Because he rejected the doctrine of election Marpeck also rejected infant baptism, since an infant cannot freely choose to obey God. Actually infant baptism compels a person to be in the church without giving that person any choice in the matter. Furthermore, before any can freely obey God, they must repent of their sins and believe that God loves them and wants their obedience, but infants can neither repent nor believe. Furthermore, we need not worry about the welfare of innocent babies. They have no sin until they are able to distinguish between good and evil. Since they are not sinners they need no redemption; God has already accepted them because Jesus said, "Let the children come to me, for theirs is the kingdom of heaven." Even the children of Christian parents, once they become responsible, have no advantage before God. It should not be assumed that they are or will be Christians. They too must repent and believe in order to be saved.

The second consequence was that Marpeck regarded the New Testament as the final authority for Christian life in the church. He agreed with Bucer that faith and love were all-important, but he went on to say that only the person who is unconditionally obedient to Christ has true faith and true love. Since in the New Testament baptism clearly follows faith, it must be so today; only those who have faith may be baptized. Jesus commanded his followers to love their enemies. That allows for no exceptions and means that Christians may not participate in war.

Third, since the New Testament is the Christian's final authority, it cancels out the Old Testament view wherever the two do not agree. Bucer appealed to the Old Testament union of church and state, but for Marpeck that was a slavish system. Since freedom is characteristic of the New Testament, freedom in matters of faith must be taken seriously, and this would inevitably mean the clear separation of church and world. To Marpeck not only God's gracious favor but also free human response mattered. The church is the society only of those who freely choose to be obedient to Christ. Joining the church is therefore not merely the acceptance of God's grace but also a willingness to live in obedience to it. It is not doing people a favor to regard them as members of the church if they do not want to be obedient to Christ of their own free will. Bucer rejected this reasoning because it would inevitably lead to the formation of a new church.

The fourth and final consequence of Marpeck's view of the Scriptures was that he rejected the idea of two servants in the church, the preacher and the magistrate, as held by Bucer. The preacher is in the church to be sure because he proclaims God's love and grace and offers it to people. The magistrate does not function within the church because there only Christ rules over the spirits of members. The magistrate is appointed by God to restrain evil. In practice this meant the rejection of all coercion in matters of faith. No magistrate has the authority even to judge in such matters, much less to force people to accept such judgments. Since God wants a free response from all people, compelling them to believe that of which they are not convinced interferes with God's order. This even applies to children of Christian parents who cannot simply be told what to believe. It applies also to those who hold views that are different from those in power. To use the magistrate to punish dissenters or blasphemers is to admit that the Word of Christ is not able to do what it is said to be capable of, to convert sinners. It is simply contrary to God's order and the spirit of Christ to persecute anyone for their faith or for having no faith at all. Not only did Marpeck state these convictions in his confession, he also appealed directly to the city council to let liberty of conscience and religious freedom prevail in Strasbourg.

Marpeck's confession convinced neither Bucer nor the council and he finally left Strasbourg in February 1532. For the next decade we know very little about his activities. He seems to have lived in Switzerland from where he continued serving as a leader, working against the encroaching legalism he found in the congregations. Many Swiss Anabaptists, however, did not appreciate his emphasis on freedom in Christ. He traveled a great deal, visiting groups in Germany, Switzerland, and Moravia. He was also busy writing letters to churches and individuals. One of the major compilations of documents from the "Marpeck Circle," the *Kunstbuch* still awaits editing and publication.

An Invisible Church?

In 1542 he suddenly emerged again with the publication of a book on baptism.[3] This volume was in fact a careful revision of a work by some Anabaptist preachers from North Germany. Marpeck's purpose in publishing it was that it might help to unite and strengthen the Anabaptist fellowship. While certainly performing this function, it also caught the attention of another dissenter, Caspar Schwenckfeld, who lived not far from Augsburg. He was not an Anabaptist but what one might call an "invisiblist." He believed concern about such visible (external) matters as baptism and the Lord's Supper was idolatry because it prevented people from being concerned for what was truly important. Since Marpeck had argued for the importance of right observance of baptism and the Lord's Supper in the church, Schwenckfeld regarded the book as an attack on himself. He replied with a book of his own charging the Anabaptists with completely misunderstanding the Bible and the Christian faith.

The position represented by Schwenckfeld proved a great temptation for the persecuted Anabaptists. Why not, some of them seriously asked, abandon baptism and the Lord's Supper since faith is what really counts? Why not become an "invisible" church so that we will not be persecuted anymore? These questions had already been asked in 1531 in Strasbourg while Marpeck was there and he had in that year written two little books against this view. Now he and some of his co-workers took up the task of replying to Schwenckfeld's criticism in a work of about 800 pages. The basic question was again the interpretation of the Bible and especially the matter of the relationship of the New to the Old Testament. There is no need to discuss this argument in detail because it was almost identical to Marpeck's argument with Bucer, which we have described.

It was his dialogue with the Spiritualist Schwenckfeld, however, which pushed him to a strong emphasis on the importance of the human Jesus, on outer (social) and inner (holiness) justice, and the importance of necessary externals in baptism and the Lord's Supper as co-witnesses (*mit-zeugniss*) of the inner experience, moving him closer to seeing the possibility of a certain objective experience in the sacraments than any other Anabaptist except, perhaps, Hubmaier. He also placed great emphasis on studying the Bible in a congregational context, the so-called "hermeneutical circle."

In 1544 Marpeck gained employment with the city of Augsburg as an engineer and did work similar to that which he had done at Strasbourg. Although efforts were made to prosecute him—he was given three warnings to cease his Anabaptist activities—he remained in his position until his death from natural causes in 1556.

Throughout his time as an Anabaptist leader and elder he was deeply concerned for the unity of the Anabaptist fellowship. This concern is clearly reflected in the fourteen remaining letters from his hand addressed to Anabaptists at Strasbourg, in Switzerland, in Moravia, and in Germany. He writes about the unity of the church.

He warns some that although the Christian is free in Christ, no one is free to live a life of sin, and he criticizes others for judging each other too harshly. He urges members separated by misunderstanding to be reconciled, writes very practically about the place of the minister in the congregation, and deals with a variety of other matters.

Pilgram Marpeck was one of the most notable German Anabaptist leaders and theologians. He contributed a great deal to the clarification of the Anabaptist interpretation of the Christian faith. Even today he inspires us with his passion for unity among believers in Christ. So also does the fact that he was able to survive and work publicly in his profession, while clearly identifying himself with Anabaptism. How was this possible?

Endnotes

1. See John S. Oyer, MQR (July 1984), 58:218-229.
2. William Klassen and Walter Klaassen, *The Writings of Pilgram Marpeck*. Scottdale, Pa.: Herald Press, 1978, pp. 107-157.
3. Ibid., pp. 159-302.

Other Resources: "Marpeck, Pilgram," ME 5:538-539. Note especially the bibliographical references. Stephen B. Boyd, "Pilgrim Marpeck and the Justice of Christ," Th.D. dissertation, Harvard University, 1984.

6

Anabaptism
in the Netherlands

IDEAS ARE POWERFUL. In a changing society they can be creatively good or tragic. Some people use well the power of new ideas; others channel them to bad ends; still others fear them and try to dam them up and hold them back. The history of the birth of the Anabaptist movement in the Netherlands, from where its people came to be known as Mennonites, is about the flow of new ideas in a society ready for change. This history not only reflects abuse and opposition, but also the creative use of new ideas.

Melchior Hoffman

Melchior Hoffman was one of the persons through whom Anabaptism arose in the Netherlands. He was a gifted but uneducated leader, a tanner or furrier by training. Born in Swabia in Southern Germany in 1493, he emerged as a self-taught Lutheran preacher active in the small countries on the east shore of the Baltic. When driven from this area he went to Sweden, to Holstein in Northern Germany, and to Denmark. But after experiencing opposition there also, he went to Emden and then up the Rhine to Strasbourg.

Hoffman began his ministries as a Lutheran evangelist, but Luther soon disowned him because of his apocalyptic spirituality and rejection of the Lord's Supper as a sacrament. He was a gifted, if unconventional, preacher who even served as preacher at the Danish court in Kiel for a time. Yet he was given to an allegorical interpretation of Scripture and prophecy based on his lay biblical studies, especially of the books of Daniel and the Revelation of John. His belief in visions also confirmed to him that the end of the world was near. He believed in the possibility of total sanctification, becoming like Christ by following him, a belief Dirk Philips was to stress under the word *deification.*

It was in Strasbourg that he was first exposed to Anabaptist thought, perhaps through Denck, Hubmaier, and others. It is assumed that he became one of their number, but we know nothing about his baptism. He soon left, however, to return to Emden in 1530. Here he found a ready response among those already inclined to reform through economic hardship, the influence of Sacramentarians, Erasmus, and simple folk piety, with the result that about three hundred were baptized. From there he then sent lay preachers into the Netherlands to announce the coming kingdom, and later traveled there himself.

In the meantime Hoffman's continuing interest in prophecy and the nearness of Christ's return was encouraged by the visions and dreams of Leonhard and Ursula Jost, Barbara Rebstock, and others. These led him to believe that Strasbourg would be the spiritual Jerusalem, and that he himself was Elijah chosen to proclaim the coming event to all people. Finding his way back to Strasbourg, he acted on his faith in these prophecies by having himself imprisoned. This was to be a necessary precondition to the coming of the kingdom. Obbe Philips, whom we will meet again later, said of these events:

> Thus, through the mediation of this prophecy, Melchior removed to Strasbourg and there began to preach and to teach here and there in the houses of the burghers. Then to be brief, the authorities sent their servants to take him prisoner. When Melchior saw that he was going to prison, he thanked God that the hour had come and threw his hat from his head and took a knife and cut off his hose (the trousers and stockings were one garment) at the ankle, threw his shoes away and extended his hand with the fingers to heaven and swore by the living God who lives there from eternity to eternity that he would take no food and enjoy no drink other than bread and water until the time

that he could point out with his hand and outstretched fingers the One who had sent him. And with this he went willingly, cheerfully, and well comforted to prison.[1]

He remained in prison until his death some ten years later. The prophecies he had so fervently believed remained unfulfilled, but his influence on other leaders in the Netherlands was of great importance for the future of the movement.

The Tragedy of Münster

Among the apostles whom Hoffman had sent into the Netherlands from Emden were Sicke Freerks, a tailor and for that reason sometimes called Snijder, who went to Leeuwarden, and Jan Volkertszoon Tripmaker, who went to Amsterdam. As a people with a long history of freedom, but now suffering under the oppressive rule of Spain, the Dutch were ready to listen to the words of these apostles. The Spanish king, who was also Holy Roman Emperor, ruled with a heavy hand. Because of this and because of the new winds of social change sweeping across Europe, the people were restless and disturbed. They resented the armies which were constantly moving across the land. A series of floods had destroyed property and killed both livestock and people. The plague also troubled them. In Leiden it was reportedly so bad that people said, "Oh, dear Lord, do not pass us by with the gift of the hot sickness, for we would rather die than live any longer." Disaster and adversity were believed to be signs of the anger of God.

There was also dissatisfaction among the people with the poor state of the medieval church. They knew of the Brethren of the Common Life, who had brought reforms and provided schools where a better religious life was taught. With the coming of printing more people could get Bibles. As many as thirty printings of different translations of the Bible as a whole or in part appeared in less than ten years before 1530. The Sacramentarians rejected the doctrine of the physical presence of the body and blood of Christ in the bread and wine of the mass. Already in 1527 the Sacramentarian widow or proto-Anabaptist Weynken of Monnickendam was arrested for heresy on this issue. When she was asked, "What do you hold concerning the sacrament?" she answered, "I hold your sacrament to be bread and flour, and if you hold it as God, I say that it is your devil." She was burned at the stake.[2]

With the coming of the Hoffmanite apostles to the Netherlands these yearnings and frustrations found new hope of fulfillment in the teachings of Anabaptism. Not all of the responses were encouraging, however. When Hoffman was imprisoned in 1533, a baker from Haarlem named Jan Matthijs claimed the leadership in Amsterdam, sending twelve apostles out in pairs to convert the people. One pair visited Leeuwarden late that year where they succeeded in winning and baptizing Obbe and Dirk Philips, two brothers who were to become key figures in the early history of the movement. Other apostles reached the city of Münster in Northern Germany and began the countdown leading to the tragedy which was to overtake the city.

Upon their arrival in Münster these apostles of Jan Matthijs found several preachers who were in close agreement with them and ready to have them remain there. This they quickly reported to Matthijs, who moved to the city early in 1534, eager to see the fulfillment of the Hoffmanite prophecy. But whereas Hoffman had claimed Strasbourg to be the site of the new Jerusalem, Matthijs used a new prophecy to change the location to his own Münster. Far more important was the change to violence. Hoffman had been peaceful and urged his followers to wait for God to set up his kingdom at the appointed time. The possibility of calling upon his faithful to help annihilate the wicked by force of arms was an option but only at Christ's return. Christ would give them the swords. But Matthijs now taught that the faithful were to prepare for the return of Christ and make a place for his kingdom by destroying the wicked. As a result, everyone was soon forced to receive baptism and join the new community, or leave the city. Military preparations were quickly made for the great battle which would usher in the kingdom.

As might be expected, the bishop of Münster, who did not live in the city, gathered an army with some support from the German princes, and laid siege to the supposed New Jerusalem. This, of course, simply increased the militancy of the Münsterites. When Jan Matthijs was killed, leadership passed to another Jan—Jan van Leiden, whose ideas were even more extreme than those of Matthijs. He proclaimed himself the new King David and ruled with an iron hand. Polygamy was introduced on the basis of examples from the Old Testament and because the battle was leaving many families without a male leader. The besieged group suffered grievously from hunger and disease. The city finally fell on June 24, 1535,

The St. Lamberti tower on the main street in Münster, Westfalen, still bears witness to the tragedy of 1534-1535. **The three iron cages** once held the bodies of radical Anabaptist leaders put on public display. Most of the male population was massacred; only a few escaped.

through the betrayal of a defector from within.

The Münsterite movement had aroused the hopes of many among the common people in Northwestern Germany and the Netherlands. Now they were not only disappointed at its failure, but even more at the bad name it gave to Anabaptists everywhere. Because of Münster Anabaptists were all now labeled as visionaries and revolutionaries. It was one of those times in history when persecution drove people to extreme action. This extreme action convinced the persecutors that they were right and justified even more severe measures against them.

The Peaceful Anabaptists

Not all of those who became Anabaptists in the Netherlands followed the Münsterites, nor even the more moderate and peaceful views of Hoffman. With Obbe and Dirk Philips, whom we have already referred to, Anabaptism followed another course even under severe persecution. In Dirk the Dutch movement was eventually to have one of its major spokesmen, theologians, and church leaders.

Obbe and Dirk Philips were sons of a priest in Leeuwarden. Their education was probably better than the average of the day. Obbe was both a surgeon and barber as was customary at the time. Dirk was associated with the Franciscans and may have had training in theology. They were both baptized by apostles of Jan Matthijs in December-January of 1533-34 and Obbe was immediately ordained as elder. This authorized him to ordain other leaders in addition to carrying other church responsibilities.

Obbe did not accept the revolutionary teachings of Jan Matthijs. He soon gathered about himself a group of potential leaders concerned for a more faithful study and use of the Scriptures. They rejected the use of force, as well as the prophecies which had led to the armed attempts of Münster. But Obbe's spiritual pilgrimage was not yet at an end. Though he worked diligently to restore order after the Münster tragedy, he became increasingly disillusioned with the Anabaptist movement which had originally spawned Münster and now, in reaction, seemed to be becoming increasingly rigid and legalistic in its demands. Because of this he pulled back from the movement in 1539-40, having earlier, however, ordained his brother Dirk as well as David Joris and Menno Simons as leaders. It is probable that he became a spiritualist who practiced an in-

Anabaptism came to the low countries around 1530 in part through the itinerant preacher **Melchior Hoffman** who first heard the ideas in Strasbourg. **Menno Simons** joined the peaceful Anabaptists in January 1536. Because of Menno's capable leadership the Anabaptists in East Friesland gained the name, "Mennists" (Mennonites).

ward religion without openly joining any church. We know very little about him after his withdrawal, except that he lived in Rostock along the North German coast and died in 1568. A confession which he wrote shortly before 1560 to explain why he left the Anabaptists is the only writing we have from his hand.[3]

Dirk worked faithfully with Obbe in opposing the revolutionary Münsterites. As his writings became known among the Anabaptists, they strengthened and encouraged the progress of the peaceful group. He might, in fact, have taken Obbe's place as leader had it not been for another who had risen in the group, Menno Simons. We now turn our attention to him as the most important leader in the first generation of Dutch Anabaptism.

Menno Simons

Menno Simons became an Anabaptist more than ten years after the first baptism in Zurich on January 21, 1525, and about six years after the apostles of Melchior Hoffman began preaching in the Netherlands. He was born in Witmarsum, a small village in the northern Dutch province of Friesland where his parents lived, most likely as farmers. We know that he studied for the priesthood and was ordained by the bishop of Utrecht in 1524, but he knew only a little Greek and no Hebrew. His first assignment was as the second of three priests in Pingjum, a kilometer west of his hometown.

In his later recollections of these early years as a village priest he tells how he spent his time in "playing cards, drinking, and in diversions as, alas, is the fashion and usage of such useless people." He did not engage in serious immoral activities but wasted away his time in careless living. Already in his first year as priest, however, he began to be troubled about the Roman Catholic doctrine of the physical presence of the flesh and blood of Christ in the bread and wine of the mass. It is likely that he had been influenced by the Sacramentarians, of whom there were many in the Netherlands. Since he could not rid himself of these doubts even through prayer and confession, he decided to turn to the Scriptures in his further search. In taking this step, he writes, he was influenced by Luther. This study of the Scriptures convinced him that the church was wrong in its teaching that Christ was physically present in the Lord's Supper.

Soon he began to doubt in another area. To his amazement he heard that Sicke Freerks (Snijder), the apostle who had been sent to Leeuwarden, had been beheaded in that city for having himself rebaptized. This time Menno turned to the Scriptures immediately but was unable to find support for the practice of infant baptism. Thereupon he studied the writings of the reformers Luther, Bucer, and Bullinger. He discovered that while they defended infant baptism, he again did not find their arguments supported by Scripture. Yet despite these doubts he remained in the priesthood. He was, in fact, promoted to become priest in his hometown of Witmarsum. It was there that his reputation as an evangelical preacher increased, for he had much occasion to refute the Münsterite doctrine which was making inroads among the people. He conferred with the Münsterite leaders and called them brothers. He was, in effect, a Melchiorite. Though he respected their zeal and sincerity, he was certain they were in error in their apocalyptic visions and violent ways. He tried publicly to correct these errors through his preaching.

The decisive moment for Menno came in one of the tragic events connected with Münster. A band of about three hundred rallied to support Münster and took over a monastery called the

Old Cloister near Witmarsum. They were besieged, captured, and many of them were killed in battle or executed. It is believed that one of them, named Peter Simons, was Menno's brother. This event, in any case, moved Menno to action. While he agreed with their criticism of the church, he deplored their misguided zeal. They were like sheep without a shepherd, while he remained in comfort and ease, even building his reputation by opposing them. And so, after some eleven years of inward struggle, and with the typical deliberateness of his Frisian people, he broke with the past. In a public statement on January 30, 1536, he told of his new commitment to the cause of Christ, and then went into hiding with the help of the peaceful Anabaptists with whom he was most in agreement.

The next year was spent in study of the Scriptures and in writing. It is, no doubt, during this period that he worked out the fuller meaning of the position to which he had come and on which he stood committed until his death twenty-five years later. At the end of this year of preparation, he was visited by a delegation of from six to eight men who asked him to become leader and elder of their people. After hesitating because of the serious implications of this call to lead a persecuted group, he finally consented to serve. He was ordained by Obbe Philips, who had also baptized him earlier (ME 5:555).

Neither Traditionalist nor Fanatic

In 1539-40, two or three years after Menno Simons' ordination, Obbe Philips withdrew from the movement, as we have seen. He had grown weary of the struggle against Roman Catholic traditionalism on the one hand, and the fanatical extremism of Münster on the other. Whereas the former seemed to be guided more by tradition than by the Scriptures, those who sympathized with the revolutionary spirit of Münster seemed to read every biblical text in the light of their own visions and expectations. Among these were the followers of Melchoir Hoffman, known as *Melchiorites*. In between were the Lutherans and Calvinists, who wanted reform but kept many of the traditions of the Roman Catholic past, and disagreed sharply with the Anabaptists on numerous issues.

To lead the fledgling Anabaptist group through this spiritual wilderness became the lot of Menno Simons. His lot in life was to sift truth from half-truth, oppose error with clear teaching, encourage the persecuted, correct the misguided, and build the young church while himself being hunted as a heretic. In this time of struggle, during the 1540s and 1550s, he had many helpers, especially Dirk Philips. But it was Menno's leadership which saved the Dutch Anabaptist movement from fanaticism and possible disintegration. Because of his leadership those who belonged to the movement were soon known as *Menists*, or *Mennonists*, and eventually as *Mennonites*.

In a way the most difficult part of the struggle during these years was not that against Roman Catholic persecution, nor against the revolutionary ideas of the fanatics. The struggle was most intense against the Lutherans, Calvinists, and even the people among his own following with whom Menno had much in common. With these it was much more difficult to know where, when, and how to take a stand. The Mennonites agreed with the Lutherans and Calvinists on many points of Reformation doctrine but with a different emphasis. Thus the latter held the Old and New Testaments about equal in authority but the Mennonites did not. For the Mennonites, justification by faith included obedience, which meant that only persons old enough to have a conscious faith and make decisions for themselves could be baptized; and only those whose life showed the results of faith were to be gathered into the church.

In contrast the Lutherans and Calvinists (Reformed) still held to the idea that a society which does not have a common religion is dangerous. They pointed to the Münsterites as evidence of the danger when people are free to choose membership in any church group, or free to refuse altogether. Menno engaged in personal and written debate with the leaders of these state churches in the decade following 1540. Many of the writings we have from his hand today reflect the issues of that period.

The first major meeting was with John a Lasco at Emden in 1544, followed by two lengthy written statements from Menno. The second debate was with Martin Micron (a/k/a Marten de Cleyne), pastor of the Reformed Church in London. When Queen Mary restored Catholicism as the official religion after the reforms of Henry VIII and Edward VI, the Calvinists had to leave England. Some arrived off the coast of North Germany near Wismar in the winter of 1553. The Mennonites, who were themselves refugees in hiding, helped the group when their boat was frozen in the ice and no one else would accept them.

At the insistence of the Reformed leaders a series of meetings was held between them and the Mennonites in February 1554. Micron, who had meanwhile located at Emden, was brought in to participate. Contrary to their understanding, he then published an account of these meetings, forcing Menno to release his interpretation also and publicly answering the charges Micron had made against him. Micron answered Menno and with that both the personal and written debate was closed, but meanwhile the authorities became aroused and Menno had to flee from the region.

Another exchange came with Gellius Faber (a/k/a Jelle Smit), who inclined toward the Lutherans, but cooperated with the Reformed John a Lasco in Emden. He had participated in the debate against Menno in 1544, and in 1552 wrote a booklet against the Anabaptists which Menno felt to be so unfair that he had to reply. This answer, which is simply entitled *Reply to Gellius Faber*, tells of Menno's conversion, and discusses his call to the ministry. In addition, it is particularly helpful for understanding how the Mennonites differed from the Reformed and the Lutherans on baptism, the Lord's Supper, church discipline, the nature of the church, and the incarnation of Christ. Both Menno and Dirk Philips were frequently charged with heresy in connection with the incarnation because they believed that Christ had not received his flesh from Mary but from God himself. Only in that way could he have been sinless and established a pure church as his body. To their opponents this seemed to deny the humanity of Christ and, therefore, the incarnation itself.

These debates made it clear that the Mennonites differed with the state churches on two basic issues: the nature of the Christian life and the nature of the church. On the first, they stressed the importance of the new birth and discipleship. Only persons who were repentant and knew by experience the grace of God should be baptized and join the church. Evidence of the new birth was to be seen in the serious attempt to live as disciples who had committed themselves fully to Christ as Lord. Vital signs of this discipleship were love and nonresistance. On the nature of the church they insisted that it must be a voluntary gathering of believers. Church members were to be bound together on the sole basis of their loyalty to Christ and their love for each other. Their life as disciples would separate them from the world. The ban served as an instrument of love to warn and chasten the erring among them. The use of the sword or other instruments of the state to enforce the will of the church was rejected as contrary to the example and teachings of Christ and the apostles. Yet Menno affirmed that a Christian could be a magistrate (ruler).[4]

Batenburgers, Jorists, and Adam Pastor

To the opposition and persecution of these state churches and of Roman Catholicism was added the pressure of the fanatics. They were not only eroding Menno's work among his own people, but bringing disrepute to the entire movement. Most active among these were the Batenburgers, Jorists, and Adam Pastor. Among these the first were the most corrupt. They tried to carry on the violent tradition of Münster, robbing and plundering churches, and seeking to kill all who could not be converted. They adopted the practices of polygamy and community of goods as practiced at Münster. Their influence did not last much beyond 1544, but their evil deeds caused great difficulties for the peaceful Anabaptists who were unfortunately identified with them.

The Jorists were the followers of David Joris, a gifted and persuasive man who had also been ordained by Obbe Philips. It was Joris who had tried, with some success, to gather the scattered remnants after the fall of Münster. His controversy with Menno arose when he began to place increasing emphasis on Spirit and prophecy while, at the same time, accusing Menno of living according to the dead letter of Scripture. Menno felt the authority of the Bible was supreme and wrote very strongly against Joris who he charged would "dare to put your dreams, your fantasies, enthusiasms, rhetorical figures, and other magic illusions ahead of the wisdom of the Holy Spirit, through which the prophetic and apostolic Scriptures have been given."[5]

Joris felt that three time periods or dispensations in the history of the human race had been revealed: the age of the Father with David in the Old Testament, the age of the Son with Jesus Christ as the second David in the New Testament, and the age of the Spirit with himself (Joris) as the David of his age.

Because Joris believed that the inner, spiritual life was all that mattered for Christians, he could pretend to be Reformed or Roman Catholic and so escape persecution. After 1544 he, therefore, moved to Basel, Switzerland, under the assumed name of Jan van Brugge, and identified himself as a Reformed merchant who had fled from Belgium. He lived as a respectable citizen and honored churchman while, at the same time, carrying on secret correspondence with his followers in the Netherlands and writing little books for their instruction. After his death on August 25, 1556, a family quarrel led to the discovery of his real identity, to the chagrin of his children who had married into respectable families of high Basel society. Because he had been a heretic his body was dug up and burned along with his books. His followers in the Netherlands maintained themselves into the seventeenth century.[6]

The third group to trouble Menno were followers of Adam Pastor (a/k/a Roelof Martens), a German priest who had joined the Anabaptists in 1533. As co-worker with the other leaders, Menno ordained him as elder soon after 1542, and he participated in the debates with the Jorists at Lübeck in 1546, as well as in the conferences at Emden and Goch in 1547. Soon, however, it appeared that Pastor did not really believe in the Trinity, having intellectual problems with the incarnation and deity of Christ. He was consequently banned from the church by Menno and Dirk in 1547. In 1552 Menno met with him again to discuss the deity of Christ, but he could not win him back. Menno held firmly to the Scriptures as authority, while Pastor tended to put logic and reason above the Scriptures. Pastor was one of the best educated leaders among the Mennonites, but Menno and his followers believed that reason must be tested and judged by Scripture, not Scripture by reason. A group of "Adamites" continued for a time after Pastor's death in the 1560s.

Thus against both the traditionalists and the fanatics, Menno and Dirk held steadfastly to the Bible as final authority in faith and life. The use of prophecy, the inner word of the Spirit, visions, or reason all had to be checked against the Bible. It was also clear to Menno and Dirk that the Bible had to be understood in light of the teachings and example of Jesus.[7]

And so Menno Simons labored after Obbe left them, to gather and defend the flock, but he did this against great odds. For most of this period he was a hunted man with a price on his head. In 1536 he married Gertrude, about whom we unfortunately know very little. Nine years later he wrote that he "could not find in all the country a 'cabin or hut' in which my poor wife and our little children could be put up in safety for a year or two." Tjaard Renicx of Kimswerd, a little village not far from Pingjum in Friesland, was executed in January 1539, for having given shelter to Menno. Of their two daughters and a son only one daughter outlived him. Menno himself was a cripple in later years, but we do not know how he became that way.

Despite these handicaps Menno traveled from Amsterdam to Danzig and perhaps further east along the Baltic seacoast, an area where Dirk Philips was to be leading elder. He was courageous in

Anabaptism flourished in Flanders, especially in the great trading centers of Ghent, Brugge, and Ypres, but after sixty years of bloody persecution the survivors moved north into Holland. Between 1535 and 1592 at least 110 Anabaptists were tortured and executed in **the castle at Ghent** alone. A display inside the castle shows a collection of **arm and leg irons** and a **canvas straightjacket.**

meeting his foes, tender in his sympathies to those in the church. He wrote devotional materials as well as treatises in the heat of controversy. He made mistakes, was not always consistent in his writings, and often felt deeply the burden of his calling, but his judgments were generally sound, as is evidenced by the wide acceptance of his leadership and writings.

Witness Through Suffering

Leaders like Menno Simons and Dirk Philips were needed for the founding of the church, but thousands of others demonstrated a heroic faith that was just as vital. They were soldiers of the cross who fought with spiritual weapons only. On this subject Menno wrote one of his best pamphlets, *The Cross of the Saints.* The meaning of the cross became very real to many of his followers in the Netherlands.

Church and state had been so closely linked in the medieval period that the state considered it a part of its duty to enforce the accepted belief of the established state church. If the church declared someone a heretic, that person was considered dangerous to the state and removed from society. Anabaptists were considered heretics. Their name, given to them by their opponents, was chosen to point to an ancient heresy. After Constantine anyone who was baptized a second time in the Roman Empire was put to death. These views continued to prevail in the sixteenth century, especially also in the Netherlands, which were under the despotic rule of Spain. Charles V had been more tolerant of Luther in Germany because he needed the military and political support of the German princes, but he was determined to stamp out the Reformation in the Netherlands. Since the Anabaptists were the major Reformation party there until 1555 when the Calvinists gained in strength, they suffered severely. Studies of the number of martyrs in Belgium and the Netherlands have shown that no less than 1,500 Anbaptists were killed, possibly as many as 2,500 from the early days of the movement to the death of the last martyr in 1574.

Typical of the spirit of the martyrs is that of Dirk Willems. He was pursued by a company of Anabaptist hunters when he escaped from prison in the midst of winter. He fled across the thin covering of ice on a river and seemed to have made good his escape when, looking back, he saw one of his pursuers break through the ice and cry for help. Dirk immediately turned back and managed to rescue

Anabaptist Dirk Willems rescues his pursuer. This etching by Jan Luyken from the Martyrs Mirror has for centuries captured the imagination of Mennonites and other Anabaptist-related groups due to its graphic portrayal of Anabaptist love for enemies.

him, but on orders of the burgomaster on the other side of the river, the man he saved arrested him on the spot. He was burned at the stake on May 16, 1569, paying for this deed of mercy with his life.

The treatment of prisoners was extremely cruel. They were broken on a torture device known as the rack to make them disclose the names of others, especially leaders. For those who remained steadfast, burning at the stake was the usual execution. Sometimes they were first strangled; sometimes a small sack of gunpowder was hung around their neck as an act of mercy since the quick fire and the smoke hastened the end. Men who renounced the Anabaptist faith were given the mercy of death by beheading, while women were drowned. But some women were buried alive, and other women, as well as men, were hanged. An account of three brethren and a sister taken in 1536 tells of the steadfastness of most of the martyrs:

They were then placed upon the rack, though contrary to their privilege, for they were mere citizens; however, they would not apostatize, though they were tortured so that the blood ran down their feet; but they trusted in and cried to God alone. After being tortured, they were brought up above again, where they comforted each other with the Word of God. 1 Thessalonians 4:18.

Finally, on the fourth of September, they were sentenced to death. They were brought bound upon the scaffold, yet came forth boldly and humbly, as lambs of Christ, and finally knelt down, saying with Stephen: "Lord Jesus, receive our spirits into Thy hands." Acts 7:59. They were all then speedily beheaded, their bodies burned, and their heads placed upon stakes. Thus they offered up their sacrifices.[8]

Persecution made believers learn to know their own faith early and well. Thomas van Imbroich, a printer's helper in Cologne, was put in prison in 1557. Two letters written to his wife have been preserved in the *Martyrs Mirror*. We also have a confession of faith from him which shows deep thought and conviction. In one of the letters to his wife and the brethren he wrote,

Yea, if the Lord should count me worthy to testify with my blood to His name, how greatly would I thank Him, for I hope not only to bear these bonds with patience, but also to die for Christ's sake, that I may finish my course with joy; for I would rather be with the Lord, than live again in this abominable, wicked world; however, His divine will be done. Amen.[9]

Thomas did testify with his death, dying on March 5, 1558, at the age of twenty-five. So powerful was the Anabaptist witness at the time of execution, that they were increasingly carried on in secret, or the martyrs were gagged. Since some of them managed to free the tongues, however, a clamp was henceforth placed over the tongue and the tip burned so it would swell up and not slip back through the clamp.

Not everyone wanted to execute the Anabaptists. Joris Wippe was mayor of Meenen in Flanders but moved to Dordrecht when he became an Anabaptist. Friends and officials warned him to flee but he refused. Consequently he was caught, tried, and ordered to be executed, but the man who was to carry out the order wept because Wippe had fed his wife and children in a time of need. Finally another man was ordered to carry out the sentence.

The letters and testimonies of these martyrs are among the finest writings. Many have been collected and published in the *Martyrs Mirror.*[10] They show that these believers looked upon their death by martyrdom as a seal of faith. God would not call them to such a fate if they were not given the grace to endure. So they gave thanks that they could witness to the truth in this way. Furthermore, they believed their sufferings to be a test that led to eternal life. They followed the way of the cross to final victory, believing fully that as they shared in the passion of Christ, they would also share in the joy of his final victory.

Endnotes

1. George H. Williams and Angel M. Mergal, eds. *Spiritual and Anabaptist Writers*. Philadelphia, Pa.: The Westminster Press, 1957, pp. 209-210.

2. T. J. van Braght, *Martyrs Mirror*. Scottdale, Pa.: Herald Press, 1938, p. 422.

3. Williams and Mergal, *Spiritual and Anabaptist Writers*, pp. 204-225. The "Confession" was located by J. Ten Doornkaat Koolman in the *Urkundenbuch der Gemeinde Heubuden* (record book, Prussia) now at the Weierhof, Palatinate, research center.

4. Leonard Verduin and J. C. Wenger, *The Complete Writings of Menno Simons, c. 1496-1561*. Scottdale, Pa.: Herald Press, 1956.

5. Ibid., p. 1019. Joris expressed joy that the Holy Spirit was finally speaking Dutch and not only Greek and Latin.

6. Gary K. Waite, *David Joris and Dutch Anabaptism, 1524-1543*. Waterloo, Ont.: Wilfred Laurier University Press, 1990.

7. Cornelius J. Dyck, William E. Keeney, Alvin J. Beachy. *The Writings of Dirk Philips, 1504-1568*. Scottdale, Pa.: Herald Press, 1992.

8. *Martyrs Mirror*, p. 445.

9. Ibid., p. 579.

10. G. C. Studer, "History of the Martyrs Mirror." MQR (July 1948), 22:163-179.

Other Resources: ME 3:824-843; 5:622-623. William E. Keeney, *The Development of Dutch Anabaptist Thought and Practice from 1539-1564*. Nieuwkoop, Neth.: B. de Graaf, 1968. Cornelius Krahn, *Dutch Anabaptism. Origin, Spread, Life and Thought (1450-1600)*. The Hague, Neth.: Martinus Nijhoff, 1968. Cornelius J. Dyck, ed. *A Legacy of Faith. The Heritage of Menno Simons*. North Newton, Kans.: Faith and Life Press, 1962. John S. Oyer and Robert S. Kreider, *Mirror of the Martyrs*. Intercourse, Pa.: Good Books, 1990. Gerald R. Brunk, ed. *Menno Simons. A Reappraisal*. Harrisonburg, Va.: Eastern Mennonite College, 1992.

7

Anabaptist-Mennonites in Northern Europe, 1550-1650

Distinctions between countries were not nearly as sharp in sixteenth-century Europe as they are now, and movement across national borders was much easier. Only in late sixteenth century did the Dutch Mennonites become clearly defined as a fellowship, and even then congregations in Northwestern Germany and as far away as Danzig had close ties with the Dutch congregations. Still we can look at the geographic spread by areas within the whole of Northern Europe to understand the size and growth of the movement to mid-seventeenth century. In this chapter we will look first at Flanders, a province in Northwestern Belgium, then move across the channel to England and on to Northern Germany, as well as east to the Vistula Delta in what is now Poland. To conclude we will return to look more closely at the original center in the Netherlands.

Anabaptism in Belgium

The origins of Anabaptism in Belgium are very similar to those in the Netherlands. There, too, people had become weary with the medieval religious life and were ready for new ideas. The same conditions described for the Netherlands in chapter 2 prevailed here as well. The apostles of Melchior Hoffman also came to these areas and found a willing audience. Though their preaching was not confined to Flanders, the main impact of their message was felt in that area.

From 1530 to 1550 the major reform party in this area was Anabaptist. The first martyrs in 1523 had been Lutheran, but Lutheranism never gained a mass following. Likewise Calvinism had little influence before 1544 but increased in significance after 1550 with its greatest influence after 1560 during the war of independence from Spain. Later it was also driven out of Belgium but still constitutes the largest Protestant body in the Netherlands.

Anabaptism spread through the efforts of merchants and weavers who could move about with greater ease than many others. Persecution arose almost immediately with mandates being issued against them on October 10, 1535; January 24, 1539; and December 14, 1541. These mandates led to the death of many, but also to the flight of many more who followed the trade routes from Antwerp and other commercial centers. Flemish refugees are found very early in England and as far east as Danzig, where Flemish ships traveled for trade with the North German cities of the Hanseatic League.

The records show that the Anabaptists were very active, but that intense persecution prevented any one person from assuming prolonged leadership among them. The Flanders story, therefore, is primarily one of many faithful lay persons building, spreading, and upholding the church. We know, for example, of Jan Claeszen who in 1544 reported that he had 600 copies of the writings of Menno Simons printed in Antwerp. Not infrequently the witness of the death of the faithful was as effective as their living witness. The movement recorded steady growth from 1550 to 1576.[1]

Some leadership help did come to these groups from the Netherlands. Gillis van Aken, a colleague of Menno and Dirk, worked here until his arrest in 1555. His story has a sad ending. Though he recanted at the threat of death, his weakness only changed the form of execution from burning to beheading. At his execution on July 10, 1557, he reportedly said, "It is too much to lose both body and soul at the same time." The great missionary Leonard Bouwens also labored here. His diary records 10,252 baptisms which he performed, giving the exact date and place of each.

Holland's greatest poet, **Joost van den Vondel** (1587-1679), was a deacon in the Waterlander congregation in Amsterdam. **Jan Adriaensz Leeghwater** (1575-1650), a brilliant engineer, architect, and inventor, directed land reclamation projects for the Dutch, Danish, French, and Prussian governments. **Jeme (Joannes) Deknatel** (1698-1759) was instrumental in founding the Amsterdam Mennonite Seminary in 1735.

Of these, 592 seem to have been in the area which is now Belgium. So far as we know this constitutes a record for the entire Anabaptist movement for any one man. A letter from Menno Simons to Bouwens' wife has been preserved, in which he encourages her not to worry about the safety of her husband who is secure in the care of God himself. She had apparently asked for a less dangerous assignment for him closer to home.

The period from 1576 to 1586 was one of relative freedom for Anabaptism. The tug of war between Calvinists seeking independence and Catholics loyal to Spain left the authorities little time for persecution of others, though neither group was actually willing to see Anabaptism flourish. But persecution began again in 1586 with the Spanish and, therefore, Roman Catholic victory over Calvinism in Belgium. With renewed pressure upon them, and the attraction of greater freedom in the Dutch provinces to the north, a gradual exodus of Anabaptists came under way again. Some moved to the larger cities in Belgium in order to hide better, but eventually even these were forced to flee. By 1640 there were few Anabaptists left in Belgium, martyrdom and emigration having decimated their ranks. Thus a promising start ended with little more than a trace of its life remaining in the homeland.

Anabaptists in England

To trace the Anabaptist movement in England is difficult but interesting. It is difficult because no separate church group can be identified as a direct result of Anabaptist efforts and because most of the records we now have come from those who opposed and persecuted them. It is interesting, however, because England differed considerably from the Germanic lands, the home for most of the Anabaptists, and because at least three major denominations show signs of influence from Anabaptism: the Congregationalists, the Baptists, and the Quakers.

As early as 1535-36 twenty-five Dutch Anabaptists were arrested and brought to trial in England. Anabaptist writings were known there even earlier. Most of these early refugees came to escape the wrath following the tragedy of Münster as, for example, Jan Matthijs of Middelburg (not to be confused with the Jan Matthijs who was at Münster). England was more tolerant later under Edward VI (1547-53) than under Henry VIII who preceded him and Mary who followed. Under Edward efforts at persuasion and some imprisonment constituted the extent of opposition to Anabaptism, as a result of which they soon worked more openly than before. Their greatest strength was in London and along the eastern coast where the refugees from Flanders landed first. The textile trade made it easy to move across the channel since it was a growing industry in England and continental weavers were much in demand.

Persecution increased under Mary (1553-58), but it is difficult to distinguish the Anabaptist martyrs from other Protestant martyrs, of whom there were many. It is significant, however, to note that the largest number of martyrs came from the areas where Anabaptism had been strongest. With Alva's "reign of terror" in Belgium from 1567 to 1573, thousands more sought safety in England, where Elizabeth was now queen. She issued an edict against them in 1560, and another in 1568, while also appointing a church commission to hunt out and bring to trial all Anabaptists in the land. The *Martyrs Mirror* has a long account of the arrest and persecution of Anabaptists in London in 1575.[2]

After 1580 a new era began for Anabaptists in England. Increased tolerance was won when other groups separated from the state church and began to organize themselves. Some of their central ideas are the same as, or similar to, those distinctive of Anabaptism, including the separation of church and state, the baptism of adult believers only, and the freedom of the local congregation from outside control. Again the leading centers for these groups were in those places where Anabaptists had been numerous earlier.

A number of these new groups had close relations with the Dutch Mennonites, and some even migrated to the Netherlands in search of greater freedom. An example of this is in the case of John Smyth, who came to the Netherlands with his group in 1608. Two congregations were organized, one in Amsterdam under Smyth and another under John Robinson in Leiden. Of these congregations it has been said: "To the Smyth congregation, which accepted adult baptism as a result of contact with Dutch Mennonites, the General Baptists owe their origin. . . . A number of members from Robinson's church were among the Pilgrim Fathers when they sailed for the new world in 1620." [3] Anabaptist doctrine is reflected most clearly in the Quakers, who arose in 1644. George Fox and other Quakers traveled extensively among the Mennonites in the Netherlands and Germany in the seventeenth century.

In summary, it may be said that Anabaptism did not become a permanent church body in England, nor was their number ever very large. Their beliefs and practices, however, did influence the history of the Protestant church in England. The Anabaptist name was lost, but other groups accepted some of the principal points which were causing the Mennonites to remain separate in Germany, Switzerland, France, and the Netherlands at that time.

Mennonites in Northern Germany

The tolerance of the rulers, together with its crucial geographic location, made Emden a major port and crossroads of northwestern Europe. Menno Simons spent much of his time from 1536 to 1544 in this area. Emden was the site of several historic meetings of Mennonites. In 1547 Menno met there with six of his colleagues for a major discussion on the incarnation, infant baptism, and on avoidance, that is, whether a husband or wife should avoid a marriage partner when the other partner was under discipline by the congregation. Usually such meetings included seven elders who had charge of the work in different areas. On January 17, 1568, the Waterlander Mennonites met at Emden and agreed on twenty-one points as a basis for working together. Still later, from February 25 to May 17, 1578, the Flemish Mennonites debated fourteen points of doctrine with the Reformed representatives in 124 sessions in Emden! Records of the debate are extant.

Mennonites could also be found in the late 1530s south of Emden along the lower Rhine, near the present Dutch border, but severe persecution destroyed the settlements eventually. Menno Simons worked there after 1544 for a time under the tolerance of Hermann von Wied, archbishop of Cologne, but when a radical Roman Catholic replaced the archbishop, all Reformation progress ceased in the area. Thomas van Imbroich, whom we met in the previous chapter, and others tried to continue the work.

Late in the sixteenth century Mennonites found refuge again in this area in the city of Krefeld. Here the history of the Mennonites has been tied closely with the history of the city itself to the present day. They contributed decisively to the economic, social, and cultural growth of the city, making it an important textile center. In the 1760s the Mennonite von der Leyen family's weaving looms employed 4,000—5,000 workers. The Krefeld congregation was the only one in this area to survive later. Two of its members

Gateway to the priory church of St. Bartholomew, Smithfield, London, outside which Anabaptists were burned at the stake in the reigns of both Queen Mary and Queen Elizabeth I. Nearby is a monument which honors the "noble army" of Protestant martyrs. The Anabaptist victims of Smithfield have no memorial.

signed the Dordrecht Confession of Faith in 1632. In 1683 thirteen families, of whom all but one family had recently left the Mennonites to join the Quakers, emigrated from here to Germantown in Pennsylvania. In the new world some returned to the Mennonites.

East from Emden, along the north German coast lies Schleswig-Holstein, where Mennonite refugees early settled on the estates of sympathetic noblemen. They knew the Mennonites to be sober and industrious people. The land was marshy, and as Dutchmen these refugees knew about dikes and the recovery of such land for farming. For these reasons they were not only tolerated but even received protection from the noblemen, who would warn them of hostile parties and other dangers. Congregations were founded near Hamburg and Lübeck, and eventually in Altona near Hamburg, where they are still strong today. Here they were legally tolerated after 1601 upon an annual payment of one Thaler tax for each Mennonite householder. By 1605 it is reported that 130 families lived in Altona.

Menno moved into this area for the last years of his life. He was in Wismar until he had to flee following the debate with Micron in 1554. He then settled on an estate of Bartholomäus von Ahlefeldt located between Lübeck and Hamburg, where he built a printshop and was active in writing. Here he also died on January 31, 1561, and was buried in his own garden. The estate was laid waste during the Thirty Years' War, 1618-48, and the Mennonite congregation scattered. Today a monument to Menno Simons, the house where his printshop was located, and a huge linden tree called *Mennolinde* mark the place.

The Vistula Delta Settlements

Mennonites found refuge in another area along the coast of the Baltic Sea. Here again they were welcomed because of their farming and irrigation skill, but there was also more religious tolerance in the free city of Danzig, and on the large estates of the nobility. Many of these estates were in Poland and, for a time, it seemed that there might be as much religious freedom there as in Strasbourg. Because of this, and because it was easy to follow the trade routes by water from Amsterdam to Danzig, many Mennonites and other Dutchmen came to the Vistula Delta in the 1530s and after.

A Mennonite congregation was soon established and grew rapidly. Close ties were maintained with the churches in the Netherlands, as the many old letters still kept in Amsterdam show. Menno Simons visited the congregation in 1549 to aid in the solving of a church problem, and Dirk Philips actually lived in Schottland, a suburb of Danzig, from about 1561 to shortly before his death in 1568. Church centers were established around the cities of Danzig and Elbing, and further east near Königsberg. Mennonites were usually not allowed to settle in the cities themselves, and were constantly subjected to oppressive measures by leaders of the state church. Still, they remained a large and significant group until World War II. Most of the Mennonites who went to Russia in the eighteenth and nineteenth centuries came from these congregations.

A Fellowship Divided

Under the pressures of finding itself as a movement in the midst of persecution, internal problems also arose to trouble the Dutch Mennonites. To some these problems simply proved that the early vision had been lost, to others they were an unfortunate but human and necessary part of growing up to Christian maturity as a fellowship. We have already seen how extreme positions arose with David Joris's belief in prophecy and Adam Pastor's tendency to unitarianism and how these movements were rejected by the main body under Menno's leadership. But where do you stop, when you begin to separate from those with whom you disagree? Much of the history of the Mennonites in the Netherlands from 1555 to 1650 shows that there was no clear and simple answer to this question.

In the disputes of this period some weaknesses became clear. The need to maintain purity in beliefs and practices, for example, is a demand which the church and the Christian ought to feel at all times. But how can this be prevented from becoming an unfair judgment of others who are also striving sincerely but find different answers? For some the church as an organization which demands complete agreement and purity overruled their love and concern for those who needed fellowship and support. There were also personal rivalries, though not immediately recognized as such. Even great leaders such as Menno, Dirk Philips, and Leonard Bouwens were not free of this weakness of an unforgiving spirit, which led to tension and schism.

A major source of their difficulties lay in their refugee life and persecutions. As people moved, they took with them the customs of their native land, customs which sometimes became a source of friction in new surroundings. Thus, for example, the Flemish from Belgium were rather quick-tempered and emotional in expression; they enjoyed fine clothing and good food. The northern Frisians, into whose territory they came, were reserved and did not easily show their feelings; they were not as open in their anger, but when aroused did not easily forget it. They were less concerned about how they dressed, but had fine household goods and linens. These differences rubbed the wrong way despite the common Anabaptist faith which these people shared.

There were also differences in how the faith was to be lived. Some people wanted to try new ideas and practices; others wanted to hold to the tried and true ways of the past. Both groups undoubtedly loved the church, but these attitudes were sufficient cause for disagreements and divisions. It must be remembered that these people had, for the most part, suffered persecution and believed strongly in their doctrines. Those who were willing to face death for their faith were also often ready to break fellowship with brothers or sisters if they thought them wrong. It was the heritage of an age in which religious convictions ran deep and tolerance was not a virtue.

The Waterlanders: The Mennonites of the Netherlands and North Germany today are unions of groups which were divided earlier. Such a division, for example, came about in the sixteenth century between the Waterlanders, who received their name from the lakes and rivers region in which they lived north of Amsterdam, and the followers of Menno Simons. The Waterlanders opposed the strict use of the ban and of shunning or avoidance. Menno himself would probably have worked with them, had it not been for pressure from Dirk Philips, and especially from the missionary Leonard Bouwens. Because the church must be kept "without spot or wrinkle" (Eph. 5:27) as the bride of Christ, the husband of Swaen Rutgers was banned about 1556 for a reason which has long since been forgotten. But she continued to live with her husband in spite of Bouwens' demand that she shun him. For this disobedience she was herself placed under the ban. In protest the more moderate believers left the movement to form their own group. Bouwens, unfortunately, immediately called them the "garbage wagon" because they no longer demanded a pure church.

The group nevertheless continued to grow, apparently repre-

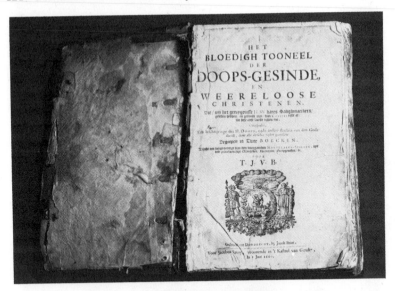

In 1660 Mennonite minister Thieleman Jansz van Braght published the **Martyrs Mirror.** The book contains two parts: accounts of the Christian martyrs from the time of Christ to the 1500s, and a record of the Anabaptist martyrs until the date of publication. The **Martyrs Mirror** went through several editions and translations and it still in print today. An engraving from the second edition (1685) shows a **multiple execution of Anabaptists on Dam Square** in Amsterdam.

senting the sentiments of a large number of Mennonites. Being opposed to Menno in this, though he was much more moderate than Bouwens, they obviously did not wish to be called Mennonites and came simply to be known as *Waterlanders*. They were the first group to hold church conferences with some regularity and with broad representation, beginning in 1568. Under the leadership of Hans de Ries and others, they actively sought unity among the various groups of Mennonites. Their own preferred name *Doopsgezinde*, meaning baptism-minded, is the name used by all Dutch Mennonites today.

The Frisian-Flemish division: Scarcely five years after the death of Menno Simons, a major division developed among those who had been united under his leadership. It was the most serious split among the Dutch Mennonites and took the longest to heal, though no major differences in belief were involved. Both parties later divided again but these divisions had less meaning for the Mennonites as a whole. The story of this split is tangled and the interpretation of events is not always clear. It may be, however, that a look at this situation can be of help in seeing how people who were probably right in principle acted wrongly and how difficult reconciliation becomes when divisions are allowed to continue.

A large number of Flemish Mennonites had come to Friesland, as indicated earlier, and placed much stress on local congregations. In 1560 the church councils in four cities—Harlingen, Franeker, Dokkum, and Leeuwarden—made an agreement to work together but, for some reason, kept the agreement a secret. Of the nineteen articles agreed upon, three dealt with the use of ministers in all four congregations, the support of the poor, and a procedure for settling disputes which could not be resolved locally. The Flemish, who had not been included, now wanted their minister included in the team with the others, but his service was called into question by the others because of the secret agreement. This disclosure of the agreement made the Flemish feel that they had been discriminated against. When the congregations were called upon to vote on the Flemish minister, the voting was not properly held and further difficulties resulted.

In this situation Jan Willems and Lubbert Gerrits of Hoorn were prevailed upon to come to Friesland to mediate, both parties having agreed to accept whatever decision they might arrive at. After a careful study, the issues seemed clear to them. They called a meeting of reconciliation on February 1, 1567, which was well at-

Hans de Ries (1553-1638) an outstanding leader among the Waterlander Mennonites. Throughout his life he worked toward the unification of the various Mennonite groups.

tended, also by outside visitors. After a careful introduction the Frisians were asked to kneel and pray for forgiveness for their error. Then they arose and the Flemish were asked to do the same; when the Flemish wanted to arise from their knees, however, they were told that the Frisians would help them up since they, the Flemish, had the greater guilt. Anyone who knew Flemish tempers should have guessed the result; some assented, but the majority were deeply indignant, and the split was far worse then before.

As the final hope, Dirk Philips came from Danzig to help, together with two other leaders from that area, but no peace could be achieved. Frisian and Flemish now no longer referred to geography but became a party label. Dirk, for example, who was Frisian by birth, was now "Flemish." The Frisian-Flemish division spread across Northern Europe, drawing other issues into it until few knew just how it had started. The disunity spread within each group as well as between them until there were "Old Flemish" and "Soft or Young Flemish," "Old Frisians" and "Young Frisians," and other smaller splits occurred again from these subdivisions. The tragic, and in a way almost comic, point was reached in Emden, where minister Jan van Ophoorn finally banned everyone in the congregation except himself and his wife! The Frisian-Flemish division went with them later to Russia and in the 1870s to Canada.

When people take their convictions seriously and seek purity, they may be tempted to make high demands on others. They may fail to recognize to what degree they have personal weaknesses. Factors such as rivalries between older and younger generations, between leaders, and between groups who rally around some particular idea or practice become occasions for pride and bitterness. Many Mennonites were lost to the Calvinists in the sixteenth century because of their quarreling and splitting. It may be that Mennonites have not yet fully solved the problem of how to be earnestly seeking purity and hold strongly to deep convictions, without splitting over differences between equally sincere believers.

Hans de Ries and Unity

The picture of the church is not as dark as the history of these splits makes it appear to have been. Leaders of broader vision and greater spirit tried to rise above the disputes and restore unity. Lubbert Gerrits, who was unsuccessful in healing the Frisian-Flemish division, later made major efforts for unity, but only the story of Hans de Ries will be told in some detail here. He stands as a symbol of others who shared his spirit.

Hans de Ries was one of the refugees who came north from Belgium. He was born in Antwerp on December 13, 1553. He was a member of the Reformed Church. He was called to the ministry among them, but objected to their use of weapons, which they even brought into church to guard against an unexpected attack. The Mennonites he knew were too divided and rigid for him to join. Later he came north and met the Waterlanders. In 1575 or 1576 he was baptized by Simon Michels and joined that group. He returned to Belgium and was married there, but persecution, which included the burning of his close friend Hans Bret, caused him to flee again. He settled in Alkmaar but spent the years from 1578 to about 1600 in Emden and in travels from that city. In a sermon shortly before his death in 1638, the octogenarian shared how the poor and suffering church of his youth had now become rich and socially acceptable but how much spiritual vigor had been lost in the process. It was out of this concern to remind children of the heritage of their martyr parents that he had already in 1615 published a history of martyrs which became the basis for the larger and more popular *Martyrs Mirror* by T. J. van Braght in 1660. He was a prolific writer, including the compilation of a hymnal which went through six editions after the first printing in 1582.

In Alkmaar he helped draft the first-known Dutch Mennonite confession of faith and subsequently became instrumental in formulating additional confessional statements. Mennonites were opposed to confessions lest they replace the Bible as the only authority but, nevertheless, many confessions did appear in the Dutch Mennonite congregations during this period. They were not intended as measures of orthodoxy but to explain interpretations on points under dispute; groups used them to discuss differences and find unity; and congregations used them both for joining with other congregations in fellowship and as expressions of a common faith for admitting others into membership. The primary test, however, continued to be a life of discipleship rather than assent to a set of propositions.

In his unity efforts Hans de Ries stands out more for his kind spirit than for his achievements. Thus, for example, he succeeded in 1601 in uniting some groups into what they called the "Pacified (Reconciled) Brotherhood." Those who did not join formed the "Separated Brotherhood." From 1610 to 1615 he worked hard to make it possible for the Brownists, a refugee group from England who had come to believe at many points as the Mennonites, to join the Waterlanders. De Ries carried on much correspondence in the interest of the church and was frequently called upon to mediate in difficulties as in Haarlem in 1608, Workum in 1618, and Amsterdam in 1626.

Hans de Ries, however, was not the only one working to bring unity to the Mennonites. As early as 1574 Jan Willems of Hoorn was able to get an agreement on the use of the ban which, many hoped, would make unity possible. The agreement was signed in the province of Groningen at Humsterland and was called the Humster Peace.

But the Flemish elders would not accept it and attempts to make peace at Emden and Hoorn in 1578 failed. In 1591 the Concept of Cologne did lead to agreement among the High German and Frisian congregations. Later they also joined the Waterlanders. In 1632 a confession was drawn up at Dordrecht and further unified the groups. This Dordrecht Confession came to be widely accepted among conservative Mennonite groups, partly because of its emphasis on discipline and foot washing, two articles which are not found in some of the other confessions. The Palatinate and Alsatian churches adopted this confession in 1660, from where it was

brought to North America and adopted in 1725.

Another step toward unity was taken in 1626, when four ministers of the Flemish branch in Amsterdam sent a letter to all churches in the Netherlands asking what the marks of a Christian church are, whether only the Flemish congregations had them, and whether peace was forbidden by the Scriptures. The answers were not too satisfactory; so on September 16, 1627, they drew up a letter to prepare for peace and sent it along with a confession of faith which they had written. The confession was called the Olive Branch, having been drafted as a sign of peace. Other steps were taken until on October 2-5, 1630, the Flemish and Frisian High German congregations joined them.

These various attempts at union did not bring all the Mennonites together. Two more centuries were to pass before that could happen in 1811, yet the forces were working for unity and overcoming the tendency to move apart. By mid-seventeenth century the Dutch Mennonites were entering more fully into the total life of the country and no longer spending most of their energy on internal disputes. They entered upon a Golden Age, if one measures it in terms of achievements in commerce and culture. Not all of this Golden Age brought gain to the church, however, as Hans de Ries had also said.

The Golden Age

The last Dutch Mennonite martyr died in 1574. With the winning of Dutch independence from Roman Catholic Spain, Prince William of Orange established a policy of toleration which soon benefited the Mennonites. In the city of Middelburg the local authorities had closed all shops owned by the Mennonites and were attempting to force them into military service, but on January 26, 1577, Prince William wrote a letter ordering the authorities to leave the Mennonites in peace so long as they remained quiet and useful citizens. The Union of Utrecht in 1579 provided that each person should be allowed to remain free in his religion.

These actions did not mean that all oppression had stopped, but the Mennonites were no longer forced to go to prison or to the stake for their faith. The Reformed ministers continued to harass them considerably, even rudely interrupting their worship services to ridicule them, but the government increasingly came to their defense. Full freedom of worship, however, did not exist for them until the nineteenth century.

Mennonites nevertheless soon made a place for themselves in the life of the nation. The overseas trade with Greenland and whale and herring fishing were almost completely in Mennonite hands. Most of them did not engage in trade with the East Indies because ships had to be armed with cannons or travel under armed escort to guard against pirates and Mennonites had still retained their non-resistant heritage. They did, however, carry on the less profitable, but still valuable Baltic Sea trade. They were also active in ship-building and in the lumber business. In Amsterdam and along the Zaan River they were leaders in the food industry, and in Drenthe they constituted the backbone of the textile industry.

For the most part, Mennonites were highly literate, partly from a desire to read the Bible and martyrologies, but also by way of overcoming their social disadvantage. In the seventeenth century a high percentage of the medical doctors in the Netherlands were Mennonite, this being one of the professions open to them. Since doctors were the best educated members in a congregation, they often served as pastors at the same time. As engineers, the Menno-nites made significant contributions to the draining of swamps. Many also engaged in agriculture and became recognized leaders in that field.

In the fine arts Mennonites soon contributed a number of well-known names also. Carel van Mander was a poet and painter from the Old Flemish of Haarlem and lived from 1548 to 1606. Jan Luyken, who lived from 1649 to 1712, was also known for his work in both fields. The etchings for the second edition of the *Martyrs Mirror* were made by him. The one who ranks among the Dutch people as Shakespeare does among the English was Joost van den Vondel, 1587-1679, whose parents fled from Antwerp because of their faith. He was a deacon among the Waterlanders, but left them to become a Roman Catholic about 1640. Other painters and etch-ers were Solomon van Ruysdael from 1602 to 1670, and Govert Flinck, at least in his youth, 1615-60. It is doubtful whether Rem-brandt, 1606-69, was ever a member of a Mennonite congregation, but he had many close associations with them which no doubt af-fected the religious content of his paintings.

All this progress in material and cultural ways was not pure gain. A century or more after the Mennonites suffered deeply for their faith, they were tolerated and many were wealthy. Many no longer believed deeply in the things for which their fathers and mothers had died. Ease and luxury had done what persecution could not do. Galenus Abrahamsz (1622-1706), a leading minister in Amsterdam, proposed that the devil had found a clever way of dealing with the Mennonites; he stopped persecution and led them to become interested in the material things of the world. The words of Hans de Ries were clearly to the point when he said, "The goods are enriched but the soul is impoverished. Clothing has become precious but the internal decorations have perished. Love has diminished and quarreling has increased."

In mid-seventeenth century the Dutch Mennonites had no serious threat to their life from without; leaders arose who tried to reverse the process of cooling off from within. They collected the stories of the martyrs, the writings of the heroes of faith, and wrote the history of their heritage in order to renew succeeding generations. In contrast to the Swiss, but paralleling the Hutterian Brethren, they were able to leave a very rich literary treasure which has served all Mennonites. All this, however, could not fully stem the tide of weariness from the quarrels within, and persecution from without. The peak of membership and activity had passed, and the following century and a half were to witness a gradual, but continuing decline.

Endnotes

1. A. L. E. Verheyden, *Anabaptism in Flanders, 1530-1650.* Scottdale, Pa.: Herald Press, 1961.
2. Pages 1008-1024. See also Irvin B. Horst, *The Radical Brethren.* Nieuwkoop, Neth.: B. de Graaf, 1972.
3. ME 2:218, 5:269-270. See also James R. Coggins, *John Smyth's Congregation. English Separatism, Mennonite Influence, and the Elect Nation.* Scottdale, Pa.: Herald Press, 1991.

Other Resources: C. Henry Smith, *The Story of the Mennonites.* Newton, Kans.: Faith and Life Press, 1981, pp. 103-188. Cornelius J. Dyck, ed., *A Legacy of Faith.* Newton, Kans.: Faith and Life Press, 1962. Peter J. Klassen, *A Homeland for Strangers. An Introduction to Mennonites in Poland and Prussia.* Fresno, Calif.: Center for Mennonite Brethren Studies, 1989. ME 5:707. Contact any MCC office or the Jan Gleysteen collection (Scottdale) for audiovisual resources.

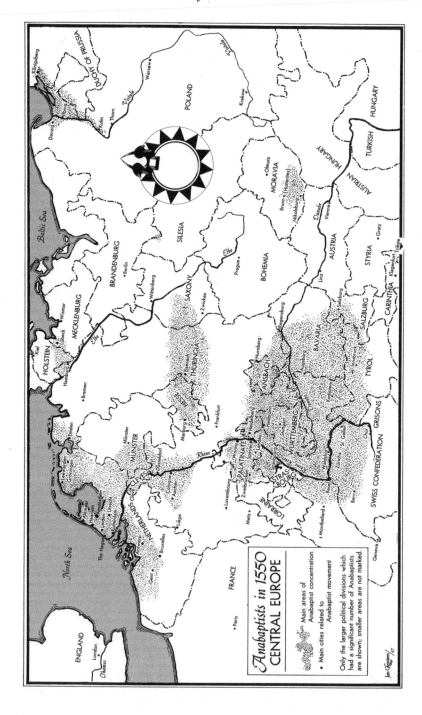

Anabaptists in 1550
CENTRAL EUROPE

Main areas of
Anabaptist concentration

• Main cities related to
Anabaptist movement

Only the larger political divisions which
had a significant number of Anabaptists
are shown; smaller areas are not marked.

8

This They Believed

WE HAVE NOTED the variety of groups in Anabaptism, their origins, geographical spread and, to some extent, their basic faith. We have not, however, developed any comprehensive list or description of theological emphases or doctrines which might be identified as uniquely Anabaptist. It is the purpose of this chapter to provide a brief descriptive summary of the things they most surely believed and, usually, were willing to die for. The almost constant possibility of martyrdom gave an existential meaning to their faith quite different from traditional rational or other theologies then and now.

In listing and defining what might be called core Anabaptist values or doctrinal emphases some important observations must be kept in mind. *First*, the context of their life and thought was Europe in the 1520s to 1560s. How we can move from there to the issues surrounding the year 2000, and in other global settings, is another question. Let us first try to understand them in their own time and place. *Second*, given the variety of persons and movements involved, it will be more helpful to look for a continuum of opinions on a given theme than for a common denominator, i.e., variations on a theme. *Third*, in an attempt to define orthodoxy against Augustine, Vincent of Lerin, a fifth century monk, described it as that which has been "believed everywhere, always and by all," (*quod ubique, quod semper, quod ab omnibus*). While this "Vincentian Can-

on" can probably never be applied, it does point to a possible grid
for Anabaptism, i.e., what can we identify as a core value in the
movement: that which has been believed by most people who
called themselves (Täufer) Anabaptists, in most places, most of the
time? Thus, for example, while Münster was violent, as were the
Batenburgers and some others, most Anabaptists, in most places,
most of the time were nonviolent, nonresistant. This then is a core
value.

Fourth, while an earlier generation of scholars saw Anabaptism
as essentially Protestant, but added discipleship, separation of
church and state, and the need for a church of believers to Zwingli's
and Luther's doctrines, it may be more helpful to define Anabaptism in its own terms. Thus it has often been said that the reformers
and the Anabaptists all believed in the primacy of Scripture—referred to as *sola Scriptura*—but this must be qualified. Yes,
Menno said, "The Word is plain; there are no glosses," but he
linked understanding to obedience.

Luther, in contrast, held a deep conviction that "the Word will
do it"—the Word will bring about the reformation of faith and then
of life, but it didn't, as he himself lamented. Also, for the reformers
sola Scriptura generally meant preaching by trained clergy, but for
the Anabaptists it meant the "hermeneutical circle"—studying the
Scriptures in small, usually secret groups. The reformers and Anabaptists certainly differed in their understanding of the function
and relationship of the Old and New Testaments, and so forth.
Thus using *sola Scriptura* as a common denominator can become
more confusing than helpful.

Finding the Essence of Anabaptism

Before turning to a description of emphases central to Anabaptism within the context of the preceding comments, our understanding of the movement will be enlarged by following the search
of scholars for what they believed to be its *essence*. This search was
carried on primarily during the years in which Anabaptism was
seen as a monolithic, peaceful "evangelical" movement and its distinguishing marks were largely religious. While later studies have
identified multiple origins and emphases, each of the essence proposals carried considerable truth in them, accenting specific unique
dimensions. While scholars today are generally committed to the
views of Anabaptist pluralism they still enjoy testing the possibili-

ties of finding a single *essence* to explain the movement, or adding another window through which to view them, the most recent being anticlericalism and "the common man" as keys to understanding their ethos and appeal.

In 1878 Albrecht Ritschl (d. 1889) first proposed that seventeenth-century Pietism was sixteenth-century Anabaptism revisited and that Anabaptism itself had arisen out of the medieval Franciscan monastic movement, especially its spiritualist wing (see ME 4:342-343). While Mennonite scholars eventually rejected both of these proposals, Kenneth Davis in *Anabaptism and Asceticism* (1974) defended Ritschl's thesis about Franciscan origins, or at least strong parallels to it, particularly in piety and the restitutionist motif, i.e., returning to the New Testament church. We know today that medieval influences were significant, as we have seen. During the 1950s Robert Friedmann (d. 1970) expended considerable energy rejecting any connection between Anabaptism and Pietist origins, noting however, that any later Pietist influence on Mennonitism would inevitably dilute the Anabaptist heritage (see ME 4:176-179; 5:703-704, 311-312).

A different thesis was developed by Ludwig Keller (d. 1915) who, as state archivist in Münster, came to see Anabaptism in a new and mostly positive light through his daily contact with the original documents. Restitutionist and renewal motifs emerged. He developed contacts with German, Dutch and North American Mennonites, carrying further the old thesis that the Waldensians of the twelfth century and similar "old evangelical brotherhoods" were the forerunners of Anabaptism and that this lineage could be traced back in apostolic succession fashion to the early church (see ME 3:162-164; 4:874-875). While this thesis lacks historical evidence it was widely believed by European Mennonite scholars for a time, including T. J. van Braght, compiler of the 1660 *Martyrs Mirror*, as the contents of the book show. More recently Leonard Verduin, translator of the writings of Menno Simons, has promoted some of these ideas in his book *The Reformers and Their Stepchildren* (1964) without claiming as much as Keller did.

Ernst Troeltsch (d. 1923) proposed his well-known church, sect and mysticism (Spiritualist) typology in which Anabaptism, as a sect, represented a dynamic Christianity in which each member had experienced the new birth, practiced nonconformity, and lived in anticipation of the coming kingdom of God. The church, in contrast, was institutionalized traditionalism. Since the latter included

Lutheranism it led to a kind of defensive Luther renaissance under Karl Holl (d. 1926), who returned to earlier polemics against Anabaptists as spiritualists and enthusiasts (*Schwärmer*). Since the 1970s Holl's spiritualist motif has been given more serious attention by scholars of Anabaptism. Among the questions raised by the Troeltsch typology, while gratifying to Mennonites, has been what happens to the second and subsequent generations who are nurtured in the faithful family and small groups and thus do not experience the pivotal "new birth"? Were there *birthright* Anabaptists or, later, Mennonites? When does the creative sect become just another church, i.e., denomination?

Among the many other essence proposals which emerged were the following: (1) Johannes Kühn, who in 1923 identified Anabaptism with discipleship (*Nachfolge*), naming love and cross-bearing as its two primary components, motifs later developed by Harold S. Bender and Dietrich Bonhoeffer, with Bender adding "a new concept of the church" to discipleship and love. (2) Max Weber (d. 1920), German sociologist, was the first to apply the term *believers church* to Mennonites and Quakers, defining it as a church of "regenerate and reborn" people. (3) Cornelius Krahn, in his 1936 book on Menno Simons, proposed the congregation (*Gemeinde*) as central to Menno and Anabaptism, a theme developed earlier by C. H. Wedel in 1900-1904 in his four-volume history of the Mennonites and continued in the 1980s by James C. Juhnke. (4) The centrality of congregational life was also stressed by Robert Friedmann, but he added another motif—kingdom theology, especially the theology of the two kingdoms of light and darkness, reminiscent of Schleitheim. (5) Walther Köhler (d. 1946) of Heidelberg, called the Anabaptists congregations of "radical Bible readers." It may be noted that none of these proposals include baptism as part of the *essence* of Anabaptism, though it may be implicit in Bender's "new concept of the church."

Two other proposals need to be added. First, while J. Denny Weaver, in his 1987 volume *Becoming Anabaptist*, lists the same three themes identified by Bender, i.e., discipleship, believing community (church), and nonresistance (love), he does not consider them as doctrinal absolutes but identifies them as "regulative principles" to help establish theological direction. This avoids the past dilemma of speaking about "normative Anabaptism," particularly since "Jesus is the norm of truth," and leaves room for creative alternatives or additions.

Because the Anabaptists held that the church is a fellowship of believers rather than a building or an organization, they referred to their simple gathering place as a **meetinghouse** rather than a church. They noted the close relationship between **communion** and community and practiced **foot washing** as a symbol of servanthood.

The second proposal, referred to occasionally in twentieth-century writings, including Robert Friedmann in 1963, has been refined and expanded by Walter Klaassen in his modest 1973 volume *Anabaptism: Neither Catholic nor Protestant.* This thesis leads inevitably to a major redefinition of all Anabaptism. In focusing on worship and the sacred, ethics, freedom and legalism; the rejection of traditional modes of doing theology without obedience to it; and the rejection of state authority in the area of faith, a new third religious option became available.

We need to remember that while we can say this in retrospect, in the time of emerging Anabaptism, Protestantism too was still finding its shape and identity. The research of the 1980s has undercut some of the power of this thesis by correlating monastic, Erasmian, Karlstadtian and mystical Müntzerian influences with Anabaptism, thus inserting both Protestantism and Catholicism, as well as their common roots, into Anabaptist origins. However, the thesis remains provocative in its indications of a totally new *essence* in Anabaptism. Yet care must be taken not to lift the movement out of context.

Emphases Central to Anabaptism

Swiss Anabaptism. In chapter 2 we referred to the Grebel circle's letter to Müntzer and in chapter 3 gave a brief description of the Schleitheim articles of 1527. These were not the only developments referred to in the Swiss context, but for our present purposes they are central.

What did the letter of September 5, 1524 emphasize? (1) Errors in the church, like the mass, must be rooted out "by the word and command of Christ." This is the locus of authority. (2) The Lord's Supper is to be a fellowship meal held in love, not taken alone, served by someone "from out of the congregation," i.e., priesthood of all believers, and preceded by admonition according to Matt. 18:15-18, i.e., discipline. (3) This text is also to be the basis for establishing a congregation of believers, i.e., intentional, covenanting. (4) Baptism is to be given to those who are "dead to sin and walk in newness of life and spirit," i.e., the new birth. (5) This baptism does not include children because "they are surely saved by the suffering of Christ, the new Adam." (6) "The gospel and its adherents are not to be protected by the sword, nor are they thus to protect themselves," i.e., nonresistance. And (7) "Christ must suffer still more in his members"; i.e., the church is the body of Christ and suffering will be a mark of its faithfulness.[1]

Similarly, what do we learn about the faith of those who drew up the seven articles at the February 1527 meeting at Schleitheim? (1) Baptism is to follow repentance and commitment to lead a new life, to those whose sins are taken away through Christ, and who "desire to walk in the resurrection of Jesus Christ," which excludes children. (2) The ban shall be used for believers who fall into error, but only after the steps of Matthew 18:15-18 have been followed, i.e., those who refuse to repent. (3) The Lord's Supper is a remembering of Christ's sacrifice and a uniting with him and the believers of the fellowship group. The impression is given that others are not welcome. (4) Separation means avoiding fellowship or contact with the powers of evil. A strong dualism is expressed in the words: "Now there is nothing else in the world and all creation than good or evil . . . darkness and light. . . . God . . . admonishes us therefore to go out from Babylon and from the earthly Egypt." (5) A competent shepherd is given considerable authority in the congregation and is also supported financially by it. (6) Any form of violence is "outside of the perfection of Christ," including being a magistrate (mayor, governor). (7) All oaths are forbidden. "Your speech shall be yea, yea; and nay, nay; for what is more than that comes of evil." [2]

A "Congregational Order" of seven points accompanied the articles, giving specific guidance for the group: (1) Meetings are to be held three or four times weekly. (2) At these meetings they shall exhort and teach one another. It is not to be a social gathering. Reading from the Psalms shall be practiced at home daily. (3) An admonition to good conduct, without frivolity. (4) Admonition is everyone's responsibility in the congregation. (5) Sharing of material goods is encouraged as practiced by the New Testament church. (6) Believers must eat and drink moderately. (7) "The Lord's Supper shall be held as often as the brothers [and sisters] are together." [3]

An important document from the Swiss circle, known as *On the Satisfaction of Christ*, stresses that faith and works are both important for salvation. Neither work-righteousness nor faith alone are sufficient. Taking the "middle path" means doing the works of faith. "How then has Christ worked satisfaction for our sins? . . . Yea, He as the head of His church, has done enough; yet He will nevertheless day by day again do enough in His members. . . .

Therefore, when one speaks of justification through Christ, one must also speak of that faith, which cannot be without works of repentance." [4]

Another Swiss Brethren treatise, perhaps by Sattler, entitled *On Two Kinds of Obedience* or *On Twofold Obedience*, has sometimes been called *"An Anabaptist Tract on Christian Freedom."* The two levels of obedience to God are filial, as a child of the family, or servile, as a servant. Legalism starves the soul. Christian freedom grows out of love and trust in the love of God. Servile obedience is an Old Testament response to the law of God; filial obedience is the joyful response of a child to its father in everything, leading to holiness and blessedness. The treatise is a brief description of the Christian life, serving Christ before Moses but without rejecting the law, which prepares the sinner for redemption.[5]

South and Central German Anabaptism. While none of the *essence* proposals mentioned earlier identified baptism as of the *essence* of Anabaptism, the Anabaptists themselves certainly did! This was undoubtedly because it was the issue on which they were challenged most and was a basic legal reason for their death sentences, but it was also stressed by them because it had to do with their vision of the church of believers.

The foremost Anabaptist writer on baptism was clearly Balthasar Hubmaier, though there are many treatises on the subject by others. Hubmaier belonged to Swiss, South German and Moravian Anabaptism in terms of context and influence. His writings on baptism stand out as the most extensive and helpful to all groups. His treatise *On the Christian Baptism of Believers* is particularly comprehensive.[6] It is also unsettling in its forthrightness when he asks, for example, "What, or how much at least, must I know if I desire to be baptized?" To what extent is baptism based on knowledge and what is the place of experience? He replies with four points initially: (1) "You [must] confess yourself a miserable sinner and guilty." (2) "You [must] also believe the forgiveness of your sins through Jesus Christ." (3) "You [must] give yourself into a new life with the firm resolution to improve your life." (4) "If you fail in this, that you will be willing to let yourself be admonished." Hubmaier was a firm believer in the necessity of instruction before baptism. His other treatises also deal more extensively with the problems inherent in infant baptism.

In his *Apology* Hubmaier gives us a succinct summary: "For I confess three kinds of baptism: that of the Spirit, which takes place inwardly in faith; the second of water, which takes place outwardly by oral affirmation of faith before the church; and the third, of blood in martyrdom or on the deathbed, of which Christ also speaks, Luke 12:50." [7] For Hans Hut, this third point was primary: baptism is the beginning of a life of suffering. Suffering purifies the believer. Christ suffers in all of his members, in all of his creation. Baptism is a dynamic experience, almost a lifelong process as in Luther. It is the real beginning of the struggle against sin. Baptism by the church is a covenant commitment and, hence, a sending forth into mission, but the true baptism is suffering, though comforted by the Holy Spirit. Baptism is a sign of rebirth, of participation in the life and death of Christ; it is the crucifixion of disobedience and the beginning of a life of love and obedience.

Hans Schlaffer (d. 1528), a former priest, wrote:

> You child baptizers say that when a child dies without baptism it is lost and will never see God. Show me, I ask you, one single letter of proof for this in the Holy Scriptures. . . . Christ says about the children that the kingdom of heaven is theirs . . . they belong to him . . . Now if they are his, the dear little children are not lost. Never! . . . Secondly, you exorcise and cast the devil out of the children before you baptize them. Eternal God! How do you know that the child just born in all innocence is possessed by the devil? Let me advise you that it is of the utmost urgency that you cast the devil out from yourselves. He has knocked your bottoms out so that no one can ever fill you.[8]

In his *Confession* of 1532 Pilgram Marpeck wrote: "In the New [Covenant], the children are pronounced holy without baptism . . . they are simply received by Christ, although Paul says: 'Without faith no man can please God.' Children and the retarded are not required to believe or disbelieve these words." [9] For Marpeck the external water baptism of believers was a co-witness with the inner Spirit, accommodating God's mystery to human frailty. Hans Denck similarly considered baptism important for believers. It cannot produce faith and is useless without it just as "water cannot wash away sin, even as one cannot wash away red color from tile," but for those who have received faith "baptism and the Lord's Supper are the completion of the work of Christ." Like baptism, the Lord's Supper was for Marpeck a co-witness uniting the external and internal, the divine with the human.

The discussion of baptism leads to Anabaptist thought about

sin and salvation. Freedom of the will and its seeming polarity grace were central to all Anabaptist understanding and definition of sin with Menno Simons, perhaps, furthest to the theological right, i.e., stressing sin most (note the ban) and Denck least, i.e., sin as negative good, certainly nothing God would create. In the South German movement the latter gave little attention in his treatise *Whether God Is the Cause of Evil* to the fall and original sin, while Hubmaier stressed these themes extensively in both of his treatises on the *Freedom of the Will*. For Marpeck also flesh and blood are not in themselves sin; God's creation was good. But then there came the Fall!

Yet all is not lost. Free will has not been totally destroyed and human nature is not totally depraved, as Augustine taught. Most Anabaptists cited Ezekiel 18:19-20: "The soul that sins shall die," but "When the son has done what is lawful and right, and has been careful to observe all my statutes, he shall surely live." The emphasis is upon personal accountability. But grace is much more important for in it God takes the initiative. Yet Hubmaier, Menno and others stress the abyss of the sin against the Holy Spirit, i.e., apostasy, returning to the broad way, Matthew 12, Mark 3, Luke 12, etc., from which there is no return, Heb. 6:4.

These themes together point to the atonement. Most Anabaptists, in most places, most of the time, believed in the Trinity. (See ME 5:342ff.) There are numerous references to the Apostles' Creed, including some by Hubmaier. Leonhard Schiemer (d. 1528) wrote a commentary on each of the twelve articles.[10] Yet we find little evidence, except in Denck and Adam Pastor, of philosophical or abstract speculation about God. They knew him best through Jesus Christ and the Holy Spirit. Christ was their Savior, Redeemer and eschatalogical hope, but most of all their model for living. The Spirit was their guide, Comforter in suffering, the living Word and guide in reading the Scriptures. Many were at different points in their understanding of the Spirit, however—on a continuum.

Hubmaier expresses the divine unity well in his *Twelve Articles in Prayer Form* when he confesses:

> "I believe and trust that the Holy Spirit has come into me, and that the power of the most high God has overshadowed my soul like that of Mary, so that I might be conceived a new man and be born again in thy living, indestructible Word, and in the Spirit and that I might see the kingdom of God."

A number of Hans Schlaffer's writings reflect trinitarian thought: "Even if Christ had died a 100 times, it would avail nothing if the spiritual Christ is not preached also." Showing the influence of Hut we read, "All Scriptures speak of nothing but of the suffering of the elect. . . . Whoever suffers in the flesh stops sinning" (perfection?). "Only he who follows Christ is a Christian." There are three kinds of grace: the divine Word, i.e., the law, which shows us what sin is; suffering, which reveals the cross to us; and joy, which is a gift of the Spirit. This is **discipleship** written in bold letters.

It is in Marpeck that we find the greatest emphasis upon the human Christ, perhaps because of his continuing debate with the Spiritualist Schwenckfeld (d. 1561), to whom externals were not important and who called the Marpeck circle "water Christians." We noted Marpeck's co-witness, i.e., the importance of externals in the ordinances. There is almost a trace of the "real presence" theology in his view of the Supper. So it is with Christ. He is much more than an ethical model. We dare not forget his humanity. It is easy to believe in a divine Christ; even the devils do that. But Christ became incarnate, took on human nature because it (we) cannot receive divine revelation except through earthly, material means. The incarnation is God's accommodation to human limitations. Christ was clearly at the center of Marpeck's theology. It appears that Marpeck accepted substantial aspects of Swiss Brethren theology into his own thought, thus providing a further bridge between the Swiss and South German movements.[11]

Marpeck, Hubmaier and Denck gave much thought to church-state relationships and to nonresistance. This theme will be discussed in the final section in this chapter on Dutch Anabaptism.

While we have not discussed the nature of the church in this section, it is clear that a vital church life was inspired by Hut, Hubmaier, Marpeck, and also Denck. There is no doubt but that the South German group were the most missionary of all Anabaptists at that time, succeeded then by the Moravians and the Dutch. They were also the most active in seeking dialogue with other Christian groups, as the careers of the four leaders mentioned, and their writings, illustrate, as well as Peter Tasch's 1538 Marburg dialogue with Bucer.

Communitarian—Moravian Anabaptism

The settlements in Moravia represented, in part, the Austrian branch of Anabaptism, but also a melting pot of refugees from the Tirol, Switzerland, and other places where persecution forced them out. Surrounded by a mostly slavic culture, which tended to isolate them, and enjoying the protection of friendly nobles, they flourished here as nowhere else. A rich group life developed, a sense of their own history emerged, which came to be recorded in the *Chronicle* begun by Kaspar Braitmichel in the 1560s, much devotional and other literature was written, and a strong sense of mission continued, even in their dispersion and decline, to the 1650s.[12]

With other Anabaptists Moravian members also stressed the new birth. Without teaching perfection they talked of being "saved *out* of sin." The new birth is grace, but beyond that comes obedience, i.e., the human response. Grace for them was the gradual restoration of the image of God in the believer. Free will was the inner consent to God's commandment. How can one come to God? Primarily with and in the brotherhood as supporting community—a rejection of individualism. The community becomes co-responsible for the salvation of its members and, by extension, for everyone through their mission calling.

As radical restitutionists these early settlements saw the church at Jerusalem as their model, Acts 2:43-47. This included having all possessions in common, but went much further to include true love, surrender, gladness of heart, worship and all of life. Externally community of goods was the most visible sign of inner commitment. This began in a time of extreme need in 1528 near Nikolsburg, now in Czechoslovakia, and continued, with a brief interruption, to the present. The present translators-editors of the *Chronicle* rightly state that this practice "became one of the most controversial points within the Anabaptist movement," and we might add, particularly with those outside of the movement who simply could not understand its motivating spirit.

Most Anabaptists shared what they could with those in need, but this practice of *community* was a total, lifelong yielding to each other, after first yielding to Christ, which saw the love of things and covetousness as *the* original sin. "Where the love of Christ does not enable me to keep brotherhood, there the blood of Christ does not cleanse from sin" (Ehrenpreis). A key word in true community was *Gelassenheit*—meaning yieldedness, self-denial, trust. And a key text was Matthew 6:33-34: "Seek first his kingdom and his righteousness, and all these things shall be yours as well. Therefore do not be anxious about tomorrow." Schiemer wrote, however, that one who has not reached this inner state and loses his valuables will worry all night even if Matthew 6 were read to him a 100 times. True freedom in Christ meant to be freed from the things of this world as objects of pride or love.

The most comprehensive account of Hutterian faith and practice was written by Peter Rideman (d. 1556) during nine years in prison: *Account of Our Religion, Doctrine and Faith*, often simply referred to as *Confession of Faith*.[13] The editors comment: "Much the same life is lived in all Hutterian communities today. . . . There are no class distinctions, no race distinctions. An order of social justice is built up arising from love for one's neighbor. Community is the fruit of this faith and the necessary expression of it." Another early document, likely written by Rideman's successor Peter Walpot (d. 1578), identifies "The Five Articles of the Great Controversy Between Us and the World." These are: the misuse of baptism, of the Lord's Supper, of True Surrender (*Gelassenheit*), government and war, and separation (divorce) of believing and unbelieving marriage partners, which is considered necessary for the spiritual welfare of the believing spouse.[14]

Dutch Anabaptism

It was doubt about the mass and infant baptism that drove Menno Simons, the priest, to the Scriptures. When increasing radicalism among the people drove people he knew to talk about a new Jerusalem about to come in Amsterdam, then Strasbourg and, finally Münster, he admonished them to read other biblical texts besides Daniel and Revelation. He again went to the Scriptures to find direction. And eventually, what he read in the Bible drove him to leave the old church at age 40 and start over. Scripture became very important to Menno. He repeatedly refers to Scripture as the infallible Word.

Others, like Hoffman and Joris, used Scripture selectively to support their own visions. Hoffman did not preach violence, but the Münster debacle grew out of his misuse of Scripture. When Menno became an Anabaptist leader in 1536 he became a hunted man with a large reward promised for his capture. Physically, and often emotionally, his 25 years as a "Mennonite" were miserable years. Yet he felt that the enemy without was no more dangerous than the enemy within his own ranks, the spiritualizers, the visionaries, the impatient reformers who misused Scripture. And to the right, hardliners Leonard Bouwens and others also made life difficult. So Menno held to Scripture as the only reliable guide that could lead him on. Dirk Philips became his close companion and shared his views.

Yet both Menno and Dirk, following Hoffman, erred in their interpretation of the incarnation, i.e., if Christ had taken of Mary's flesh and blood he would be a sinner also and unable to redeem; therefore Christ had only heavenly flesh which God provided. But was he then truly human, incarnate as well as divine? Yes, they said against much ridicule. If ever a course was needed in biblical interpretation (hermeneutics) it was then. Yet the same could have been said about Hut and his visions or, again on the right, the legalism of some of the Swiss who, Marpeck said, counted every fold in an apron as necessary for salvation. But he angered some of them with that and was not allowed to speak or pray in their meetings. Hutterian communalism soon became equally legalistic until renewal came.

The question of authority, whether biblical, the authority of office (elder-bishop), charismatic-personal, or congregational continued to plague all Anabaptist groups long after Menno (d. 1561) and Dirk (d. 1568) were gone. In the Netherlands tension between elder and congregation remained real, but the latter eventually won out. In most other areas strong leaders continued to dominate, including groups of Dutch lineage. Anabaptists had good biblical method as indicated above; they mostly believed the New Testament to be the fulfillment of the Old, as Marpeck also taught, but what ultimately helped them most was that they read it "through Christ," believing that if they obeyed as best they knew the Spirit would lead them on. Menno's motto was 1 Corinthians 3:11: "Other foundation can no one lay than is laid, which is Jesus Christ." (See also ME 5:45-47.)

Nowhere is a continuum of interpretation more visible than in the Anabaptist understanding of church-state relations. All agreed that government was ordained of God (Rom. 13; 1 Tim. 8; 1 Peter 2:13-14) (Zofingen debate, 1531), that it now belonged to the fallen order but that God was still able to use it for good (Col. 1:15-17); all believed in some form of church-world dualism, i.e., that only the ban and not violence has a place in the congregation, and that government should have no role in the church, except Menno, who believed government should punish heretics but not shed blood. All agreed with Acts 5:29 that loyalty to God comes first. Questions were those of function, limits and power. And how can the Sermon on the Mount be reconciled with Romans 13?

The continuum might begin with Hubmaier on the right: defense is necessary and the "sword" justified; there may be just wars but no holy wars. Then might come Menno: government can be Christian and a Christian can be in government. It will suppress evil and reward good. There must be no bloodshed. Then Hut—he carried a staff, not a sword until the Lord returns and gives him one. Then he will help to slay the godless. Then, perhaps, Marpeck, who had a long career as a civil servant. Christians can be in government, but not for long; they will soon be forced to act as the world does, using non-Christian violent methods.

And the rest? Sattler: separation from this evil world! Denck: it will be good to talk with authorities about their options, but violence must never be used. Hutterian Brethren: withdrawal, but pay taxes, except for war and the executioner; basically a two-kingdom dualism. Powerlessness by worldly standards, suffering became the ultimate answer as the *Martyrs Mirror* testifies. Nonviolent resistance does not seem to have been an option then, but needs further study. In the Netherlands there was no more "world" left by 1650, but then Pietism, and later rationalism largely internalized it. (See also ME 5:637-638.)

Did these considerations exhaust the meaning of discipleship? Love, obedience, following Jesus, community, helping the needy, abandoning security and risking death in faithful witness? This certainly seemed to combine ortho-doxy with ortho-praxis. For Menno and Dirk the new birth and regeneration were central to their faith. There could be no true discipleship without first being *reborn*. Regeneration was the larger term, a continuing process, including conversion. "In your life you must be so converted and changed that you become a new person in Christ, so that Christ is in you and you are in Christ" (Menno). "The new birth . . . is a powerful and active work of God and makes the person a new creature in Christ Jesus" (Dirk).

True repentance is seen in new life, which is a sign of regeneration. The believer is not only declared righteous through faith in the work of Christ, but much more, becomes a new person whose being and nature actually change in walking with Christ. Sin loses its grip as holiness and sanctification increase. In the generation after Menno a few persons talked about the possibility of perfection. (See ME 4:414; 5:787-788; 5:756-757; 5:238-239.)

No doctrine was more important to Menno and Dirk than the nature of the church. However, Dirk used the term *church* for sterile traditionalist institutions; for Anabaptism he used the term *congregation*. Dirk had an unusual conception of congregational origins. "The congregation of God was first begun in heaven with the angels" and continued with Adam and Eve in paradise. But that is also where the fall and apostasy came, first with the angels in heaven, then in paradise. The promise of deliverance (Gen. 3:15) was the first preaching of the gospel, through which Adam and Eve had their divine image restored. The congregation is the body of Christ, the bride of Christ, the new Jerusalem.

In addition to the ordinances of baptism and Supper, Dirk stressed "the foot washing of the saints." The fourth ordinance is separation from the world, the fifth is love, the sixth obedience, and the seventh suffering. Menno listed six signs of the true church and six of the false church.[15] Both were restitutionists, i.e., return to the New Testament church, not reformers trying to improve existing structures. Their message was "start over." (See ME 1:594; 5:150-152.)

While the desire for a pure church is present in the Schleitheim articles and other parts of Anabaptism, it was expressed most forcefully in the Dutch movement, particularly through the use of the ban and avoidance (shunning). Both Dirk and Menno wrote several treatises defending its necessity. Yet the pure church eluded them! The ban led to numerous schisms, perhaps in part because it was often imposed unilaterally by a stern elder rather than redemptively by the entire congregation. Menno believed that a church without discipline (ban) is like a house without walls or a garden without fences. Perhaps the church was seen more as an ark than a lighthouse in a wicked world. Yet at its best it was the necessary support group in a counter-culture lifestyle.

Both Menno and Dirk carried a strong missionary concern. Their co-worker Leonard Bouwens kept a list of 10,252 persons he had baptized. In a moving passage Menno wrote:

> Therefore, we preach, as much as is possible, both by day and by night, in houses and in fields, in forests and wastes, hither and yon, at home and abroad, in prisons and in dungeons, in water and in fire, on the scaffold and the wheel. . . . For we feel his living fruit and moving power in our hearts. . . . We could wish that we might save all mankind from the jaws of hell, free them from the chains of their sins, and

by the gracious help of God add them to Christ by the gospel of his peace.[16]

The relatively rapid growth of toleration in the Netherlands led to the early acculturation of many Anabaptists. It led to a large body of literature, the writing of innumerable confessions, of which the *Dordrecht Confession* of 1632 had widest influence, also being adopted in Germantown, Pennsylvania, in 1725. Their first martyrology *Het Offer Des Heeren* was compiled in 1562, followed later by several larger ones, including the classic edition of 1660. In the following generations theological, historical, devotional, catechetical and poetic writings proliferated enormously, as did works of art and other cultural contributions. But this is another story.

In Summary

The above summary of core values, or the essence of the Anabaptist groups described earlier, is not intended to be a systematic or even comprehensive description. Its purpose is rather to accent those aspects of faith important to them, many of them important enough for them to die for. Biblical authority is there as basic, normative for most, and Christ as both Savior and norm for Christian living. Christ, Scripture, the congregation as supporting community of faith, and discipleship appear, in one form or another, in all of the movements. Are these the heart of their faith? It would certainly seem so.

Endnotes

1. Williams and Mergal, *Spiritual and Anabaptist Writers*, pp. 73-85.
2. From Yoder, *Legacy*, pp. 34-42.
3. Ibid., pp. 44-45.
4. Ibid., pp. 108-120.
5. Ibid., pp. 121-125.
6. Pipkin and Yoder, *Hubmaier*, pp. 94-149, but see also his other treatises on the subject, pp. 166ff., 245ff., 275ff., and 386ff. References to baptism also appear in his other writings.
7. Ibid., pp. 301.
8. Walter Klaassen, *Anabaptism in Outline*. Scottdale, Pa.: Herald Press, 1981, p. 171; from Lydia Müller, *Glaubenszeugnisse oberdeutscher Taufgesinnter*. Leipzig, Germany: M. Heinsius Nachfolger, 1938, p. 100.
9. Klaassen, *Outline*, p. 176; from William Klassen and Walter Klaassen, *The Writings of Pilgram Marpeck*. Scottdale, Pa.: Herald Press, 1978, p. 129. A study of ten Anabaptist men and women, 1525-1536, led to an estimated average age of 36.4 at baptism, with none under 20, two between 20-29, four between 30-39, and four between 40-49. ME 5:53.

10. Müller, *Glaubenszeugnisse*, pp. 44ff.

11. Neal Blough, "Pilgram Marpeck und die Schweitzer Brüder um 1540," *Mennonitische Geschichtsblätter*. 47/48 Jahrgang. 1990/91, pp. 162-163.

12. *The Chronicle of the Hutterian Brethren*, volume I, Rifton, N.Y.: Plough Publishing House, 1987.

13. Rifton, N. Y.: Plough Publishing House, 1970. A new edition is in preparation.

14. *Chronicle*, pp. 251-294. See also ME 5:406-409.

15. Dyck, et al. *The Writings of Dirk Philips*, pp. 350-382; CWMS, pp. 743-744.

16. CWMS, p. 633.

Other Resources: Alvin J. Beachy, *The Concept of Grace in the Radical Reformation*. Nieuwkoop, Neth.: B. de Graaf, 1977. C. Arnold Snyder, *The Life and Thought of Michael Sattler*. Scottdale, Pa.: Herald Press, 1984. Donald F. Durnbaugh, *The Believers' Church*. New York, N.Y.: Macmillan, 1968. Robert Friedmann, *The Theology of Anabaptism*. Scottdale, Pa.: Herald Press, 1973. Cornelius J. Dyck, editor. *A Legacy of Faith: The Heritage of Menno Simons*. Newton, Kan.: Faith and Life Press, 1962. Robert Friedmann, *Hutterite Studies*. Goshen, Ind.: Mennonite Historical Society, 1961. Rollin Stely Armour, *Anabaptist Baptism*. Scottdale, Pa.: Herald Press, 1966. Clarence Bauman, *The Spiritual Legacy of Hans Denck*. Leiden, Neth.: E. J. Brill, 1991.

9

Mennonites in Europe, 1648-1815

UNDER THE IMPACT of martyrdom, internal divisions, and accommodation to their environment the strength of original Anabaptism had gradually been lost in the four generations from 1525 to 1650. New movements were arising, however, and capturing elements of their spirit. The Baptists emerged with a concern for believers baptism and congregationalism and the Quakers with a strong peace emphasis. Pietism came to stress the importance of an inner relationship to God. These movements were not without influence upon the Mennonites, but rationalism also came and had a particular effect upon the congregations in the Netherlands. The Swiss and South German Mennonites were best able to preserve their traditional way of life during this period and, to some extent, also the congregations in Eastern Europe in Prussia.

The South

Switzerland: Though Zurich had been the first center of Anabaptism, only the groups in the *rural* cantons of Zurich and Bern remained in 1648. This decline in membership was due, in part, to the strong emphasis upon military preparedness among the Swiss and the consequent pressure upon nonresistant Anabaptists. But the separateness of the congregations from the rest of the people and their culture also made them appear unpatriotic to the Swiss population. The resulting pressure to conform led many to give up their faith and many others to emigration. But emigration itself was very difficult. It became possible only after 1642 through the intercession of the Dutch Mennonites with the Swiss authorities. Until 1661, most of these emigrants came to the Palatinate from Zurich.

As a result of these developments only the Bern Mennonites remained in Switzerland in the late seventeenth century. Efforts to win them to the state church through persuasion and persecution continued. Innumerable mandates of suppression were issued against them in the seventeenth and eighteenth centuries. The persecutions of 1671, 1691, and 1711 were particularly tragic. A special commission was established to deal with them from 1699 to 1743. While the death penalty was no longer applied, other severe measures were taken against them. Many were sent to the sea as galley slaves. Many were imprisoned. They were frequently branded on the forehead to identify them as undesirables. No one was allowed to give them board or room. Those who reported them to the authorities received a reward. Mennonite children were considered illegitimate and had no rights before the law, not even the inheriting of their parents' property. They could not be buried in the community cemeteries. Thus those who could emigrated, especially since they were welcome in South Germany and in Prussia because of their agricultural skill.

Most of the Swiss Mennonites were farmers, though there were some craftsmen, especially linen weavers, among them. Because of the persecution few were able to secure an education, and as a consequence very few writers arose among them. In matters of faith they simply adhered to the 1527 articles of Schleitheim, and in their worship the martyrologies of their forebears, to which they added from time to time, were important. The *Ausbund* was their hymnal. Eventually they also began to use a Reformed Church hymnal containing translations of the psalms, but they usually tore out the front page to eliminate the identity of the book. Use of the 1632 Dordrecht Confession may have begun as early as 1691. Later, pietism influenced the congregations in the direction of a simple, emotional and inner piety, possibly through the reading of the devotional tract, *The Wandering Soul,* written by the Dutch Mennonite Jan Philipsz. Schabaelje in 1635 and printed later in the German language.

Alsace: In 1648 the Treaty of Westphalia gave Alsace to France, except Mulhausen, which returned to the Swiss Confederacy. This political division also had its effect upon the Mennonite congregations, but they continued to meet as best they could. The record of a ministers' meeting held in 1660 shows the seriousness with which they worked at matters of faith. Names represented at the meeting were Egley, Frick, Habich, Husser, Muller, Ringer, Schmidt, and others. The Dordrecht Confession, which the Flemish Mennonites had prepared in 1632, was adopted for use by the Alsatian congregations. We note further from the record of the meeting that a vigorous discussion was held on the nature of the church, including baptism, swearing of oaths, the ban and avoidance, foot washing, and the nature of Christ. Foot washing, which had been neglected, was reinstated as a biblical ordinance. Questions about the nature of Christ were not fully resolved at this meeting. At issue, presumably, was the question about whether Christ had received his flesh from Mary or from heaven, a question discussed vigorously among the Dutch Mennonites during and following the ministry of Menno Simons.

Meanwhile Mennonite refugees continued to come into the region. Among them was Jacob Ammann (b. 1644), who soon became minister and elder of the congregation in Markirch. There he became troubled over the lack of church discipline in his and other Alsatian and Swiss congregations. Appealing to the Dordrecht Confession which the congregations had now adopted, he insisted that church discipline should include avoidance. In its strictest form this meant that even family members must avoid excommunicated persons, making them eat, sleep, and live completely alone. The goal of this action was to bring them to repentance. Ammann also insisted that all congregations should practice foot washing, that members wear simple clothing including beards for the men.

Though he met with considerable opposition, particularly from elder Hans Reist in Switzerland, Amman traveled through the churches in Alsace and Switzerland to share his convictions, frequently banning those who disagreed with him. Numerous attempts were made at reconciliation, even Gerhard Roosen came from Hamburg for that purpose, but without success. Gradually this division became sharper among the churches with most of the Alsatian congregations following Ammann, and with most of the Swiss and South German congregations opposing his teaching. From this time (1694-1697), his followers have generally been known as Amish Mennonites, or simply Amish.

Soon after this division the Amish were faced with an expulsion order from Alsace by the French authorities in 1712. Though they appealed the order they were told to leave. It is likely that the order was given to please Roman Catholics in the area who felt that the authorization of Lutheranism and Calvinism was going too far. Some did leave, but most of them managed to stay, though the instruction to leave was repeated in 1744, 1766, and 1780.

Three Amish conferences were held during this period, one at Steinseltz in 1752, and two in Essingen in 1759 and 1799. The leader among them during this period was Hans Nafziger, who was elected minister in 1731 and ordained as elder soon after. It is he who wrote the detailed statement of how an Amish congregation was to be organized and which has become the pattern for most of their congregations from that time to the present. The first Amish Mennonites probably came to Pennsylvania in 1720. Large migrations to America came later in the eighteenth and to mid-nineteenth century. Settlements were also established in Canada, as well as in Ohio and other Midwestern states.

The Palatinate: The Palatinate of South Germany seemed to be a veritable crossroads for Mennonites in the seventeenth and eighteenth centuries. During this period one finds Swiss Mennonites, Hutterian Brethren from Moravia, Dutch Mennonites, and refugees from other areas all together in this region. The estate owners apparently even welcomed heretics such as the Mennonites were considered to be, if they could work to restore the land after the devastation of the Thirty Years' War (1618-1648). An edict of toleration was issued in their behalf in 1664 by elector Karl Ludwig of the Palatinate. This allowed them to worship in their homes but not to baptize and required the payment of an annual tax for the privilege of toleration.

There is a story of how the elector was riding across his lands one day and come to a Mennonite farm. One of his aides whispered the rumor that the Mennonite was so wealthy because of his skill in making counterfeit money. When the elector confronted the Mennonite with this charge, the farmer simply showed him his blistered hands and said, "All the money I possess has come from this soil through the work of my hands under the blessing of God." According to the records there were twenty-seven congregations with a total of 618 families in this area by mid-eighteenth century. One of their number, David Möllinger (d. 1787), is known to this day as the "father of Palatine agriculture." The Mennonite name Detweiler likewise became synonymous with good farming at this time.

Here as in other congregations of Southern Germany, pietism came to have particular influence among the Mennonites. Leaders in this movement were Peter Weber (d. 1781) and Adam Krehbiel (d. 1804). The leading pietist, John Henry Jung-Stilling, was a personal friend of Möllinger. It was among these congregations also that the prayer book, *Ernsthafte Christenpflicht* (serious attention to Christian duty), was published in 1739, followed by other prayer books later. Of great significance for their congregational life was the publishing of the *Martyrs Mirror* in 1780 through the efforts of Weber and Hans Nafziger.

The North

The Netherlands: In the south the inner life of the Swiss congregations was less open to outside influences than that of those who left to settle in Alsace and the Palatinate. In the north, however, it was the mother congregations in the Netherlands who were influenced, rather than the colonies in Prussia which had sprung from them. Here Galenus Abrahamsz de Haan (d. 1706) assumed leadership after the Thirty Years' War. He was known as "the last prophet among the Anabaptists." He was a medical doctor ordained to the ministry in the Flemish congregation known as *The Lamb* in Amsterdam. Through him the Mennonites soon came into contact with the English Quakers. In an account of a visit with Galenus the Quaker patriarch George Fox reported that the former asked Fox to take his eyes off him, for they bothered him! Through Galenus many Dutch Mennonites also had contact with the Collegiants, an unorganized lay movement concerned with deepening of the spiritual life. It was his openness to the Socinian brethren from Poland, however, who were anti-Trinitarians, which brought him into difficulties, though he did not agree with them about the nature of Christ.

In time a serious division arose among the Mennonites in Amsterdam. Those worshiping at *The Lamb* church, and led by Galenus, were inclined toward a more liberal interpretation of the authority of the old confessions and stressed the importance of right Christian living under the leadership of the Holy Spirit. Those worshiping at *The Sun* church, the conservative wing, with the same intentions as the others, stressed the importance of right doctrine,

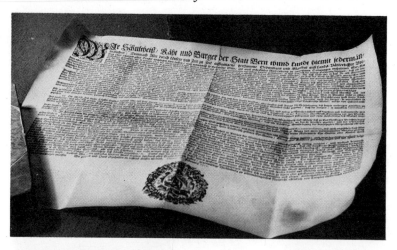

Local, regional, and imperial mandates calling for the extermination of Anabaptist-Mennonite heretics were issued in great number. The city and canton of Bern alone issued 47 mandates between 1527 and 1743. The **mandate of 1711** calls for the compulsory emigration of all Anabaptists. Only a small number of Anabaptists reported for the exile, but on July 13, 1711, four boats sailed down **the Rhine.** Near Mannheim half the passengers escaped to settle in the Palatinate.

calling for adherence to the old confessions and traditions of the past. Galenus finally wrote a clarifying statement in 1699, in which he listed the differences between Mennonite doctrine and Reformed or other groups as consisting of (a) the supremacy of the New Testament over the Old Testament, (b) believers baptism, (c) non-swearing of oaths, (d) nonresistance. The conservatives soon replied with their own statements and a history, written by Herman Schijn (d. 1727), which erroneously linked Anabaptism to the twelfth-century Waldensians.

In addition to these somewhat polemical writings a host of devotional and worship literature appeared among the Dutch Mennonites at this time. These included the *Wandering Soul* and *Martyrs Mirror*, numerous hymnals, and a collection of writings from Menno Simons known as the *Little Menno*. These selections from Menno, which were chosen to stress the importance of conversion and discipleship, helped to shape the life and thought of European Mennonites for many years. They were edited by John Deknatel (d. 1759), a minister at *The Lamb* church who was clearly a pietist and a close friend of the leading pietist Count von Zinzendorf of the Moravian (Herrnhuter) Brethren. A pietist emphasis soon came to be felt in a number of congregations. (See ME 5:703f.)

The Dutch Mennonite congregations were also influenced by their economic experiences. Since they had earlier not been allowed to enter such professions as teaching, nor to hold any public offices, many had become traders, i.e., businessmen. By mid-seventeenth century many of them, having now long enjoyed toleration, became quite wealthy. This in turn led to social, cultural, and educational interests and influence. With many members becoming well educated, the demand for trained ministers arose. For a time members who were medical doctors were often ordained, since they had received the most training, though it was not theological training. By 1735, however, a seminary was founded in Amsterdam under the leadership of *The Lamb* congregation to provide leaders and to prevent the continuing loss of their young men who were seeking theological training in the Remonstrant Church seminary. Beautiful churches were built, including the one built in Rotterdam in 1773. With the new buildings came the desire for musical instruments. In 1765 the first organ was installed in Utrecht. Haarlem followed in 1771. Eventually organs were found in most Dutch Mennonite churches. Audible prayer also gradually replaced the traditional silent prayers of the congregation.

Out of the stress upon discipleship among the Dutch Mennonites arose a concern for mutual aid. Not only did they seek to meet
the needs of unfortunate members among themselves, they also
sent relief to the congregations in the Palatinate in 1696, as well as
to Prussia and Poland in 1711 and 1713. The aid given to the Swiss
has already been referred to. An administrative organization for relief abroad was established in 1725. A society was founded to aid
the families of men lost at sea. Pieter Teyler van der Hulst, a Mennonite merchant, established a foundation in Haarlem in 1778 to
support museums and scientific research. This foundation is still
active. There was genuine concern to use their wealth responsibly
as Christian disciples. Through these activities and resources Mennonite cultural, social, and even political influence in the Netherlands grew stronger than Mennonites have enjoyed anywhere else
at any time.

In spite of these developments, or perhaps because of them, a
decline set in among the congregations. Church discipline became
lax, as did the observance of traditional ordinances such as foot
washing. Mennonite traders and shipowners began to arm themselves, mounting guns onto their ships, because of pirates. When
the privilege of nonresistance was withdrawn by the state in 1799,
very little objection was heard from the Mennonites. Membership
declined sharply, forcing congregations to join together to maintain
their programs. Some left for social or economic reasons, some because their heritage no longer meant much to them, some because
the Reformed Church seemed to offer more spiritual stimulation.

And so, while there had been some 160,000 Mennonites in the
Netherlands in 1700, in 1808 there were only 26,953. One hundred
congregations became extinct in those 108 years. A gradual recovery was to set in, but was followed by another decline, leading to a
baptized membership of 25,589 in 1978 and 18,000 in 1990. The
founding of an all-Mennonite conference known as the *Algemeene
Doopsgezinde Societeit* (ADS) in 1811 became the first of many developments which helped to reverse the decline.

The Lower Rhine: The city of Krefeld was destined to become
one of the key centers of Mennonite activity in the Lower Rhine region in the seventeenth century. Because it was under the sovereignty of the Dutch House of Orange many Dutchmen, including
Mennonites, found their way to the city. Among these was Herman
op den Graeff, a competent Mennonite businessman, who came
there either in 1607 or 1608. He not only founded his business but

established a Mennonite congregation. Numerous new members were added in 1654 and the following years of that decade when Mennonites were expelled from the neighboring duchies of Juelich and Berg. Since these refugees were more High German than Flemish, they gradually turned the life of the congregation in the direction of north German Mennonitism. An open and tolerant attitude in matters of faith became a distinguishing mark of the Krefeld congregation from this time on. In 1693 they were allowed to build a fine church on one of the main streets of the city.

A period of intense prosperity began for Krefeld and the Mennonites when the city came under Prussian control in 1702. Most of the Mennonites in this area were linen weavers, though some, like the von der Leyen family, specialized in silk. In 1731 this family founded the Frederick and Henry von der Leyen company which came to be known internationally for its silk products. For a time the company employed over 3,000 workers, almost half of the population of the city. Special privileges were granted to the Mennonite congregation by Frederick William I of Prussia because of the von der Leyens and in 1721 and 1738 he visited their plant. Later Frederick the Great likewise visited them in 1751 and 1763, presenting them an oil painting of himself. In due course the family was knighted because of their achievements and became a part of the German nobility.

Meanwhile the life of the congregation also changed, particularly through the influence of other religious movements. From 1670 to 1683 the English Quakers worked in that area, influencing some and actually causing some to leave the Mennonite church. Eventually thirteen families followed the invitation of William Penn and settled in Pennsylvania in 1683 to become the first group of German settlers in America. From 1705 to 1725 some of the Mennonites came under the influence of the Dunkards, now known as the Church of the Brethren, who practiced immersion.

The mysticism of the poet and hymn-writer Gerhard Tersteegen also influenced the congregation from 1735 to 1769. The Mennonite meetinghouse was one of the few places where he was allowed to preach. This mystic piety soon prepared the way for rationalism. Through the generosity of the von der Leyen family an organ was installed in the church in 1768, and from 1770 graduates of the Amsterdam Mennonite seminary were engaged as ministers. By late eighteenth century one Mennonite mansion after another was being built on Frederick Street, the most imposing one being

Twice-uprooted Swiss families settled near **Wintersheim in the Palatinate** where they restored neglected fields to fruitful vineyards and abundant fields of grain. In 1770 the Mennonites were given reluctant permission to build a meetinghouse on **the Weierhof,** provided it looked like a farm structure and not like a church.

the von der Leyen "castle" which today serves as the Krefeld city hall. To it Conrad von der Leyen would invite representatives of all confessions in the city for conversations in an effort to encourage tolerance and mutual understanding. A cluster of small congregations formed around Krefeld in the Duchy of Cleve, including one in Emmerich in 1676, Cleve itself in 1683, Rees in 1738, and others. Most of these groups received financial help and spiritual encouragement from the Amsterdam and Krefeld congregations.

South of Cologne, on the right bank of the Rhine, lay the Duchy of Wied. Following the destruction of the Thirty Years' War, Count Frederick (d. 1698) build a new capital on the Rhine in 1653, calling it Neuwied. To rehabilitate his lands he invited whoever would come to settle, including Mennonites, to whom he granted special privileges in 1680. His nephew, Count Alexander, who ruled from 1737 to 1793, caused the Mennonites to build a church near his castle in the same architectural style. Leader of this congregation during this period was Lorenz Friedenreich of Switzerland, a pietist who maintained intimate contact with like-minded brethren in Holland and the Palatinate. The German literary giant Goethe once visited the congregation and subsequently wrote about the "wonderful honesty and integrity" he had seen in the faces of the Mennonites.

East Friesland: In mid-sixteenth century East Friesland became a haven for Mennonites who fled the Netherlands to escape the tyranny of the Spanish occupation. Consequently there were Mennonites in this area throughout the seventeenth century, and several congregations continue to this day. During the early days numerous families had located in the villages of the Krumhorn west of Emden, but by mid-eighteenth century only four city congregations remained in East Friesland, namely, Leer, Emden, Norden, and Neustadt-Goedens. Among these Emden was the center of most activity. Though several graduates of the Amsterdam seminary served these congregations, the members were careful to resist outside influences. Menno Simons' understanding of the incarnation was not forgotten. Church discipline was taken seriously.

While the Mennonites were generally tolerated in this area, every change of government required a renegotiation of their privileges and the paying of additional compensatory taxes. Nevertheless, these families prospered. As in Krefeld, so here most of them were also weavers, though some became quite wealthy in the whaling industry. Here too the Mennonites began to build beautiful church buildings, installing organs, and calling trained seminary graduates to serve them. One of these men, Hinderk Waerma (d. 1741), representing the old Flemish tradition, prepared a Dutch-French confession of faith in 1757 for use by his congregation. The Emden church experienced a division 1692-1732 over the issue of silent or audible prayer during the worship services. While the traditional form had been silent prayer, the progressive Waterlander Mennonites had shifted to audible prayer early in the seventeenth century under the influence of elder Hans de Ries (d. 1638). This influence was now asserting itself in Emden, itself a Waterlander congregation.

In 1720 Joachim Christian Jahring (d. 1729), a Lutheran pastor in the area, described the Mennonites as follows:

> As it generally known, their life and conduct is praised by many, and it is indeed true that they lead an honest and disciplined life. If differences occur with others over financial affairs, they seek private settlement rather than a decision of the courts. They are never heard to swear, nor do they have disputes and violence among themselves. They seek with all diligence to avoid immorality in every respect. So far as their economic life is concerned most of them are engaged in trade, which they carry on in as large a scale as opportunity provides. Because of this many are very wealthy, which is also enhanced by their frugal living. Some support themselves through farming, linen weaving, bakeries, etc.

Hamburg and Schleswig-Holstein: Anabaptists from the Netherlands and the Lower Rhine had been fleeing to Holstein as a sanctuary from the early days of the movement in the sixteenth century. In Fresenburg near Oldesloe, where Menno himself had spent his last days, a congregation flourished until 1656, in Luebeck until 1720. Particularly attractive were the lands under Danish sovereignty. Congregations arose at Glueckstadt on the Elbe, at Friedrichstadt on the Eider River, and in Altona near Hamburg.

Though Mennonites had received an invitation with special privileges from Duke Frederick in 1623 and settled in the Friedrichstadt area, the high point of their congregational life was reached only in early eighteenth century. Already in 1698 the Frisian, Flemish, and High German groups had united as one congregation. By 1708 they had their own meetinghouse with a cemetery. They also established two homes for orphans, widows, and others without income. Here, as elsewhere, they acquired an excellent reputation through quiet living and intense devotion to agriculture and other peaceful vocations. For a time the same issues confronting the Amsterdam congregations were faced here, but their decisions eventually favored the more conservative position of *The Sun* congregation rather than that held by de Haan. In mid-seventeeth century a serious problem also arose when the magistrates refused to give legal sanction to marriages performed by Mennonite ministers, making their children legally illegitimate, but toleration was finally won.

Mennonites were entrusted with public offices in this area sooner than almost anywhere else in Europe. As early as 1607-8 Jan Coodt Classen near Eiderstedt achieved public recognition in municipal affairs. In 1680 a Mennonite became a member of the city council, followed by others including Nicholas der Ovens who became mayor of Friedrichstadt in 1711. At the same time, however, serious reverses were being felt within the congregation itself. Many young people had apparently been marrying members of the Lutheran state church who thereupon also became Mennonites. In 1751, however, a royal mandate decreed that all marriage partners had to become members of the state church if not already so. This led to a rapid decline of Mennonite membership. Thus, while Friedrichstadt counted 178 members in 1703, they counted only 30 members in 1803, one hundred years later.

A larger congregation also arose in Altona. With its adjoining city of Hamburg, Altona enjoyed free city status, both cities governing their own affairs. As traders Mennonites soon found their way to Hamburg-Altona. A special edict favoring them was issued in Altona in 1601 and four years later in Hamburg, as a result of which many Mennonites came to settle there. Though these groups belonged to different traditions, i.e., Frisian, Flemish, and High German, they soon merged into one congregation which located in Altona, while many of the members lived in Hamburg. Coming from the Lower Rhine and the Netherlands, these immigrants naturally brought with them the textile industry and also an interest in shipping and commerce. Some were engaged in whaling expeditions to the coast of Greenland and apparently did very well financially. The profits of the Mennonite whaling crews in 1675, in fact, enabled them to build and completely pay for a new church structure.

An insight may be gained into the life of the congregation through the experiences of two prominent families among them, the Roosen and van der Smissen families. The Roosens came to Altona in 1611 and for 300 years provided strong leadership in the congregation. Prominent among them was Gerhard Roosen (d. 1711), who firmly resisted the immersionist teachings of the Dunkers and the mystical piety of the Quakers around them. At the age of ninety he published a catechism for use in membership classes. This catechism went through many editions and was even translated into the English language. The tenor of this catechism, as of his other writings, was one of accommodation, however, it being Roosen's concern to make Mennonitism appear harmless and as nearly like other Protestant groups as possible. One might describe his catechism as Mennonitism in a minor key (Friedmann).

The van der Smissens came from a patrician family in Brussels and settled in Altona in 1632. Henry (d. 1737) brought fame to the family name through his involvements in the textile and bakery industries. He became so active in rebuilding the city following the Swedish-Danish War of 1712-13 that he was given the honorary title of cofounder of the city. The van der Smissens have been active in the Hamburg-Altona congregation since that time. The life of the congregation would, in fact, be almost unimaginable without the van der Smissen and Roosen families. In 1868 members of the General Conference Mennonite Church persuaded C. J. van der Smissen to come to America as director of the Wadsworth Institute (Ohio), the first Mennonite school for higher theological education in America.

The Mennonites in Prussia—Poland

West Prussia: In 1642 King Wladislaw IV of Poland issued an edict favoring Mennonite settlements in his lands. From the wording of this edict it becomes clear that they had won the respect of their government, and of their neighbors. This became true particularly through their work in draining the swamp lands bordering the Vistula and Nogat rivers, turning erstwhile useless lands into profitable pastures and wheat farms. The cost, however, was high and countless numbers died of swamp fever during the first generation, the estimate of deaths going as high as 80 percent of the settlers for a time. Toleration was the reward granted them for their labors. (See ME 5:314-317.)

This tolerant attitude can be seen, for example, from their experiences in the city of Elbing which belonged to the Hohenzollerns. As early as 1585 two Mennonites were given citizenship in the city, and five years later the congregation was allowed to build their own church. The city council in Danzig likewise was tolerantly disposed toward them but frequently forced to exert pressure upon them to retain favor with the guilds and others who were jealous of Mennonite prosperity. Because of these pressures Mennonites could not receive citizenship in the city of Danzig as late as 1800 and normally had to live on the outskirts of the city.

Persecution was particularly persistent in Danzig. During the Swedish-Polish War of 1655-60, and the Polish War of Succession, 1733-35, many of their houses were destroyed by the war and by those who resented them as a people. In 1660 they were charged by the city with having proselyted and baptized a Roman Catholic woman. Expulsion seemed imminent. The charge could not be proved, however, since the woman herself denied having been rebaptized at all. Similar problems arose again and again, usually initiated by those who were envious of their economic successes. Perhaps the Mennonites, on the other hand, failed to take time for their poorer, non-Mennonite neighbors and scorned them for their poverty. It was also unfortunate that anti-Trinitarianism was strong in that area and that Mennonites were sometimes confused with this movement. Repeated hearings were held to discover their theology, but no anti-Trinitarianism could be found in their doctrines and they stoutly denied it as well.

With the eighteenth century came greater tolerance. This immediately led to the building of churches in many places, though only simple sheds were permitted at first. Thus Thiensdorf was built in 1728, Rosenort in 1754, and Fuerstenwerder, Heubuden, Ladekopp, and Tiegenhagen in 1768. In 1783 a second meetinghouse was built in the country, near Elbing. During this period also the congregations gradually shifted from the use of Dutch to German in their worship services. Of significance for the Mennonites was the transfer of sovereignty of this area from Poland to Prussia in 1772 and the subsequent edict of toleration issued by Frederick the Great in 1780. This and later edicts, nevertheless, did not long satisfy the Mennonite conscience, and by 1789 the great migration to Russia was under way.

East Prussia: In early eighteenth century the plague decimated the population of East Prussia. To revitalize his lands Frederick I invited any who would come, but especially the Mennonites, to settle in that region. The first Mennonites arrived from Switzerland in

1711 but did not stay long. They were followed by others from West Prussia in 1713, who settled in the Memel region near Tilsit. By 1724, however, they were forced to leave again because they refused military service. This expulsion was revoked in 1740, and they returned to establish thriving agricultural communities in the Memel River valley. By 1765 there were 570 members in this region. Congregations had now been established in Königsberg, Brenkenhofswalde, Franztal, and other locations. It was here also that they came into close contact with the Moravian Brethren (Herrnhuter), from whom they learned the practice of child consecration but also acquired a new concern for missions and for the establishing of their own schools in order to preserve their heritage. Gerhard Wiebe (d. 1796) of West Prussia wrote a catechism which was used much in this area and which later found its way to America among the Amish congregations.

Poland: As a buffer state between Germany and Russia, Poland has experienced many boundary changes in its history. West and East Prussia, for example, were added to Poland in 1466. Thus when Mennonites from the Netherlands came to settle along the Vistula River after 1530, they settled in Polish territory. From that time onward until their flight-expulsion from the area in 1945, Mennonites seem to have fared better under the rule of the Polish nobility and kings than under the pressures of state church Lutheranism and Prussian militarism when the latter were in control of the area.

When lands in the Vistula delta and Danzig (Gdansk) area became crowded, or unavailable, the Mennonites moved south along the Vistula River into the interior of Poland, settling at Schwetz, Graudenz, and Culm and eventually near Warsaw at Kazun and Wymysle, as well as southeast to Michalin and into Volhynia. Mennonites and Amish from Switzerland, South Germany, and Alsace settled near Lemberg in Galicia in the eighteenth century, but most of the Swiss-Volhynian and Swiss-Galician settlers later joined the migration of the 1870s to America.

Summary: As we observe the Mennonites in Europe from 1648 to 1815 we note the following phenomena among them: (1) dispersion continues, but toleration is gradually achieved in most places; (2) general economic prosperity which makes them attractive to governments, but stirs envy in the hearts of their neighbors; (3) in the major cities some Mennonites achieve civic prominence and are honored as leading citizens; (4) there is a general numerical decline among them which, if it had continued, would have made them extinct in Europe today; (5) numerous outside influences help to shape their religious life in addition to their economic environment, notably pietism, Quakerism, and rationalism; (6) prominent leaders arise from time to time who, through their writing and active participation in the life of the congregations, give new vision to their people; (7) some of these leaders, and some of the outside movements, bring divisions into the life of the congregations, but by 1815 the impact of tolerance and enlightenment make it possible for most of the Mennonites to overcome their earlier schisms; and (8) some of this new unity must also be attributed to the influence of pietism, which led to a recovery of Bible study, prayer, and a sense of mission among them.

Other Resources: Pietism: ME 5:703-704; Switzerland: ME 5:868; Alsace: ME 1:66-75; Amish: ME 1:90-92; Palatinate: ME 4:106-112; David Möllinger: ME 3:731; *Ernsthafte Christenpflicht*: ME 2:244-245; Lamb's War: ME 3:271; Wandering Soul: ME 4:884-885; Netherlands: ME 3:824-844; Krefeld: ME 1:733-738; Waterlanders: ME 4:895-896; Hamburg-Altona: ME 2:639-643; Prussia: ME 4:224-225, ME 4:920-926, ME 2:123-125; Poland: ME 4:199-200. Smith, *Story*, pp. 75-248. Dyck, *Legacy*, pp. 119-168.

10

The Mennonites in Russia[1]

THE FORMER *Union of Soviet Socialist Republics* (USSR), also referred to
traditionally as Russia, dissolved in late 1991 under the impact of
policies initiated in the late 1980s by its then President Mikhail
Gorbachev. The land and its people remain, of course, except the
Mennonites, most of whom have emigrated to the West.[2] Their exodus makes it even more important to know and to remember the
200-year story of Mennonite life in that land as an important part of
the larger Anabaptist-Mennonite story of pilgrimage, pioneering,
success, failure, suffering, compromise and hope. The Mennonites
leaving Russia in the 1980s and '90s were certainly a different people socially, culturally and spiritually from those who came there
two centuries earlier, or those who left in the 1870s and 1920s.
Knowing this story will also provide background for understanding "Russian Mennonites" and their descendents in Germany and
North and South America.

In 1762-63 Catharine II invited Germans and other Europeans
to settle lands in Southern Russia wrested from the Turks in war,
thus assuring their continued possession. Catherine II was the
German-born wife of Peter III and succeeded him as ruler of Russia
in 1762. Within ten years her invitation had resulted in the establishment of about one hundred German colonies in Southern Russia, but the Mennonites were not to come until the 1780s. Even

then they were not motivated so much by the attractive settlement opportunity as by the pressure of events at home in Prussia. They did not seem to have been aware that they were being used as political pawns in the "New Russia" lands. (Mennonites who settled in the Chaco of Paraguay in the 1930s were also innocent pawns; Mennonite settlers in the United States and Canada seemed unaware that they were taking land from the Indians.) Their vision was sectarian and, hence, inner-directed. We also cannot rightly apply today's agenda to earlier eras.

Growing military preparations, in the face of a Europe made restless by the political upheaval in France, made the Mennonites apprehensive. Then, too, many were without land. The problem arose from the fact that both military and church taxes were based on land ownership, and Mennonites would pay neither for support of the military nor of the state church. The more land they owned, the more difficult it became for the state to finance military and church activities; they already owned approximately 300,000 acres. Consequently, government controls prevented Mennonites from buying more land. But they had large families to support and what should young couples do for a living?

It is not surprising, therefore, that George Trappe, the special representative of Catherine II, found a very cordial reception among the Mennonites when he came to their Prussian communities in 1786. His reports of the settlement possibilities in the new Russian lands were enthusiastic, kindling a like response among those who heard him. At his urging some of the Mennonites appointed Jacob Hoeppner and Johann Bartsch to visit Russia and bring back a firsthand report. This they did, leaving on October 19, 1786, and returning just over a year later. They had many things to report—a visit with Catherine II herself, real travel difficulties, Hoeppner's broken leg—but most important of all, they reported very favorably about the lands they had visited and the agreement they had been able to reach with authorities in St. Petersburg.

The special charter of privileges granted to the Mennonites on March 3, 1788, and later reaffirmed by Tsar Paul I on September 8, 1800, did not vary signficiantly from the privileges granted to other immigrants. Russian colonial policy at the time aimed at a complete separation of all foreigners from the native population, with the result that colonies were quite independent in their affairs. This pattern appealed to the Mennonites, who cherished the right to control their own religious, educational, and civic affairs as they had done in Prussia. Among the privileges was the guarantee of complete religious freedom and exemption from military service for all time. There was also an interesting provision granting the Mennonites special permission to brew beer and vinegar and distill brandy, a trade for which they had already been famous in Danzig and Prussia. These special considerations were justified, especially because they would be model farmers, in the preamble to the charter as follows:

> Conceding to the petition of the Mennonites settled in the New Russian territory, whose excellent industry and morality may, according to the testimony of the authorities, be held up as a model to the other foreigners settled there and thereby deserve special consideration; now therefore with this Imperial Charter we most graciously wish not only to confirm all their rights and privileges specified in the preliminary agreement concluded with them, but in order to stimulate their industry and concern in agriculture even more, to grant them also other advantages, as follows: (the listing followed).[3]

The First Colony at Chortitza

Under these favorable conditions the first eight families, totaling fifty souls and including Hoeppner, left Danzig (present-day Gdansk, Poland) by wagon train on March 22, 1788. It took the group five weeks to reach Riga, less than 300 miles away, where they rested their horses for a month. The next 300 miles took six weeks, bringing them to Dubrovna on July 24. Since Russia was again at war with Turkey, they were forced to spend the winter there. More immigrants joined them in the months following, until there were 228 families in the Dubrovna camp.

Prussian authorities were opposed to the emigration, but the Mennonites went anyway. The prohibition applied particularly to landholders. While there were many landless Mennonites these would likely not have included ministers; the landless were on a lower social level. Since the first to leave were the landless, this may explain why there were no ministers among them.[4] An attempt to elect a minister before the first group left failed because of ancient Frisian-Flemish rivalries. Consequently four men were elected to read sermons they had brought with them, but this did not seem satisfactory.

Soon there were also twelve couples wishing to get married. An offering was finally taken and sent back to Danzig with the re-

A **Mennonite home** on the outskirts of Millerowo, South Russia. In 1924 almost all the Mennonites of Millerowo migrated to Canada. The **Mennonite Hospital and School of Nursing** at Muntau in the Crimea was built in 1889. In 1927 the hospital was placed under communist control and the last Mennonite manager, Franz Wall, was exiled to Siberia.

quest that it be used to send a minister to them. At the same time, however, the Danzig church had written that they should conduct their own elections for a minister. This was done and twelve names were submitted to Danzig, from which four were approved for ministry. One of them, Bernhard Penner, was later commissioned by letter to serve as elder. The awareness of being a "priesthood of all believers" community was obviously muted, while the desire for order and recognized institutional authority was strong.

Three weeks before Easter, 1789, six families set out for their final destination by sleigh and wagon. Travel was slow, however, and the rest of the group caught up with them. It had grown larger with other families coming direct from Danzig. Upon arrival at the land selected earlier by Bartsch and Hoeppner, they were advised to settle on the west side of the Dniepr River, though the two men had chosen the east side, because the latter was still under military operations. This site was miles upstream from the former choice near Kherson. A Russian settlement director was appointed to help them. The new colony, which by now consisted of 400 families, finally located on the banks of the Chortitza River, a tributary of the Dniepr River. The entire settlement came to be known as the Chortitza Colony, or also Old Colony since it was the first Mennonite colony in Ukraine.

Pioneering difficulties were so many in these early years that most of the immigrants became quite dissatisfied. Disease and death took a heavy toll. Rains made the mud huts even muddier. Horses were stolen or lost for lack of fences. Wood for construction was slow in arriving and of inferior quality. The promised government assistance of 500 rubles per family was delayed, much of it arriving eight years later. The people were very poor; even elder Bernhard Penner had to wear homemade sandals to church instead of shoes. There were unsettling clashes with marauding tribes. Nevertheless, by the turn of the century the 400 families had become established in fifteen villages and were farming approximately 89,100 acres of land.

The problems of pioneer life were made more difficult by a lack of unity among the settlers. In time the frustrations of a large number focused on Jacob Hoeppner, who was accused of withholding funds from the others and of using the knowledge gained on his exploration trip for selfish ends. He became the scapegoat of their frustrations, eventually being excommunicated from the church and denounced to the Russian authorities, who imprisoned

him and made plans to send him into exile in Siberia. He was eventually released, however, and joined the church which had been established by the immigrants of Frisian extraction, though he himself was of Flemish origin.[5] His land had been sold while he was in
prison, and he lived the remaining years of his life in silence at
Kronsweide, a casualty of jealousy, suspicion and, perhaps, tension
between the new civil and religious authorities in the colony.[6]
Some years after his death a monument was erected in his honor
on the island of Chortitza in the Dniepr River. The monument was
brought to Canada and erected at the Mennonite Village Museum
in Steinbach, Manitoba, in 1973.

Educational facilities and leadership were also totally inadequate in these early years. Schools were established, but the children were frequently needed at home, and teachers were appointed in a haphazard manner. The curriculum was limited, centering
around the Bible and catechism. In most villages the same building
was used for school and church meetings. These schools, as all affairs of the colony, were under the control of the Mennonites themselves, with little interference from the Russian authorities. To facilitate this control each village elected its mayor or *Schulze* with an
Oberschulze governing the entire colony. Through the *Oberschulze*
contact was also maintained with the Russian authorities in Odessa.
He was their window to the world.

The Molotschna Settlement

Meanwhile, economic and religious restrictions were increasing in Prussia, and the reports from Chortitza were not sufficiently
negative to discourage others from coming. Elder Cornelius
Warkentin of Rosenort in Prussia had visited the Chortitza settlement in 1798, and had discovered the availability of a large tract of
land 100 miles southeast of Chortitza on the Molochnaya River.
With this news, others prepared to leave, and the first Molotschna
group arrived in Chortitza in the fall of 1803. Their stay with these
pioneers during the winter taught them many things which would
make their own settlement less difficult. In the spring of 1804 they
occupied their lands. Others soon joined them, a total of 365 families from 1803 to 1806.

By now the Prussian authorities were becoming alarmed about
the loss of some of their best citizens. The restrictions on land and
taxes, which had been so troublesome to the Mennonites, were re-

After initial years of hardship and discouragement, the Mennonites in South Russia built up excellent farms and helped make the Ukraine "the bread basket of Europe." Their buildings were well-kept and orderly; here a Russian employee shows off a prize **Oldenburger stallion** on a Mennonite farm.

laxed but a 10 percent tax was imposed on all emigrants leaving the country. These provisions, together with the Napoleonic War and Napoleon's march on Moscow in 1812, slowed down the movement but did not stop it. By 1835 some 1,200 families had made their home in the Molotschna colony, settling in fifty-eight villages with an acreage of 324,000, thus constituting the largest settlement Mennonites were to establish in Russia. The villages of Halbstadt and Gnadenfeld served as administrative centers. Because this second movement included teachers, ministers, and other community leaders, as well as being more prosperous than the 1788 movement, progress was rapid and the colony was soon thriving in every respect.

Am Trakt, 1853, and Alexandertal, 1859

Two other colonies were established in Russia before the flow of immigrants from Prussia stopped, the Am Trakt colony in 1853, and the Alexandertal colony in 1859. The Am Trakt settlement was located east of the Volga River in the province of Samara, receiving its name from the *Salztrakt,* a road which was used primarily to haul salt from the Aral Sea and which ran near the settlement. The first nine families arrived in 1853, followed by others until 197 families had located in ten villages by 1872. The original settlement privileges were limited somewhat in that the immigrants had to make a deposit with the Russian embassy in Berlin against costs the government might incur in their behalf. Exemption from military service was limited to twenty years but available after that on payment of a tax assessment. This did not seem problematic in their two-kingdom theology where the military was of the world and they were of the church. Yet there was also a continuing erosion of non-resistance among them in the Prussian context and the influence of the Enlightenment.

Alexandertal, the last of the original Mennonite settlements to be established in Russia, was also located near the Volga River, not far from the Trakt colony. It was named after Czar Alexander II, who was ruling Russia at that time, and who showed special favor to the Mennonites. Settlement privileges were more limited, and the settlers had to buy their own land, but nevertheless by 1870, 106 families had come to the colony. Marketing problems, and some internal tensions due to the religious fanaticism of Claasz Epp, Jr., limited progress in both colonies for a time, but strong leadership helped to place them on a permanent basis by 1900. Among the outstanding leaders of the Am Trakt settlement were Johannes D. Dyck (d. 1898) and Johann Bergmann, the former being decorated three times by the Russian government for pioneering achievements. He had spent a decade in the United States before settling in the Volga region.[7]

With these settlements the Mennonite immigration to Russia came to a close. By this time the threatened loss of exemption from military service in Russia became the stated reason for the emigration of 18,000 to North America as will be seen in the following chapter. The real threat seems to have been the growing emancipation of the Russian serfs and their threat to Mennonite social autonomy. That some Mennonites were sufficiently attracted to come to Russia, while others were, at the same time, sufficiently threatened to leave, is an interesting commentary on Mennonite (and human) nature. In part it was a question of values. Sometimes spiritual values came first; sometimes material values seemed to dominate. Usually it was difficult to distinguish clearly between them.

In all four colonies the difficult pioneer years gradually gave way to years of remarkable prosperity. Whereas the settlers had originally occupied themselves primarily with small crafts and industries including silkworms, the development of Black Sea ports by Russia gave the Mennonites the possibility of grain production and export. The rich Ukrainian soil was ideally suited for the production of hard winter wheat, for which there was increasing demand all over Europe. With economic prosperity also came greater attention to educational, religious, and cultural affairs. Able leaders with training in Russian and European universities began to emerge, and the economy was better able to support the increasing cultural and socio-religious activities.[8] Work was still next to godliness but some dared to engage in the arts—music, literature, painting and other "unproductive" pursuits. Some even discovered the rich Russian cultural heritage.

Johann Cornies, 1789-1848

Among the emerging leaders none influenced the settlements more than Johann Cornies, who was appointed mediator between the Russian government and the Mennonites by the czar at the age of twenty-eight. In that capacity he became, in a sense, director of the growth and development of the Mennonite communities in their economic and educational activities, thereby also influencing their religious life.

Johann Cornies was born in Prussia in 1789 and accompanied his parents to the Molotschna settlement in 1804. After his preliminary grade school education he worked for a year as a laborer in a flour mill, then began marketing agricultural produce in nearby towns. Following his marriage in 1811, he settled on a farm in Ohrloff, a village of the Molotschna colony, but without intending to limit his activities to that location. Soon he was renting large tracts of government land for sheep and cattle grazing, including a 9,000-acre tract by 1830. Among his primary interests were the improvement of horses and livestock and the establishing of nurseries for trees and other horticulture. The government soon recognized his outstanding abilities and gave him almost unlimited authority to promote good agricultural practices among the Mennonites and beyond. In 1817 he was made permanent chairman of the Agricultural Association, which came to include all of the educational activities in the Mennonite colonies.

Under the umbrella of this association Cornies founded a society for Christian education in 1818, an organization which eventually controlled all of the educational activities in the Mennonite colonies. The first secondary school was founded in Ohrloff in 1820. Through his efforts curriculum reform was undertaken, as was better teacher training, and the groundwork was laid for an excellent school system. Among his specific contributions was a major document on "General Rules Concerning Instruction and Treatment of School Children," with counsel for teachers in relation to their school responsibilities.

With his knowledge, drive, and power of position Cornies influenced not only the Mennonites but also the Hutterites and various Russian ethnic groups including the Doukhobors and Molokans.[9] Special instruction in agriculture was given to Russian boys and girls in the Cornies home and to others where they were apprenticed. At the time of his death in 1848, he was farming about 25,000 acres, keeping some 500 horses, 8,000 sheep, and 200 head of cattle.

Growth in Russia

The large number of children in most Mennonite families in Russia led to a rapid increase in population and thus a continuing need for more land since the vast majority gave little thought to occupations other than farming. The original 10,000 settlers had grown to 34,500 by 1859 but had added little land to the original acreage. There were, of course, men like Cornies who rented or purchased estates and farmed on a large scale. It is estimated that by 1900 there were as many as 384 such estates, totaling approximately one million acres, but these estates were the exception. Government regulations were that the original 176-acre plots of land per family were not to be subdivided.

The result of this policy was that many families were soon landless, and without land they became second-class citizens. They were given a garden plot at the outskirts of the village and were, for that reason, known as *Anwohner* (marginal people). The landed farmers, on the other hand, were known as *Wirte* or landlords. While the former had no vote since the franchise was based on land ownership, they were obliged to pay taxes which were based on population. The situation became most acute in the Molotschna colony where there were 2,356 landless workers and 1,384 landed farmers in 1865. Younger *Anwohner* brothers worked for the older brother who had inherited the parental farm, side by side with Russian day laborers. The situation was ripe for social upheaval, even violence and revolution.

With a vision they had not shown before, perhaps born of fear and desperation as well as by government threat and prodding, the two oldest colonies initiated a program of fundraising for the purchase of land in other areas. Here they established the landless and young people in what came to be known as "Daughter Colonies." The new settlers were given ten years to pay for their lands, the proceeds being used for the purchase of more land. The first daughter colony to be established was Bergthal in 1835; a century later more than forty-five had been added in Ukraine, Crimea, Caucasus, south central Asia, and Siberia. In Siberia Mennonites from all of the four old settlements founded the large Slavgorod-Barnaul colony in 1908, with fifty-nine villages on 135,000 acres of land.

Religious Developments

The plight of the landless in mid-nineteenth century gave impetus to a growing restlessness within the church itself. In those years religious organization paralleled community organization; citizens of the community were almost certainly members of the church also.

As the *Oberschulze* (mayor) was in charge of civil affairs, so his counterpart the elder was in charge of the church and, therefore, a powerful figure. The elder was assisted by ministers and deacons who together constituted the *Lehrdienst* (teachers) who, as preservers of the tradition, frequently became defenders of the status quo. In describing the difficult pioneer era, one writer has said:

> Under these circumstances a slow stagnation crept into the intellectual and spiritual life of the group. When missionary David Schlatter visited the colonies in 1825, he reported that the church had lost its salt. But the spiritual life was to sink even lower during the next two decades. What impact could have come from the Russian culture was lost since the settlers did not know the Russian language. . . . By 1845 only one item had been printed by the Mennonites in Russia. . . . Continued intermarriage within the group led to a unique self and group consciousness. To be a Mennonite meant not primarily religious but ethnic relations.[10]

The dissatisfaction of many with this low spiritual state was increased by the failure of the church to champion the cause of the poor among their own ranks. The economic and educational progress made under Cornies' leadership clashed increasingly with the spiritual traditionalism of the church and finally stirred the people to action.

Kleine Gemeinde: As early as 1814 a break had occurred in the unity of the Mennonites in Russia. Klaas Reimer, a young minister who came to the Molotschna Colony in 1804 from Danzig, was appalled at the low level of spiritual life among the immigrants, especially the lack of personal morality and ethical concern. He also opposed Mennonite contributions to the Russian government in the war against Napoleon. He was particularly opposed to the use of corporal punishment by the civic Mennonite leaders, believing that since all were church members, only excommunication should be used to discipline offenders. In reaching these conclusions he was guided by a serious study of the Scriptures, a diligent reading of the *Little Menno* volume, and the *Martyrs Mirror*. This indicated that his central concern was primitivism, the restoration of authentic New Testament and Anabaptist Christianity.

Finding little response in the church, he began meeting separately with like-minded members in 1812, and by 1814 they were organized as a separate group. The others mockingly called this minority group the *Kleine Gemeinde* (small church), a name which the group itself soon accepted fully as indeed indicating the true nature of the faithful church in a hostile world. (The group is today known as the Evangelical Mennonite Conference.) In 1869 a group broke with the *Kleine Gemeinde* over the mode of baptism and formed the Krimmer (Crimea) Mennonite Brethren.

Mennonite Brethren Church: Another division which eventually affected all of the Mennonite communities was the organizing of the Mennonite Brethren Church on January 6, 1860. In 1834 Wilhelm Lange, a Mennonite elder in Germany and former Lutheran, had led a group to the Molotschna settlement to found the village of Gnadenfeld (field of grace). Through contact with Moravian pietism in Germany, these settlers brought with them deep spiritual concern and, in turn, provided contact with other evangelicals traveling through the area. Among these latter travelers was Eduard Wüst, a German pietist, who was soon conducting a series of meetings among the Mennonites. His messages stressed repentance and conversion and called for a life consistent with Christian faith. His meetings led to Bible study and prayer cells. When these Brethren, as they called themselves, despaired of working renewal among the Mennonites, they organized their own fellowship in 1860, with eighteen charter members. Social and economic factors were part of the ferment. Their story will be told in chapter 15.

Other signs of renewal: The invigorating forces which gave birth to the Mennonite Brethren Church did not bypass the other Mennonites known simply as *Kirchliche,* i.e., church Mennonites, or Mennonite church. In 1883 all of these congregations united to form a conference in order to work together in the fields of education and charity. The conference took as its motto, "In essentials unity, in nonessentials liberty, in all things love." In addition to renewed attention to education, concern developed for missions and evangelism. Though the Mennonites were forbidden to proselyte among members of the Russian Orthodox Church, a significant outreach began among their neighbors, at times leading to imprisonment and exile for Mennonite evangelists.[11]

Although the Mennonites in Russia had been supporting the Amsterdam Mennonite Missionary Society since 1854, no missionary had been sent by them until 1871, when Heinrich Dirks went to Sumatra. His return ten years later, and appointment as elder among the home congregations, added considerably to their sense of mission. Dirks was followed by at least twenty-eight workers to Java and Sumatra, and one to Egypt. The much smaller Mennonite Brethren Church was also active in mission work during this time, having sent twenty-two workers to India, and two to Africa by 1914.

This new vitality was sparked by the work of numerous members who deeply felt the inadequacies of their church but decided not to break with it. One of the foremost among them was Bernhard Harder (d. 1884). Harder had also been inspired by the preaching of Eduard Wüst and became a powerful evangelist among the congregations without stressing separation as a mark of renewal. He was roundly criticized by many in the Mennonite church for sounding too much like a Mennonite Brethren and by the Mennonite Brethren for not joining them. But he coveted all the open doors he could find and had ready access to most Mennonite congregations of that time. Though he was a teacher by profession, he occasionally interrupted his teaching to pursue evangelism, being supported during those times by a special group of friends. He has been called the greatest evangelist and pulpit man to arise among the Mennonites in Russia. In the course of his ministry he wrote many poems and hymns, of which over 1,000 have been published.[12] On September 27, 1884, he returned ill from a series of meetings in which he had preached four times daily and died of pneumonia five days later.

Two other developments in the life of the church at this time were the flight into the wilderness of a group under the visionary Claasz Epp, Jr., in 1880, and the establishment of the Evangelical Mennonite Church, generally known as the *Allianz Gemeinde,* in an attempt to overcome the separatist spirit in the settlement, in 1905. Epp was an able leader and farmer who became captivated with the books of Daniel and the Revelation. Under pressure of the events which caused many to leave for America, Epp was led to believe that deliverance from the great tribulation of the last times would come in the East, not in the West. Thus to go to North America was to run away from the Lord. Consequently he led a small group deep into Asiatic Russia in search of the haven *(Bergungsort)* which the Lord had prepared for his people, the Mennonites. Another group, which had joined them from the Molotschna Colony, settled in Alma-Ata in Kasakhstan, while Epp pressed on to Ak-Mechet in the Khanate of Khiva. After untold hardship and suffering some eventually found their way to North America anyway, but Epp died lonely and under excommunication in 1913, having climaxed his vision by proclaiming himself to be the Son of Christ and the fourth person of the Trinity.[13]

The *Allianz Gemeinde* arose in the villages of Lichtfelde and Altonau as a unity movement opposed to the increasing separatist tendencies among the Mennonite Brethren. Its founders were prominent leaders within the Mennonite Brethren Church. They advocated and practiced open communion of all true believers in Christ, accepted as members without rebaptism persons who clearly professed and evidenced faith, regardless of their mode of baptism, and broadened the authority base in the congregations by abolishing the one elder system in favor of a council of elders. The well-known historian P. M. Friesen (d. 1911) was an advocate of this unity movement, but not one of the original founders. Their bridge-building efforts of love were inspiring, but not too successful. In later migrations those in Canada joined the Mennonite Brethren, those in Paraguay remained separate, while those in Brazil joined the General Conference Mennonite Church.

Economic and Social Progress from 1850 to 1920

The high point of community development among the Mennonites of Russia was reached during this period from mid-nineteenth century to the Bolshevik Revolution. The most comprehensive statistics of Mennonite life in Russia were taken for the decade of the 1920s and constitute an invaluable study of the socio-economic conditions at that time. From them it appears that there were 120,000 Mennonites in Russia after World War I, of whom 75,000 lived in Ukraine and 45,000 in Siberia and other parts of Russia.[14] This does not include the 18,000 who emigrated to North America in the 1870s.

The agricultural development promoted by Johann Cornies also made possible and necessary a limited industrial program. Mennonites concentrated on the production of agricultural machinery and the processing of their own agricultural products. Thus by early twentieth century they had seventy large steampowered flour mills, factories whose combined output included 15,000 mowers and 10,000 plows annually, creameries, and other industrial projects. Six percent of the industrial production in Russia was carried on by the Mennonites. But the vast majority of them were farmers. It has been estimated that the industrial wealth, which accounted for 50 to 75 percent of total Mennonite assets, was in the hands of 2.8 percent of the people. Some of them were very wealthy; they traveled or studied in Europe, read Russian books and magazines and, on ocassion, socialized with the elite of Russian society in a variety of cultural settings.[15]

This flourishing economy made possible civic and educational programs unmatched anywhere in the Mennonite world at that time. Mutual aid, homes for the aged, orphanages, hospitals, including a psychiatric hospital, a school for deaf-mutes, a girls' school, and a school of business for young men were only a part of the vast provisions the communities made for their people. By 1914 they had 400 elementary and thirteen secondary or high schools, two teachers' colleges, four trade schools, one Bible school, and negotiations were carried on with the government for permission to establish a seminary. In addition there were approximately 250 Mennonite students attending higher Russian educational institutions and some fifty in seminaries and universities abroad. It is clear that all of these institutions could not have been supported adequately except by congregations who were experiencing a recovery

A prosperous Mennonite **farmstead** (Hof) in Ukraine, ca. 1900. Painted by Woldemar Neufeld. Commissioned by Milo Shantz. Used by permission.

of their spiritual life and were willing to sacrifice for these causes. This willingness was verified further by their support of some 12,000 Mennonite young men in the forestry and medical corps service during World War I which, in 1917 alone, cost the congregations three million rubles.

Developments to 1930

Meanwhile the Russian reform and nationalization program which had begun in 1866 was also affecting the Mennonites. The government-sponsored agricultural reforms led, for example, to a change in regional administrative boundaries. As a result Mennonites began to find themselves a minority in a local Russian administrative unit. Where they were in the majority they were now forced to keep all records and official correspondence in the Russian language. They had also to contribute to the tax support of local political, welfare, and educational institutions, as well as support their own. The fact that many of the landless now received the franchise, moreover, threatened the traditional balance of power in the Mennonite communities.

The biggest threat to the Mennonite way of life, however, lay in the requirement that Russian be taught in all schools and that Russian teachers would be provided where Mennonite teachers were not qualified. Russian had been used in some Mennonite schools as early as the 1830s, and many more used it by the 1860s, but from 1881 the State Department of Instruction kept close watch over the Mennonite schools, and in the 1890s all instruction came to be in the Russian language, with the exception of Bible and German as a language. It is possible that this development conditioned the Mennonites to see the German language as an essential part of the Mennonite faith itself. Elder Leonhard Sudermann spoke for many in 1873 when he said, "Those of our young people who enter Russian higher schools are lost," but a Mennonite opponent of this view wrote in 1874:

> It has been shown that the dear, honorable, bishop was wrong. Our American brethren confess that it is much more difficult to keep their young people in the congregations than in Russia. . . . The number of those who have left the Mennonite faith while studying at Russian schools, or later . . . is very small. More have been lost from those who did not attend Russian schools . . . although these too have been few.[16]

Still most of the Mennonites had learned to identify themselves completely in terms of their totally self-sufficient and exclusive communities. The changes which were coming threatened to assimilate the Mennonites into the Russian population. This seemed to many to forecast an end to their historic faith as a people. Would they indeed necessarily have lost their faith if assimilation or acculturation had taken place? The Mennonite experience in other cultures does not seem to confirm the need for geographical boundaries to maintain identity, but it does change the dynamics of relationships and faith itself. (See ME 5:635-636.)

The climax of this development was reached with the passage of the universal military service law of 1874. In anticipation of its passage the Mennonites sent five delegations to St. Petersburg from 1871 to 1873 to plead for the old privileges. We can appreciate the displeasure of the president of the Imperial Council when he discovered that two of the leading elders could not speak Russian even though they had lived in Russia all their lives. Eventually the delegations were promised alternative service instead of military training, but even this was more than some could tolerate. They asserted that they did recognize government as necessary, they did obey it whenever possible, and they did pray for it. They also cited the official recognition given to them following the Crimean War of 1854-56, when they had made major medical and food contributions and cared for 5,000 wounded which were brought to their colonies from the nearby front. Section 157 of the law of 1874 did provide for alternative service by the Mennonites, but those who felt this to be a violation of conscience, or an indication of further threats to their faith, emigrated to the United States and Canada. This group totaled 18,000. Among those who remained was a critic who charged that too many Mennonites identified their faith with the German language, whereas in Christ there should be neither Jew, nor Greek, nor Scythian, and then he added:

> Thank God that they left. It was good for them, for their children, and for America. Their conscience was eased . . . and America now has received many of our people which are enriching Kansas, Nebraska, Dakota, Minnesota, etc., they are good . . . farming people. . . . for us it was also good . . . and it was good for Russia which was now free of these . . . pious foster children whom it was impossible to satisfy.[17]

Meanwhile the involvement of Mennonites with their Russian environment increased. Mennonite hospitals served many non-Mennonites, business contacts with others increased, and friendships developed as the Russian language ceased to be a barrier. Thousands of Russians served the Mennonites as farm laborers and household help and, in many cases, became very fond of each other. Among Mennonite intellectuals were many who admired Russian literature and read deeply in Russian history to understand the soul of the nation. In the Russo-Japanese War of 1904-5, the families of Russian soldiers from Mennonite areas received substantial monetary and food aid from the colonies. This involvement, however, was not sufficient to close the social, cultural, and economic gap that existed between the Mennonites and their neighbors. The peasants and many Russian officials were jealous of Mennonite achievements, piqued also no doubt by a certain Mennonite hauteur and condescension which they regarded as a feeling of superiority. There were few Mennonite-Russian marriages.

These attitudes, together with Mennonite wealth, brought great difficulty to the colonies with the coming of the Bolshevik Revolution in 1917. As German-speaking people the Mennonites were suspect as enemies of the state in its war against Germany; and as prosperous farmers and businessmen they were soon suspect as enemies of the revolution as well. For a time the struggle between the Red and White Russian armies centered in Ukraine, the battle front having moved back and forth as many as twenty-three times in some Mennonite areas. With this devastation came pillaging by ruthless bands of robbers and opportunists. One of the most dangerous leaders was Nestor Machno, a political prisoner, a philosophical anarchist whom the revolution had released from Siberian exile and who was out to take his revenge on society. Machno knew the Mennonites well, having worked for them as a young man; he even spoke the Low German language. In his opinion they had underpaid him and he was now collecting his wages with the help of thousands of peasants. As a result of this reign of terror hundreds of Mennonites were killed (240 alone in Zagradovka in November 1919) and countless villages completely destroyed.

During these dark hours most of the Mennonites sought to remain true to the principle of nonresistance and of love for the enemy. For a minority of young men, however, this was too difficult to accept in the face of the murder of parents, rape of wives and sisters, and wholesale plunder. With earlier advice and some equipment from the German forces they organized what was known as the *Selbstschutz* (self-defense), and gave armed resistance to Machno, particularly during the winter of 1918-19. Mennonite church conferences later condemned the *Selbstschutz* as both a tactical blunder and a violation of historic biblical nonresistance. A number of these young men were later able to escape to the United States via Constantinople. The *Selbstschutz* experience has since become a favorite case study among Mennonites.[18]

A terrible famine swept over the newly formed USSR from 1919 to 1920 in the aftermath of the revolution and millions of Russians, as well as some Mennonites, died. In desperation the Mennonites sent four men to North America to plead for help from the Mennonite churches. The Mennonite Central Committee was organized in 1920 in response to this request and sent immediate help. This averted heavy casualties among the Mennonites, as well as aiding non-Mennonites as possible. Clayton Kratz, one of the relief workers from Pennsylvania, disappeared mysteriously late in 1920 and was never heard from again. It is estimated that no less than 2,200 Mennonites perished during these years as a result of war, famine, and the typhus epidemic which scourged the land. The four men who had been sent for help had, in the meantime, explored settlement possibilities in Canada and by 1923 a steady flow of immigrants was on their way to join those who had settled there in the 1870s.

Those remaining in the USSR began the difficult task of re-

Legally exempt from military service, Mennonite young men served as hospital orderlies or as **foresters** instead of serving in the army. To escape the terror of the Stalin era (1919-1953) tens of thousands of Russian Mennonites attempted to migrate to North and South America, but only a small percent succeeded. **Railroad boxcars held 25 to 28 refugees each,** with meager personal belongings placed on shelves at each end of the boxcar.

building their communities. An agricultural association was organized to coordinate their concerns and to speak unitedly in their behalf. It also became a channel for emigration which made it suspect in the eyes of the authorities. An office was established in Moscow to provide liaisonship with the new government. In 1925 this office began publishing *Der Praktische Landwirt* (The Practical Farmer) to encourage the Mennonites and keep in touch with them. Another publication, *Unser Blatt* (Our Paper), was begun the same year to speak to spiritual needs and issues.

The last large Mennonite church conference in Russia was held in Moscow in 1925. As part of its business it elected two representatives to the first Mennonite World Conference meeting in Switzerland, and drafted an extensive, optimistic statement to that conference, calling for a MWC treasury to assist needy congregations as well as missions, education, relief, and the promotion of spiritual life globally. The delegates in Moscow proposed beginning this treasury by repaying the relief aid they had received just as soon as possible! But the emissaries Jakob Rempel and Benjamin H. Unruh were not admitted to Switzerland.[19]

With the initiation of the Soviet's first five-year plan on October 1, 1928, which included forced collectivization of their farms, new efforts were made by many to leave the USSR. In a desperate attempt to escape some 13,000 Mennonites made their way to Moscow in the fall and winter of 1929, but only 5,677 managed to get to Germany, due in large measure to the heroic work of B. H. Unruh, by then in Karlsruhe. From Germany they were sent to Canada and South America. More might have been allowed to leave if Germany and Canada had been quicker to grant visas, but these nations had unemployment and other problems of their own as a result of the depression. A few were able to leave in 1930 before all emigration was stopped, bringing to 20,201 the number who had come to Canada from the time the movement began in 1923. Approximately 600 made their escape eastward across the Amur River into China from where they later went to Paraguay and the United States.

The 8,000 Mennonites who had gone to Moscow but had been unable to leave returned to their homes. But many did not arrive there, being sent on to prison or exile and hard labor in the forests of the north. These were followed by countless others who were considered obstacles to the complete collectivization of Soviet agriculture. Most of the exiled never returned. Meanwhile the terrors of collectivization were followed by another famine in 1932-33, in

which from five to eight million Russians died, including over 100,000 German-speaking people. The world Mennonite fellowship again tried to send help. A special MWC was convened in Danzig (now Gdansk) in 1930 to explore how help might be given, but little could be done.

From 1930 to the Present

Spiritual poverty followed close on the heels of physical suffering. In the new society Christian concepts of right and wrong, property, marriage, education, responsibility, and freedom were changed. Revolutionary rights replaced human and civil rights. It became a time of great suffering. Many wives whose husbands had been deported had all they could do to provide daily bread for their children. The children grew up without proper parental attention and without Christian training. By 1935 a majority of the churches were closed and the buildings used as clubhouses, stables, theaters, or granaries. Membership in these congregations had declined rapidly because of the antireligious propaganda and other threats to the faith. Many strong leaders had escaped to Canada, and those who remained were soon in exile.

Non-Mennonites settling in Mennonite villages contributed further to the cultural disintegration of their communities. Some Mennonites also participated actively in the new social revolution. The purges of 1937-38, which victimized over seven million Soviet citizens, also affected the Mennonites. It is now estimated that twenty million Russians were *liquidated* during Stalin's regime. Mennonites suffered with the others, especially leaders and ministers. While the exact number will never be known, we do know that in 1937-38 alone the Chortitza settlement lost 800 men. The stories of some of these are available in a work translated as *Mennonite Martyrs.*[20]

With the coming of World War II in 1939, the complete dissolution of the Mennonite communities was only a matter of time. Many were evacuated into Asiatic Russia in 1941, to escape the German front. For those remaining, the German occupation gave a brief period of relative freedom. While Russians suffered miserably at the hands of the Nazis, German-speaking peoples enjoyed numerous privileges; churches were reopened and religious instruction introduced into the schools. Soon, however, the rigors of war and occupation made the German rule almost as oppressive as communism.

With the German retreat following the battle of Stalingrad in the winter of 1942-43, many ethnic Germans including some 35,000 Mennonites were evacuated westward by the retreating German armies. This retreat soon turned into a mass disorganized flight characterized by panic and terror. Hundreds of refugees died, while scores of families were separated. In the closing days of the war and its aftermath thousands were also forcefully sent back to the USSR as part of the allied Yalta agreement. Only some 12,000 Mennonites were later found in the western zones of Germany. Most of these subsequently migrated to South America and to Canada.

One of the most dreaded experiences of Germans in the USSR, including Mennonites, was to fall into the hands of the *Spetskomandantura* (Special Command) run by the secret police. Beginning in 1941 it led to loss of civil liberties, deportation to northern wastelands, loss of educational and other similar opportunities, loss of families and, in general, an internal reign of terror. The agency was abolished in 1955, with gradual rehabilitation of survivors until 1972. (See ME 5:849-850.)

Little was known about the Mennonites in Russia immediately after World War II ended in 1945, except that there was continued suffering during the fourth five-year plan, 1946-50. Following the death of Joseph Stalin in 1953, internal relaxation and amnesties were granted to the inmates of many of the labor camps in 1953, 1955, and 1957. Although they were not permitted to return to their former homeland in Ukraine and the Volga region, they were at liberty to establish new homes. Many of them moved to Kazakhstan in central Asiatic Russia, frequently worshiping with Baptist congregations. An additional concentration of Mennonite families occurred in southwest Siberia. Some were allowed to join their families in Canada, and some were reunited, fewer than ten, when those living in Canada returned to Russia.

Meanwhile contacts had also been established between the Baptists in Russia and the Mennonites in North America. Beginning in 1956 official exchange visits began to take place with Baptist delegations, frequently including Mennonites, visiting North America and North American Mennonite delegations visiting Russia. These contacts confirmed that Mennonites were losing some of their traditional doctrinal distinctives, as well as their former ethnic identity, but that strong spiritual vitality was evident among many of the estimated 55,000 members scattered across the nation. Many worked intimately with the All-Union Council of Evangelical Christians-Baptists (AUCECB), but others considered these too co-operative with the state and made common cause with the protesting "Reform Baptists," the Council of Churches of Evangelical Christians-Baptists (CCECB) since 1961.

The tragic dimensions of the cultural and spiritual collapse of the remnants of Mennonite life, due in large part to the devastation of the *Spetskomandantura*, were not really understood in the West. Discrimination against believers continued at all levels during the '60s, '70s and into the '80s leading, for example, to a high incidence of functional illiteracy, permanently torn and lost family relationships, unemployment and despair.

A 200-Year Legacy

By 1992 all this had changed. In that year there seemed to be fewer than 10,000 Mennonites left in Russia, with emigration to the West continuing. Once thriving congregations were gone or reduced to a remnant of elderly and ill believers. Russian Mennonite churches, identifying with the culture and using the Russian language, have not been established. Cooperation with the Baptists continues, more readily with the Mennonite Brethren than church Mennonite (*Kirchliche*) groups. Mennonites remaining in the land can and do find fellowship and nurture with these Baptist believers. Young people's activities continue in that context. Some ministers who emigrated to Germany return to their communities in Russia for a period to help as possible, yet by emigrating they forfeited an earlier status; to those remaining, leaving is seen as a kind of betrayal of trust.

It is generally believed that this 200-year chapter of Mennonite history will be closed by the end of the century, though some persons with Russian spouses, non-believers of Mennonite heritage, and a few brave families who believe God has called them to witness there precisely in this time, remain. Several Western Mennonites are attempting a ministry also, and MCC has an office in Moscow. It is amazing how remaining groups fall back upon old traditions of worship and relationships. Why, for example, should there be Mennonite Brethren and church Mennonites after 70 years of intense suffering? Was it faith or primarily tradition which survived? Yet who can predict where and how the Spirit may bring new life and vitality, new birth and hope?

In August of 1989 Mennonites from all over Russia met in what was formerly Chortitza, near the great old oak tree, to celebrate the bicentennial of their beginnings in 1789 and to reflect on the "graciousness and the strictness of God." There was singing, preaching and the distribution of eight tons of Christian literature. An evening evangelistic meeting saw 10,000 people gather in a nearby stadium, most of them Ukrainian evangelicals. One Mennonite who had pastored a Russian congregation for forty years, said:

> Russians are a very nationalistic people. It is impossible to merge the two cultures: German/Dutch and Russian. They will not mix. . . . Now if Mennonites could become like Russians, totally adjusted to their way of thinking, feeling, speaking and acting . . . and at the same time retain their Anabaptist-Mennonite faith, then they would have a future, but that is utterly impossible.[21]

Must Mennonites in North America believe that? Yet who are we to second guess those who have been through it all? The two alternatives posed by the 1989 gathering was either emigration or mission. Mennonite emigration continues despite pleas like one from the Ukrainian evangelical who said, "Please don't leave us alone."

Meanwhile massive demographic shifts are ocurring within Russia. The South Asiatic republics are determined to be Muslim, over fifty million strong; people are returning to their historic lands within the former empire. Mennonites would not have much chance of reclaiming their former colony lands. What is the potential shape of a Mennonite identity in that context? In their "Golden Years" every kind of need was met somehow with a new institution —education, economics, health . . . Can we think of a non-institutional future, as missionaries are now doing around the world? Are the 200 years of experience now an asset or a liability, or does it simply mean a time of totally new beginnings? Mennonites still in Russia should not be left alone with these questions.

The lessons to be learned from the story of the Mennonites in Russia are many and beyond the scope of this chapter, but not beyond careful analysis and reflection. What is it that the church and Mennonites as a people need to learn here? Should the last Mennonite leave Russia, this 200-year experience in all its strength, agony and sorrow needs to be faced as "our" history as clearly as that of the sixteenth century.

Endnotes

1. The *Union of Soviet Socialist Republics (USSR)* established in 1917 dissolved in 1991. Under the leadership of Russia, the largest of the republics, a new tentative union called the *Commonwealth of Independent States (CIS)* was organized. Because of the uncertainty of future developments the traditional name *Russia* will be used in this chapter for the former USSR though separate republics like *Ukraine* will also be referred to.

2. Many ethnic Germans and Jews also left, of course.

3. Quoted in David G. Rempel, "The Mennonite Colonies in Russia: A Study of Their Settlement and Economic Development from 1789 to 1914." Unpublished Ph.D. dissertation, 1933, Appendix II. On the charter of privileges see also John Friesen, "Mennonites in Poland. . ." *Journal of Mennonite Studies*, vol. 4, 1986, esp. pp. 101-103. "Privilegia": In Poland, as in many European countries in the late middle ages, citizenship was not by country or place of birth. A "Privilegia" was a contractual arrangement between a king or nobleman and minorities, e.g., Jews or Mennonites, in his realm, granting specific privileges and requiring commensurate duties; it set forth the legal conditions for residency. Full citizenship was another matter altogether. See also Lawrence Klippenstein, "The Mennonite Migration to Russia, 1786-1806," in John Friesen, editor, *Mennonites in Russia 1788-1988.* Winnipeg, Man.: CMBC Publications, 1989, pp. 13-42.

4. See Adolf Ens, "The Tie That Binds: Prussian and Russian Mennonites (1788-1794)," *Journal of Mennonite Studies*, vol. 8, 1990.

5. For details of the Frisian-Flemish division see Cornelius J. Dyck, et al., *The Writings of Dirk Philips*, 1504-1568. Scottdale, Pa.: Herald Press, 1992, pp. 468ff.

6. Friesen, "Mennonites," pp. 43-53.

7. ME 2:115.

8. See, for example, Al Reimer, *My Harp Is Turned to Mourning.* Winnipeg, Man.: Hyperion Press, 1985. Also John B. Toews, *Czars, Soviets & Mennonites.* Newton, Kan.: Faith and Life Press, 1982, chaps. 3 and 4.

9. See Harvey L. Dyck, "Landlessness in the Old Colony: The Judenplan Experiment 1850-1880." John Friesen, editor. *Mennonites in Russia, 1788-1988.* Winnipeg, Man.: CMBC Publications, 1989, pp. 183-201.

10. Gerhard Lohrenz in C. J. Dyck, editor. *A Legacy of Faith.* Newton, Kan.: Faith and Life Press, 1962, p. 173.

11. Gerhard Lohrenz, "Mennonites in Russia and the Great Commission," in Dyck, *Legacy*, pp. 171-191; cf.: MQR (January 1968), 42:57-67.

12. Heinrich Franz, ed., *Geistliche Lieder und Gelegenheitsgedichte* (1888), and P. B. Harder, ed., *Kleines Liederbuch: Geistliche Gelegenheitslieder* (1902).

13. Fred R. Belk, *The Great Trek of the Russian Mennonites to Central Asia*, 1880-1884. Scottdale, Pa.: Herald Press, 1976. See also Waldemar Janzen, "The Great Trek: Episode or Paradigm?" MQR (April 1977), 51:127-139.

14. Adolf Ehrt, *Das Mennonitentum in Russland.* Langensalza: Julius Beltz, 1932, pp. 91-95.

15. Al Reimer, "Peasant Aristocracy: The Mennonite *Gutsbesitzertum* in Russia," *Journal of Mennonite Studies*, vol. 8, 1990.

16. P. M. Friesen, *The Mennonite Brotherhood in Russia (1789-1910).* Fresno, Calif.: Board of Christian Literature, 1978, p. 593.

17. Ibid., p. 594.

18. Helmut-Harry Loewen and James Urry, "Protecting Mammon. . . ." *Journal of Mennonite Studies*, vol. 9, 1991, pp. 34-53. ME 4:1124; 5:807-808.

19. *Bericht über die 400-jährige Jubliäums-Feier der Mennoniten. . .* Karlsruhe, 1925, pp. 156-57. Cf.: MWC *Handbook* 1978, pp. 3, 8. They met daily at the border with people from the conference. The statement brought from Moscow caused considerable discussion and some controversy at the sessions.

20. A. A. Toews, *Mennonite Martyrs*. Hillsboro, Kan.: Kindred Press, 1990.

21. Walter Sawatsky, "From Russian to Soviet Mennonites, 1941-1988," in Friesen, *Mennonites*, pp. 299-337.

Other Resources: James Urry, *None But Saints. The Transformation of Mennonite Life in Russia, 1789-1989*. Winnipeg, Man.: Hyperion Press, 1989. John B. Toews, *Czars, Soviets & Mennonites*. Newton, Kan.: Faith and Life Press, 1982. Idem, *Lost Fatherland. The Story of the Mennonite Emigration from Soviet Russia, 1921-1927*. Scottdale, Pa.: Herald Press, 1967. C. Henry Smith, *The Coming of the Russian Mennonites*. Berne, Ind.: Mennonite Book Concern, 1927. Walter Sawatsky, *Soviet Evangelicals Since World War II*. Scottdale, Pa.: Herald Press, 1981. William Schroeder and Helmut T. Huebert, *Mennonite Historical Atlas*. Winnipeg, Man.: Springfield Publishers, 1990. Contact any MCC or conference office for audiovisual resources.

11

The Mennonites Come to North America

MENNONITES began coming to North America after direct persecution had ended in Europe. They came to escape the continuing oppression, discrimination, and intolerance they were experiencing, especially the pressure of rising militarism. They also came to seek economic opportunity and adventure. Like the Puritans, who came to Massachusetts Bay by mid-seventeeth century to plant a new Eden in the wilderness, the Mennonites came to preserve the faith, to plant the seeds of a true New Testament church, and to fulfill the vision for which their fathers and mothers had suffered. God was giving them another refuge.

Those who came were part of two broadly related yet culturally unique streams, the Swiss-South German and the Dutch-Prussian-Russian, with the latter coming first but the former soon dominating the scene until well into the nineteenth century. There are references to Dutch *Menists* being in Manhattan (New York) as early as 1644, and on Long Island (New York) in 1657. In 1663 Pieter Cornelisz Plockhoy, a Mennonite Collegiant from Amsterdam and London, established a communitarian settlement of 41 persons, including Mennonites, at Horekill on the Delaware River. But the colony was destroyed a year later by British troops.

On October 6, 1683, a group of thirty-four Mennonites and Quakers from Krefeld, Germany, arrived in America after a 10 1/2-week journey and settled in Germantown, just north of Philadelphia. It was from this group that the first formal protest against the slavery system in America was issued in 1688.[1] By 1705 the Germantown settlers had been joined by others from the Lower Rhine area until they totaled approximately 200. A log meetinghouse was erected in 1708. It was replaced in 1770 by a stone building which is still in use.

From these early beginnings until 1824 European Mennonites settled primarily in the United States. First among these were some 4,000 Swiss and South German Mennonites and about 200 Amish. All went to eastern Pennsylvania. The Seven Years' War (1756-63) between England and France ended further immigration. Continuing unrest in Europe prevented renewed movements until after the Napoleonic wars were over in 1815. From that time on some 3,000 Amish Mennonites came from Alsace-Lorraine and South Germany to Pennsylvania. They also moved further west to Ohio, Illinois, and Indiana. By the time of the Civil War in 1860 a group of at least 500 Mennonites and Amish Mennonites had come to Ohio and Indiana directly from Switzerland.

Meanwhile some Mennonites had also begun moving north to Canada after the Revolutionary War of 1776. By 1800 a considerable group had left Pennsylvania for the Niagara area in Ontario. In 1807 Benjamin Eby founded Ebytown, now Kitchener. These were joined later by Amish groups coming directly from Alsace-Lorraine and Bavaria, as well as additional Mennonites and Amish from Pennsylvania. The need for more land and a desire to remain loyal to the British crown were the primary reasons for the northward movement. The total number of South-German, Swiss, and Alsatian Mennonites and Amish immigrants to the United States and Canada probably did not exceed 8,000, including a small group which came after 1865.

In contrast to this the number of Dutch-Prussian-Russian immigrants were far more numerous, but most of them came in mass movements, except for the initial small group mentioned earlier. From 1873-1884 approximately 18,000 immigrants came from Russia to the Midwest. Many of these were inclined to be conservative, finding the alternative service offered to them in lieu of military service in Russia unacceptable. They settled in Manitoba, Minnesota, South Dakota, Nebraska, and Kansas. Some 300 immigrants from Prussia and about 400 from Polish lands also arrived in Kansas and South Dakota.

Fifty years later, in the decade of the 1920s, these were followed by an even larger number when some 21,000 from the Soviet Union entered Canada. A small group went to California via China. The number coming to Canada since the end of World War II in 1945, directly from the Soviet Union via Western Europe or indirectly via South America, exceeded 20,000. Thus the total number of immigrants in this ethnic-cultural tradition was likely around 60,000. When added to the earlier Swiss-South German figures, some additional Prussian Mennonites, and Hutterites, the immigrant total of all groups from the beginning to the present stands between 70,000 and 75,000.

The Environment of the Early Settlers

The Mennonites came to America at the invitation of William Penn who granted 18,000 acres to six men of the 1683 group on condition that they establish a colony. On their arrival they soon met Francis Daniel Pastorius (d. 1720), who had himself bought 25,000 acres from Penn and served as land agent for the Frankfurt Land Company. Through his efforts and the enthusiastic letters of the settlers, other German minority groups found their way to America and became the neighbors of the Mennonites. These included the Dunkers (Church of the Brethren) in 1719, the Moravians in 1735, and the Schwenckfelders in 1734.

These groups, especially the Mennonites, soon almost covered what is now Lancaster County and continued to branch out. They had many things in common religiously, especially the moral earnestness and Bible-centered emphasis of both Anabaptism and pietism. At first Mennonites were not separatist. "You can hardly imagine how many denominations you will find here . . ." wrote Christopher Schultz, a Schwenkfelder; "Everybody speaks his mind freely. . . . We are all going to and fro like fish in water."[2] At first the Mennonites and Quakers shared a common meetinghouse for worship, but by 1705 the Quakers built their own, as did the Mennonites three years later. At first the Mennonites also shared in the duties of governing Germantown but soon left it to the Quakers who, in turn, were to leave it to the Presbyterians and Anglicans. Germantown had been incorporated in 1691 but lost its charter in 1707, during its Mennonite-Quaker period, because not enough

William Penn, an English Quaker, received land in America from King Charles II in payment of a debt. Penn extended a cordial invitation to the Quakers, Mennonites, and other oppressed minorities to join him in his noble experiment of a peaceful society. In the same spirit, Penn worked out a **treaty with the Indians** already living in the area.

members could be found who were willing to hold office.

Yet Mennonites gradually tended to prefer isolation, either because of the dynamics of sectarianism or the legacy of persecution, and tried to preserve it through geographic and language boundaries, though they could not escape the influence of their environment. Often immigrants also tend to conservatism to preserve the heritage they brought with them, especially in frontier situations. Yet without realizing it or wanting it, Mennonites were becoming part of the North American social, political, and economic scene. Mennonite history cannot be rightly understood without understanding this context. There were no land reserves or autonomous colonies for the Mennonites on the colonial frontier, as there were to be in Russia.

Long before the Mennonites came, earlier settlers had begun to occupy huge tracts of Indian lands, pushing the Natives west ward slowly but surely until, in the course of time, those who remained could be relocated onto reservation lands which white people did not want. Most Mennonites tried to befriend the Indians and some suffered greatly because they would not resort to vio-

The first permanent Mennonite settlement in North America was established in 1683 at Germantown, Pennsylvania. The log meetinghouse which served the pioneers was replaced in 1770 by this fieldstone building, the **oldest Mennonite meeting-house** in continuous use in North America.

lence. But they did enjoy farming the good land and were probably unaware of what they were doing to the culture and future of the Indian nations.

It is estimated that there were some 900,000 Indians in what is now the United States and 400,000 in what is now Canada when Columbus landed in 1492. But instead of increasing in number three fourths of them had been killed by 1800 until there were fewer than 250,000 in the USA and fewer than 95,000 in Canada. Spanish and French Roman Catholic missionaries were active among the Indians from the beginning. A few Protestants, including John Eliot, the Mayhew family, and the Moravians were also at work. The Mennonites did not begin organized evangelistic outreach among the Indians until the late nineteenth century. None of these groups seemed to take the spiritual legacy of the Native peoples seriously at that time.

Negative feelings of Mennonites toward Native Americans were undoubtedly stirred by unfortunate incidents resulting from the clash of interests on the frontier. A settlement of thirty-nine

An early leader among the Germantown Mennonites was William Rittenhouse, who also became the first papermaker in North America. **The Rittenhouse home** still stands along the creek, but the mill was not rebuilt after floods washed it away the second time.

Mennonite families in Page County, Virginia, experienced an Indian raid in 1758, followed by a second raid in 1764. In this second raid the Indians were led by a white man on a bloody rampage which was to cost many lives. Preacher John Roads was killed in the doorway of his home and his wife and son in their yard. A son who climbed a tree to see what was happening was shot in the tree and killed. Still another son was shot and killed as he tried to swim across a river. Later they killed two daughters and another son whom they had taken as captives. A fourth captive was later released by treaty.[3]

An attitude of unconcern and of overcoming obstacles to pioneering was dominant along the frontier and naturally influenced the Mennonites. This was true not only of the early "American" Mennonites, but also of the later immigrants from Russia, as the "Metis incident," which occurred near present-day Winnipeg on July 1, 1873, illustrates. During their travel in what is now Manitoba the delegates, sent from Russia to explore settlement possibilities in

North America, were set upon by an angry mob of Natives who rightly sensed that their future was at stake. The delegates might never have lived to return home had it not been for the gun of their guide and the quick arrival of a contingent of troops. But this did not deter the delegates from recommending the area as a place for settlement. The incident was apparently considered to be the kind of problem pioneers ought to be prepared to expect. Violation of the rights of others—as we see it from the perspective of the 1990s—was not a central issue for them.

The story of the black minority experience in America is also part of the context for the Mennonite experience. In 1619 the Dutch ship *Jesus* arrived at Jamestown, Virginia, from the West Indies and landed twenty black Africans. These were to serve from three to seven years as "indentured servants" to pay for their passage. Then they would be free. Indeed one of them, Anthony H. Johnson, later himself became one of the largest holders of servants in the colony, both black and white. But only too soon the tobacco and cotton economy, requiring cheap labor, brought about the slavery system. By 1710 there were some 50,000 slaves in the USA, by 1776 some 500,000, and by 1860 some 4,000,000.

The petition of 1688 had placed Mennonites on record as opposed to slavery. So far as we know this attitude governed Mennonite conduct during the entire Colonial Period. The Quaker John Woolman (d. 1772) told of a Mennonite who traveled a great distance to visit a friend, but when he saw that he owned slaves he refused his hospitality and slept in the forest. So also the later Burkholder confession of 1837 (Virginia) stated that "as all are free in Christ, they must take no part in slaveholding or in trafficking with them in any wise."

These were not isolated Mennonite statements or actions of that time; they were becoming increasingly conscious and concerned about racism. But often by quietly acquiescing to the racism of their surrounding culture they also participated in it. It is encouraging to note that what is now the Allegheny Mennonite Conference passed a strong resolution against the Ku Klux Klan in 1924 because it discriminated against "Jews, Catholics, and Negroes." In that same year, however, another district conference encouraged the establishing of separate congregations for blacks and cautioned against "close social relations" or intermarriage. It was only after World War II that Mennonites, as part of the Civil Rights Movement in America, began to speak and act courageously here and there against the sin of racism and began to help solve some of the enormous social problems with which racism had saddled the nation.

The Mennonites and Amish Spread Out

Surrounding the Mennonites during the Colonial Period, up to the Revolutionary War in 1776, were a growing number of other church and nonchurch people. While the Mennonites did have large families, the descendants of the original 4,000 immigrants were still a very small part of the total population of the United States, estimated at three million in 1776. Of these only about one in twenty was a church member, yet the piety of the early pioneers and "fathers" is an important myth in American history. The size of the denominations in 1774 were approximately as followers: Anglican 480 congregations, Presbyterian 543, Congregationalists 658, Baptists 498, Quakers 295 "meetings," Dutch Reformed 251, Lutheran 151, and Roman Catholics with ca. 24,500 members in 50 parishes. The sum total might have been approximately 3,000 congregations, which would theoretically have meant at least 1,000 members in each—except for the one in 20 problem.

Yet most Mennonites kept largely to themselves. The desire to avoid contacts with others, the need for more land, and other factors led to their rapid spread across the land. In the 1760s and 1770s Mennonites and Amish settled in southwestern Pennsylvania and in Maryland to form what has been known since 1954 as the Allegheny Conference. As early as 1735, Lancaster Mennonite families located in Franklin County, and by the time of the Revolutionary War also in adjoining Washington County, Maryland. By 1810-1830 they formed the Washington-Franklin Conference.

The movement to *Ontario*, referred to earlier, was not without its problems. A few families had moved there as early as 1786. By 1800 about sixty persons had settled at Vineland, and a settlement was begun that year in Waterloo County. It was in the latter county where the Mennonites bought land only to discover that it had a $20,000 mortgage on it. This was more than they could pay, so two men returned to Lancaster County for help, which they received. In the 1820s these groups were joined by Amish Mennonite immigrants from Europe, who formed the Ontario Amish Mennonite Conference a century later, in 1922. In 1959 they joined the Mennonite General Conference and in 1963 changed their name to

The **Pioneer Tower** near Kitchener, Ontario, marks the spot where the first Pennsylvania Mennonites settled along the Grand River in the spring of 1800. The **Clemens family mirror** survived the trip from Montgomery County, Pennsylvania, to Waterloo County, Ontario, in a Conestoga wagon.

Western Ontario Mennonite Conference. In 1988 they joined two other conferences to form the Mennonite Conference of Eastern Canada. (See ME V:569-70.) From these groups settlers began moving westward in the 1890s to Alberta and Saskatchewan. The Alberta-Saskatchewan Conference was organized in 1907.

Another problem facing the immigrants to Canada was the Militia Act of 1793, which stipulated that all persons between the ages of sixteen and fifty were required to pay a militia tax of twenty shillings per year in time of peace and five pounds per year in time of war. Even more threatening to the Mennonites was the fact that many of their young men did not join the church until some time after age sixteen and would, therefore, be eligible for the draft. A petition in 1810 to the Crown relieved them of this latter problem, but the militia tax remained in effect until 1849 when a bill was passed abolishing the possibility of paying a tax or a fine in lieu of military service and exempting the Mennonites from military service requirements. Meanwhile, however, they had encountered war firsthand when the British demanded their horses, wagons, and supplies in repelling the American invasion of 1812-14.

While the Ontario movement was under way, others moved west to *Ohio, Illinois,* and *Indiana.* Both Mennonites and Amish settled in *Ohio,* with the first families arriving in 1799. While the Old Order Amish formed no conferences and worshiped in homes, the Amish Mennonites gradually adopted the English language, Sunday schools, and church buildings. In the years 1916-27 they merged with what is now the Mennonite Church. Oak Grove in Wayne County became one of its major congregations.

As in Ohio, both Mennonites and Amish Mennonites settled in *Illinois,* largely in the 1830s and 1840s. The Amish Mennonites arrived first, coming from Alsace-Lorraine, Hesse, the Palatinate, Bavaria, and Switzerland, with the greatest number from Alsace. The first congregation to emerge was Partridge, which is represented today in the Metamora church. One of the strongest leaders in the history of the Illinois Amish Mennonites was Joseph Stuckey (d. 1901), often called "Father Stuckey." In the course of time he found himself out of step with other leaders of the Midwest and ultimately withdrew from the Amish Mennonites to form the Central Conference Mennonite Church (name adopted in 1914). In 1946 this group affiliated with the General Conference Mennonite Church. A second leader among the Amish Mennonites was John Smith (d. 1906), whose son C. Henry Smith (d. 1948) has been called the "dean" of American Mennonite historians.[4]

Mennonites and Amish also came to *Indiana* in the 1840s. A few settlements had been established in 1838, when Swiss immigrants from the Jura in the canton of Bern began to settle in Wells and Adams counties. The Adams County Swiss Mennonites are now well known through the large Berne congregation with over 1,300 members. This congregation affiliated with the General Conference Mennonite Church in 1872. A strong leader in the Berne church was S. F. Sprunger (d. 1923). A few families from Lancaster County and the Shenandoah Valley began to settle near Arcadia, between Kokomo and Indianapolis, in 1838 but the congregation remained weak and died out by 1900.

The strongest settlement of Mennonites in Indiana was made west of Goshen in Elkhart County, beginning about 1840. Two early major leaders in this area were John F. Funk (d. 1930), who came to Elkhart from Chicago in 1867, and the outstanding evangelist, John S. Coffman (d. 1899).[5] In 1853-54 a number of Frisian families came from the Netherlands to settle in Elkhart County. Amish families began moving into Indiana in 1841, settling primarily in Elkhart and Lagrange countries.[6]

By 1839 the westward migration of the Mennonites and Amish reached *Iowa* with the arrival of John C. Krehbiel from the Palatinate in Germany. The first church was to be organized in Lee County in 1845, but was postponed to 1849 because of the murder of their minister. The movement to *Missouri* came about the time of the Civil War, and to Kansas early in the 1870s. By 1900 the descendants of the colonial Mennonites, and those coming directly to the west from Europe, had reached the Dakotas, Montana, Colorado, Washington, and Oregon, as well as Oklahoma, Arkansas, Texas, Florida, and California. By the mid-1960s few states remained where descendants of the early immigrants from Switzerland and Germany had not established thriving communities and congregations. In Canada, Quebec had been added as the fourth province in which congregations were established.

During this century or more of frontier experience the Mennonite self-image as the faithful remnant amid growing denominational proliferation remained relatively strong. The transition from Pennsylvania German to English was slow in the church and family, the Dordrecht Confession of 1632 served as guide in doctrine, church discipline was generally mild and loving, and discipleship was taken seriously in a tradition where little new biblical or historical study was being carried on.

The Revolutionary War of 1776, and the Civil War of 1861 were a time of testing for the Mennonites, but also strengthened their identity. Since about one third of the population in the United States was loyalist in 1776, and about one third indifferent to the issues, it was not difficult for the Mennonites to affirm loyalty to King George III, as well as to affirm their nonresistance. Here and there public feeling ran high against them, but already in 1775 the Continental Congress passed a resolution assuring nonresistant persons of their right not to bear arms, while encouraging them to be active in the meeting of human need caused by war.[7]

The Civil War of 1861-65 brought into sharp focus that the Mennonites had grown lax in their teaching of nonresistance. Some hired substitutes to serve in their place, but the church soon discouraged this practice of paying someone to do what one's own conscience forbade. In the North most Mennonites ended up paying a $300 fee and in the South $500 in lieu of military service. Most Mennonites considered this a legitimate government-imposed tax, in contrast to the Quakers who mostly refused to pay it. The shock of the war and its pressure upon the Mennonites became a major factor leading to new spiritual life among them, but many potential members from among their own families were lost to the church in this period.

The Coming of the Mennonites from Russia

We have seen in chapter 10 how and why the Mennonites went to Russia from Prussia beginning in 1789 and continuing to the mid-nineteenth century. By the time the last immigrants had arrived in Alexandertal in 1870, the first contingents were ready to move on to America. One of the major events in North American Mennonite history in the years from 1873 to 1950 was the coming of over 50,000 Mennonites from Russia to the central provinces and states. While their coming added significantly to Mennonite life, the locating of 36,000 of them in central Canada actually began an entirely new chapter in their own religious life, as well as in the life of their new homeland. Most of these immigrants eventually affiliated with the General Conference Mennonite Church or the Mennonite Brethren Church, though some remained independent or belonged to the *Kleine Gemeinde*—now the Evangelical Mennonite Conference.

From 1873 to 1884: During this period approximately 18,000

Mennonites came to the central states and provinces from Russia, of whom 8,000 settled in Manitoba, 5,000 in Kansas, 1,800 each in Minnesota and the Dakota territory, and the rest in Nebraska with a few in Iowa. They came because a new military law which became effective in 1874 seemed to threaten their exemption from military service. Section 157 of that law actually provided for alternative service in forestry or medical work. But they were not accustomed to alternative service and were afraid this was simply the beginning of an end to their coveted religious freedom. Other motives were also involved in their leaving: the increasing pressure upon minority groups to assimilate with the Russian population, the need for more land, and an inability to deal creatively with the problems of a changing society.

The way to North America had been prepared by twelve deputies sent to spy out the land. These men were much encouraged by the friendly attitudes of the American Mennonites and by favorable settlement opportunities. Their return in September 1873 marked the beginning of the emigration. While Canada had gone further in guaranteeing religious freedom than the United States because each state had in the USA had to pass its own legislation, more settled south of the forty-ninth parallel in order to escape the isolation and harsh winters they anticipated in Manitoba. At least one of the deputies would be extremely surprised if he saw Manitoba today, for he wrote very negatively about his impressions. Winnipeg, he said, "is only a small town," and as he traveled across the lands reserved for them, his diary reports:

> The people are lazy farmers of mixed Indian blood. . . . The land does not seem bad. . . . The wheat stand was small but looked fresh and healthy. One could also see considerable unthreshed wheat left from the previous year. . . . We continued our journey through many muddy and marshy places. . . . The roads were very bad. . . . We came to a house where only the wife was at home. . . . They had been living in Canada for two years. . . . She praised the country, very likely because she wanted neighbors. . . . This region seemed more subject to drouth. . . . The mosquitoes were so bad that one could hardly defend himself.[8]

His inspection report concluded with the remark, "To most of us Manitoba country was not to our liking, but seven of the brethren liked it." Since there were only twelve deputies, the majority actually preferred Manitoba. On his return trip through the Dakotas the

A massive migration of Russian Mennonites to the Canadian and American West began in 1874. They soon established new homes and farms, schools and industries. **The mill at Steinbach, Manitoba,** reveals a three-century accumulation of Dutch, North German, and South Russian innovations in its design.

deputy wrote that they saw some grasshoppers, "but not as many as in Manitoba." In strong contrast to this pessimism is the report of the Governor General Lord Dufferin after a visit to the Mennonite settlements in Manitoba in 1877, only a few years after their arrival:

> Although I have witnessed many sights to cause me pleasure during my various progresses through the Dominion, seldom have I beheld any spectacle more pregnant with prophecy, more fraught with promise of a successful future than the Mennonite settlement. When I visited these interesting people they had been only two years in the province, and yet in a long ride I took across many miles of prairie, which but yesterday was absolutely bare, desolate, untenanted, the home of the wolf, the badger, and the eagle, I passed village after village, homestead after homestead, furnished with all the conveniences and incidents of European comfort, and of a scientific agriculture; while on either side of the road, cornfields ripe for harvest, and pastures populous with herds of cattle stretched away to the horizon. Even on this continent—the peculiar theater of rapid change and progress—there has nowhere, I imagine, taken place so marvelous a transformation.[9]

Reports from settlements in the United States were equally glow-ing. In 1883 one Kansas writer said that "the sight of their [Menno-nite] fields and orchards, their trim buildings hedged in with mul-berry, is like a glimpse of some fair new land of promise." A few years later *The Daily Record* of Lawrence, Kansas, reported:

> After sixteen years those Mennonites are with us still. They abided and toiled in Marion, McPherson, and Harvey counties . . . went on tilling their 100,000 acres of land . . . and every fall, no matter what the season, wheat has been brought to the Newton market in untold quantities from that settlement. . . . The Mennonite says nothing, but goes on marketing his fat cattle, his corn and wheat.[10]

The wheat was the new, hard winter wheat which they had brought with them from Russia, and for which they were to become famous.

The Mennonites in Ontario and in the United States had given real encouragement to the immigrants, having raised over $100,000 for their transportation and settlement costs. In 1873 they had set up a Board of Guardians to administer this aid in the United States and a similar committee in Ontario. John F. Funk, the publisher-editor in Elkhart, Indiana, who had been a most vigorous and able champion of the immigration, began a new paper called *Die Men-nonitische Rundschau* in 1880 for the Mennonites from Russia. The new settlements continued to prosper and congregations arose quickly. In 1882 they founded a school for higher education, which was to become Bethel College of Newton, Kansas. Several years lat-er a deaconess hospital was established in the same city. Another school, which was to become the Mennonite Collegiate Institute, was founded in Gretna, Manitoba, in 1889. Soon the new immi-grants seemed to be not only fully at home in the North American environment, but also surpassing the economic, social, and spiritu-al levels of their former home.[11]

From 1922 to 1930: Meanwhile events in Russia were leading to the second major Mennonite exodus, bringing an additional 21,000 persons to Canada and some 4,000 to South America. It must be re-membered that 70 percent of them had not emigrated in the first movement. Some had stayed because they were too comfortable to leave, some because they did not sense a threat to their freedom in the way those who left did, and some stayed because they felt that to be the will of God. Among these last were those who believed that God had called the Mennonites to Russia for a purpose and that leaving would be running away from God. One elder wrote,

"Some consider it a matter of conscience to go; I consider it a matter of conscience to stay. . . . We are to be the salt of the earth, and salt is needed here as much as anywhere else." He added that the Mennonite witness had opened the door to religious freedom in Russia, and who could tell what God would yet do in that land because of this.

Even the most sturdy became concerned, however, with the bitter civil war and the establishment of a communist government in Russia after World War I. They sensed immediately that more would be at stake than the loss of exemption from military service, an exemption which was, in fact, maintained until the late 1920s by the new government; at stake would soon be the right to an undisturbed church life; the right to have their own church institutions to care for the sick, handicapped, and aged; the right to nurture their children in the Christian faith; and other rights which they considered essential to their identity and survival as a Mennonite people. Consequently a commission of four men was sent to North America by the Mennonite congregations; they made arrangements for their coming to Canada.

Others, however, still hoped to stay and carried on difficult negotiations with the young government. A petition in 1925, for example, pleaded, "Give us our children, give us freedom to train and educate them in accord with the commands of our conscience," but their hopes were not to be fulfilled in the new emerging social order. Thus they began to leave the land they had grown to love, at first reluctantly and in small groups, selling their lands to other Mennonites eager to extend their holdings; but soon reluctance turned to haste, and haste to panic until all emigration was stopped in 1930.[12]

The life of those settling in South America will be told in chapter 17. Those coming to North America all settled in Canada except perhaps 100 who were allowed to enter the United States for special reasons. The Canadian Board of Colonization, which had been organized under the chairmanship of David Toews to raise the necessary funds for travel, made valiant efforts in settling the newcomers on prairie farms. With the depression and drought years of the early 1930s, however, many relocated in Ontario and British Columbia. In keeping with their life in Russia, they again established schools, homes for the aged, and hospitals together with their constantly increasing congregations from the Pacific Ocean to the Great Lakes. An increasing number of their children acquired advanced training as teachers, doctors, social workers, and in other professions, but they remained essentially a rural people until World War II. With few exceptions, they were only moderately successful financially during the first two decades, but a strong spiritual life was apparent in many of their congregations. During this period most of their worship services were conducted in the German language, with lay ministers carrying primary responsibility.

From 1946 to 1954: Approximately 35,000 Mennonites in Russia were evacuated to Poland and Western Europe by the retreating German army following the Battle of Stalingrad in 1943. Of these, some 23,000 were later forcibly returned to Russia by the Russian and Allied troops, but approximately 12,000 remained in the west. Most of these wished to join their relatives in Canada, but health and other reasons prevented many from going. Rather than stay in Europe, they chose to settle in South America and nearly 5,000 located in Paraguay, Uruguay, and Argentina. Over 7,000, however, did come to Canada and were soon scattered across the land with friends and relatives, most of them preferring to live in cities where work could be found. With hard work and high postwar wages most of them were soon financially independent. Because of their urban living, acculturation was extremely rapid among them as they settled down to become Canadians in the full sense of the word.[13]

For Conscience' Sake

All of these migrations, both to North America and within its boundaries, show the Mennonites to have been a people on the move. A study of their history reflects an endless pilgrimage from one corner of the earth to the other. We have seen, for example, how the first immigrants were ready to leave Russia for America by the time the last had come to Russia from Prussia. Similarly, the immigrants to Canada in the 1920s and again in the 1940s came just in time to buy up the farms of Mennonites leaving for Paraguay and Mexico. From their sixteenth-century European origins the Anabaptist-Mennonites have spread to Asia, North America, South America, and even Australia. Until recently the Mennonite self-image which has emerged because of these migrations has been that of pilgrims and strangers in a hostile world, the church in the wilderness seeking to remain pure for the coming of the Bridegroom, Christ. Harold S. Bender once wrote:

It is not that Mennonites do not love the soil or have no sense of home and homeland. Nor is it that they have not loved the men and women of the lands in which they have lived, or that they were unwilling to stay and carry on even after difficult circumstances. It was the hostile world around them which would not tolerate them, which forced them to go, which was unwilling to let them stay and maintain a faith and a spirit which was a challenge to its own system.[14]

It is clear that freedom of conscience was central to these migrations, particularly if conscience is defined to include the economic, social, and other conditioning factors which shaped their life together as much as pure religious convictions. And conscience worked differently with different people, urging some to leave for the sake of their faith and some to stay for the same reason. How can it be shown that those who left a country first were more faithful to God than those who stayed the longest and often perished for their faith? The faith and beauty but also the agony and pathos of those who were forced to make a decision one way or another are reflected in the words of a young colonist in Mexico:

> Great-grandfather migrated with his family from Prussia to South Russia via the wheelbarrow route. He lies buried there. Grandfather with married sons and daughters came to Canada in 1873. He sleeps beneath the soil in Manitoba. Now father, an old man has brought his family to Mexico where he is starting all over again.[15]

Endnotes

1. See Richard K. MacMaster, *Land, Piety, Peoplehood. The Establishment of Mennonite Communities in America, 1683-1790.* Scottdale, Pa.: Herald Press, 1985, pp. 42-43.

2. Ibid., p. 138.

3. Ibid., p. 118.

4. See C. Henry Smith, *The Story of the Mennonites.* Newton, Kan.: Faith and Life Press, 1981, first published in 1941, pp. 359ff. Also Willard H. Smith, *Mennonites in Illinois.* Scottdale, Pa.: Herald Press, 1983.

5. Helen Kolb Gates, et al., *Bless The Lord, O My Soul. A Biography of Bishop John Fretz Funk, 1835-1930.* Scottdale, Pa.: Herald Press, 1964, and Barbara Coffman, *His Name Was John.* Scottdale, Pa.: Herald Press, 1964.

6. J. C. Wenger, *The Mennonites in Indiana and Michigan.* Scottdale, Pa.: Herald Press, 1961.

7. Richard K. MacMaster, et al. *Conscience in Crisis. Mennonites and Other Peace Churches in America, 1739-1789. Interpretation and Documents.* Scottdale, Pa.: Herald Press, 1979.

8. J. M. Hofer, ed., "The Diary of Paul Tschetter, 1873," MQR (July 1931), 5:204.

9. E. K. Francis, *In Search of Utopia.* Glencoe, Ill.: Free Press, 1955, p. 79.

10. Helen B. Shipley, "The Migration of the Mennonites from Russia, 1873-1883, and Their Settlement in Kansas," MA thesis (1954), p. 184.

11. Theron F. Schlabach, *Peace, Faith, Nation. Mennonites and Amish in Nineteenth-Century America*. Scottdale, Pa.: Herald Press, 1988, pp. 231-294. Frank H. Epp, *Mennonites in Canada, 1786-1920*. Toronto, Ont.: Macmillan, 1974.

12. Frank H. Epp, *Mennonite Exodus*. Altona, Man.: D. W. Friesen & Sons, 1962; Idem, *Mennonites in Canada, 1920-1940*. Toronto, Ont.: Macmillan, 1982.

13. Peter J. and Elfrieda Dyck, *Up from the Rubble*. Scottdale, Pa.: Herald Press, 1991.

14. In S. C. Yoder, *For Conscience' Sake*. Goshen, Ind.: Mennonite Historical Society, 1945, p. viii.

15. Ibid., p. 234.

Other Resources: ME 3:684-687; ME 5:586-587. David V. Wiebe, *They Seek a Country: A Survey of Mennonite Migrations*. Freeman, S.D.: Pine Hill Press, 1974. Beulah Stauffer Hostetler, *American Mennonites and Protestant Movements*. Scottdale, Pa.: Herald Press, 1987. J. C. Wenger, *The Mennonite Church in America*. Scottdale, Pa.: Herald Press, 1966. C. Henry Smith, *Mennonite Country Boy*. Newton, Kan.: Faith and Life Press, 1962. William Schroeder and Helmut T. Huebert, *Mennonite Historical Atlas*. Winnipeg, Man.: Springfield Publishers, 1990. Contact any MCC or conference office, Mennonite museum or information office for audiovisual resources.

12

The Mennonite Church

WE SAW in the previous chapter that the first Mennonites to settle in North America were Dutch Mennonites from Krefeld in 1683. They were called Mennists or Mennonites because by the 1540s a considerable group in Holland, though not all, were identified as followers of Menno. One of the earliest Mennonite documents in America is the 1724 deed for the land on which the first Germantown meetinghouse was built in 1708. In it the land is described as belonging to the "Meeting of the people called Mennonist (alias Menisten)."

The name used for the Mennonites in Pennsylvania deeds of the 1700s was Mennonist Society. This was a curious development since most of the subsequent immigrants were from Switzerland and the Palatinate who, though they had had nothing to do with Menno, were now called by his name. Mennonites did not use the German word *Kirche* (church) for their fellowship since it implied the state church establishment. So in English they used the Quaker term *society* instead. This was particularly appropriate since many of the early group had joined the Quakers.

Finally, perhaps before 1800, the Mennonites of Pennsylvania began to call themselves Old Mennonites. The later schismatic groups, such as the Herrites in Lancaster County, or the larger Oberholtzer body in Franconia in 1847, were then called New

214

Mennonites. The main body actually became fond of the name Old Mennonites. They used it on cornerstones of meetinghouses, on tombstones of ministers, and in common speech.

The name was acceptable until various bodies of Mennonites who withdrew from the Old Mennonites from 1872 to 1901, because they rejected the Sunday school and other changes as the result of the "Awakening," came to be called Old Order Mennonites. Then some Old Mennonite leaders became sensitive about the word "Old," fearing that it would confuse the larger body with the Old Order traditionalists. Leaders like Daniel Kauffman, editor of the church paper, often wrote the name in parentheses: (Old) Mennonite Church. Harold S. Bender, a more recent leader in the group, did not want the word *Old* in any shape or form; so he insisted that *The Mennonite Encyclopedia* refer to the group as the Mennonite Church (MC). In 1971 the Mennonite General Conference, which was organized in 1898, became the Mennonite General Assembly, with a new constitution which specified that the official name of the group was to be the *Mennonite Church.*

Original Settlements

The first settlers naturally met together for worship, often with the Quakers or others and might be called the Germantown congregation north of Philadelphia. Dirck Keyser, a Mennonite, and perhaps others, would read a sermon from a book at these meetings. About 1690 elections were held in which William Rittenhouse was chosen as the first minister and was authorized by letters from the Mennonite congregations in Altona (Germany) and Amsterdam to baptize and serve communion, but he died early in 1708 before he could follow through with it.

Meanwhile Swiss and Palatine Mennonites were arriving, a total of 473 by 1709. Already in 1708 some of these, after initial hesitation, joined the Germantown congregation. Others had moved earlier to what became known as Skippack and founded a congregation there in 1702. Following the death of Rittenhouse the Germantown assistant minister Jacob Gottschalk baptized eleven members and served the Lord's Supper. That same year the small congregation built a log meetinghouse in Germantown, which was replaced in 1770 by a stone building which is still in use. The congregation today is inter-Mennonite in conference affiliation and is truly part of the heritage of all North American Mennonites; it belongs to them all. An inter-Mennonite board governs the use of the facilities as a historical and living landmark.

In the decades after 1708 other congregations were established, mostly in what are now Montgomery and Bucks counties. Settlements were also made in the counties of Chester, Berks, Lehigh, and Northampton. But the bulk of the Mennonites of what is now the Franconia Conference live within a fifteen-mile radius of Souderton, in Montgomery County. When was the Franconia Conference organized? Semi-annual ministers meetings were held in the Franconia meetinghouse by mid-eighteenth century, "before 1769," and these were referred to as conferences. When it was formally organized is not clear.[1]

In 1710, just eight years after the Germantown Mennonites started the Skippack settlement, Swiss and Palatine families settled near the present town of Strasburg in what is now Lancaster County. Here the Willow Street or "Brick" congregation developed. Other congregations soon emerged. New groups also formed in York, Adams, and Lebanon counties.

Within two decades after settling in Lancaster County, Mennonites had found their way to Virginia. The early settlements in Page, Shenandoah, and Frederick counties died out, but the congregations in Rockingham and Augusta flourished. The scattered congregations of the Allegheny Conference, largely in southwestern Pennsylvania, were founded for the most part around the time of the Revolutionary War (1775-83) and the following years. The Mennonite churches of Washington County, Maryland, and Franklin County, Pennsylvania, were established for the most part a little before 1800. The Ohio congregations began to spring up in the early years of the 1800s, and the Amish followed the Mennonites into Ohio as early as 1808. The Amish settled in Illinois in the 1830s and the Mennonites in the 1840s. Mennonites began to locate in Indiana in 1838, and the Amish followed in 1841. It is impossible to separate the history of the Mennonite Church from that of the Amish.

Mennonite Church baptized membership in North America in 1992 was as follows: 9,510 in Canada and 93,069 in the United States plus 45 in Mexico for a total of 102,624 in conferences participating in the General Board; 2,237 in Canada, 13,629 in the United States, and 385 others world-wide in independent conferences, for a grand total of 118,875.[2]

Church Government

When the Mennonites left Europe for America before 1700 and until the middle 1700s, there were no district conferences in Europe. The first American Mennonites were congregationalists in church government. Occasional ministers' meetings had been held in Europe to discuss issues, however, and the same was soon true in Pennsylvania. In the year 1725, for example, sixteen ministers from five congregations or settlements in southeastern Pennsylvania held a ministers' meeting and adopted the Dutch Mennonite Dordrecht Confession of Faith (1632) as their doctrinal standard. They also wrote an endorsement of the Confession:

> We the hereunder written Servants (that is, ministers) of the Word of God, and Elders in the Congregation of the People, called MEN-NONISTS, in the Province of Pennsylvania (*sic*), do acknowledge, and herewith make known, that we do own the foregoing CONFES-SION, APPENDIX, AND MENNO'S Excusation, to be according to our Opinion; and also, have took the same to be wholly ours. In Testimony whereof, and that we believe that same to be good, we have here unto Subscribed our Names.

Then follow the names of five Lancaster (Conestoga) bishops, two Franconia bishops, and nine Franconia preachers. It is interesting that *Dordrecht*, not the *Schleitheim* articles were adopted.[3]

Other ministers' meetings were held, both in the Franconia and Lancaster settlements. In the course of time these meetings were held regularly, each spring and fall. The first man to sign the above mentioned confession in 1725, was the first man to serve as an American Mennonite bishop, Jacob Gottshalk (d. 1763), who began to baptize and administer the Lord's Supper in 1708 at Germantown. There was no prepared program of addresses at these ministers' meetings, no written agenda, no constitution, no secretary, and no minutes, indeed, no officers of any sort. In a general way the bishops served as leaders, with the senior bishop presiding. What are now spoken of as the semiannual meetings of conference were therefore at first unofficial and informal ministers' meetings to discuss the life and welfare of the congregations of the area. In time, however, these ministers' meetings grew in influence and eventually became church synods or district conferences which increasingly set the disciplinary standards for the congregations. For a century and a half, or longer, no disciplinary standards were

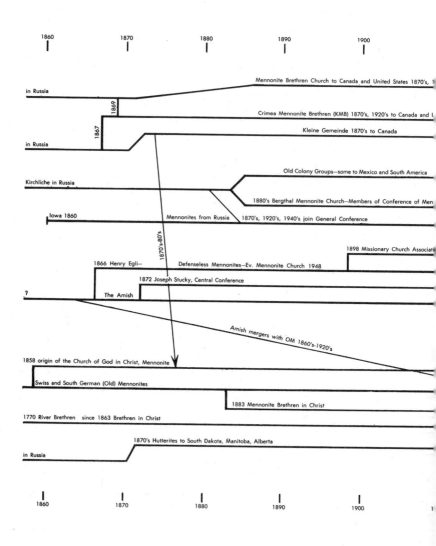

1860   1870   1880   1890   1900

Mennonite Brethren Church to Canada and United States 1870's,
in Russia

1869

Crimea Mennonite Brethren (KMB) 1870's, 1920's to Canada and U

1867

Kleine Gemeinde 1870's to Canada
in Russia

Old Colony Groups—some to Mexico and South America
Kirchliche in Russia

1880's Bergthal Mennonite Church—Members of Conference of Men

Iowa 1860   Mennonites from Russia   1870's, 1920's, 1940's join General Conference

1898 Missionary Church Associati

1870's-80's

1866 Henry Egli—   Defenseless Mennonites—Ev. Mennonite Church 1948

1872 Joseph Stucky, Central Conference

?   The Amish

Amish mergers with OM 1860's-1920's

1858 origin of the Church of God in Christ, Mennonite

Swiss and South German (Old) Mennonites

1883 Mennonite Brethren in Christ

1770 River Brethren   since 1863 Brethren in Christ

1870's Hutterites to South Dakota, Manitoba, Alberta
in Russia

1860   1870   1880   1890   1900

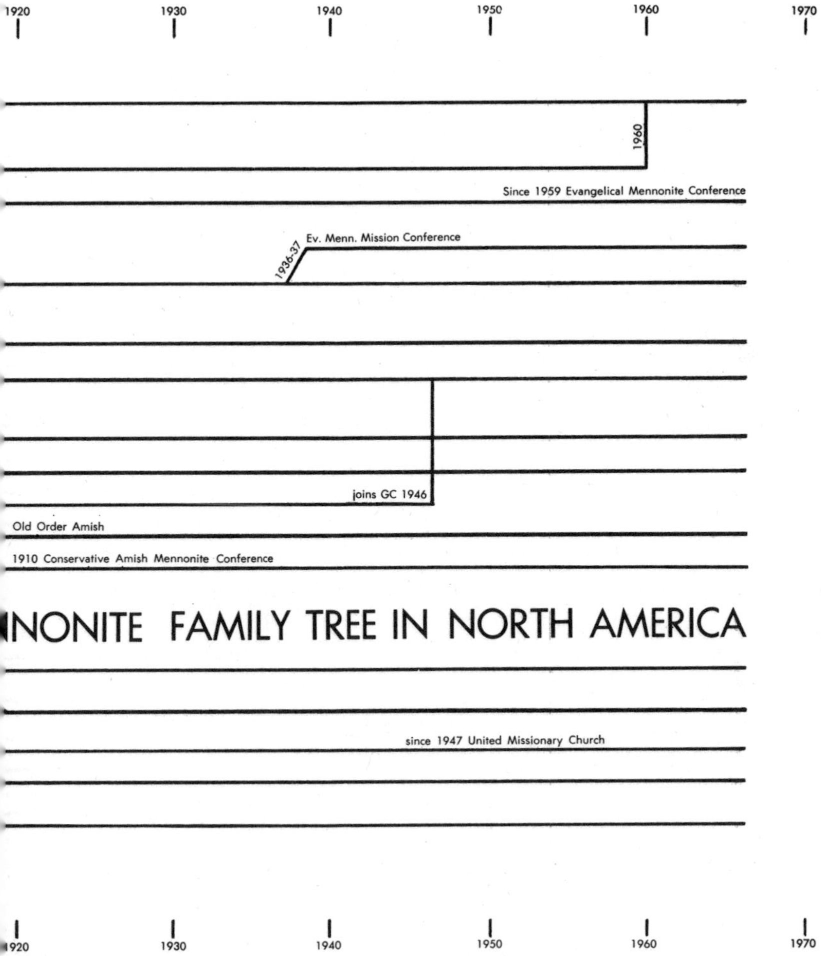

1920   1930   1940   1950   1960   1970

1960

Since 1959 Evangelical Mennonite Conference

Ev. Menn. Mission Conference

1936-37

joins GC 1946

Old Order Amish

1910 Conservative Amish Mennonite Conference

NONITE FAMILY TREE IN NORTH AMERICA

since 1947 United Missionary Church

1920   1930   1940   1950   1960   1970

printed and adopted. Lancaster adopted its first *Rules and Discipline* in 1881 and Franconia followed a few decades later.

The Mennonite Church, therefore, has a form of church government which is difficult to name. It is neither purely episcopal, synodal, nor congregational, but a combination of all three. The district conferences now set the basic disciplinary standards for the congregations. The bishops or pastors, assisted by the deacons or elders, attempt to carry out these standards in the congregations of their charge. Major matters of policy are, however, subject to congregational discussion and decision. This type of church discipline involves an intricate system of checks and balances, with some variations in different parts of the church. Some conferences put more weight on the authority of the bishops and on the decisions of the conference; others are more inclined to stress congregational government. In many locations the bishop or elder (the latter is generally the preferred term) has been replaced by a conference minister, but functions have been redefined. Authority has shifted in the direction of the congregation and district conferences.

Organization

The organizational structure of the Mennonite Church has changed over the years with the changing needs of the congregations and their mission. In 1720 there were no Mennonite organizations in North America other than the several dozen congregations. By 1820 the older district conferences, such as Franconia, Lancaster, Washington-Franklin, and possibly Ontario, had emerged, and Virginia and Ohio soon followed. Between 1875 and 1895 three boards were organized: Publication, 1875; Missions, 1882; and Education, 1895. These, in turn, became the Mennonite Publication Board in 1908, the Mennonite Board of Missions and Charities in 1906, and the Mennonite Board of Education, also in 1906. In their earliest forms these three boards, therefore, antedated the Mennonite General Conference, which was organized in 1898.

As the church grew in its identity and sense of mission, these forms again seemed inadequate. There was need for greater freedom on the part of the congregations to do their work but, at the same time, an increasing need for conferences and boards and committees which could serve the congregations in fulfilling their mission. The old General Conference, which not all the district conferences had joined anyway, lacked the flexibility and openness for growth in the 1970s and beyond. Consequently the Mennonite General Conference was succeeded by the General Assembly in 1971, as mentioned above.

With the new structure five program boards were established under the direction of a general board. Other agencies, including the Historical Committee, also relate directly to the General Board. The five program boards are the Mennonite Board of Missions, the Board of Education, the Board of Congregational Ministries, the Publication Board and the Mennonite Mutual Aid Board. Not all members favored the new structures, with some forming their own organizations, including a group calling itself the Fellowship of Concerned Mennonites (1983) with specific concerns about the theological direction of the Mennonite Church and other Mennonite groups. FCM is not a separate conference body, however, but a renewal group-movement. Since 1975 Mennonite Renewal Services has facilitated cooperation of Assembly groups with congregations and individuals in the charismatic movement. (See also ME 5:564-567.)

Mennonite Mutual Aid was organized in 1946, initially to help young men returning from Civilian Public Service (CPS) camps, but soon branched out into many areas of aid in keeping with the Mennonite belief in helping others. The board and most of its activities soon became inter-Mennonite, facilitating its ministries for good to all in the "MCC family" and beyond while working on the difficult boundary between church and world, business and Christian service.[4] For an organizational directory of the Assembly consult the *Mennonite Yearbook*.

Four Major Leaders

John Fretz Funk, 1835-1930: The most important figure in the life of the Mennonite Church in the nineteenth century was John F. Funk. Born in Bucks County, Pennsylvania, he took summer courses in a Mennonite school, Freeland Seminary (now Ursinus College), and taught school three years. In 1857 he moved to Chicago and entered the lumber business. Converted in 1858, he returned to his home church, Line Lexington in Bucks County, and was baptized. In 1864 he started the first successful church periodical of the Mennonite Church, the English *Herald of Truth*, and its German twin, the *Herold der Wahrheit*. That same year, 1864, he also married his second cousin, Salome Kratz (d. 1917), one of his former pupils. They had six children, four of whom died in childhood. He was ordained by John M. Brenneman in 1865. Two years later Funk, then thirty-two, sold his lumber business in Chicago and established his home and printing business in Elkhart, Indiana. Here he lived the remaining sixty-two years of his life, dying in his ninety fifth year.

Funk started the publication work of the Mennonite Church, first as an individual then in partnership with his brother Abraham, and finally as the Mennonite Publishing Company in 1875. It was a powerful instrument and there was some uneasiness in the church that one man controlled it. In 1908 he was asked to sell his periodicals and subscription lists to the young Mennonite Publication Board which had its publishing house at Scottdale, Pennsylvania, which he did.

Funk also had a vision for building up the spiritual life of the church through Sunday schools. He had been a Sunday school worker for D. L. Moody in Chicago and had regularly attended three Sunday schools there: as a pupil in one, as a teacher in a second, and as the superintendent of a third. By personal urging and by public appeals through the *Herald of Truth,* Funk was a leading figure in helping the Mennonite Church to establish Sunday schools throughout the church from east to west, initially against considerable resistance, largely in the period 1865-95.

As early as 1882 Funk led the Indiana Conference to set up an Evangelizing Fund to send preachers to neglected communities and members. In this he found strong support in his co-worker John S. Coffman. The fund was administered by an Evangelizing Committee which ultimately developed into the Mennonite Board of Missions and Charities.

Funk also felt that it would help the unity of the Mennonite Church to create a General Conference. Consequently he mailed a letter to the ministers of the church asking for their reaction to the plan of setting up such a conference. The response was favorable and a number of district conferences appointed representatives to do the initial planning. After preliminary meetings, a major consultation at the Pike meetinghouse, Elida, Ohio, in 1897 prepared the way. The first regular session of the Mennonite General Conference was held in 1898. Funk preached the conference sermon.

It is difficult to estimate the influence of John F. Funk on the Mennonite Church. One scholar wrote, "John Fretz Funk found the Mennonite Church still in the seventeenth century, and brought it

John L. Ruth—author, filmmaker, and storyteller—answers questions at an Anabaptist Heritage Seminar. Architect **Leroy Troyer** favors community participation in shaping meetinghouses and educational facilities. **Mennonite Information Centers,** museums, and heritage centers help to share the story of our spiritual pilgrimage with interested outsiders.

into the twentieth century, preserving its great values, and helping it to live in the future, not in the past." [5]

Yet another felt that in his later years he resisted new ideas and was not sensitive enough to inter-personal relations.[6] In any case, he was suspended as bishop in 1902 and never restored. This was a particularly difficult decade for him. During this period he also suffered a fire at his printing press and eventually lost ownership of it, as well as experiencing bankruptcy and some continuing mistrust of his leadership. Fortunately he lived long enough to experience full reconciliation. An impressive marker erected at his grave later testfies to the general recognition of his contribution.

John S. Coffman, 1848-1899: One of Funk's most effective colleagues was John S. Coffman of the Shenandoah Valley, Virginia. Coffman early became a successful schoolteacher and an effective preacher. Funk urged him to locate in Elkhart and help in his publication work, which he did in 1879 and for twenty years he was an influential teammate of Funk, promoting all good causes in the church, serving as assistant editor of the *Herald of Truth*, and writing Sunday school lesson helps.

But Coffman's greatest contributions came in still other areas. Daniel Brenneman had promoted an emotional type of piety and evangelism through which he eventually lost the confidence of many of his fellow ministers in Elkhart County. He was expelled in 1874 for his unwillingness to accept direction from them. Coffman knew this history well, yet he was convinced that the church had to engage in evangelistic work or perish. He therefore fasted and prayed for the Lord to open the door for the desired "Protracted (extended) Meetings."

In 1881 the small Bowne congregation in Michigan invited him to hold a series of meetings, which he did, with good success. Other churches heard of this pioneer evangelist, and they too invited him. A handsome, well-built man with clear gray eyes, and a pleasant personality, Coffman was also a man of much prayer. Sometimes he prayed all through the night. And yet he was also a man with a keen sense of humor with which he held and delighted his audiences. Thus he was a man of unusual effectiveness in the pulpit—undoubtedly the most effective preacher in the Mennonite Church in the last quarter of the nineteenth century. He brought hundreds of young people into the church.

It was in the field of education that Coffman made his final contribution. A Mennonite physician, Dr. Henry A. Mumaw

(d. 1908), had founded a small school in 1894 and called it the Elkhart Institute of Art, Science, and Industry. A year later he turned it over to a board of trustees known as the Elkhart Institute Association. In 1896 Coffman became the president of this board and guided the school with an able hand until his death three years later. This service on the part of Coffman cost him much, for some of his former friends and supporters turned away from him when he became the open champion of higher education. Coffman's address on the occasion of the dedication of the Elkhart Institute building in 1896 was entitled "The Spirit of Progress," an address which testified effectively to the strength of his vision.

In many ways Coffman served as a balance wheel to his employer and fellow minister, John F. Funk. Funk's junior by thirteen years, Coffman possessed a remarkable number of the gentler virtues Funk may have lacked. Words which might characterize Coffman are "gracious" or "winsome," while Funk gave the impression of an iron will, although accompanied by a large heart and creative spirit.

Daniel Kauffman, 1865-1944: The third major figure in the molding of the Mennonite Church was Daniel Kauffman, one of the many converts won by John S. Coffman. A native of Juniata County, Pennsylvania, he was the son of David D. Kauffman, who moved to Elkhart County with his family in 1866 and three years later to Morgan County, Missouri. There David served as a preacher and bishop. Son Daniel attended Missouri State University and earned the degree principal of pedagogics. Then from age eighteen to thirty-two, he taught school in Missouri, serving part of this time as county superintendent of schools. For a time he conducted a private business college at Garden City, Missouri.

In 1887 Kauffman married Ota J. Bowlin, who died three years later. That same year, 1890, he was converted. He was ordained in 1892, having given up his planned political career soon after conversion. He also remarried in 1892. In 1896 he was ordained a bishop in the church and served in that capacity for forty-eight years. He was editor of the *Gospel Witness*, published at Scottdale from 1905 to 1908. After the purchase of Funk's *Herald of Truth*, he edited the merged *Gospel Herald*.

In the long span, 1905-1943, "D. K.," as his friends knew him, served as the chief leader and major voice of the Mennonite Church. A man of great poise and dignity, quiet by nature, he was nevertheless an effective team worker. At one point he is said to have been a member of twenty-two committees and boards. He was moderator of Mennonite General Conference four times, including the first official sessions in 1898. He was the author of twenty-two books and pamphlets. Among these are *Manual of Bible Doctrine,* 1898; *A Talk with Church Members,* 1900; coauthor, *Mennonite Church History,* 1905; author-editor, *Bible Doctrine,* 1914; *The Conservative Viewpoint,* 1918; *My Vision of the Future,* 1938; *Fifty Years in the Mennonite Church,* 1941.

The 1914 *Bible Doctrine* volume became the norm in the church for faith and conduct with its three-fold division of doctrine into "Plan of Salvation," "Ordinances," and "Restrictions." In keeping with evangelical revivalism faith now became propositional and discipleship was separated from salvation. Yet to violate any of the ordinances, as for example the head covering, or any of the restrictions, like amusements or lawsuits, was to have failed in them all and, in effect, to be inclining to modernism. Faith and works were separated and put into a sequence with discipleship last of the three. This did not mean that discipleship was unimportant but it was not a part of salvation.

Under revivalist influence the dividing of time into definite periods or dispensations, in each of which God worked differently with his people, also became popular, particularly through the influence of Bible conferences. Men like A. D. Wenger used timeline charts to illustrate their lectures. While some teachers like Wenger were premillenialists, Kauffman was not. Nevertheless, in 1937 he could say: "The Mennonite Church is firmly committed to the Fundamentalist faith." While Kauffman cannot have meant the strident, militant Fundamentalism raging in Protestantism at that time, in thus skirting its edges the stage was set for Harold S. Bender's later effort to define Anabaptism as a new third way between liberalism on the left and fundamentalism on the right.[7]

Daniel Kauffman was a church statesman. He knew how to use power, which he certainly had during his thirty-five years as editor of the *Gospel Herald.* Liberalism seemed to him to be the basic spiritual issue which the church was facing and he took a courageous stand for what he believed was right. He loved people, and was a good arbiter in cases of tension and misunderstanding. He was basically conservative, yet he would make concessions in religious practice, provided these would not violate the ordinances and restrictions, in order to maintain the unity of the church. But there could be no concessions in the area of doctrine, as the issues surrounding Goshen College in the troubled mid-1920s and the founding of Eastern Mennonite College proved.[8]

John F. Funk was the great organizer of the church, founding its publication work, and its mission outreach, as well as the Sunday school movement in the Mennonite Church. John S. Coffman was the pioneer evangelist and man of prayer, and the chief promoter of the Elkhart Institute, which in 1903 was moved to Goshen, Indiana, and renamed as Goshen College. Daniel Kauffman was the statesman of the church who worked to consolidate the gains of the "Awakening," which came to the church in the latter decades of the nineteenth century, to clarify the doctrinal position of the church, and to maintain its unity.

Harold S. Bender, 1897-1962: The fourth leader to be identified here was Harold S. Bender. Born in Elkhart when Funk was sixty-two, Coffman forty-eight, and Kauffman thirty-two, Harold was a brilliant and gifted boy. At the early age of twelve he accepted Christ as his personal Savior and was received by baptism into the membership of the Prairie Street Mennonite Church. He graduated from Elkhart High School in 1914, and from Goshen College in 1918, in spite of taking out a year to teach in the Thorntown (Indiana) high school, 1916-17. In August 1922, he received the bachelor of divinity degree from Garrett Biblical Institute; in May 1923, the master of theology degree from Princeton Theological Seminary; in June 1923, the master of arts degree from Princeton University; and the doctor of theology degree from Heidelberg University, Germany, in 1935. In 1923 he married Elizabeth Horsch, daughter of Mennonite historian John Horsch of Scottdale, Pennsylvania.

Harold Bender was first of all an outstanding teacher, at Hesston from 1918 to 1920 and at Goshen from 1924 to his death. He had the art of mastering his field of study so thoroughly that he was not bound to the textbook or to the outline of anyone. He came to class with a clear grasp of what he wished to share with his students, and he was able to do so effectively. He was a competent lecturer, rather than a teacher who "discussed" the field with his students. Yet he stimulated interest and learning. He taught in many fields but excelled in Bible and church history.

Second, Harold Bender was also an able college administrator. He succeeded Dean Noah Oyer on the latter's death in 1931, which led to his becoming known generally as Dean Bender. During his years in office the college received accreditation from the North Central Association.

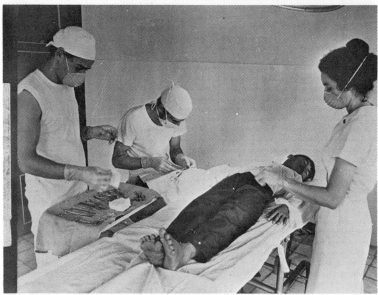

Active participation in **congregational life** locally, or active involvement in study and service opportunities elsewhere, are assumed as part of committee, voluntary, and adult membership. The ideals of being peacemakers in a broken world, and servants to one another, help Mennonites to seek **constructive work** in a world of destruction, to minister to the needs of the most disadvantaged.

Third, Dean Bender inaugurated a four-year theological course at Goshen College in 1933, leading to the Th.B. degree. Gradually this course was strengthened until a college degree was required for admission, the B.D. degree was offered, and the name of the Bible School was changed to the Biblical Seminary. The Seminary also achieved accreditation from the Association of Theological Schools.

Fourth, Dean Bender was an outstanding writer and editor. His most outstanding book was his definitive biography of the chief founder of Swiss Anabaptism, Conrad Grebel, written in German in 1935, and published in English in 1950. But we must go back to 1924 for the founding of the Mennonite Historical Society at Goshen College, and to 1927 for the establishment of the leading journal in its field, *The Mennonite Quarterly Review*. Dean Bender served until his death as president of the society and editor of *MQR*. He was also the longtime chairman of the Historical and Research Committee of Mennonite General Conference. But his really huge contribution was as primary editor of the four-volume *Mennonite Encyclopedia*, published 1955-59.

Fifth, Dean Bender was an ecumenical Mennonite leader. He was assistant secretary and executive committee member of MCC from 1931 until his death in 1962. In 1939 he became secretary of the Mennonite Central Peace Committee; and in 1942 chairman of the MCC Peace Section, and he retained that position until his death. In 1944 he was ordained in his "Mennonite Church (MC)," as he preferred to call it, and at about that point he entered the most strongly ecumenical phase of his ministry. Beginning in 1945 he made annual trips to Europe for shorter or longer visits, largely devoted to MCC and MWC concerns. He was president of the 1952, 1957, and 1962 sessions of the Mennonite World Conference. In 1949 he became chairman of the International Mennonite Peace Committee. His 1943 presidential address at the American Society of Church History was entitled "The Anabaptist Vision," which soon became internationally known as a statement of what Anabaptism really was: discipleship, a church of believers only, with love and nonresistance in all relationships.

Perhaps the cause dearest to his heart was the Biblical Seminary at Goshen College, and when its deanship was separated from the office of the college dean in 1946, he elected to go with the seminary, rather than to stay with the college. He was also delighted when Goshen College Biblical Seminary and Mennonite Biblical

Seminary of the General Conference Mennonite Church became the Associated Mennonite Biblical Seminaries in 1958.

He had his critics, of course, for how could a man be as active as he was without arousing criticism? Students were sometimes annoyed that he seemed so certain of what courses they ought to take, or what positions they should accept, and someone half-humorously one day dubbed him with the label "the pope," which title was well known on the campus, beloved as he was at the same time.

And so Harold S. Bender was the outstanding scholar leader of the Mennonite Church. In much of his scholarly work he relied heavily on Elizabeth Horsch Bender, his wife, particularly in the editing of MQR, translating of articles for the *Mennonite Encyclopedia*, and in many other ways. (See ME 5:66.) While personally a staunch (Old) Mennonite, Harold Bender had great ecumenical concern, a man who was able at the same time to put a warm arm of love around the Mennonites of all lands.

It is unlikely that there will be any one person as outstanding in the life of the Mennonite Church, as the four leaders just described were in their time. Times have changed. The leadership of the church is becoming much more diffused, which is a wholesome development. The church is growing larger, there are more able leaders. As the institutions of the church grow, fewer and fewer leaders have the time, energy, or inclination to immerse themselves in so broad a spectrum of activities as did Funk, Coffman, Kauffman, and Bender.

Group Characteristics

The 1989 Kauffman and Driedger study, *The Mennonite Mosaic*, provides us with important information about Mennonites, including Mennonite Church identity as individuals and as a group. The findings, of course, depend on questions asked or not asked, and on how answers are interpreted. We turn briefly now to this study but will, at the end, also suggest other readings based more on historical and theological considerations.

It is significant to note initially in chapter 3 of *The Mennonite Mosaic* that 88 percent or more of all Mennonites studied marked the most conservative response option on every item, indicating greater orthodoxy in matters of faith than Catholics and all mainline Protestant groups except the Southern Baptists. Thus even a

Passing on the story to the present and the coming generations has always been of vital importance to Mennonites—witness the *Martyrs Mirror,* the *Hutterite Chronicles,* and the *Mennonite Quarterly Review.* The **Historical Committee** of the Mennonite Church founded in 1911 meets twice yearly to report on an active program of research, teaching and publishing. Shown here are James O. Lehman, Carolyn C. Wenger, Steven D. Reschly (chair), Beulah Stauffer Hostetler, Samuel Steiner, Albert N. Keim, Hope Kauffman Lind, and Gerald Hudson.

"liberal" Mennonite would likely be conservative by comparison! Taking only the figures for the Mennonite Church here, this applies to items like belief in the divinity of Jesus (86%), miracles (90%), the resurrection (90%), a personal devil (89%), biblical inerrancy (75%), creation of the earth in six 24-hour days (47%), etc.

In measuring devotional practices 77% reported praying daily or oftener, 89% say grace at meals, 62% read the Bible at least weekly, 56% have family devotions weekly or oftener, and 53% "feel close to God." In terms of religious experience 82% reported a conversion experience, 48% had received the "baptism of the Holy Spirit," but 12% "often feel discouraged in living a Christian life." (Is this normal or the result of a Mennonite tendency towards a perfectionist ethic?) An amazing 92% attend church weekly or "almost weekly" and 81% Sunday school. On a range of from zero to eight in Bible knowledge, Mennonite Church members had a mean score of 5.6.

Comparing three belief systems identified as general orthodoxy, Anabaptism, and fundamentalism, the responses of all five groups surveyed showed that high scores on Anabaptism correlated with high scores on Bible knowledge, church participation, peacemaking, service to others and support for MCC. Those scoring high on Anabaptism were also somehow better able to resist the secularizing influence of urbanization, economic success, and mobility factors.[9]

Chapter 9 explores moral and ethical issues, both personal and as a group. What do Mennonites believe about issues crucial today and in the 16th-century Anabaptist vision of a church "without spot or wrinkle" (Eph. 5:27)? How do they fit into an increasingly urbanized social order? The researchers rightly identify one problem as that of deciding moral issues rationally or on biblical (or church) authority. It became clear that the 19th century widened the gap between conservative and progressive Mennonites, and that education was a major factor. This trend continued in the 20th century.[10]

On issues of personal morality "always wrong" was marked by 72% on smoking tobacco and 92% on marijuana, 90% on homosexual acts, 50% on moderate drinking, 88% on income tax evasion, 51% on buying lottery tickets and 84% on swearing. Opposition to abortion ranged from 17% if a woman's health was in danger, to 42% in case of rape, to 50% if there was a strong chance of serious defect in the baby, to 89% if she did not want the baby. A homosexual would be accepted as a member of the church by 70%, but only if non-practicing; if active, the figure dropped to 22%.

On social issues 72% believe all people in the human race are equal and 71% would sell their house to anyone regardless of race or the reaction of neighbors. Negatively 55% believe the Bible does not teach the separation of races, 77% believe it is wrong for races not to mix socially, and 79% believe it wrong to keep people of other races out of their neighborhood. Those scoring higher on general orthodoxy or fundamentalist belief systems were not nearly as open on these issues as were those more strongly favoring Anabaptism. Similarly 30% (of all five groups combined) agreed that if people are poor it is their own fault, and 24% felt that welfare support to them should be decreased. Again for all groups, 34% believed in capital punishment.

Finally, 31% in the Mennonite Church believed that women were suffering discrimination in both society and the church, 50% felt they should have larger roles in church leadership, and 45% approved of the ordination of women to the pastoral ministry.

In general, greater openness to change and "liberal views" were found among young, urbanized, and more educated members, who were also more involved in community affairs. However, the range of views varied more *within* each of the five conference groups than *between* them. These are a sampling of the issues investigated in this study. We become particularly aware of their significance when we remember that ethics was at the very heart of the discipleship of 16th-century Anabaptism, a biblical norm to which Mennonites today still claim to be committed.

Members of the Mennonite Church have a strong historical consciousness. They are keenly aware that their spiritual forebears suffered and died for the faith and fled from one land to another in search of religious liberty. This has led to a strong concern for faithfulness to the heritage.[11] Some in the church feel, perhaps with some justification, that their group, more than other Mennonite groups, has historically been the "custodian of the heritage of faith," without denying that other groups have also been faithful. This can, but need not, lead to a conserving, traditionalist stance where faith is boxed in by a variety of "boundary maintenance" devices rather than coming truly alive by being shared on the market place. A noted historian offers the following dictum: "Tradition is the living voice of the dead; traditionalism is the dead voice of the living" (Jaroslav Pelikan).

Mennonite Church people find deep satisfaction in their simple worship services. The entire congregation joins in the singing of four-part music, usually sung a cappella, even though musical instruments are in the worship center. The pulpit is placed in the center of the platform symbolizing the centrality of God's Word. Historically, everyone knelt for prayer, but this changed in the 1950s to standing in most congregations. Midweek Bible study meetings in church have become fewer, but many members meet in homes for small-group sharing, study, and prayer. A number of house church fellowships emerged during the 1960s and '70s, as well as informally organized assemblies, bringing together numerous house group meetings. The Mennonite Camping Association also facilitates meeting and dialogue through approximately 50 retreat and conference centers and campgrounds. The influence of the charismatic movement was felt for good throughout the church in terms of new freedom to witness and a loosening of the remnants of legalism. Being a member of the church increasingly meant, not only discipleship and hard work, but also a simple, unashamed joy in the Lord.

Endnotes

1. J. C. Wenger, *The Mennonite Church in America*. Scottdale, Pa.: Herald Press, 1966, p. 61. Idem, *History of the Mennonites of the Franconia Conference*. Telford, Pa.: Franconia Mennonite Historical Society, 1937, p. 52. Idem, "No date is known for the formal organization of the conference, if indeed there ever was a formal organization," ME 2:368.

2. James E. Horsch, *Mennonite Yearbook & Directory*, 1992-93. Scottdale, Pa.: Herald Press, 1992, p. 208. See subsequent editions for up-to-date statistics and other conference information.

3. See Beulah Stauffer Hostetler, *American Mennonites and Protestant Movements*. Scottdale, Pa.: Herald Press, 1987.

4. The term "MCC family" is frequently used to refer to all groups who agree with the MCC mission statement and its theology and can, therefore, be included in the "believers church" family. See the MQR (July 1970) "MCC Anniversary Issue."

5. Helen Kolb Gates, et al. *Bless the Lord, O My Soul*. Scottdale, Pa.: Herald Press, 1964, p. 8.

6. Ibid., p. 181.

7. See, for example, Juhnke, *Vision, Doctrine, War*, chapter 4, "Swiss-American Mennonitism," pp. 106-135. Cf.: Schlabach, *Gospel Versus Gospel*, chapter 4, pp. 109-47.

8. John S. Umble, *Goshen College, 1894-1954*. Goshen, Ind.: Goshen College, 1955.

9. Kauffman and Driedger, *Mosaic*, chapter 3, pp. 65-85.

10. Ibid., chapter 9, pp. 185-209. Cf.: Schlabach, *Peace, Faith, Nation*, chapter 8, pp. 201ff.

11. See Marlin E. Miller, "Musings on 'Integration' and 'Essentials' and 'Faithfulness' " in *AMBS Bulletin*, May 1990, pp. 3-5.

Other Resources: See relevant ME articles, especially in Volume 5, including bibliographies and cross references. John L. Ruth, *Maintaining the Right Fellowship.* Scottdale, Pa.: Herald Press, 1984. Theron F. Schlabach, *Peace, Faith, Nation.* Scottdale, Pa.: Herald Press, 1988. Idem, *Gospel Versus Gospel.* Scottdale, Pa.: Herald Press, 1980. James C. Juhnke, *Vision, Doctrine, War.* Scottdale, Pa.: Herald Press, 1989. J. Howard Kauffman and Leo Driedger, *The Mennonite Mosaic.* Scottdale, Pa.: Herald Press, 1991. Calvin Wall Redekop and Samuel J. Steiner, Editors. *Mennonite Identity.* Lanham, Md.: University Press of America, 1988. Beulah S. Hostetler, *American Mennonites and Protestant Movements.* Scottdale, Pa.: Herald Press, 1987. Contact Mennonite church or regional conference offices for audiovisual resources.

13

The Amish and the Hutterian Brethren

The Amish

THE AMISH-MENNONITES or Amish, as they have come to be known, originated from the only major division among the Swiss Brethren in Europe. The Dutch Mennonites had experienced many divisions during the sixteenth and seventeenth centuries, frequently over issues of church discipline. They may have inadvertently helped to precipitate the Amish division through the article on discipline in the (Dutch) Dordrecht Confession of 1632, which demanded shunning or avoidance *(Meidung)* of a transgressing member of the fellowship. Such a member was to be expelled from the fellowship, but also "according to the doctrine of Christ and his apostles, be shunned and avoided by all members of the church . . . whether it be in eating or drinking, or other like social matters."

The Confession itself had not been formally adopted by the Swiss Brethren, but was frequently referred to by them as a guide to faith. It was precisely on the subject of discipline that the Swiss had held discussions with the Dutch Mennonites, including Menno Simons, and urged them to moderation. In late seventeenth century, however, a young Swiss Brethren elder by the name of Jacob Ammann, became deeply concerned over laxity of discipline in the

Swiss and Alsatian congregations, when a woman who admitted speaking a falsehood was not shunned. He also identified as wrong the belief that sincere people *(treuherzige)* who were sympathetic to the Swiss Brethren doctrines but did not join the group would be saved.

In due course Ammann began traveling from his home near Bern, Switzerland, to visit all the congregations in the Swiss, South German, and Alsace areas to find support for his concern. He also criticized an older fellow elder, Hans Reist, for not disciplining the woman and other evidences of undue tolerance. Reist undoubtedly underestimated Ammann's zeal when he told others "not to consider seriously the teaching and ordinances of youths." Meanwhile Ammann's concerns grew to include other issues. Though the Swiss had never practiced foot washing, article XI of the *Dordrecht Confession* did teach it, and so Ammann did also. He saw worldliness coming into the fellowship in the clothes being worn and urged both simplicity and uniformity. Men should not trim their beards since this was an obvious sign of pride. To attend the services of the state church was also grounds for discipline. Communion service was to be observed twice annually, not once, Ammann insisted, and began the actual schism by observing it "out of order" in the summer of 1693.

Eventually Ammann excommunicated all ministers who did not agree with him, including Reist, as well as many individual members. He found his strongest support in Alsace. Many attempts at reconciliation were made, even by North German Mennonites, but without success. While Ammann did apologize later and admitted acting too quickly, he did not retreat from the substance of his position. The 1693 division seemed to be final by 1697. It was a reform attempt to recover doctrines which Ammann thought were being neglected, but it also included personality conflicts and the struggle for power. Sectarian divisions normally occur most frequently at the conservative end of the theological continuum.

The earliest records of Amish coming to North America are for 1727, but no congregation was organized until 1749 when Jacob Hertzler (d. 1786) came to Berks County, Pennsylvania, followed later by many others to Lancaster and Chester counties. Others continued coming directly from other parts of Europe, including Hesse in Germany, and moving inland to Ohio and Indiana. By 1812 a large settlement was developing in Holmes County, Ohio, and by the 1840s in Lagrange and other counties in Indiana. The westward movement continued to Illinois, Oregon, and Kansas, but also including the Dakotas, Iowa, Nebraska, and other states. The largest settlements in the twentieth century, however, continued to be in Lancaster, Holmes, and Lagrange counties.

The Amish came to Ontario through the initiative of Christian Nafziger, a poor farmer in Bavaria, Germany. Mennonites in Amsterdam provided him with travel funds to New Orleans; from there he went to Pennsylvania in 1821. There, however, he discovered that land was too expensive for him to buy, but his Amish and Mennonite friends told him of ample, cheap land in Canada and provided the necessary travel funds for him. By 1822 he had indeed been able to make favorable land purchase arrangements in Waterloo County. He apparently negotiated directly with the governor of Upper Canada and on his return journey succeeded in having an audience with King George IV in London, who confirmed the reliability of the governor's offer. While Nafziger himself could not come immediately, the good news he brought put many on the way to Ontario from Europe and, eventually, even some from Pennsylvania.

Old Order Amish: From 1850 to 1880 the process of accommodation to the surrounding culture became the cause for a division among the Amish themselves. As those labeled Progressives began to modify the strict Amish disciplines on dress, on the use of modern inventions, and on other daily life issues, as well as on beginning the use of English in worship and on building church buildings, a rift became inevitable. In contrast to those now known as the Old Order, the Progressives came to be called Amish Mennonites and eventually did join the Mennonite Church in the twentieth century. In 1990 there were approximately 56,200 members in a total community of 127,800 in Old Order Amish groups in North America. They are among the fastest growing population in the world. A few have also emigrated to Paraguay.

Most Old Order Amish communities meet in homes, that is, in a large house, shed, or barn for worship every other Sunday. Families with adequate facilities take turns inviting the group. Services last from three to four hours with several ministers speaking without notes. The language used is Pennsylvania "Dutch," sometimes sprinkled liberally with English words and some *Schrift-deutsch* (Bible German). An Old Order congregation or district consists of from forty to fifty-five families and is divided when it becomes larger. A bishop, two ministers, and a deacon preside over each district.

The largest concentrations of **Old Order Amish** are found in Pennsylvania, Ohio, Indiana, Iowa, and Kansas. They live a simple life, retain their German dialect, and resist large-scale mechanization. Their farming methods combine family effort and animal power.

It is not correct, as many think, that the Amish believe in salvation by works instead of grace, but it is correct that obedience to Jesus Christ is for them the real test of faith (James 2), and that the will of God is known to the believer both through the Scriptures as well as through the present living body of the church and the faithful church of all time, i.e., the tradition. The four questions of the Amish baptismal vow are as follows (with slight variation from place to place):

1. Are you able to confess with the Ethiopian eunuch that you believe that Jesus Christ is God's Son? (Answer: Yes, I believe that Jesus Christ is God's Son.)
2. Do you confess that you are uniting with the true church of the Lord? (Yes.)
3. Do you renounce the devil and the world with all its wicked ways, and also your own flesh and blood, and commit yourself to serve Jesus Christ alone who died for you on the cross? (Yes.)
4. Do you promise to keep the ordinances *(Ordnung)* of the Lord and the church, to faithfully observe and to help administer them, and never to depart from them so long as you shall live? (Yes.)[1]

It is also not correct, as many think, that the Amish do not believe in education. It is true that they hold a certain amount of education to be sufficient for their rural community needs, but within these limits the total emphasis is upon an integration of life and learning to equip the student to become a faithful member of the church and a useful member of society. As one former Amishman writes: "Where public schools emphasize competition and pride of achievement, the Amish stress cooperation and humility (not exactly unbiblical themes)."[2] This, it has been noted, requires qualified rather than "certified" teachers, i.e., the church rather than the state determines the qualifications:

Although the Amish school is separated from "the world" outside, it is not separated from Amish life. The school supports the family and the traditions and economy of the Amish community and enables the child to learn both the facts and the roles he needs to function as an Amish person in twentieth-century America.[3]

It may well be argued that the Amish, despite weaknesses which can be found in any group, have much to teach society in the last decade of the twentieth century about the wise use of energy, near self-sufficiency together, and mutual aid, integrity, simplicity, and not least about love of the soil and its care. They have been the subject of many sociological studies. Those who seem to understand them best identify faith in God and a commitment to obey his will as they understand it as the primary foundation of their existence.

Unfortunately, some Amish communities experienced a time of stress and division during the latter half of the nineteenth century. Issues in one community quickly spread to others. From 1865-75 the "Egli Amish," known as the Defenseless Mennonite Church until 1948 and then as the *Evangelical Mennonite Church* (chapter 15), separated from the Old Order Amish in the Berne, Indiana, area after Henry Egli reported a new regeneration experience and made it normative for all. Another group in Michigan sought reform of Old Order life and thought, but not in the way the so-called Progressives were going; the reform group came to be known as the Conservative Amish Mennonite Conference in 1910. In 1957 they dropped the "Amish" from their name and are known as the *Conservative Mennonite Conference.* They are loosely affiliated with the Mennonite Church, support an active education program, including Rosedale Bible Institute, Irwin, Ohio, as well as an extensive mission program. Their membership in 1986 was 7,918, in 99 congregations. The *Brotherhood Beacon* is the conference paper (ME 5:192).

Beachy Amish Mennonite Fellowship: The record seems to indicate that this was more a development of separation by mutual consent than a schism. When Moses M. Beachy (d. 1946) became bishop in southwestern Pennsylvania, he could not find it within himself to shun all members of the Old Order who left for Mennonite churches as his predecessor had done. After a decade of struggle over the issue the retired bishop and about one half of the congregation began meeting separately for worship in 1927, but for the next twenty-six years both groups used the same meetinghouse, on alternate Sundays, though the Beachy group had introduced Sunday school and other innovations. The condoning of the use of automobiles by the Beachy group, however, created more serious tension. Other groups in Pennsylvania, Ohio, and Indiana merged with the Beachy Amish, bringing their membership to 7,238 in 105 congregations by 1990. Some congregations still use the German language. Most have Sunday school and midweek prayer meetings. Mutual aid is important: "a religion that works is encouraged." Something of the spirit of the group is captured in the following words written by a member in 1978.

Doctrinally the church emphasizes repentance, conversion, blood atonement, the new birth, believer's baptism, justification by faith, practical discipleship, and progressive sanctification. Eight Christian ordinances are practiced: baptism, communion, foot washing, woman's veiling, the holy kiss, anointing with oil, laying on of hands, and marriage.

In spite of the differences, we love the Lord and we love one another. "For he that loveth not his brother whom he hath seen, how can he love God whom he hath not seen?" (1 John 4:20). We do sense a dire need for more spiritual growth, that we might love God and our fellow brethren enough that we might be one! Jesus is coming soon[4] (ME 5:60-62).

The Hutterian Brethren

The sixteenth-century origins of the Hutterian Brethren were described briefly in chapter 4. Persecution decimated their ranks in the seventeenth century and ultimately destroyed the communities in Moravia, though cultural remnants (*Habaner*) remained until World War II. Many, however, had continued their westward migration into Slovakia and Transylvania but the entire movement was on the verge of extinction when a Russian general invited the small remnant of 123 to settle in Ukraine in 1770. Fifty-six of these were Lutherans who converted to the Hutterians and gave new life to the movement.

This was to be their home for 100 years. Some measure of prosperity returned to them, but internal tensions led to a giving up of their historic communal lifestyle from 1819 to 1859. At this point a spiritual revival led to new community life, but it was of short duration. The growing emancipation of the Russian serfs led to an egalitarianism which seemed to threaten the cherished privileges of the Hutterians, Mennonites, and other foreign colonies. The threat of a military conscription law passed in 1872 convinced the Hutterians, and many Mennonites, that it was time to leave even though the law eventually provided for alternative service for conscientious objectors to war. In 1873 a twelve-man delegation was sent to North America to explore the possibilities for resettlement. Two of the delegates were Hutterians. Paul Tschetter, the older of the two, kept a most informative diary of the journey.[5] Their recommendation was to settle in the Dakota territory. By July 1874 the first group had arrived and by 1877 all of them, numbering between 700-800 persons, were on the selected sites.

In 1528 two hundred Anabaptist fugitives from South Tirol settled at **Austerlitz** (today: Slavkov in the Slovak Republic), where they pooled their resources and started communitarian Anabaptism. They are named after their most influential leader, Jacob Hutter. The **Great Chronicle of the Hutterites** was begun by Caspar Braitmichel in the 1560s at Neumühl (today: Nové Mlyny). It was later carried to Vishenka in Russia by the fleeing Hutterite remnant, from where it came to America in 1874. So well known were the Hutterites for their artistic **ceramics** that even their fiercest enemies would often choose Hutterite pottery as wedding presents for their children. This plate is dated 1674.

The original communities in the Dakotas consisted of three groups in addition to those who wished to live alone on their own properties. The first group came to be known as the *Schmiedleut*—the blacksmith people—after their leader Michael Waldner, who was a blacksmith. The second group was called the *Dariusleut* after their elder Darius Walther. The third group was called the *Lehrleut*—teacher's people—after their elder Jacob Wipf, who was a teacher. The first group located near the Missouri River at what is still known as the Bon Homme colony, the second near the James River, a tributary of the Missouri, while the third settled north of Wolf Creek as the (Old) Elmspring colony.

The three communities now entered a period of rapid growth and economic success. Their population doubled during the next forty years and their settlements increased to seventeen. The near isolation of their communities from the surrounding culture was undoubtedly what they had been longing for and now experienced with gratitude.

This changed, however, with the coming of World War I in 1914. People looked with suspicion upon German-speaking conscientious objectors. Their refusal to buy Liberty Bonds was resented severely, even though they made donations to the Red Cross and other relief agencies. Acts of violence against the settlements increased. A group of angry patriots came to the James colony and drove off a herd of 100 steers and 1,000 sheep, ostensibly to sell them in order to purchase bonds, but they did this without censure from law enforcement agencies. Ugly rumors were circulated against the colonies.

The most suffering, however, was endured by the young men who were drafted for military service and taken to army camps, but refused to put on uniforms or follow the orders of their commanders. There were no provisions for alternative service at that time. The case of the three Hofer brothers, Joseph, David, and Michael, and Jacob Wipf shook the communities particularly. After two months in the military guardhouse they were sentenced to thirty-seven years in prison. They were taken to Alcatraz, handcuffed by day and chained by night. Here they were placed in wet dungeons in solitary confinement, wearing only their thin underwear, since they refused to put on the uniform which hung in the cell. For five days and nights they stood, sat, and slept on the wet floor without a blanket or other comfort. They received a glass of water daily, but no food. Then their situation eased somewhat.

The Hutterians, established in Moravia around 1533, arrived in North America in 1874 after a three-century odyssey through Eastern Europe. These limestone buildings of the **Bon Homme** Colony near Yankton, South Dakota, were their first American home. Most of the Hutterian colonies are located in the Canadian and American West.

Four months later they were transferred to Fort Leavenworth, Kansas. After four days and five nights of misery in travel they were marched on the run from the station to the camp, then made to strip their outer clothing and stand in the winter cold dripping with sweat. Two hours later they were issued prison clothing, but forced to stand outside. By morning Joseph and Michael Hofer collapsed and were taken to a hospital. The other two were placed in solitary confinement and issued a starvation diet. For nine hours each day they stood with their hands tied to an overhead beam and their feet barely touching the ground. Somehow Wipf had managed to send a telegram to the wives of the two hospitalized men. When they arrived they found their husbands near death. By next morning Joseph had died, but his wife, Maria, was not allowed to see the body. After much pleading she was taken to the coffin where she discovered that the uniform he had refused to wear in life had been put on him after he was dead. Michael died two days later. The other two were eventually released.[6]

Meanwhile negotiations in Washington, including discussions with the Secretary of War and a petition to President Woodrow Wilson, had not received a significant response. Consequently, the Hutterians saw no alternative but to emigrate to Canada where religious freedom was promised to them. The move began almost immediately and included all of the settlements except the oldest one at Bon Homme. The *Schmiedleut* settled in Manitoba, the *Dariusleut* and *Lehrleut* in Alberta. Within a few years sentiment, and eventually legislation, in the Dakotas began to change. By the time of the depression in the mid-1930s there was actual encouragement for them to return, largely for economic reasons, and many did until most of the earlier colonies were once more under cultivation. The Canadian settlements continued to serve the needs of the rapidly growing communities.

The Land Problem: The need for more land has gone hand in hand with Hutterian growth and prosperity. In contrast to the Amish, the Hutterians use the most modern machinery available for their farming, shops, and other production needs. The founding of a new community requires a large tract of land, often 5,000 acres or more, and Hutterian economic strength made it possible to "buy out" smaller farmers. Settlements gradually became a threat to farming communities and to small towns who saw their markets disappear through Hutterian self-sufficiency and bulk buying at larger, more distant urban centers. As a result restrictive legislation was enacted in Alberta, but later modified to the present liaison office where Hutterian and provincial representatives agree upon new land purchases before they are made. Restrictive legislation was also proposed but never enacted in Manitoba and Saskatchewan, as well as in Montana and Minnesota.[7] Hutterian sensitivity to community feelings in areas of proposed purchases, as well as their reputation of being both good farmers and good neighbors, has seemed to resolve this problem. However, it continues to remain a source of concern to all parties potentially involved. For a time people believed that as a religious community the Hutterians did not pay any taxes. They do indeed pay, but as a colony rather than individuals, obviously. In 1990 Hutterian baptized membership in Canada and the United States was 15,000, within a total population of 35,000.

The Hutterian Brethren (Society of Brothers): A fourth group known as the *Arnoldleut* was added to the Hutterian community in 1930. Eberhard Arnold (1883-1935), a German writer and teacher,

These **Hutterian girls** are members of the Milltown Colony near Elie, Manitoba, the oldest colony in Canada.

became attracted to the sixteenth-century Anabaptist-Hutterite model and founded a community in Germany in 1920. In 1930 he visited the Hutterian communities in North America, having first heard of them in 1928, and was accepted, as well as ordained, by them before his return. Difficulties arose in the group soon after Arnold died. Under the pressures of World War II they were forced to leave Germany and settled in England, but after encountering considerable hostility there also because they were Germans, and nonresistant, they eventually migrated to Paraguay, locating near the Mennonite colony of Friesland east of the Paraguay River.

The peak of *Primavera* (spring) colony life came in the early 1950s with a membership of around 650, of whom approximately one half were children. They were noted particularly for their thorough educational system, which was trilingual (Spanish, German, English), the diversity of membership background, with some ninety family names represented, and their hospital which became known far and wide for its excellence and compassion. A decline of spirit and then membership began to erode the community by the mid-1950s and eventually led to its dissolution in Paraguay.

Some of these members joined a reconstituted community (Woodcrest) under the leadership of Heini Arnold, son of the founder, at Rifton, New York. This group, formerly the Society of Brothers, is now known officially as the Hutterian Brethren, and is again in full membership with the Hutterians in the West since 1974, but not before another crisis of identity and mission had to be overcome in the colonies in the East in the 1960s. In 1987 there were 350 colonies scattered across North America, but concentrated in Alberta (119), Saskatchewan (39), Manitoba (76), Montana (41), and South Dakota (48). There were also three colonies in New York State, two in Pennsylvania, and one each in Connecticut, England, Germany, and Japan. The Hutterian (Eastern) colonies counted a population of 1,800, of whom approximately 800 were members, a total of about 15,000 members in 1990.[8]

Colony Life: Hutterian life is much more than sharing a common treasury and living together in a given communal setting. It is a total way of life with regulated lines of authority and responsibility and a specific place for every member. The time and abilities of the members is no more their own than money is. It is clear that order becomes a very central concept if many people are to work together harmoniously all their life. This order is rooted in God's orderly creation and influences the Hutterian understanding of order in space, in time, and in society. Buildings and living arrangements for families are not arranged haphazardly in the colony. Daily time schedules are precise, so also are the grouping of ages according to time (years) in terms of work, respect, and trust. There is social ordering ranging from education to young people's activities, marriage, male-female relationships, and the role of the elderly.

The ordering of all of these relationships does require authority, and there is a hierarchy of responsibility, but it is servant-oriented for the good of all. Within the larger colony community the church is the primary authority, with a spiritual leader or minister at its head. He in turn seeks the counsel of the other ministers and the total church. A council of from five to seven men chosen by the church, always including two ministers, the field manager, and the householder, is responsible for the daily running of the colony and making routine decisions. All major decisions are made by the church, in which only baptized males may vote. Church discipline includes excommunication and possible expulsion from the community.

Like the Amish, the Hutterians run their own schools whenever possible, with certified teachers, but supervision by the larger area school board or superintendent. Some of their young people do attend college in order to return to the colony as teachers. Filmstrips and other visual aids are normally not used. Television sets are not found in the colonies. Most children attend school through grades eight or nine. This is considered sufficient to help them adjust to the religious and social life in the colony and to cope with their place in the larger society and the world. The daily devotional services also serve an important role in furthering spiritual growth.

The *Baptismal Vow* normally used by the Hutterians today for admission to membership is as follows. Its questions indeed call for a total commitment. Questions asked of the applicants before the prayer:

1. Do you acknowledge the doctrines, which have hitherto been taught to you, as being the truth and right foundation for salvation?
2. Do you also believe in and agree with the twelve articles of our Christian faith which comprise: "We believe in God the Almighty . . ." [Each repeats the Apostles' Creed]
3. Do you also desire the prayer of intercession of the pious that God may forgive and remit the sins committed by you in ignorance?
4. Do you desire to consecrate, give, and sacrifice yourself to the Lord in the covenant of Christian baptism?

Here follows the prayer.
[After this prayer, while kneeling, follow these six questions:]

1. Do you now sufficiently understand the word of God and acknowledge it as the only path to life eternal?
2. Do you also truly and heartily repent of the sins which you have in ignorance committed against God and do you desire henceforth to fear God, nevermore to sin against God, and rather to suffer death than ever again to sin willfully against God?
3. Do you also believe that your sins have been forgiven and remitted through Christ and the prayer of intercession of his people?
4. Is it also your desire to accept brotherly punishment [discipline] and admonition and also to apply the same to others when it is needful?
5. Do you desire thus to consecrate, give and sacrifice yourself with soul and body and all your possessions to the Lord in heaven, and to be obedient unto Christ and his church?
6. Do you desire thus to establish a covenant with God and all his people and to be baptized upon your confessed belief?

[Note: All these questions must be answered with a "yes." The minister, laying on his hands and sprinkling with water, speaks the following words:]

> On thy confessed belief I baptize thee, in the name of the Father, the Son, and the Holy Ghost. God Almighty in heaven who has given you grace and mercy through the death of Christ and the prayer of his saints, may clothe you with fortitude from on high and inscribe your name into the book of eternal life, to preserve thee in piety and faith until death. This is my wish to thee through Jesus Christ. Amen.[9]

The age of baptism is normally between nineteen and twenty for girls and from twenty to twenty-six for boys. Individuals wishing to be baptized need to ask for it from the ministers. An instruction period of from six to eight weeks precedes baptism itself. The rite itself, as seen in the questions, promises unqualified obedience to Christ and to his church, i.e., the Hutterian church.

In the sixteenth century the Hutterians carried on itinerant missionary activity long after the other Anabaptist groups had withdrawn to sheltered places for survival. This pattern seems to be regaining momentum, but in a different mode, through initiating dialogue with a wide range of groups including Waldensians, Quakers, Mennonites, Church of the Brethren and including distant countries like New Zealand, India, Sweden and visits to Central America. Prison and relief ministries are also carried on, the latter often in cooperation with MCC and Oxfam. The activity of the *Plough Publishing House* is seen as mission with its literature distribution and translation of early Hutterian historical and devotional writings.[10]

An Anabaptist study center has been established in Tokyo through the initiative of Isomi Izeki who was ordained by the Alberta Hutterians in 1977. Gan Sakakibara, a Japanese scholar, has written numerous volumes on Anabaptism and secured a major Anabaptist library collection for the center.

A unique witness is also being given by their very existence as communities and by a lifestyle so different from that of the surrounding culture. One of their leaders has written: "Some [Hutterians] say that the mission field is in their daily work and way of life. When researchers come and go and when the press reports about the Hutterian way of life, that is mission outreach. It is annoying to some that so much is published about Hutterians and that so many busloads of tourists come almost daily to the colonies."[11] One keen observer of the Hutterian way of life has written: "Hutterians are rarely alone and seldom lonely."[12]

Endnotes

1. John A. Hostetler, *Amish Society*, Baltimore, Md.: The Johns Hopkins Press, 1963, p. 55. An older form added "whether it be for life or death" at the end of questions three and four as part of the commitment.

2. Levi Miller, "The Amish Word for Today," in *The Christian Century*, vol. XC, no. 3, January 17, 1973, p. 71.

3. Quoted in ibid., from John A. Hostetler and Gertrude Enders Huntington, *Children in Amish Society*. New York, N.Y.: Holt, Rinehart, and Winston, 1971, p. 2.

4. *Mennonite World Handbook*, 1978, p. 369, by Ervin N. Hershberger.

5. MQR (April 1931), 5:112ff.; (July 1931), 5:198ff.

6. Recounted in John A. Hostetler, *Hutterite Society*. Baltimore, Md.: The Johns Hopkins University Press, 1974, pp. 128ff., from the original account in A. J. F. Zieglschmid, *Das Klein-Geschichtsbuch der Hutterischen Brüder*. Philadelphia, Pa.: Carl Schurz Memorial Foundation, 1947, pp. 477-489.

7. Hostetler, *Hutterite Society*, p. 134-135.

8. ME 5:406-409. MWC *Handbook* 1990, pp. 413, 416.

9. Hostetler, *Hutterite Society*, appendix VII, pp. 337-338; reprinted from Peter Hofer, *The Hutterian Brethren and Their Beliefs*. Starbuck, Man.: The Hutterian Brethren of Manitoba, 1955, pp. 26ff.

10. See e.g. *The Chronicle of the Hutterian Brethren*, vol. I, Rifton, N.Y.: Plough Publishing House, 1987, pp. 887.

11. John A. Hostetler and Gertrude Enders Huntington, *The Hutterites in North America*. New York, N.Y.: Holt, Rinehart, and Winston, 1967, p. 110.

12. Paul S. Gross, MWC *Handbook* 1978, p. 356.

Other Resources: See items referred to in the endnotes, especially also the ME 5:406-409 article and bibliography. Contact any MCC office or Mennonite information center for audiovisual resources.

14

The General Conference Mennonite Church

MILITARY CONFLICTS sharply limited the flow of European immigrants to North America during the second half of the eighteenth century. There was first the Seven Years' War of 1756-63, between England and France over control of New World lands, particularly Canada. This was followed by continuing Indian wars encouraged by the two European powers. Then came the American Revolution of 1775-83, the French Revolution of 1789-99, and the Napoleonic Wars, which finally ended in 1815. A renewed flare-up of hostilities across the forty-ninth parallel between England and the United States had led to the War of 1812, but by 1815 tensions had subsided—until the American Civil War, 1861-65—and immigration again came into full swing.

Among the new waves of immigrants were also some 3,000 Mennonites from Alsace, Bavaria, and Hesse, who settled in Ontario, Ohio, and further west in Indiana, Illinois, and Iowa. While they carried the same names as those who had come to Pennsylvania a century earlier, and many came from the same communities in Europe, they were different because of different experiences. While those who came in the eighteenth century lived in relatively closed, self-sufficient Mennonite settlements, those who came after 1830 had experienced the spiritual and intellectual freedom which had arisen in Europe. They were beginning to be citizens of this world while still being pilgrims on their way to the world beyond. This new mood is reflected in the gentle but perceptive comment of Jacob Krehbiel, a minister from the Palatinate who settled in New York State but associated with the Franconia Conference. He wrote in a letter to his friends in Germany in 1841, ten years after his arrival in America:

> I do not wish to deny that in some American congregations too much emphasis is placed on outward forms and at times, therefore, some points seem exaggerated. But this is admitted by most of the preachers here themselves, and I would not want to say that there is no good intention at heart. Rather it is the case with a good many that they possess only to a small degree the gift of differentiating between the greater and the less, wherefore nonessentials are made to be essentials and consequently too much strictness is laid upon these matters, forgetting that Paul laid the first emphasis on a "new creature in Christ." [1]

Some of the immigrants who had come to Illinois settled near Summerfield, across the Mississippi River from St. Louis. In 1851 a group settled in Lee County, in southeast Iowa. True to their Mennonite tradition they began to organize churches as soon as they arrived. One congregation was organized at West Point, Iowa, in 1849, with two men chosen as ministers. A small log cabin church seating thirty people was built four miles from town. Because it was located on the edge of a wooded area the congregation was often referred to as the *Busch Gemeinde,* i.e., bush church. Another congregation, called Zion, was organized nine miles from the first, in Franklin Township, in 1852. They were allowed to use a German Lutheran church building on alternate Sundays until their own building was completed in 1855. A third congregation was organized at Summerfield in 1858. Krehbiels were among the leading men in all three congregations. There were other Mennonites and Amish in these communities also, families who had moved west from Pennsylvania and Ohio, but because of their different background and experiences these German immigrants did not seem to have much contact with them.

Because fellowship is necessary for Christian growth the three congregations at West Point and Summerfield tried hard to overcome their geographical and spiritual isolation. In 1853 the West

Point and Franklin Township congregations united to form the
German Evangelical Mennonite congregation with a total of 181 members. Since the two churches were nine miles apart, they continued
to meet separately but had annual conferences together. By 1859
they felt it necessary to do something concrete in home and foreign
missions. They had become alert to the need for missions through
the work of an itinerant British Baptist who had visited their communities while they were still in Europe,[2] and especially through
the impact of pietism (see ME 5:703-704) in their home communities. They became convinced that they needed to be united in order
to undertake such work. Three resolutions were adopted at the
conference that year: first, to take an offering for missions on the
first Sunday of every month; second, to take offerings for the support of a minister who could be asked to visit the scattered Mennonites in the Middle West; and third, to appoint a business committee to take care of these affairs and to "correspond with other Mennonite churches and invite them to join this union." When minister
Jacob Krehbiel I sent these resolutions to be published in the Mennonite paper, *Das Christliche Volksblatt,* he added a letter saying:

> May the Lord lend his blessing to this small beginning, that eventual-
> ly a common bond of brotherhood bind all our Mennonite communi-
> ties to work unitedly that the brethren living in isolation may receive
> the pure gospel, and thereby the scattered sheep be held for our fold.[3]

Almost unknown to these congregations was the fact that four
years earlier, in 1855, a similar unity had been achieved by the congregation in Wadsworth, Ohio, with several Mennonite congregations in Ontario. The minister of the Wadsworth congregation was
Ephraim Hunsberger, a frontier preacher who felt Mennonites
were too slow in spreading the gospel. The leader of the participating Ontario congregations was Daniel Hoch, an evangelist who disturbed many Mennonites with his emphasis upon prayer meetings,
freedom of expression in church meetings, and holiness. Here too
missions and unity received primary attention. Hoch himself was
commissioned as an itinerant evangelist and union negotiations
were begun with the East Pennsylvania Conference.

At the third meeting of this group, known as the Canada-Ohio
Conference, approval was given to a proposal which had appeared
earlier in *Das Christliche Volksblatt.* The proposal began with the
words, "Let all ministers of the various branches of the denomination cultivate a fraternal confidence toward each other and

abandon all prejudice." It further urged the preparation of a confession of faith and added that "all those who will accept this confession and unite upon it shall be considered the real Mennonite denomination." The desire for unity among Mennonites, which was to become a major concern of the General Conference Mennonite Church, was already present.

John H. Oberholtzer, 1809-95

There was another group involved in unity negotiations. This group was under the leadership of John H. Oberholtzer, minister of the Swamp Mennonite Church near Quakertown, Pennsylvania. It is interesting to note that while this group was interested in *union* with other Mennonites, their own little East Pennsylvania Conference had originated in 1847 after a *break* with the older and larger Franconia Conference.

Oberholtzer was born on January 10, 1809, in Berks County, Pennsylvania. His great-grandfather Jacob Oberholtzer had come to Philadelphia from Switzerland in 1732. Young John received the best education a farm boy could acquire during the winter months in the German church school. By the time he was sixteen years of age he was himself employed as a teacher every winter until he was ordained as a minister in 1842. But this teaching had its own problems. For a time his classroom was the second floor of a hog barn on the farm of John Ritter. It seems that the older boys enjoyed asking for permission to leave the room and then used the occasion to stir the swill barrel down stairs until the hungry pigs were in a real uproar waiting to be fed. Classes naturally had to be dismissed for the remainder of the period because of the noise and dust. This practice became such a nuisance that the school had to be discontinued at that location. Since the school year was short and the salary small, young John also learned the locksmithing trade, later establishing his own shop near Milford Square. This skill became his main financial support for thirty years.

His call to ministry came through the lot. Since the minister of the Swamp church was over eighty years old, the congregation nominated fifteen members of the church as possible ministers, John among them. Though he had misgivings about calling ministers by the lot, there was nothing he could do about it since that was the tradition. When the fifteen candidates were together, each was given a Bible, but only one had the lot in it. This was a slip of paper on which the words of Proverbs 16:33 were usually written: "The lot is cast into the lap, but the decision is wholly from the Lord." The lot was drawn by John.

One Sunday morning about six weeks later John was told, upon arriving at the church, that he was to preach his first sermon that morning. He chose as his text Ephesians 2:8, "For by grace you have been saved, through faith." After the service he overheard the remark, "That was a scholarly sermon," and since scholarship was seen as a sign of pride the remark probably meant that it had been a bad sermon. Yet he himself shared later that he had experienced real divine help in this hour, having claimed the promises of Joshua 1:5 and Hebrews 13:5.

Nevertheless, he continued in his ministry but felt increasing opposition to his thinking. He was an able preacher and administrator, with many new ideas which he believed to be biblical. He was young and possibly somewhat impatient with the old forms of worship and community life. More and more he found himself distinguishing between practices which were followed from force of habit only, without clear biblical precedent, and those which he found in the life of the early church according to Acts and the epistles. Why, he asked, should ministers wear different coats than laymen, why should no minutes be kept of church meetings, why is a church constitution sin, and why could Mennonite ministers not have Christian fellowship with other ministers except Quakers? There were other lesser things which troubled him, and personality clashes must have been inevitable. He could not get used to the authority of bishops, believing rather that the entire congregations should decide all major issues in the church. And slowly the fellowship was broken, though several attempts were made at reconciliation.

This had indeed been a difficult time for the Mennonites in Pennsylvania. Being both hard-working and frugal, they had become quite wealthy. Religious freedom meant for them the freedom not to change their old customs. The War of Independence had cut them off from stimulating contacts with their European brethren, and the democratic American environment seemed foreign to them. Missions were not undertaken, education was suspect, and prayer meetings were frowned upon. Members were forbidden many things that seemed harmless, such as picnics or celebrations, farm exhibitions and poultry shows.

But all this must not be taken as a lack of spiritual interest.

There was, on the contrary, very strong Christian conviction, but it was not nourished by fresh Bible study and prayer and fellowship with other believers. The unfamiliar constituted a threat to the faith because they were so conscious of a heritage to preserve. And so the faith was seen as a timeless deposit to be guarded zealously from the world, rather than as a living power meant precisely for the world in its lostness. The consequent stress upon external forms and customs left too little freedom for the renewing work of the Holy Spirit.

A particular problem among the two groups was the constitution Oberholtzer had written for adoption by the conference. Known as the *Ordnung*, it not only gave full authority to the entire congregation instead of to the bishop but also proposed the keeping of minutes, regular elections, and a modification of the use of the lot in choosing ministers. It urged a greater openness to other Christians, also suggesting that Mennonites might marry outside their church so long as it was "in the Lord." It was clear that the *Ordnung* would lead to less separation from the world and greater adaptation to their American environment. With this, it seemed, would come a loss of the heritage of faith through outside influence. By 1847 the rupture was complete and the representatives of fourteen congregations met to form a new organization which they called the East Pennsylvania Conference of the Mennonite Church. Soon this group became known as the *New* Mennonites to distinguish them from the *Old* Mennonites, though neither group really considered the other to be true disciples of Menno any longer.

In addition to leading the affairs of the new conference and ministering to his own congregation, Oberholtzer now worked tirelessly for spiritual renewal. He was to establish one of the first American Mennonite Sunday schools. He ordered Mennonite literature and catechism materials from Europe to teach young people the meaning of their faith, and he carried on correspondence with Mennonites scattered throughout the Middle West. Particularly important was his founding in 1852 of *Der Religiöser Botschafter*, a newspaper by which it became possible to reach the most scattered believers with greetings and spiritual help. Four years later the name was changed to *Das Christliche Volksblatt* and it continued successfully under the editorship of Oberholtzer.

A General Conference Is Born

The initiative toward union came from the two congregations at West Point, Iowa, with the editorial support of Oberholtzer. Having themselves united in 1853, they published the minutes of their 1859 conference which invited others to join them and announced the next meeting for "the second day of Pentecost in 1860 at West Point." Neither the Canada-Ohio Conference nor the East Pennsylvania Conference took much notice of this invitation. Shortly before it was to meet, however, the latter group adopted a motion stating that "since the Iowa conference has come to notice, it is agreed that ministers who wish may attend voluntarily." At the last minute friends raised enough money for Oberholtzer to go to the conference.

When the conference convened, only the two sponsoring churches and four visitors, including Oberholtzer, were present. Five sermons were preached before they turned to the agenda of four points. These were the organization of a missionary society, the establishment of a training school for Christian workers, the formation of a historical society, and the publication of tracts. During the conference a committee of five was appointed to draw up a plan of union by the following morning. This they did and the resulting plan, with six points, was adopted without much change. Its provisions were to make it possible to work together on all important matters without violating the congregational freedom of the churches. Uniformity in all things was not considered necessary for cooperation. It was agreed to work earnestly in home and foreign missions and establish a school for the training of Christian workers as soon as possible. It was also agreed to meet again the following year at Wadsworth, Ohio. John H. Oberholtzer was elected chairman of the new conference.

On February 11, 1861 president-elect Abraham Lincoln left Springfield, Illinois for his March 4 inaugural in Washington, "not knowing when or whether I ever may return." Because an assassination plot had been discovered he was put aboard a secret train traveling at night and arrived at 6 a.m., February 23rd. On April 12 the shore batteries at Fort Sumter went into action. The Civil War had begun. This was the climate in which the new conference began also.

A few months later a significant decision was made by the 1861 conference in appointing Daniel Hege as *Reiseprediger,* i.e., a traveling minister for the conference. It was to be his duty to travel through the Mennonite communities to promote unity, evangelism, and the need for a stronger educational program. In speaking of this need before the conference he said:

> If we Mennonites are not to increase our guilt by longer neglecting the duty of missions as commanded by our Lord . . . we must, not singly, but as a denomination, make missions the work of the Lord by our people. If we would undertake our mission duty, we first need Christian educational institutions. But to found and carry on institutions . . . demands not only active interest, but also much money, and for that, churchwide participation and unremitting sacrifice is required as well as unity.[4]

Because of the Civil War Hege was unable to begin his journey immediately, but in May 1862 he set out to visit the churches in the Middle West, the East, and in Ontario. He normally conducted at least four preaching services each week and as many as fifty to sixty house calls. In every home he challenged them to give to missions and education, sharing with them his vision of a united Mennonite church forgetting its differences in the work of the kingdom. He was very well received in most places after he had presented his case, though questions and criticism were often leveled at him before they discovered his fine Christian spirit.

In November he returned home to Summerfield, planning to finish the work in Iowa by the end of the year, but he took ill and died of typhoid fever on November 30. His itinerant ministry had made a deep impression upon the churches, however, so forceful that Oberholtzer wrote, "If the aims of the general conference of Iowa and Ohio are ever accomplished, then Brother Hege stands forever as one of the first men who helped break through the opposition."

We have seen earlier that the initial membership in the conference consisted of two kinds of groups: South German and Alsatian immigrants coming after 1815, and the American Mennonites of the East Pennsylvania Conference originating in 1847. The conference founded in 1860 was thus not a split from the so called (Old) Mennonites of that time, but, at its founding, drew in the Oberholtzer group as one of its participants. It was, in fact, only after the *Reiseprediger* Daniel Hege visited the Oberholtzer group in 1862 that they developed some enthusiasm for the union.

Ten years after its founding the General Conference thus consisted of some twenty congregations with approximately 1,500 members. To these were later added as a third group, the congregations in Ohio, Indiana, and Missouri which had come directly from Switzerland between 1817 and 1854. It was from the Swiss congregation at Berne, Indiana, that S. F. Sprunger (d. 1923) was to come. "Sammy," as he was known, had a great influence upon the conference through his spiritual concern and evangelical power.

The fourth and by far the largest group to join the conference were the Mennonites from Russia. The history of their experiences has been told in chapters 10 and 11. Leaving Russia to escape the military draft and the threat of gradual assimilation into the surrounding culture, the first groups arrived in the United States and Canada in 1873. During the ten following years a total of 18,000 were to come, 10,000 settling on the frontier lands west of the Mississippi in Dakota, Nebraska, and Kansas, and 8,000 locating in Manitoba. A large number of these soon joined the General Conference.[5]

It has sometimes been asked why these 1870s immigrants joined the General Conference rather than the American or (Old) Mennonites who had given them so much moral and financial help. The answer lies partly in the fact that the latter had not unified as a conference which they could have joined, but even more in two other factors. The immigrants felt a greater cultural affinity for the more Germanic element in the General Conference, in terms of language, social attitudes, convictions about education. Second, they did bring with them a mission concern which identified them with the young conference, and which they did not find among the others. When they asked John F. Funk about this, he referred them to the Dutch Mennonite missionary program in Indonesia.

The Mennonite mosaic which emerged in Kansas in the 1870s may have been even more unique than that in Germantown in the 1680s. There were Dutch-Prussians direct from the Vistula Delta who had never gone to Russia (Elbing, Emmaus), Dutch-Russian Mennonites (from the Molotschna, the majority), Swiss-South Germans (Halstead . . .), pure Swiss (Whitewater), Volhynian-Amish-Swiss, Swiss-Galician (Arlington, Ransom, Hanston), Dutch-Polish (Grace Hill, Canton, Galva . . .) traces of Hutterian in the Volhynian groups, some MC Pennsylvania Dutch. These were culturally separate groups with different food systems, dialects, politics, worship patterns, economic status, modes of dress, criteria for simplicity, etc. Yet they came together for hymn sings, formed a teachers' association and launched the first mission efforts in Oklahoma.

This was certainly not a monolithic General Conference Mennonite Church but a cross section of the mosaic that the GCMC was to continue to be.

The Conference of Mennonites in Canada

The immigrants of the 1870s had found the Manitoba frontier congenial and progressed rapidly. An additional 21,000 persons from Russia joined them during the 1920s and many thousands came after World War II. While the first group of the 1870s stayed mostly in Manitoba, those of the 1920s located primarily in Saskatchewan and Alberta, though some stayed in Ontario. Since the depression and its crop failures came soon after their arrival, many experienced extremely difficult pioneering years. In time, large numbers left their prairie farms for the fruitlands of British Columbia and Ontario.

By the close of World War II farming had become so mechanized that few immigrants after the 1940s could afford to buy land or machinery. Consequently they located in urban areas. This, in part, accounts for the large Mennonite congregations in the cities of Canada in contrast to the pattern in the United States, a fact that was to add to unique social dynamics in General Conference relationships. Thus some two-thirds of the General Conference came to be of Russian Mennonite background and over 40 percent of its membership was in Canada: 28,994 members in Canada, 34,693 in the United States and 3,306 in South America, for a total of 66,993 in 369 congregations in 1990, plus 8,350 members in 69 associate congregations in Eastern Canada, and over 3,000 in nonaffiliated but participating congregations in 1990.

The coming of the Mennonites to Canada is described in Frank H. Epp's *Mennonite Exodus* (1962), and their history in Canada in his volumes I (1974) and II (1981), *Mennonites in Canada.* A sociological analysis of some of them has been provided by E. K. Francis, *In Search of Utopia* (1955). Each of these movements called forth men of vision who were willing and able to direct them and who frequently risked a great deal to bring them to pass. Prominent in the movement of the 1870s was Cornelius Jansen (d. 1894), a man of courage and ability who was exiled from Russia for encouraging the Mennonites to leave and who himself settled in Beatrice, Nebraska.

Central to the movement of the 1920s to Canada was the life

Mennonite Heritage Centre, an inter-Mennonite archive operated by the Conference of Mennonites in Canada, located on the campus of Canadian Mennonite Bible College, Winnipeg, Manitoba. The Centre also houses the library and historical library of the college.

and work of David Toews (d. 1947), who came to Kansas from Russia via Asia at the age of fourteen, moved to Canada as a young man to teach school, and, before he died, came to be known as the Moses of the Mennonites. Traveling far and wide from his modest home in Rosthern, Saskatchewan, in the interests of the emigration, he soon had many friends and helpers, even in Ottawa. When he borrowed nearly $400,000 in the name of the Mennonites to make the coming of these immigrants possible, he also had numerous opponents among his own people. Total borrowings and interest were to grow to 1.9 million dollars before all was repaid in 1946, one year before his death. The work of the Canadian Board of Colonization which had been established by Toews was of particular significance. The human drama of these migrations was filled with pathos, faith, but also humor, and is gradually finding expression in biographies and novels.[6]

The Conference of Mennonites in Canada had its origin in the concerns of two multi-congregational groups, the Bergthal group near Winnipeg in Manitoba and the Rosenort group north of Saskatoon in Saskatchewan. The former had come from Russia as an entire colony group in the 1870s, the latter included immigrants from both Russia and Prussia. Since Bergthal members continued to move west they were encouraged to affiliate with the Rosenort group. Eventually a meeting to regularize pastoral concerns and discuss closer cooperation between the two groups was held in Elder Peter Regier's garden near Laird in 1902. The following year the Conference of Mennonites in Middle Canada was organized at Hochstadt, Manitoba. The name was later changed to the Conference of Mennonites in Canada.

Numerical growth has been steady in the Conference of Mennonites in Canada through natural increase and immigration but also through evangelism. Conference activities have proliferated in education, relief, mission, native ministries, camping, and other programs. It must be remembered that each of the five western provinces have their own conference structures and also carry on ministries in these and other areas. When the General Conference is added as a third layer of organization and activities the problems of duplication, jurisdiction, and bureaucracy increase at times to significant levels of frustration. To this situation must yet be added the activities of MCC at the provincial, national, and North American levels.

Interest in education in the conference is seen in the support given to Canadian Mennonite Bible College, Winnipeg, Manitoba; Menno Simons College, Winnipeg, Manitoba; Columbia Bible College, Clearbrook, British Columbia (inter-Mennonite); Conrad Grebel College, Waterloo, Ontario (inter-Mennonite); Mennonite Collegiate Institute, Gretna, Manitoba; Rosthern Junior College, Rosthern, Saskatchewan; Swift Current Bible Institute, Swift Current, Saskatchewan; United Mennonite Education Institute, Leamington, Ontario; and Westgate Mennonite Collegiate, Winnipeg, Manitoba.

A first in integration occurred on March 1, 1988 when the Mennonite Conference of Eastern Canada (MCEC) replaced the

Conference of United Mennonite Churches in Ontario (GC, 5,192 members), the Mennonite Conference of Ontario and Quebec (MC, 5,110 members), and the Western Ontario Mennonite Conference (MC, 3,195 members), for a total MCEC membership of 13,497 at that time. There were five MCEC congregations in Quebec (plus 11 Mennonite Brethren congregations) and seven in the Maritime provinces: four Mennonite Brethren, one Kleinegemeinde, one Church of God in Christ, Mennonite, and one MCEC at Petitcodiac, New Brunswick.

Other Groups in the General Conference

Other smaller groups also joined the General Conference. There was immigration from Prussia to both Canada and the United States in small numbers from the 1870s to the 1940s. In 1946 the Central Conference with 3,211 members primarily of Amish background joined. Approximately one half of the Bergthal congregations decided to join more recently, bringing the totals to the numbers indicated above. Of particular interest is the growing tendency for congregations to have dual membership by joining the given regional conference of the Mennonite Church also. In North America the heaviest concentration of General Conference membership has been in the Middle West, stretching from the Prairie Provinces in Canada through the Dakotas and Nebraska to Kansas and Oklahoma.

Defying these early regional settlement patterns are not only the French-speaking congregations in Quebec, but also the non-European origin congregations arising in urban centers. These include numerous Chinese, as well as Vietnamese, Laotian, Native Christian, black and Hispanic congregations. The inter-racial and inter-Mennonite Learning Center of Chicago also illustrates this trend. The advocacy of minority rights, particularly of Native Canadians by MCC Canada during the 1980s and early 1990s revealed the growing sensitivity of many Mennonites to issues of social justice. Congregations arose from this identification with human need.

United to Serve

"From the very beginning of the General Conference," wrote J. W. Kliewer, chairman of the Mission Board for twenty-five years, "missionary interest has been the cement that has held this structure together." Missions, unity, and education were indeed the primary motives leading to union. The wide variety of ethnic and cultural backgrounds of the groups joining the conference indicated that something stronger than family relationships was drawing them together. Nor were they uniting simply for the sake of unity, as their minimal organizational machinery verifies. They did not adopt a formal constitution for thirty-six years! They united in order to do together that which none of them could do alone.

American Christians were long familiar with the idea of missions, but the Mennonites were too isolated by their own cultural patterns to be inspired by them and the mission zeal of the sixteenth-century Anabaptists had long been lost. The Dutch Mennonites, however, being more open to the influence of others, had organized a missionary society in 1847, and sent their first missionary Pieter Jansz (d. 1904) to Java in 1851. The Mennonites in Germany and Russia soon supported this work.

The immigrants coming from South Germany to West Point and Summerfield in mid-century brought an interest in missions with them. In 1853 Oberholtzer published an article about Methodist mission work, the first of many on this subject. At the 1858 meeting of the East Pennsylvania Conference he was asked to write to the European Mennonites for information about their missionary activities. Their response was an invitation to join in the work with the Dutch, German, Austrian, and Russian Mennonites who were already supporting it. The following year the Ontario Mennonites organized the "Home and Foreign Mission Society of the Mennonites," and in 1866 the Pennsylvania Mennonite Mission Society with seventy-two charter members was organized in Oberholtzer's church. Nevertheless, it was to take until 1872 before the first missionary candidate was available.

The founding of an educational institution was seen as part of their interest in, and preparation for, missions. Mennonites had generally been opposed to higher education. They believed that much learning made people proud and prevented them from seeing simple spiritual truths. The persecutors of the sixteenth-century Anabaptists had, for the most part, been learned men. Faith, the Mennonites had come to believe, was not so much intellectual understanding as a matter of the heart and of obedience to the call of the gospel. The new conference, however, saw education as inseparable from missions; those chosen for this work should be well prepared. The institution they wanted to establish was to be a missionary training school, missions meaning not only bringing the gospel to distant lands, but working with the unevangelized at home, and even gathering indifferent and scattered Mennonites.

At the conference sessions of 1863 a report was received from the committee which had been appointed to study the school question. This report called for a school to be built at Wadsworth, Ohio, as soon as possible and to be named the "Christian Educational Institution of the Mennonite Denomination." Funds were immediately solicited and the building was finished in time to be dedicated at the next conference session in 1866. Classes began in 1868 with twenty-four students and six teachers. That same year Carl J. van der Smissen was called from a pastorate in northern Germany to be principal.

The curriculum was divided into three departments—theology, German, and English. Under the latter department were included most of the subjects normally taught in academies and colleges at that time. That the field of education was indeed new to the Mennonites in North America, became clear when the school had to be closed in 1878, after eleven years of operation, because of financial and internal problems. But this first attempt was not without result. A total of 209 students had come under its influence, including the first missionaries to be sent out and many others who were to assume leadership in the conference. The school taught the people to give their money and to think in terms of missions. Consequently the same session which closed the school in 1878, authorized the Mission Board to establish another school at a more favorable location but no immediate steps were taken.

With the coming of the Mennonites from Russia in 1874-83, many new congregations were added to the conference, together with fresh enthusiasm for missions and education. Because they had conducted their own schools in Russia for over one hundred years, they were familiar with school problems and procedures. By 1877, a committee had been appointed to study the possibility of founding a school for higher education in Kansas. That school opened its doors in 1882 as the Emmental school north of Newton, but transferred to Halstead in 1883; it eventually became Bethel College in 1893. With the Mennonite Collegiate Institute opening in Gretna, Manitoba, in 1889; Bluffton College, Ohio, in 1898; and Freeman Junior College (South Dakota) in 1903 there was no longer any doubt that the General Conference people were interested in education.

Mennonite settlers in Kansas, Minnesota, and Manitoba built homes in their accustomed styles out of available materials. This **adobe house** still stands in Hillsboro, Kansas; the **adobe brick molds** now rest in a Mennonite museum at Freeman, South Dakota. The newly constructed transcontinental railroads actively invited immigrants to settle along their lines. The Santa Fe brought the Russian Mennonites and their wheat to **Newton, Kansas.** Bernard Warkentin built his mill alongside the main line.

The immigrants also brought an interest in mission with them, stimulated in Russia by German pietism and by the work of the Dutch Mennonites. In 1868 Henry Dirks, the first Mennonite missionary from Russia, had gone to the Java field. The financial help which the immigrants received from their American co-religionists upon arrival in the Middle West accustomed the latter further to sacrificial giving, which directly benefitted the mission cause a few years later. All of these factors caused the Pennsylvania minister N. B. Grubb to write "It was not until the Russian brethren had come to America and united with the General Conference that the cause of missions took definite action and the spirit of missions became fact." [7]

Judged by modern standards the beginning was slow and painful. The mission societies of 1859 and 1866 had confined their activities primarily to fund raising and the publishing of articles about mission. Now, in 1872, S. S. Haury, a former student of the Wadsworth school, declared his intention to become a missionary and to prepare for this by further studies in Barmen, Germany. The conference thereupon promptly established a Mission Board of five members to work with him, also agreeing to support him financially during his studies. Following his return in 1875, he was ordained and commissioned to find a suitable field.

The Mission Board preferred to begin their own work rather than lend him to the Dutch for work in Java. He therefore spent five difficult years in this search. When the door seemed to close for work among the American Indians, he made a 9,000-mile trip to Alaska, but since the Presbyterians were already locating there, he returned to explore the Indian territory further. Finally, in 1880, the way opened for him to locate at Darlington, Oklahoma, to work among the Arapahoes. There were many hardships. A fire claimed four lives, including his own child, and destroyed the new mission building. But the work prospered and by Christmas, 1882, fourteen workers were on the field.

Overseas work began in 1899 when famine relief was sent to India, followed by mission workers in 1901. In 1911 the Central Conference, which later merged with the General Conference, began work in the African Congo (Zaire). In 1914 the work begun earlier in China by private persons was taken over by the Mission Board. Soon after World War II, work was begun in Colombia, Japan, and Taiwan. Later work was extended to Paraguay, Uruguay, and Brazil in a cooperative arrangement with Latin-American Mennonites. In the 1970s work was also begun in Bolivia and Costa Rica. The 1990 conference budget of 5.3 million dollars allocated 63 percent for overseas and 20 percent for home ministry projects. North American workers serving abroad numbered 118, and 150 at home, plus 250 with MCC. The era of mission was by no means over, but a new chapter was being written in how this witness was to be carried out in the late twentieth century.[8]

With the increase in conference activities came the need for a clear understanding of responsibilities such as a constitution helps to provide. The first formal constitution was consequently written and accepted in 1896. In order to preserve congregational autonomy the constitution provided that the conference could *advise* but not *legislate*, with the final authority remaining in the hands of the congregations. After continuing revision to meet new situations, the constitution established the commission for overseas ministries (COM), home ministries (CHM), and education (COE), as well as a board of directors for Mennonite Biblical Seminary, which worked together with Goshen Biblical Seminary as the Associated Mennonite Biblical Seminaries at Elkhart, Indiana. Staff offices are located in Winnipeg, Manitoba, and Newton, Kansas, with a General Board responsible for overall guidance in cooperation with an annual Council of Commissions meeting. The Conference of Mennonites in Canada meets annually, as do the provincial conferences, the South American Conference, and the five district conferences in the United States: the Central, Eastern, Northern, Pacific, and Western districts. The conference as a whole meets in plenary session every three years. Its official papers are *The Mennonite* and *Der Bote*, with the bi-weekly *Mennonite Reporter* meeting a real need in Canada and beyond.

Significant changes came to the conference in the affluent decades following World War II. Not least of these was the re-opening of a seminary, this time in Chicago in 1945, and with it a trend toward the professionalization of pastoral ministry and, inevitably, the growth of conference organizations, budgets and programs. However well-trained and capable the seminary graduates were, they were salaried, i.e., "hired," and could not possibly bring to their calling the kind of benevolent authority that a lifetime lay minister or *lehrdienst* (ministers/bench) had. In due course the congregationalism to which the conference was firmly committed led to the need for more structures but also to a dilution of authority and, at times, unhealthy, tiring congregational autonomy in supporting conference causes, the calling of ministers and, occasionally, even decisions by congregations to simply leave the conference.

Fortunately a wealth of leadership potential also emerged from the ranks of CPS (Civilian Public Service), MCC experience, new immigrants to Canada, increased numbers with graduate degrees, "new," i.e., non-Dutch-Germanic ethnic members, inter-Mennonite cooperation, and especially the long overdue freeing of women and their gifts. This wealth of leadership gave a new burst of energy to mission activities at home and abroad, to a less apologetic peace witness, voluntary service, a general empowering of the laity and many other activities, including a series of study conferences to discern vital issues of faith in a way in which the very non-creedal conference had never done.

Faith and Life

At a centennial study conference in 1960 the following statement of goals was adopted to express the hopes and vision of the people of the General Conference for its *second century*:

> As we of the General Conference stand at the threshold of our second century, we look back to the work of those who walked before us, faithful in the cause of Christ and his church. We also look up in gratitude to our heavenly Father for his merciful guidance in the century now closing; and we look forward humbly to the century ahead, aware of the far-reaching warfare we may be called upon to wage against unprecedented demonic power.
>
> So we stand at the threshold, seeking inspiration from the past and praying for God's strengthening in the present and the future as we surrender ourselves in deeper discipleship to him who is our Saviour and Lord, dedicating ourselves to
>
> WITNESS
> to the saving power of Jesus Christ our Lord
> to the unity of all believers in Christ
> to the gospel of peace and reconciliation through Jesus Christ
> to the priesthood of all believers
>
> to the growing multitudes in our cities
> to all who have not heard the gospel
> to each succeeding generation

against the spirit of materialism of this age
against the spirit of exclusivism in our fellowship
against the spirit of division in the Christian Church
against the rising tide of moral laxity

through personal evangelism
through the witness of the printed page
through our institutions of higher learning and all
    conference institutions
through the efforts of the conference in the area of Christian service

by reaffirming our faith in the inspiration and authority
    of the Scriptures
by dedicating ourselves anew as disciples of Christ
by living a life of dedicated stewardship
by keeping open our hearts to the regenerative and sanctifying work
    of the Holy Spirit

by strengthening the Christian family
by manifesting concern over social evils of our culture
by a prophetic witness to state and society.

These goals represented dedication to greater faithfulness. A spirit of repentance and hope was evident at the study conference which adopted them. A sign of this repentance was the adoption of a statement asking forgiveness of the Mennonite Brethren Church for wrongs the forefathers of the General Conference had committed in Russia during the painful experience of division, and the sending of a representative to bring this message to the Mennonite Brethren Conference in session. Repentance has been the first requirement for renewal in every age.

Study conferences and commissions became a significant vehicle for the continuing search for greater unity and faithfulness. The Believers' Church Study Conference in 1955 identified nine suggestions for recovering biblical fellowship within and among congregations, and in a letter to the churches said:

It [the church] is composed of those who have voluntarily accepted Jesus Christ as Savior and Lord and have committed their lives to him. . . . It is a fellowship of brotherly love and discipline controlled by the Holy Spirit. . . . Its authority lies in the Scripture seen particularly in the revelation of God and Jesus Christ. . . . It reveals itself as a missionary church with each believer as active witness.[9]

The Study Conference on Evangelism in 1958 located responsibility for outreach and witness squarely in each congregation and its members when it said: "Even as the crucial link in the church of Christ is the local fellowship, so the crucial link in effective evangelism is the lordship of the living Christ in the local fellowship."[10] It made a particular point of stressing the unity of word and deed when it said: "Teaching, preaching, Christian nurture, as well as the ministry to human need through healing rehabilitation, and relief are but different phases of the total task of the church."[11] This same concern was underscored even more in the Church and Society Study Conference of 1961, the findings of which included the following words:

> We often deny the Incarnation by the very methods of evangelism which we deploy. Should our ministers act in the same way in which Christ did, and seek out the town drunk in the local saloon, they would most likely receive from their congregations the same condemnations that were heaped upon Christ himself. What we plead for is not evangelism on the one hand and social service on the other, but a getting through to human beings in their total need with the one gospel to the whole man [person].[12]

A particularly important *Study Conference on the Church, the Gospel and War* was held in 1953. World War II (1939-45) had shown that the teaching of biblical nonresistance had been neglected by the churches, in that one half of the young men of draft age rejected that position. Part of this response may have been due to the usual nationalist pressures of wartime society, but part of it was also the legacy of the Modernist-Fundamentalist controversy in the conference during the 1930s and 40s. As a progressive body the conference was open to liberal theology and scientific modernism, though the spokesmen for this position were actually few and often misunderstood. Social concern was not, for example, as some opponents insisted, a sign of modernism.

There had been the inevitable clash of personalities. Beyond this, numerous good men and women who no longer felt accepted in their respective Mennonite affiliations joined the General Conference, which did not help its image with other Mennonites. In any case, considerable segments of the conference came increasingly under the influence of Fundamentalism which, at that time, meant the end of any thought of nonresistance. Romans 13:1-7, often misinterpreted, rather than the Sermon on the Mount and the

Mennonites of Russian origin also came to **Mountain Lake,** Minnesota, on the Chicago and North Western Railroad. The Mountain Lake train depot in the top photo was built in 1873, one year before the arrival of the Mennonites. The bottom photo shows the town in the mid-1920s.

life of Jesus, became the guide in citizenship decisions. The conference of 1953 became a turning point back to nonresistance. It closed with the following moving appeal to the congregations:

> Therefore, we call upon you, to help reexamine and strengthen our peace position. We believe that by making an unqualified commitment of allegiance to Christ, a genuine searching of the Scriptures, an early training of our children, the building of churches as consecrated brotherhoods who love their Christ, the development of Christian communities with spiritual patterns of living, the move toward redemptive church discipline, and a mighty thrust of preaching, teaching and healing, that these will help to revive the doctrine of love and nonresistance in our fellowship. May God lead and bless us in this endeavor, is our prayer.[13]

In addition to these and other study conferences, study commissions worked at specific issues at the heart of General Conference concerns. These included church discipline, the inspiration of Scripture, race relations, the Christian and nuclear power, capital punishment, inter-Mennonite cooperation and unity, evangelism, nationalism, poverty and world hunger, church renewal, divorce and remarriage, and others. Statements were adopted for discussion and printed on most of these issues.[14] In 1979 a special mid-triennial session of the General Conference was called in Minneapolis to deal with the question of paying taxes for war in view of nuclear proliferation and the growing worldwide arms race.

There were other signs of spiritual vigor. The Canadian schools referred to, as well as Freeman, Bluffton, and Bethel colleges, were receiving strong student and financial support. The inter-Mennonite seminary program at Elkhart, Indiana, received gratifying encouragement and support. In the decade from 1967-76 the conference experienced a 10 percent membership increase, of which a proportionately larger share occurred in Canada because of immigration, but also through the adding of new members, including minorities congregations.

Meanwhile in the United States over 11 percent of the members had parents of non-Mennonite background. A particular concern for Native ministries was evident in Canada. Small groups were being formed in most congregations for sharing, confession, and mutual support. New intentional communities, covenanting house fellowships, and persons in the charismatic movement brought new vitality and joy in many places without the threatening divisions of earlier history.

There were, of course, also continuing concerns. A shortage of pastoral and other church workers continued. Women were ministering increasingly in new ways in the church and traditional roles were slowly changing. A 1989 study reported 59 percent of the conference favoring their ordination.[15] Midweek Bible study and prayer meetings had all but disappeared, Sunday evening services received modest support, and adult interest in Sunday school studies seemed to be declining, but family clusters and other alternate activities were increasing. Nonresistance continued to grow,[16] but troubling questions about divorce and remarriage, abortion, sexuality, family abuse and other ethical issues were part of the continuing conference dialogue. Retreat centers, marriage enrichment sessions, singles groups, senior citizens groups, and other events provided context for this dialogue.

In the midst of these developments the gap between rich and poor was widening locally, as well as globally. A 1989 study asked for a response to the following statement: "For the most part, people are poor because they lack discipline and don't put forth the effort needed to rise above poverty." No separate General Conference statistic is available, but 21 percent of all Mennonites believed this statement to be true, while 24 percent believed benefits to the poor should be decreased.[17] The question of possible greater cooperation or integration with the Mennonite Church emerged as two options of a significant agenda item for the conference by 1992.

Nevertheless, these concerns were not unusual for persons concerned for faithfulness and obedience even while they lived in an urban, mobile, and secular society. The recognition of these problems, and the openness with which they were being faced, were an encouraging sign of the power of the Holy Spirit at work among the churches.

Endnotes

1. S. F. Pannabecker, *Open Doors. A History of the General Conference Mennonite Church*. Newton, Kan.: Faith and Life Press, 1975, p. 14.
2. James C. Juhnke, *A People of Mission*. Newton, Kan.: Faith and Life Press, 1979, p. 4.
3. Pannabecker, op. cit., p. 45.
4. Ibid., p. 52.
5. C. Henry Smith, *The Coming of the Russian Mennonites*. Berne, Ind.: Mennonite Book Concern, 1927.
6. Cornelius Neufeld, *The Russian Dance of Death*. Winnipeg, Man.: Hyperion Press, 1977.
7. E. G. Kaufman, *The Development of the Missionary and Philanthropic Interest*

Among the Mennonites of North America. Berne, Ind.: Mennonite Book Concern, 1931, p. 103.

8. Juhnke, op. cit.
9. Quoted in Pannabecker, *Open Doors,* pp. 399-400.
10. Ibid., p. 401.
11. Ibid.
12. Ibid., pp. 404-405.
13. Ibid., p. 397.
14. See ME 5:329-332, especially 331:2.
15. J. Howard Kauffman and Leo Driedger, *The Mennonite Mosaic.* Scottdale, Pa.: Herald Press, 1991, p. 207.
16. Ibid., pp. 174ff.
17. Ibid., pp. 204-205.

Other Resources: ME 5:329-332 and other articles, including their bibliographies and cross-references. MWC *Handbook* 1978, 1984, 1990. MacMaster, *Land, Piety, Peoplehood,* 1985. Schlabach, *Peace, Faith, Nation* 1988. Juhnke, *Vision, Doctrine, War,* 1989. Kauffman and Driedger, *Mosaic,* 1991. John L. Ruth, *Maintaining the Right Fellowship,* Scottdale, Pa.: Herald Press, 1984. Beulah Stauffer Hostetler, *American Mennonites and Protestant Movements,* Scottdale, Pa.: Herald Press, 1987. Contact conference offices or information centers for audiovisual resources.

15

The Mennonite Brethren Church

ALTHOUGH spiritual life was at a low ebb in the Mennonite colonies of South Russia, there were also strong influences for renewal. The sermons of Ludwig Hofacker were read by many ministers in private as well as in public meetings. These sermons were not spectacular in style but stressed the need for repentance and forgiveness. Tobias Voth, the first teacher of the Ohrloff high school, was influenced by pietism. As steps to new spiritual life he organized evening services, mission fellowships, and youth meetings. (For Pietism see ME 5:703-04.)

The village of Gnadenfeld, which had been influenced by Moravian pietism in Germany, began observing harvest-thanksgiving Sundays annually at which particular emphasis was given to missions. Preachers from surrounding non-Mennonite churches were sometimes invited to speak at these occasions, among them Eduard Wüst, a Lutheran pietist serving a nearby separatist Lutheran church. Wüst was a dynamic speaker, with strong convictions, stressing free grace (not dependent upon works) and holy living. His style and message presented a sharp contrast to the more unassuming, conventional preaching of the Mennonite ministry. He led many Mennonites to a conversion experience, following which they witnessed to their faith in a free and open manner.

Under the influence of these believers, lay evangelism was introduced into the villages from Gnadenfeld. House visitations were made and meetings held in homes to which unbelievers and nominal Christians could be invited. Larger prayer and Bible study meetings were initiated on Saturday afternoons in order not to conflict with the regular Sunday worship services. Pastor Wüst was present at many of these meetings, usually assuming responsibility for preaching and teaching.

Many of the elders in the church appreciated Wüst's message. Even August Lenzmann, an influential elder at Gnadenfeld, expressed his willingness to cooperate with Wüst. When criticism was expressed over the unaccustomed emotionalism in the group meetings, Lenzmann defended Wüst by attributing the deviations to a misunderstanding of the nature of free grace. This criticism was, however, confirmed by P. M. Friesen when he wrote that "sanctification, to which he [Wüst] referred and which he earnestly practiced, was not preached in a systematic way nor was it in proper relationship to his joyful and evangelical sermons of grace."

Wüst died in 1859, but his conventicle groups continued to meet. Since they addressed each other as brother, they came to be known as the Brethren. Increasingly they became discouraged with the opposition of many of the leaders in the church and charged them with unspirituality. This, in turn, led to estrangement and separation, which prevented the new spirit from working its way into the church as a whole. With the growing separation, the new group felt drawn more closely to each other. This encouraged them to observe the Lord's Supper together late in 1859 under the leadership of Abraham Cornelsen, a schoolteacher. Since none of the church elders were present, though they had been invited, this procedure was considered highly irregular. As a result, calls for discipline were heard. Elder Lenzmann consequently invited the offenders to a hearing, at which six of the brethren promised to refrain from further irregularities, pledging obedience to all things not contrary to their conscience and the Word of God.

Elder Lenzmann and other ministers in Gnadenfeld were, however, deeply concerned for reconciliation and worked to this end. Their efforts were thwarted by the demands of the church majority that private communion services must be discontinued, while the new group insisted they could no longer have fellowship with the entire membership of the large church. On January 6, 1860, the

new group met in a private home to discuss the possibility of organizing a separate fellowship of believers. A document, addressed to
the elders of the church, had been drawn up by Abraham Cornelsen and was considered carefully. Attention was called to the persecution which might follow formal separation. A prayer session
followed. Finally, toward evening, the document was laid on the ta-
ble and signed by eighteen of those present with several of those
present refraining. However, nine of these added their signatures
two days later.

The document accused the church of being in a state of growing corruption and its leaders of tolerating this condition of spiritual decay. There seemed to be little quarrel over doctrine. The primary concern centered around moral and ethical laxity among
church members. While the charges brought against the ministers
may have been too sweeping and severe, they were not without basis in fact. The statement consciously stood for historic
Anabaptism-Mennonitism in its discussion of baptism, communion, foot washing, election of ministers, church discipline, and
other issues. In addition to the signatures, the document named a
committee of three who had been appointed to speak for the new
group.

The signers of the document could hardly have anticipated the
results which were to follow. Since the elders either refused to admit the moral and spiritual decay charged to the church, or were
defensive about it, the document was considered a serious attack
against them and the establishment. Consequently, at a meeting of
elders on January 18, a statement was drafted which placed the entire matter into the hands of the civil authority in the colony, the
Gebietsamt, i.e., the state. This statement was signed by five elders,
several others saying they needed "more light on the matter." It
was clear that the five wanted the new group to be disciplined in
order, as the statement said, "to bring them back from the error of
their ways."

In thus turning a religious issue into a state, viz., colony matter,
the elders did what the Anabaptists had experienced so harshly at
the hands of the establishment in the sixteenth century: they identified the cause of the church with that of the state. But this violated a
very basic conviction of the Anabaptists, who rejected the jurisdiction of the state in matters of faith. Not all of the elders in the old
church were in agreement with the action of the five. Even before
the January 18 meeting, the Ohrloff-Halbstadt church council had

pleaded for tolerance and urged that efforts should not be directed against the new group but against the evils they were criticizing. Many were troubled by the issue but seemed unable to do anything about it. Little was known about the entire problem in the two colonies on the Volga River.

Meanwhile the colony administration accepted the responsibility given to it by the elders and asked the new group for an explanation. In their response of January 23, they declared that they would gladly have remained in the church, but since the ministers were not obedient to the Word of God, they felt compelled to leave. They also declared their intention to remain Mennonites. The colony administration, however, invoked Article 362 of the Penal Code of 1857, which dealt with secret societies, against the Brethren. Religious meetings not sponsored by the established church were forbidden. Physical suffering followed. P. M. Friesen speaks of "continuous examinations, threats, imprisonments, sentences to hard labor, and starvation." Abraham Cornelsen, the father of a large family, was banished from the colony and spent a long time among one of the surrounding nomadic tribes. Others were deliberately ruined economically. Since legal travel documents were denied them by the administration, members of the new group were unable to leave the colony, yet staying became unbearable.

The revival which began in the Molotschna Colony had its counterpart in the Chortitza Colony, though the two movements were not related at first. Unfortunately the Chortitza movement, centering in the village of Kronsweide, embodied emotional excesses which led to a false freedom and to an incident of immorality which, of course, brought further disrepute upon the movement. In the village of Einlage, however, sanity prevailed and the renewal group there disassociated itself from the others. It appears that the Einlage group was influenced by the German Baptists through periodicals which they had been receiving from them. In spite of these distinctions, the Brethren in Chortitza had as hard a time of it as those in the other colony. Wilhelm Janzen was given ten lashes and jailed in an unheated room, while his overcoat was taken from him.

Early Organization and Recognition

One of the first problems which faced the new movement was a lack of strong leadership. On May 30, 1860, an election of minis-

An **M. B. evening Bible school class** in Woldemfürst, Kuban, South Russia (ca. 1925). Johann J. Toews (1878-1933), seated near the middle, was a highly gifted itinerant teacher. **Four of the leading M. B. preachers** visited the Kuban region in 1913: Peter Koehn from Waldheim, Molotschna; Kornelius Wiens, an elder of the Kuban church; Jakob Reimer from Rükenau, Molotschna; and Johann Fast of Alexanderfeld, Kuban.

ters was held by the Molotschna group. Three of them immediately disqualified themselves for office, though they had seemed likely candidates, because they had earlier given a promise to the Inspector of Colonies not to organize a church without official permission. Consequently Heinrich Huebert and Jacob Becker were elected and ordained three days later. While there are no official records of the ordination itself, unofficial reports indicate that the oldest member of the group, Franz Klassen, upon the request of the others, laid his hands on the two candidates and, with earnest prayer, dedicated them to the ministry of the church. Though the elders had been invited to the ordination service, none were present. The historian P. M. Friesen considered this election and ordination to constitute the official organization of the Mennonite Brethren Church.

Now began a long struggle for official government recognition of the new group, which would then also force the Mennonites to recognize them. Failing this, they stood in danger of losing all their special privileges as Mennonites. Repeated trips to St. Petersburg showed the government to be both friendly and helpful, and contact was also made with the Baptists. The colonies, on the other hand, tried to prevent the government from granting the desired recognition and identified them as no longer being Mennonites but "a new sect." At home the Molotschna colony administrator asked the elders to choose between two options for the new group: expulsion from the colony or recognition, apparently hoping thereby to prepare the way for the first option to be implemented. Meanwhile the new group had also presented a petition to the czar in the spring of 1862.

A break came in the tense situation through the leadership of the well-known teacher and minister Johann Harder. In a letter of November 12, 1862, to the colony administration he wrote:

> The October 11, 1862, conference of municipal leaders in the Area Administrative Office regarding the matter of the Mennonites who seceded from the decadent (!) churches advanced the alternatives that either these people will have their colonial status rescinded and be exiled, or they will have to be recognized as a church with rights similar to those of other Mennonite churches in the future. Faced with these alternatives, our church declares that since the first alternative is not based on God's Word, we agree to the latter on the condition that when these people publish a confession of faith, it should correspond substantially with ours. Since upon investigation the se-

cessionists declared their confession to be the same as ours, namely the confession of faith of the so-called united Flemish, Frisian and High German Anabaptist Mennonite Church, published by the Rudnerweide Church in South Russia, the Ohrloff-Halbstadt Church sees no hindrances to recognizing these Mennonites as a church and notifies the Area Administrative Office to that effect. Blumstein, November 12, 1862. Johann Harder, Elder.[1]

This recognition was a direct challenge to the five elders who had signed the objection, and they drafted a lengthy reply. In it they accused the new group of acting without the sanction of ordained leadership, particularly in observing communion. The reply further referred to improper conduct in their meetings and to the practice of rebaptizing persons who had already been baptized in the Mennonite Church. A last attempt to suppress the movement was made by the administration of the colony late in 1863, by ordering village officials not to recognize marriages performed in the new group, and to record the children of such marriages under the mother's name as in the case of illegitimate births. This instruction roused the group to send a petition to the government, which was answered on March 5, 1864, with the coveted official government recognition that they were still considered Mennonites in the full sense of the word.

The period of litigation had come to an end, but the division remained. Bitterness and strife continued for a time, but gradually church leaders of both groups again began working together in matters of common interest to them all.

Doctrine and Church Government

Baptism: The question of the mode of baptism was not an issue for the first group of Brethren; the original document had simply stressed the importance of believers' baptism. Jacob Reimer, one of the signers, had, however, come to question pouring as a biblical mode already in 1837. As an eighteen-year-old, before his baptism, he had read the biography of Anna Judson and had expressed the desire to be baptized by immersion. When he asked whether there were still people who baptized by immersion, his father answered that he had known such people in Prussia.

The first baptism by immersion occurred in the Molotschna Colony in September 1860. The memoirs of Jacob Becker, one of two baptized at that time, throw some light onto the developments which led to the introduction of the practice of immersion in the Mennonite Brethren Church. He writes:

> We knew nothing of immersion until the first Sunday in September, 1860, when two sisters who had not been baptized in the Mennonite Church applied for baptism. After the church had examined them, I received the charge to baptize them. Then brother Johann Claassen came to me and asked me: "According to which form do you intend to baptize?" He went on to say: "The way the church baptizes is not scriptural." These were strange words to me.[2]

Claassen then gave Becker a pamphlet on baptism which he studied carefully and gave to his neighbor, Heinrich Bartel. From it both received the conviction that they themselves would need to be baptized before they could baptize others. Fearful lest the leaders would interpret this as proof that they were indeed introducing a new religious fellowship, they read the works of Menno Simons to see whether he confessed baptism in water. Becker found a reference in which Menno stated that although the mode of baptism had changed several times since the apostolic age, it had originally been in running water. (Jesus was, of course, baptized in the Jordan River. The second century *Didache* marked specific reference to running water.) From this the group concluded that they were in agreement with Menno and that they now had good historical backing for immersion, while still remaining Mennonites.

When Becker brought his convictions to the attention of the Brethren, many agreed with him, and it was decided that he should baptize the women by immersion. He himself, however, felt that he would first need to be immersed, before he could so baptize others. Consequently he wrote:

> Soon thereafter, during the middle of the week, in the month of September, 1860, a wagon loaded with members drove to the water and knelt for prayer at the bank. Thereupon Bartel and Bekker went into the water. Bekker first baptized Bartel, then Bartel baptized Jakob Bekker, and the latter then baptized three others.[3]

The early Mennonite Brethren did not make immersion obligatory for those who had already been baptized by pouring in the Mennonite Church. Heinrich Huebert, one of the eighteen and later the first minister and elder of the church, was rebaptized in May 1861, the year following his election as a minister. Johann Claassen, who

The noted Mennonite Brethren minister, educator, and historian, **Peter Martin Friesen** (1849-1914), shown here with his wife, Susanna. Friesen served the Zentralschule at Halbstadt as teacher and principal, and formulated the M. B. Confession of Faith in 1902. He was a strong promoter of Allianz (see page 288).

was always highly recognized in the new group, was not rebaptized until June 30, 1862.

Early Mennonite Brethren historians note the fact that the conviction to baptize by immersion came to them independent of direct Baptist influence from the outside. However, since Johann Claassen had been in fellowship with the Baptists in St. Petersburg, it is quite possible that they influenced him in his understanding of the Scriptures at this point. In the Chortitza Colony the question of baptism emerged later, after Abraham Unger, a leader in the new group, had corresponded with a German Baptist minister in Hamburg. Eventually the insistence upon immersion as a prerequisite for membership also came from Chortitza, where the Einlage group made immersion a requirement for participation in communion. The churches in the Molotschna Colony were more tolerant on this issue and, until 1863, it was still possible for non-immersed persons to fellowship with the church. However, the advocates of immersion as a prerequisite for membership were finally successful in establishing these practices in the church.

Extremism Is Overcome. Meanwhile the emotional excesses referred to earlier were leading to a crisis in the young movement. Members involved in this overenthusiasm, which came to be known as the *fröhliche Richtung* (joyous movement), called themselves the "happy" ones, and "strong" ones. Several of the leading men were drawn into this circle, though Elder Heinrich Huebert was a staunch opponent and declared it unbiblical. The moderates, however, were unable to stem the tide of emotionalism and soon leadership fell to the radicals both in Chortitza and Molotschna. Those who did not participate in the movement were excommunicated. All social contacts were forbidden to the elect, and even the greeting of a relative on the street was considered to be fellowship with the world.

Johann Claassen, who was in St. Petersburg at this time, wrote strong and pleading letters to these new leaders, but without effect. By spring, 1862, their excesses reached tragic proportions. This doctrine of "liberty in Christ" was interpreted to mean that the usual proprieties between men and women could now be disregarded. The saved, after all, were free from the flesh. This attitude led to the immorality referred to earlier. The sinner was excommunicated by his own group, and the case served as a deterrent to the entire radical movement among them.

In June 1865, five meetings were held by the new group and a sixth one on August 4. One meeting, begun on Saturday morning, lasted throughout the night. The following day, Sunday, was observed as a day of repentance and prayer. Letters of repentance were written to church and government leaders. And so ended a most unfortunate chapter of suffering, but also of triumph, in the early development of the Mennonite Brethren Church.

Baptist influence: During these early years the inexperienced new group leaders often turned to their Baptist contacts for help and counsel. Those in the Chortitza Colony were particularly open to them. It was natural, therefore, that Abraham Unger should write to Hamburg for counsel in connection with the extremist problem. Baptist August Liebig from Hamburg arrived to help them in the spring of 1866. Finding the Chortitza group somewhat unsure and disorganized, he began to preach and to organize special meetings to bring order into the movement.

Many in the new group were opposed to formal organization of any kind, lest it hinder the free work of the Holy Spirit. But Liebig chaired the meetings and took the opportunity to show them parliamentary procedure. Minutes were also kept at his request. After two weeks' stay, however, the authorities arrested him and deported him back to Germany, but even in that brief time he had given invaluable aid and counsel to the Brethren. Unger stayed in touch with him by letter, and in 1869 the German Baptists sent J. G. Oncken to South Russia to help organize the scattered groups. A special meeting was called for October 18, 1869, at which meeting Oncken ordained Unger as elder, Aron Lepp as minister, and two men as deacons. The Molotschna Brethren also desired Oncken's services, but the aging minister was anxious to return to Germany before the rigors of winter set in.

Oncken's visit proved to be a mixed blessing. He stimulated the new movement spiritually, and helped to organize them further. But he smoked, and his influence encouraged several of the group to follow his example. Since he was Baptist, many considered those who had been ordained by him to be Baptists as well. Furthermore, he seems to have had a negative influence upon the traditionally Mennonite belief in biblical nonresistance. The anti-Oncken group finally won, and the ordained men were considered still to be Mennonites. The smokers were excommunicated. The new Mennonite Brethren continued to cherish fellowship with the Baptists but favored organizational separation from them. They wanted to remain Mennonites but the implications of Baptist help did continue to complicate their idenity.

Allianz Gemeinde: Very little genuine fellowship existed between the Mennonite Brethren and other Mennonites. With the growing convictions about immersion an increasing rigidity led to exclusivism and consequently isolation. After the crisis of emotionalism had passed the influence of Johann Claassen and Jacob Reimer waned and a new set of leaders emerged. Many of them were limited in their theological understanding and carried the pure church concept to such extremities that fellowship with other Christians was impossible. A reaction came to this in the *Allianz* or alliance movement.

There were other Brethren in addition to Claassen and Reimer who favored wider contacts than the new leadership wanted. One of them was Christian Schmidt, an evangelist sometimes called "the Wüst of the Mennonite Brethren." Schmidt worked toward fellowship with all true believers, irrespective of their church affiliation. At one of their annual conferences several of these ecumenically minded persons announced their intention to practice open communion, and the service was held in 1899. The repercussions were almost immediate. The congregation of which the evangelist Jacob W. Reimer was a member was asked to discipline him. But the congregation loved Reimer and refused.

As this spirit of tolerance spread, a group of the Brethren met on May 16, 1905, to organize the "Molotschna Evangelical Mennonite Brethren Church," a fellowship dedicated to serve all Mennonite believers, regardless of the mode of baptism practiced by them. The group soon came to be known as the *Allianz Gemeinde,* i.e., alliance or unifying church. Its single requirement for membership was a new birth, and this also meant open communion. Immersion was practiced, but members who had been baptized by another mode were not required to submit to immersion. The office of elder was abolished. In one way this group represented another division, but in another it served as a wholesome corrective to Mennonite Brethren exclusiveness. It constituted a bridge between them and the other Mennonite churches.

Krimmer [Crimea] Mennonite Brethren: Another group born in the midst of revival and closely related to the Mennonite Brethren Church in thought and practice was the Krimmer (Crimea) Mennonite Brethren Church (KMB). The village of Annafeld in the Crimea experienced a revival and Jacob A. Wiebe was converted. A potential leader, Wiebe became a dominant figure in the new

An outstanding leader in helping Mennonites move out of Stalin's Russia to Canada in the 1920s was **B. B. Janz.** He himself settled near Coaldale, Alberta.

movement. He had had previous contacts with the *Kleine Gemeinde* and had been impressed by their piety. He invited Elder Johann Friesen to visit Annafeld and to organize the new group into a *Kleine Gemeinde* congregation. This was done in 1867, with Wiebe as its first minister.

Since many of the members had been baptized before experiencing a conversion, the question of rebaptism was raised. Elder Friesen would not condone a second baptism; so the group commissioned one of its own brethren to baptize Wiebe, who in turn baptized eighteen others, on September 21, 1869. The group chose the name *Brüdergemeinde* (Brethren church) and, to distinguish it from the other Mennonite Brethren, added the geographical designation *Krimmer,* i.e., from the Crimea. The contacts with those other

Mennonite Brethren, however, were few, though they agreed doctrinally except on immersion. The new group practiced kneeling for immersion forward. Rigorous austerity in dress and life, coupled with strict church discipline, marked the KMBs even more than the Mennonite Brethren. The KMBs were to join the MBs in 1960 at the centennial conference in Reedley, California.

Mennonite Brethren in North and South America

With the immigrants of the 1870s, who have been described earlier, were also numerous Mennonite Brethren and KMB families. One of the first of these was Peter Eckert, a Mennonite Brethren elder who arrived in Kansas in 1875, bringing a number of families with him. The group was of Lutheran background and had become Mennonite through the early revivals and evangelistic efforts which followed 1860. Eckert was a tolerant and open-minded Christian and, therefore, made an attempt to form one group with the KMB families who had located nearby in the village of Gnadenau. They lived fourteen miles northwest of Peabody, in Marion County, but preferred to remain separate.

In 1876 some seventy-five additional families arrived from Russia. Although the majority were from the Volga area, a number had also come from the Kuban and Chortitza colonies. Those from the Volga and the Kuban settlements immediately joined Eckert's group, but the Chortitza families remained separate. The reason for this seems to have been the close feelings not shared by the others. From 1874 to 1880 a total of approximately 200 Mennonite Brethren families came to the Middle West, including Elder Abraham Schellenberg of the Molotschna, who exerted a stabilizing influence in the new settlements.

After these congregations had become established, a general desire was expressed for the organization of a conference of local churches. The first meeting for this purpose was called by Peter Regier and eleven delegates representing the churches in Kansas and Nebraska came to it. Because of inadequate representation and decisions made which later conferences could not approve, this meeting has not been accepted as an official conference. The first official conference was held in Henderson, Nebraska, in 1879. From that time on they were held annually until 1909, and triennially thereafter.

The Mennonite Brethren church in Canada began through the

The **M. B. Seminary** in Fresno, California, is located on the campus of Pacific College.

missionary activities of David Dyck of Kansas and Heinrich Voth of Minnesota in 1884. The first converts coming from this work were baptized near Winkler, Manitoba, in 1886. There were no Mennonite Brethren among the immigrants of the 1870s to Canada. Later, Gerhard Wiebe, an immigrant of 1888, was supported by the conference in an evangelistic ministry. The first congregation was organized at Burwalde, with smaller congregations organized at Plum Coulee in 1897 and Kronsgart in 1898. From these centers workers were sent to Saskatchewan where the first congregation was established in Laird with sixty members in 1898. Congregations were also soon organized in the Rosthern and Herbert areas.

By 1900 membership in the Mennonite Brethren churches in North America was a little over 2,000. Annual conferences made it possible for them to carry on projects in missions, evangelism, and literature. In 1903, the conference delegates were asked to consider the possibility of dividing the total constituency into district conferences which would convene annually, and to have the entire conference meet every three years. No agreement was reached, however, and the question was tabled. Meanwhile a constitution was written, and accepted in 1908. The following year the projected division was carried out with the establishing of the Southern, Central, and Northern District conferences. At the 1911 conference in Rosedale, California, the Pacific District was added as a fourth conference.

The migration of the 1920s brought many additional Mennonite Brethren families to Canada and, from 1930 on, also to Paraguay and Brazil in South America. Those settling in Canada established congregations in the Prairie Provinces. After the depression many were forced to move to British Columbia and Ontario, where conferences were also organized. On the prairies, Winnipeg emerged as the largest urban concentration of Mennonites, including the Mennonite Brethren. Many became leaders in business and a wide variety of the professions.

On June 9, 1930, a group of fifty-five brethren met in the village of Gnadenheim, Fernheim Colony, Paraguay, to organize the Mennonite Brethren Church in the country. Leaders in this movement were Heinrich Pauls and Gerhard Giesbrecht. The newly organized group adopted the constitution they had brought along from Russia. With the founding of Friesland Colony in Paraguay in 1937, active Mennonite Brethren congregations were established in that area also, under the leadership of Kornelius Voth. When more settlers arrived after World War II, the Volendam Mennonite Brethren Church was organized in 1947 and the one at Neuland Colony in 1948.

The first Mennonites to settle in Brazil arrived in January, 1930. An intimate relationship was maintained among the Mennonite Brethren, Evangelical Mennonite Brethren, and Mennonite churches. However, efforts to organize a united Mennonite church failed and the Mennonite Brethren Church was officially organized in the Krauel Valley under the leadership of Elder Jakob Huebert.

Several Mennonite Brethren churches were then organized in other districts. The district around Curitiba had attracted many Mennonite settlers from the Krauel, and the Boqueirão Mennonite Brethren Church was organized, with Peter Hamm as its leader. Later, the churches at Guarituba and Neu-Witmarsum were established; also, the churches of Vila Guaíra and Xaxim. One of the larger Mennonite Brethren churches in Brazil is the Bage church, founded in 1949 in the state of Rio Grande do Sul. Congregations also exist at Blumeneau, Sao Paulo and other locations.

Several Mennonite Brethren churches have been established in Uruguay as well. The first church was organized by the immigrants coming there in late 1948 with the Mennonite refugees from Danzig and Prussia. These, however, were Polish Mennonites from areas near Warsaw. Their primary leader was Tobias Foth. An initial settlement attempt was made by them at Canelones, near Montevideo. Congregations were later also established in the capital city and in the colonies.

According to the official statistics for 1989, the total number of members in North America was 43,452 of whom ca. 17,000 were in the United States and 26,452 in Canada. However, the Mennonite Brethren Church has more members outside of North America than any other Mennonite group. In 1989 there were: 300 members in Austria and ca. 3,000 in Germany; 24 in Spain; 3900 in Brazil; 1,000 in Colombia; 150 in Mexico; 700 in Panama; ca. 4,200 Spanish-, Indian-, and German-speaking members in Paraguay; 150 in Peru; 160 in Uruguay; 1,250 in Angola; ca. 63,250 in India; 1,619 in Japan; and 46,906 in Zaire for an estimated total of 126,609 baptized members, not including those in North America, nor Russia, nor those who resettled in Germany from there. The work among the Indians in Paraguay was carried on by an inter-Mennonite agency "Light to the Indians" *(Licht den Indianern)* and the members, therefore, belonged to all conferences of the agency, but for many years the leading workers were Mennonite Brethren.

Distinctive Characteristics

The Mennonite Brethren Church stands fully in the Anabaptist tradition together with the other Mennonite groups. Though Baptist and pietist influences were evident in their early history, as other influences were clear in other Mennonite groups, the intention has been and remains to be true to the sixteenth-century heritage of biblical Anabaptism. This has been restated clearly in the following:

(1) The early Mennonite Brethren were definite in their desire to remain Anabaptist in their confessions. Every attempt was made to declare themselves in harmony with the basic tenets as set forth by Menno Simons.

(2) The advances toward affiliation with the Baptists were made by individuals who may not have fully processed these moves with members of the new community of believers.

(3) It seems rather clear that the Mennonite Brethren revival was meant to be a return to the Anabaptist vision, rather than a deviation from it. The desire to build a community of believers who had per-

sonally committed themselves to follow Jesus Christ, and who were willing to live a separated life of holiness, was certainly in keeping with what the Anabaptist forefathers felt was the New Testament pattern for a believers' church.[4]

Baptist influence on the mode of baptism by immersion is clear. The influence of pietism on the nature of Christian experience expected is also evident. Wüst has been called the "second reformer" of Mennonitism after Menno. Because of his influence, some of which continued later in American revivalism, the Mennonite Brethren Church has sometimes been described as "Mennonite in doctrine, pietistic [individualistic?] in spirit."

This statement confirms that what are sometimes called *distinctives* in a group, here particularly the Mennonite Brethren Church, are often more a matter of style and emphasis than doctrinal difference. The following points are often cited as central to "MB faith," without implying that other Mennonite groups do not also hold to these affirmations.[5]

Practical Biblicism. Frequent Bible study sessions give direction to members for faith and life. The stress upon the practical affirms that faith is more than a set of theological propositions, and that the Scriptures are given for daily spiritual nurture and guidance. The temptation has occasionally arisen to stress the *letter* rather than the *spirit,* to consider "proof-texts" as being the biblical approach, but the centering of all faith in the Bible and to make it the test of tradition has been healthy.

Experiential Faith. Emphasis upon a definite conversion experience has been central to Mennonite Brethren doctrine from the beginning. This represents a different course than entry into the church through nurture (mastery of the catechism). The convert is normally expected to be able to state time, place, and specific insight into God's Word as the spiritual turning point. This has sometimes led to the "dated" conversion experience, or to being conditioned to think and say what is expected. Christian nurture has sometimes been neglected in favor of the subjective experience (cf.: the comment of Philip Jakob Spener, German pietist [d. 1705], that he had learned more in one dramatic night with God than in all his years at the university), but ideally both experience and nurture-growth are expected.

Christian Discipleship. Practical holiness was not a new teaching for nineteenth-century Mennonites in Russia. But there was lax-

M. B. historian **J. B. Toews** and a young student browse through the English translation of P. M. Friesen's voluminous *History of the Mennonite Brotherhood in Russia, 1789-1910.*

ity in emphasizing actual, loving, corrective discipline. Yet new life is to be seen in a new direction taken under the leading of the Holy Spirit. Frequently this concern has taken the personal route of not smoking, drinking, dancing without a concomitant concern for the social evils of poverty, injustice, racism. The old doctrine of separation from the world would require a new definition in the present age of social, economic, and political acculturation-assimilation. Nonresistance has frequently become a casualty of this accommodation, though it remains the official doctrine of the church today.[6]

Brotherhood Emphasis. Early use of the term *Brethren* indicated their intention for the nature of the church in 1860. Much of this spirit has been retained to this day, but in North America considerable individualism is also evident. This is not surprising as a legacy of pietism and within the context of a capitalistic economy. The church becomes less important; admonition, the congregational functions of binding and loosing, tend to disappear. The M. B. *Confession of Faith* lists the characteristics of the true church as including "fervent brotherly love, fellowship and submission among themselves and love of their neighbors." The powerful unity which the Spirit brings has been evident in numerous decisions of the Mennonite Brethren Church in recent years.

In his definitive *History of the Mennonite Brethren Church* the late John A. Toews identifies Fundamentalism and dispensationalism as two major influences on Mennonite Brethren theology in the twentieth century. He finds a primary reason for this in the opposition these movements represented to modernism, which most Mennonites also rejected, and especially in the high view of Scripture the former advocated. But Fundamentalism "concentrated on Christian dogmatics, rather than on Christian ethics and . . . has weakened the historic evangelical Anabaptist foundations of Mennonite Brethren faith and practice." [7] On dispensationalism Toews wrote as follows:

> Although Mennonite Brethren, like the earlier Anabaptists, have consistently held to the view of a progressive revelation in Scripture and to the finality of the New Testament, they have at the same time accepted the significance and relevance of the whole Bible for the faith and work of the church. The artificial and arbitrary division of Scripture found in dispensationalism is foreign to historic Mennonite Brethren theology.[8]

Freedom of Spiritual Expression. An open sharing in the warmth of Christian fellowship is encouraged in expressions of testimony, prayer, aspirations, calls for intercession, and new insights from God's Word. There is a closeness of clergy and laity. When it became apparent in Russia by 1900 that the elders among them tended to defend the status quo, the office of elder was abolished with the comment, "The system is sick, that is why our men get sick." Lay ministers continue to be elected from the congregations, though many receive formal theological training also. One writer stated: "It is hardly possible to see the New Testament church without a multipastoral system. The ministry in the early Christian church was shared ministry. Paul appointed elders for the new churches, always in the plural. There was a uniqueness in sharing the ministry." [9]

The Present Witness

In the first decades, the Mennonite Brethren of Russia participated with Baptists in a missionary program in India. Similar cooperation with other agencies has continued through the years, including relief-related activities with the Mennonite Central Committee. Zaire and Indonesia have been added to a number of other areas in which missionary cooperation is practiced. In North America the Mennonite Brethren are associated with the Evangelical Foreign Missions Association (EFMA) and with the Evangelical Fellowship of Canada (EFC). In local areas, churches associate themselves with evangelicals of similar doctrinal positions in social concerns, service, outreach, and witness.

Publication activities began in 1884, when the conference elected a committee of three to arrange for the editing and printing of a church paper, the *Zionsbote*. The paper was published in German until January 1, 1965, when it was discontinued. *The Christian Leader* was first published in English as a monthly periodical (1936-48) and since 1948 twice a month. In Canada the German family paper, *Die Mennonitische Rundschau*, originally founded by John F. Funk of Elkhart, Indiana, is published by the Board of Faith and Life of the Canadian Conference of MB Churches and printed by Christian Press of Winnipeg. *The Mennonite Brethren Herald* is the English-language Canadian periodical. Kindred Press of Hillsboro, Kansas, and Winnipeg, Manitoba, is the official publishing house. The Mennonite Brethren of South America cooperate in the publishing of the *Menno-Blatt*.

The Centennial Conference of the Mennonite Brethren, 1860-1960, in Reedley, California, brought together MBs from far and wide, in this case from Japan, Paraguay, and India.

Mennonite Brethren have a history of strong interest in education. At one time or another, for varying numbers of years, five Bible schools were or are operating in the United States and twelve in Canada, including Columbia Bible College, Clearbrook, British Columbia, which has been operated jointly with the General Conference Mennonites of British Columbia since 1970. Five high schools were also established in Canada. Two four-year liberal arts colleges are also maintained: Tabor College in Hillsboro, Kansas (1908), and Pacific College in Fresno, California (1944). The Mennonite Brethren Biblical Seminary began operations in Fresno in 1955.

The Mennonite Brethren Bible College, founded in Winnipeg in 1944, changed its name to Concord College in 1992 with a more university-oriented curriculum, while retaining its traditional emphasis in Bible, theology and music. During the mid-1970s the seminary and the colleges at Hillsboro and Winnipeg established three centers for Mennonite Brethren Studies, with offices in Winnipeg,

Hillsboro and Fresno, to serve as archival center, heritage research and promotion center, as well as being a resource for local congregations. The centers are governed independently, with Winnipeg serving the Canadian Conference, Hillsboro the U.S. Conference, and Fresno the entire MB Conference. One of the first major achievements of the Fresno Center has been the translation and publication of P. M. Friesen's monumental (1,065 pages) history of *The Mennonite Brotherhood in Russia (1789-1910)* in 1978.

In discussing the relevance of the Anabaptist heritage for Mennonite Brethren today one writer stated, "To be Anabaptist-New Testament we must be willing to become a Jesus movement once again . . . we must be willing to become a believers' church movement once again. . . . To be Anabaptist necessitates the rejection of ethnicity as in any way determining Christian faith and faithfulness." He continues:

> Anabaptism is not identical with contemporary Mennonite Brethrenism. In many ways it is in serious conflict with it. Therefore, for us to flesh out the New Testament heritage means we must make a choice. We can face the difference between the New Testament visions and present Mennonite Brethren reality and conclude that out of faithlessness to the vision we are no longer Anabaptist-New Testament Christians. Or we can repent and be renewed. That will mean recommitting ourselves to the New Testament vision of faith and church, being judged by it and thereby being justified by it.[10] (See also ME 5:557-559 and listed cross-references.)

Endnotes

1. P. M. Friesen, *The Mennonite Brotherhood in Russia* (1789-1910). Translated from the German. Fresno, Calif.: Board of Christian Literature, 1978., p. 254.

2. Adapted from Jacob P. Bekker, *Origin of the Mennonite Brethren Church*. Previously Unpublished Manuscript by One of the Eighteen Founders. Hillsboro, Kan.: Mennonite Brethren Historical Society, 1973, pp. 70-71.

3. Ibid., pp. 72-73. For a parallel account see Friesen, *Mennonite Brotherhood in Russia*, pp. 284ff.

4. J. A. Toews, *A History of the Mennonite Brethren Church*. Hillsboro, Kan.: Mennonite Brethren Publishing House, 1975, p. 367, quoting Frank C. Peters. Some MB historians question how deep the commitment to Anabaptism actually was.

5. For the following grouping of subheadings I am partly indebted to the above-mentioned volume by J. A. Toews, pp. 367-379.

6. But see ME 5:559 (1990). Also J. Howard Kauffman and Leo Driedger, *The Mennonite Mosaic*. Scottdale, Pa.: Herald Press, 1991, p. 174.

7. Toews, *History*, pp. 376-377. Cf.: ME 5:559.

8. Ibid., p. 379.

9. Waldo Hiebert in Ibid., p. 307.

10. John E. Toews, "The Meaning of Anabaptism for the Mennonite Brethren Church," in Paul Toews, ed., *Pilgrims and Strangers*. Essays in Mennonite Brethren History. Fresno, Calif.: Center for Mennonite Brethren Studies, 1977, pp. 167-168. In his *History. . . ,* J. A. Toews cites B. B. Janz as saying: "Never use the gospel-horse to pull the culture-wagon; but hitch culture to the gospel and let it promote the cause of Christ," p. 341.

Other Resources: See especially the bibliography in ME 5:559. Also Friesen, *The Mennonite Brotherhood in Russia (1789-1910)*, 1978. Paul Toews, ed. *Pilgrims and Strangers*. Fresno, Calif.: Center for Mennonite Brethren Studies, 1977. Kauffman and Driedger, *Mosaic*, 1991, especially pp. 217-230. Redekop, *A People Apart*, 1987. MacMaster, *Land, Piety, Peoplehood*, 1985. Schlabach, *Peace, Faith, Nation*, 1988. Juhnke, *Vision, Doctrine, War*, 1989. Volume 4 of this *Mennonite Experience in America* (MEA) series is in preparation with Paul Toews, Fresno, as author. Contact MB conference offices for audiovisual resources.

16

The Smaller Mennonite and Related Groups in North America

IN ADDITION to the larger Mennonite groups, the Amish, and the Hutterian Brethren, which have been discussed in the preceding chapters, there are other branches of the Anabaptist-Mennonite family tree. For a proper understanding of the legacy of sixteenth-century Anabaptism in our day, these branches should be discussed also. The total baptized *membership* of these smaller Mennonite groups in North America is about 61,500 not including some 40,000 persons of Germanic background in Mexico and 3,500 in Belize. The two Mennonite-related groups discussed in this chapter had a combined membership of 53,463 in 1989. Thus the total of all groups discussed in this chapter is about 115,000 baptized persons plus the 40,000 "souls" mentioned above. The Bergthal groups are included in the Conference of Mennonites in Canada and General Conference statistics.

The uniqueness of these smaller groups will be seen in the discussion of their historical development and present emphasis. Often the specific emphasis of a group arose in response to the particular cultural and geographical environment in which it found itself, rather than in a negative response to what other Mennonites were saying. Other differences emerged from the variety of ways in which congregations in the same environment responded to the same challenge because they were independent and free to act as they thought best.

Different leaders also had different visions for the church, and obedience meant different things to them depending on their background, character, and use of Scripture. To some obedience meant the establishing of communities which were isolated from the world either by geographical location or by language and other cultural barriers. In time this isolation obviously had its effect on their life and thought. To other groups obedience meant going into the world with the good news, and the ensuing influence of their environment changed them, some even leaving the Mennonites in their desire to be faithful to the heavenly vision.

We cannot conclude from these reasons for the differences among them, however, that the Mennonites were not interested in unity. Rather, they gave a higher priority to obedience as they saw it. It may be that the heritage of suffering and persecution influenced them more than they suspected. Or that their stress upon the importance of love as a doctrine made it easier to forget it in practice as they labored to establish the disciplined and faithful church. If spiritual unity is considered a primary goal of the church, most of the Mennonites were more united than might appear from an organizational chart. It was, in fact, their very oneness which accented the image of their diversity.

Groups of Swiss Ethnic Origin

• *Reformed Mennonite Church:* John Herr of Lancaster County, Pennsylvania, founded the Reformed Mennonite Church in 1812. His father, Francis, had been excommunicated from the Mennonite church earlier for reasons which are not entirely clear. They seem to have centered around his conviction that the Mennonites had forsaken the faith of Menno Simons, especially in their lax discipline of erring members. Francis had subsequently met in homes with his followers until his death in 1810, after which his son John continued as leader. In 1812 the group elected him minister and bishop, though he was unbaptized. One of the members subsequently baptized him even as the Swiss Brethren had done in 1525. The group was variously spoken of locally as "New" Mennonites, or *Herrites,* but eventually came to be known as the Reformed Mennonites.

In doctrine the Reformed Mennonites seek to return to what they believe was taught by Menno Simons, whom they regard very highly. Their basic position is spelled out in the *Restitution,* a book which indicates clearly where they believe the church needs restoring. It seems to them that the rest of the Mennonites have left the true faith because most of them vote, some take part in local political issues, they have fun and tell stories, and many neglect the biblical requirements of foot washing, the kiss of peace, and strict discipline, including shunning.

The church has no Sunday school work, no youth work or mission activities, concentrating its efforts primarily in the Sunday morning worship service. Young people are active participants in the normal life of their community until they join the church. Then a serious transformation in attitudes, dress, and social relations is expected. This may be one reason why many find it difficult to join the church of their parents. As a result, there has been a steady decline in membership in the twentieth century, until only some 400 remain (1987). Of these, about 155 are located in Ontario, and most of the rest in Pennsylvania, with a few scattered families in Ohio, Indiana, Illinois, Michigan, and New York. A church paper, *Good Tidings,* was published from 1922 to 1932. (See also ME 5:753).

• *Church of God in Christ, Mennonite:* Originating in Wayne County, Ohio, in 1859, this group is also known as the *Holdeman Mennonites* after the founder John Holdeman (d. 1900). Like the preceding group it protested against the seemingly low level of spiritual life in the church. Unlike the former, its central thrust arose from a religious experience rather than from a concern over discipline. John Holdeman had a deep religious experience at the age of twelve. At twenty-one he was baptized and reconsecrated himself to the work God would have for him. He felt a strong calling to preach, but the church had not, and might never call him to the ministry. At the same time, he was appalled at the traditionalism he found as he entered into the life of the congregation as a new member. His concerns were not shared by the leaders, however, and he soon faced the necessity of either giving up his vision of what the New Testament church should be like or breaking the fellowship.

After much prayer and inner struggle he chose the latter course, calling separate meetings in homes for those of like concern. Because he wanted to see his church directly in line with the New Testament church, he called it the Church of God in Christ. To avoid being confused with other churches of God, and to show that they cherished the Anabaptist heritage, the name "Mennonite" was added later. The Dordrecht Confession of 1632 was adopted as spiritual guide. Added to this was a particular emphasis on nonconformity to the world in dress and all of life, one of the more obvious marks being the wearing of beards by all male church members. Emphasis was placed on the study of the writings of Menno and Dirk Philips, and of the *Martyrs Mirror*.

The spiritual concern of John Holdeman led to missionary activities from the beginning. After a slow start in 1859, the church won numerous members from other Mennonite churches, especially the *Kleine Gemeinde*, now the Evangelical Mennonite Conference, in Manitoba and Kansas soon after their arrival from Russia in the 1870s. An energetic mission program, including a hospital and several schools, was begun in Mexico in 1927. Work later expanded to Haiti, Nigeria, Belize, the Dominican Republic, the Philippines and Brazil. In 1965-66 a delegation was sent around the world to pursue contacts arising from radio and Bible lessons, and to explore the possibility of new mission programs in Egypt, India, and other countries. Out of this grew the Gospel Tract and Bible Society which carries on a global Christian literature program. This work is seen as preparing the soil for missionary work. Overseas membership in 1988 was 1,379.

During the 1970s many church schools were established to achieve greater nonconformity to the world. "The church seeks to maintain the 'stranger-pilgrim' stance" in society. Because the *Holdeman* consider themselves to be in the true spiritual lineage of the apostolic church, the impression is sometimes conveyed that they consider themselves to be the only true church. An emphasis on conversion, proper baptism (pouring), excommunication and avoidance, and the careful calling of ministers are considered important in achieving the Pauline ideal pure church "without spot or wrinkle" (Eph. 5:27). The church participates in the work of MCC in relief and peace programs, but is also careful to cite a favored text from Amos 3:3, "Can two walk together except they be agreed?"

The administrative offices of the church are located in Moundridge, Kansas. A hospital and printing press are also located there, with *The Messenger of Truth* being the official church periodical. Nursing homes and a child care facility are also maintained. In 1989 the membership of the church was 12,694 in North America, of which about one-fourth lived in Canada. (See also ME 5:154-157.)

• *Evangelical Mennonite Church:* The impetus leading to the founding of this group in 1864 was again a personal experience of deep spiritual significance, this time on the part of Henry Egly, an Amishman near Berne, Indiana. Because of his leadership they were frequently known as the "Egly Amish" but called themselves the Defenseless Mennonite Church of North America until 1948 when they adopted the present name. This use of the name *Defenseless* was probably the most accurate translation of the German *wehrlos,* which is today translated as nonresistant. As in the case of John Holdeman, so Egly charged the church with indifference in things spiritual, especially in forsaking the genuine inheritance of the Mennonite faith. Among the important essentials was the new birth. Soon those who felt as he did, and who had experienced conversion themselves, joined him in separate meetings which led to their formal organization as a group.

A strong conservatism prevailed in dress and doctrine during the early years, but gradually the distinctive external marks of faith were discarded, including bonnets and beards. The practice of the holy kiss was largely abandoned, musical instruments were introduced into worship services, and English replaced the German language. The early zeal, however, continued. Several preaching services were held every Sunday, Sunday schools were organized in the 1870s, and regular evangelistic meetings were held once or twice annually. Missionary work was begun in what is now Zaire in 1896. Out of this program the Africa Inter-Mennonite Mission was organized in 1912, in cooperation with the Central Conference of Mennonites, now part of the General Conference. Since 1949 mission activities have been carried on in the Dominican Republic and, more recently, in other countries also.

The first annual conference of the Defenseless Mennonites was held in 1883, but formal organization was not completed until 1908. Publication of the first conference paper began with the *Heils-Bote* in 1897, but the name was later changed to *Zion's Tidings* and is now called *The Evangelical Mennonite.* In 1989 the total membership was 3,888 located especially near Berne, Indiana; Archbold, Ohio; and Gridley, Illinois. (See also ME 5:276, 278.)

• *Old Order Mennonites:* The term *Old Order Mennonites* does not refer to one specific group but to those Mennonites of Swiss-South German lineage who resisted acculturation more than others

An **Old Order Mennonite meetinghouse** at Churchtown, Lancaster County, Pennsylvania. The largest concentration of Old Order Mennonites is around St. Jacobs and Elmira, Ontario. During the winter months they use both **buggies and sleighs** for their transportation.

and eventually organized into numerous independent groups. These groups adhere to the basic tenets of Anabaptism, which they consider the "Old Order" of customs, behavior, and worship.

The origin of the two initial groups can be traced to two schisms—the Stauffer schism from the Lancaster Mennonite Conference in 1845 over excessive social involvement, and the Wisler schism of 1872 in Indiana over Jacob Wisler's refusal to sanction Sunday schools and other innovations. Both groups have numerous autonomous congregations in their lineage, usually named after their first bishop. They differ in their concerns on a variety of issues as the following paragraphs will show.

The Stauffer Mennonites are also called Pike Mennonites because the old meetinghouse near Hinkletown, Pennsylvania, was close to a pike, i.e., road. Nonconformity is outlined in eleven articles ranging from a rejection of secular office holding, jury duty, voting, insurance, lawsuits, and lightning rods to modesty in dress, housing, and a stress on the need for shunning of excommunicated persons. Automobiles are not permitted. Of the eleven groups in this lineage most are found in the Ephrata, Pennsylvania, area but some also in Maryland, Missouri and Kentucky. The Noah Hoover group is located not only in Pennsylvania and Kentucky, but also in Belize. The number of members in the Stauffer groups may be about 800 (1987).

The Wisler schism in 1872 soon spread into Ohio, Ontario, Pennsylvania, and Virginia. Two major lines emerged—the English churches open to more accommodation to their environment, and the German churches with less openness. The former have also been known as *Black Bumper Mennonites* and the latter, who do not drive cars, as *Team* (horse and buggy) *Mennonites*. In Pennsylvania the progressive Wisler group is also known as the Weaverland Conference or *Horning* group and the German group as the *Groffdale* or *Wenger Mennonites*. Because of the need for more land these groups have also spread out to Missouri, as well as to Ohio, Kentucky, Wisconsin, and other states during the 1970s. In 1987 there were some 4,200 members in the Weaverland group and an equal number in the *Groffdale* conference. Thus the total *Old Order Mennonite* membership, including the Waterloo-Markham Conference in Ontario, founded in 1939, with a membership of 1,035 in 1989, is estimated at 10,000 - 11,000, including Belize. (See also ME 5:654.)

In doctrine they affirm the Dordrecht Confession of Faith of 1632. Simplicity in all areas of living is emphasized. *Gemeinschaft,* meaning fellowship, mutual interdependence, and love is important in all groups. Since there have been as many as fifteen separate groups or movements among them they have seemed unduly divisive and unloving to many outsiders. Some of these groups, however, are not the result of schism, but simply groups meeting separately for geographic reasons. The issues which have led to separation, or perhaps it should be called *swarming,* like bees forming a new group, were not usually doctrinal but the practical application of the faith, especially in the area of nonconformity to society, which involved cars, telephones, electricity, amusements, clothing, homes, and total lifestyle. All of the groups are *restitutionist* in spirit, that is, wanting to return to the original Anabaptist and New Testament church in spirit and in form. They differ on how this might best be achieved, but are one in their desire to be faithful to Christ, the Scriptures, and to the heritage received. (See also ME 5:654.)

Groups of Dutch Ethnic Origin

• *Old Colony Mennonites:* Many of the immigrants coming to Manitoba in the migration of the 1870s were from the Chortitza settlement which was also known as the Old Colony, since it was the oldest Mennonite settlement in Russia. They were joined in Canada by immigrants from the two daughter colonies of Chortitza, Bergthal and Fürstenland. The Bergthal group settled on the East Reserve, about sixty kilometers south of Winnipeg, and came to be known as *Bergthal Mennonite Church.* The Chortitza and Fürstenland groups settled on the West Reserve, west of the Red River, and came to be known as *Reinland Mennonite Church* after the municipality of Reinland, in which many of them lived.

A decade later, in the 1880s, about one half of the Bergthal settlers moved into the West Reserve areas occupied by their people from the other two groups. Problems soon developed because of the progressive spirit of many of the Bergthal members who were willing to abandon the old pattern of settling in villages in favor of the individual farm pattern prevalent in Manitoba. Many of the Chortitza and Fürstenland leaders saw a real danger to the faith in the scattered farm life. As early as 1880 the *Reinland Mennonite Church* had made willingness to live in closed villages a test of membership, causing many to join the *Bergthal Church.* Some of the progressive Bergthal members constituted an additional threat in their attitudes to education. Instead of being content with the simple seven-month school led by untrained teachers under the supervision of the elder, they desired teachers who could pass government inspection. They were also not opposed to receiving tax support.

By 1890 a major regrouping of loyalties occurred among all of them, including the *Bergthal Church*. Bergthal members living in the West Reserve and opposed to the new progressive movement came to be known as the *Sommerfeld Church*, after their elder who lived in the village of Sommerfeld. Bergthal members living in the East Reserve and sharing the same fear of progress came to be known as the *Chortitza Mennonite Church*, after their elder who lived in the village of Chortitza. The progressives in both Reserves retained the name of *Bergthal Mennonite Church*, while the largest and most conservative group of all came increasingly to be referred to as the *Old Colony Mennonites*.

Following this regrouping, the *Bergthal Mennonite Church* moved forward rapidly. Local schools were improved and a high school, later to be known as the Mennonite Collegiate Institute, was established in Gretna in 1891 with the help of H. H. Ewert (d. 1934), a government inspector of all Mennonite schools in Manitoba. In 1903 he became one of the founders of the Conference of Mennonites in Canada, now affiliated with the General Conference Mennonite Church, together with Peter Regier of the Rosenort church in Saskatchewan and David Toews, the "father" of the Mennonites in Canada. In 1972 the *Bergthal Church* voted itself out of existence as an umbrella organization by granting local autonomy to each congregation. All of them joined the Conference of Mennonites in Canada. About half also joined the General Conference. (See also ME 5:67.)

In the meantime many Old Colony families had moved to Saskatchewan, settling in the Rosthern and Swift Current areas. The coming of World War I in 1914, however, revived their concern over education. Schools failing to meet government standards were to be subjected to official control, and English was to be the language of instruction in all subjects except religion. It was clear that most of their schools would not meet these minimal government standards. Numerous petitions to provincial authorities in Manitoba appealed to the privileges guaranteed them at the time of immigration.

When these failed to bring any promise of relief in this threatened area of the faith, a delegation left for South America on July

15, 1919, to explore the possibility of settlement there. Neither Brazil, Uruguay, nor Argentina seemed willing to grant the desired privileges, however, and the search continued. By 1921 it was clear that Mexico was to be the new haven of refuge to which these people could escape and by 1926 some 4,500 moved to that land, the first trainload leaving Canada on March 1, 1922. Nevertheless, the continuing pressures in Canada led to further search, and in 1926 the first contingent left for Paraguay, where good settlement possibilities seemed to exist. This will be discussed in the following chapter.

According to the statistics available in 1989 there were approximately 6,500 baptized *Old Colony Mennonites* in Canada, 5,500 *Sommerfelder*, 2,400 *Chortitzer*, 2,100 *Reinlander*, and other groups totaling some 3,000 for a combined total of 19,500 members. This does not include over 40,000 persons (members and children) who migrated to Mexico, as will be seen in the following chapter, nor those who went to Belize, Bolivia, and Paraguay.

As with the divisions among the *Old Order Mennonites*, so these migrations were caused by concern about separation from the evils of society and conformity to the will of God. However, there seemed to be less reliance upon Scripture than among the Old Order and a greater reliance upon tradition and the authority of the elders. Both the Old Order and the Old Colony Mennonite movements were attempts to be faithful in an unfaithful church as they understood it, but sociologically many other elements would be added to understand the far right of the progressive conservative continuum. (See also ME 5:651-653.)

• **Evangelical Mennonite Mission Conference:** In the preceding paragraphs we have seen the *Old Colony Mennonites* as the most conservative and the *Bergthal Church* as the most progressive of the immigrants of the 1870s, with the Sommerfeld and Chortitza groups somewhere between these two on questions of change. In 1936-37 a split occurred in the *Sommerfeld Church* as a result of the evangelistic work of I. P. Friesen of Rosthern, Saskatchewan. Under the impact of his three-year ministry people were changed and became willing to break with the traditionalism of the past. Their church, however, remained intransigent. Eventually the new believers formed a separate group called *Rudnerweide Mennonite Church*, after the village of Rudnerweide in Manitoba, Russia, and Prussia. In 1961 the name was changed to the Evangelical Mennonite Mission Conference (EMMC).

In contrast to the mother church, the new group immediately carried a strong missionary concern, as also interest in education and discipleship. It appeared to be a genuine recovery of the vision of the sixteenth-century Anabaptists at many points. The EMMC became particularly active in working with the brethren they had left in the old church and eventually also established churches among them in Saskatchewan. In 1989 the EMMC included approximately 3,470 members with missionaries in Belize, Bolivia, Mexico, Texas, and Ontario, ministering both to Old Colony Mennonites and nationals. A strong concern for members of the old church continued, evidenced in Low German radio programs and other mission activities. A Bible school has been established at Aylmer, Ontario. The official conference paper is the *EMMC Recorder*.

• *Fellowship of Evangelical Bible Churches:* Another of the groups working for renewal among the immigrants of the 1870s was the *Evangelical Mennonite Brethren Conference*, founded at Mountain Lake, Minnesota, in 1889. After several name changes the EMB designation was adopted in 1937, but changed to the present FEBC in 1987 after "a 25-year debate on conference identity." Reasons given for the initial break were insufficient emphasis upon the new birth in their old church, too much conformity to the world, and the lack of scriptural church discipline. The form of baptism has remained optional, either by immersion or by pouring.

With the break came a strong emphasis on education and missions, though most of their missionaries served under non-Mennonite boards. The A. F. Wienses were among the first Mennonites to work in urban areas when they located in Chicago in 1906. In addition the conference cooperated in the support of numerous Bible schools, including those at Dalmeny, Saskatchewan, Steinbach, Manitoba, Meade, Kansas, and a College of the Bible at Omaha, Nebraska. Its congregations were scattered through the entire Middle West, from Manitoba to Kansas, with some also in the Pacific Northwest. Attempts at federation with the *Evangelical Mennonite Church* in the 1950s did not succeed. The conference paper is the *Gospel Tidings*. Membership in the church was 4,538 in 1987, of which 1,981 were in Canada, 62 in Argentina, and 361 in Paraguay. (See also ME 2:262-264; 5:296-297.)

• *Evangelical Mennonite Conference* (Canada): The origin of the conference was in the same kind of spiritual restlessness we have seen in most of the preceding groups. Klaas Reimer, ordained in Prussia in 1801, emigrated to Russia four years later. He was appalled at the lack of spiritual concern and the ethical laxity he found in the Molotschna Colony. Soon others felt drawn to his deep faith commitment, and in 1813 eighteen families formed their own renewal group, which was derisively referred to as the *Kleine Gemeinde* (the little church) by others. In addition to the Bible, Reimer had found particular inspiration in reading the *Martyrs Mirror* accounts of how early Christians and later sixteenth-century Anabaptists had been willing to die for their faith.

In 1874 most of the group emigrated to North America, with sixty families settling in Manitoba and thirty-six at Janzen, Nebraska. In 1881-82 one third of the Manitoba group joined the Holdeman group from Ohio (*Church of God in Christ, Mennonite*). The Nebraska group, meanwhile, had migrated to Meade, Kansas, where they soon dissolved as a group. Some joined other groups, but others formed a new congregation, the Emmanuel Mennonite Church, in 1943. In 1948-49 about 400 members emigrated to Mexico from Manitoba to avoid the pressures of acculturation. In 1952 the *Kleine Gemeinde* adopted the name *Evangelical Mennonite Church*, changed to *Evangelical Mennonite Conference* in 1960. Membership in 1989 was 5,813

The conference has continued to promote serious commitment to Christ in keeping with Klaas Reimer's early concern. Because of this tensions have arisen in the area of public school education from time to time. Steinbach Bible College (1979) has provided a partial answer to this concern. Graduates are encouraged to attend the four-year colleges of other Mennonite groups. The early concern for nonconformity also remains but, instead of stressing the evil of certain externals, emphasis is placed upon regenerate attitudes and behavior. A missionary program is being carried on with workers in Germany, Mexico, Nicaragua and Paraguay. Some *Kleine Gemeinde* members from Belize have expanded to Canada, settling in Nova Scotia. The official publication of the Conference is *The Messenger*.

Groups Related to the Mennonites

• *The Missionary Church:* The *United Missionary Church* and the *Missionary Church Association* merged in 1969 to form the *Missionary Church* with a 1990 membership of 33,610 of which 6,700 were in Canada and 26,910 in the United States. From 1947 to 1969 it was known as the *United Missionary Church*. Before that it was the

Mennonite Brethren in Christ Church which, in turn, originated in 1883 through the merger of the *Evangelical United Mennonites* with a *Brethren in Christ* group in Ohio known as the Swankites. The *Evangelical United Mennonites* had originated from earlier divisions and mergers.

The *Missionary Church Association* originated in Berne, Indiana, in 1898, when several members of the group now known as the *Evangelical Mennonite Church* were excommunicated. The reason for this discipline was their belief in the necessity of baptism with the Holy Spirit after regeneration as a separate work of grace. They had also stressed the importance of divine healing, immersion as the only valid form of baptism, and had developed new insights into the second coming of Christ. Several ministers of the General Conference Mennonite Church were also influenced by these questions and joined the movement in its early years.

Much of the impetus for the new spiritual vigor of the *Mennonite Brethren in Christ Church* came from contacts with Wesleyan piety and church organization, together with an emphasis upon holiness prevalent among some Methodist churches. Under this influence the Anabaptist ingredient of the faith grew less with the passing of time, and few contacts were sought with the Mennonites. The Pennsylvania Conference withdrew from the *United Missionary Church* in 1952 and adopted the name *Bible Fellowship Church* in 1959.

In addition to the usually accepted evangelical doctrines, a strong emphasis is placed on sanctification as a second work of grace following regeneration. The spirit of the *Missionary Church* might be described as the search for a religion of the heart, for a faith that makes a difference in all of life. Baptism by immersion continued after the merger. Annual camp meetings have become important for the renewal of members and the winning of new converts. The emphasis in these meetings is upon both salvation and sanctification. These camp meetings also form an integral part of a missionary program around the world. Both Fort Wayne Bible College in Indiana and Bethel College in Mishawaka, Indiana, serve to train workers for this global ministry. The latter is an accredited four-year liberal arts college. The official periodical of the *Missionary Church* is called *Emphasis*.

• *Brethren in Christ:* The beginnings of the Brethren in Christ movement go back to about 1780, when a revival movement spread through the Lutheran, Baptist, and Mennonite communities in Lancaster County, Pennsylvania. Out of this revival a small group, mainly Mennonites, began to meet separately. They came to be known as the *River Brethren* after one of their groups which met near the Susquehanna River. During the Civil War they registered with the government and went on record as a peace group. In the process they changed their name to *Brethren in Christ*. In Canada they became known as *Tunkers* for a time, a kind of nickname, because of their trine immersion baptism which is practiced in all Brethren in Christ churches. Immersion is forward three times, representing an act of humility and submission to God.

The men first involved in the Lancaster County revival were Philip Otterbein, a pietist, and Martin Boehm, who had been excommunicated from the Mennonite church for participating in the revival work. They met in common conventicles. Around 1780, however, the River Brethren or *Brethren in Christ* pulled away from the conventicles, which stressed the experiential over obedience, forming their own organization. The remaining group formed what came to be known as the United Brethren around 1800. A stress on simple living as "the plain people," and on discipline according to Matthew 18, which in the Brethren in Christ Church was called "keeping house," remained strong, as did nonconformity, nonresistance, non-swearing of oaths, rejection of public office holding, careful and discriminate use of modern technology, and in all things a sharp distinction between church and world (society).

From about 1880 to 1910 many changes were introduced, including Sunday schools, home and foreign missions, protracted (extended) meetings, a church school, and a church paper, the *Evangelical Visitor*. The change that made for the greatest denominational uniqueness, however, was that of Wesleyan holiness. It encountered considerable resistance and continued to be an issue on which members held different understandings. The holiness movement included an emphasis on justification, usually a crisis conversion experience, followed by a second experience of sanctification.

The emphasis on a crisis conversion experience grew out of the influence of pietism. The holiness movement tended to deemphasize the conversion experience, making sanctification the primary experience. In the early days of the movement those who had only a conversion experience were considered rather second rate Christians. Some believers held to gradual sanctification, others to an instantaneous, total experience. In either case the *River Brethren* believed that the Holy Spirit empowered the believer to resist sin

and live a victorious Christian life. The possibility of sinlessness was taught by the more radical holiness advocates, as Wesley himself had taught—but never claimed for himself. These advocates stressed the eradication of the sin principle, but this never became the official position of the church.

In contrast to Mennonites, greater emphasis was placed upon emotion and feeling, and on becoming perfect. The holiness camp meeting became an important part of Brethren in Christ life, a week or more of intense preaching and counseling to achieve conversion, sanctification, and spiritual growth. This proved to be an effective missionary tool. It helped win many non-Mennonites, which may have made the group less ethnic and, perhaps, more individualistic than the Mennonites. It has been said that whenever Mennonites wanted a little more life in their religion they went to the *Brethren in Christ*.

The period from 1910 to 1950 was one of stress but also consolidation and expansion in Brethren in Christ history. The impact of American culture was eroding some of the historic convictions about nonconformity, nonresistance, and discipleship, leaving more and more issues to personal rather than group decision. In an attempt to stem this trend a series of rules for dress and conduct were drawn up during the 1930s, but it led to the loss of a significant number of young people.

Fresh life came when this so-called legalism was ended in the 1940s and when new associations were formed—with the MCC in 1942, and both the National Association of Evangelicals (NAE) and the Christian Holiness Association (CHA) a few years later. A new organization divided the church into six regional conferences, one of them in Canada, each served by a full-time bishop. Each congregation received representation at the annual regional and biennial General Conference sessions. By 1950 new and growing support for education and missions was evident. In 1989 the total membership stood at 19,853 in North America and some 16,000 in other lands.

Social and missionary concern also increased by mid-century, stimulated by a strong missionary emphasis at Messiah College. To the earlier work in Zambia, Zimbabwe, and India were added teams of workers in Cuba, Japan, Nicaragua, Venezuela, Colombia, Malawi and England, but also a significant new interest in church extension in North America itself. While there had been a continuing concern for racial justice, the discovery in 1970 of a segregated

Brethren cemetery led to a rigorous challenge to racism throughout the conference. The implications of world hunger became an increasing concern among members. In 1976 the General Conference agreed to have a person spend at least one year among the congregations stressing "the stewardship of possessions, the simple life, and the underlying causes and unjust structures which contribute to widespread poverty and hunger in the world."

The first woman delegate to conference was elected in 1964, but by the late 1970s women were members of the major boards and exercising influence at regional levels. The diverse early roots in Anabaptism and pietism continued to find echoes in vigorous discussions about the relationship between discipleship and holiness, social action and revivalism and other related issues. At times democratic process tended to replace earlier covenanting in congregations. But there was conference-wide commitment to the authority of the Bible, the importance of the congregation of believers, and the need for a strong witness to the power of Christ in the words and deeds of every conference member. (See also ME 5:96-98.)

Other Resources: See the articles and bibliographies for each item in ME 5. Also MWC *Handbook* 1990, pp. 404ff. Clarence Hiebert, *The Holdeman People: The Church of God in Christ, Mennonite, 1859-1969*, South Pasadena, Calif.: William Carey Library, 1973. Stan Nussbaum, *You Must Be Born Again: A History of the Evangelical Mennonite Church*, Fort Wayne, Ind.: Evangelical Mennonite Church, 1979. Calvin Wall Redekop, *The Old Colony Mennonites*, Baltimore, Md.: Johns Hopkins Press, 1969. Jack Heppner, *Search for Renewal: The Story of the Rudnerweider/EMMC, 1937-1987*, Winnipeg, Man.: EMMC, 1987. Eileen Lageer, *Merging Streams: The Story of the Missionary Church*, Elkhart, Ind.: Bethel Publishing Company, 1979. Harold P. Shelly, "The Bible Fellowship Church." Unpublished manuscript of the author, Alliance Theological Seminary, Nyack, N.Y.: 1991. Carlton O. Wittlinger, *Quest for Piety and Obedience: The Story of the Brethren in Christ*, Nappanee, Ind.: Evangel Press, 1978. Contact Messiah College, Grantham, Pa., for audiovisual resources.

17

Mennonite Churches in Latin America

NORTH AMERICANS have generally been so busy with themselves that they have remained largely unaware of the vast lands south of the Rio Grande River, yet in this region live nearly twice as many people as the approximately 285,000,000 (1992) who live in Canada and the United Sates. By the year 2000 the total population of Latin America is expected to reach 619,934,100.[1] These people are also Americans. All together these nations make up a land area almost as large as Europe and the United States combined.

This region is generally known as Latin America, comprising Central and South America, but it also includes the West Indies (or Greater and Lesser Antilles) with the islands of Cuba, Haiti-Dominican Republic, Jamaica, and various United States possessions, including Puerto Rico, the Virgin Islands, and others. Sometimes Trinidad and Tobago are added to this group. The nations of Central America are Belize, Costa Rica, El Salvador, Guatemala, Honduras, Nicaragua, and Panama. North of these is the closest neighbor, Mexico, while South America includes Argentina, Bolivia, Brazil, Chile, Colombia, Ecuador, French Guiana, Guyana, Paraguay, Peru, Surinam, Uruguay, and Venezuela. The name Latin America is a cultural term derived from the fact that the two primary languages used there, Spanish and Portuguese, as well as French, are *Latin* in origin.

In this vast region climate and topography have played a decisive role. Latin America is 25 percent mountainous, almost 25 percent swampy, and about 10 percent desert land. The gigantic Andean mountain range on the West Coast, the steaming jungles in Brazil, and the four great rivers—Amazon, Magdalena, Orinoco, and La Plata—have largely determined the flow of the population and political boundaries. European economic interest in exploiting the natural and human resources of specific regions also helped to determine the life and culture of Latin America.

Agriculture is still the dominant activity of many people, but most farms are very small. Some farms, on the other hand, are gigantic in size, given to ranching or parceled out in small plots to peasant farmers by a small wealthy and privileged class. The system is known as *Encomienda* in which the peasant is easily exploited. Some 90 percent of the land is still owned by about 10 percent of the people; land reform or redistribution has been difficult to achieve. The poverty created by this unequal land ownership has been a major cause of the civil wars in Central America during the 1980s. In recent years great emphasis has been placed on industrialization as a means to economic prosperity. Latin America is rich in natural resources. But industrialization has also encouraged the movement of peasants to the cities, where many live in extreme poverty. Huge trade imbalances and national debts have aggravated the situation. However, a small but growing middle class is arising in most of the nations.

The economic problems of Latin America are accentuated by a birth rate ranging between 2 and 3 percent in the various nations. This means that the population nearly doubles every twenty-five years. Paraguay, an extreme example to be sure, had a population of only 225,000 at the end of the Lopez war in 1870, but reported 3.5 million people in 1992.

In most of these nations over one-half of the people live in urban areas, and over one-half are under twenty years of age. Poverty, a high rate of infant mortality, and a short life expectancy encourage large families. Social and economic services cannot keep pace with this growth. Schools continue to be completely inadequate for vast numbers of children even at the elementary level, though the universities of Peru, Mexico, and the Dominican Republic are the oldest in the Western Hemisphere. In many areas health facilities reach only a relatively small number of people with preventive or even emergency care. Welfare burdens likewise break down under excessive demand and the given political-social priorities.

Politics become volatile when people are hungry, unemployed, and marginalized. From the 1960s to the 1980s Marxism was often seen as the only alternative by disillusioned social theorists and many others. Its defenders argued that the violence of oppression was worse than the violence of possible liberation by revolution. These attitudes led to large expenditures for military equipment by many governments who felt threatened, as well as to the suppression of civil liberties.

Liberation theology, initially indigenous to Latin America, has emerged as the voice calling for justice in behalf of the oppressed. While it uses certain Marxist categories in its socio-economic analysis, it has, in fact, not usually identified itself with the radical and violent political left, nor should it be identified with Marxism. It is providing a strong voice calling for social and economic justice, often at great risk to those involved. These voices are usually encouraged and led by priests and other "religious" within Roman Catholicism, though the church is not unanimous in its support. Few Protestants (*Evangelicos*) have taken these risks. There have been many martyrs. A social revolution of major proportions is under way in Latin America. With the near-global demise of communism in 1990-92 most Latin nations have turned to modified forms of democracy, but their socio-economic and demographic problems are increasing.

Most Latin Americans consider themselves Roman Catholics, but for the majority this is little more than a cultural tradition. The number of active communicant members ranges from a low of 10 percent to a high of 30 percent of the population. There is an acute shortage of priests and many who do serve in Latin America have been brought from Europe. As in North America secularism is the dominant orientation of the majority of the people, though the cultural aspects of Roman Catholicism—laws, social institutions, language—permeate their life and thought.

Roman Catholics themselves referred to this situation as tragic not many years ago. There are encouraging signs that renewal has come to many aspects of church life and work. The impact of Vatican Council II (1962-65) and several papal visits to the continent since then, the use of lay people in the work of the church, and the

SOUTH AMERICA

LEGEND
MENNONITE CHURCHES IN SOUTH AMERICA
- ■ Organized bodies
- ★ MCC involvement
- ◻ Other missions and programs (not including those relating to organized bodies)
- ● 500 members (approx. locations)

Kilometers   0   500   1000   1500

prophetic voices and actions of many clergy and bishops are having a profound influence on educational, social, and economic problems. Local grass-roots "base communities" (*comunidades de base*) working, praying, and suffering together have had a major impact on church renewal and growth. A total ministry to body, mind, and spirit is underway in many places, often under lay leadership.

Protestantism was slow in coming to Latin America, but has been growing rapidly. At the International Mission Conference in Madras, India, in 1938, Protestant missionaries saw the possible loss of their fields in Asia because of Japanese military exploits on the eve of World War II (1939-45), and looked for other areas in which to work. Many turned to Latin America, where some Protestants were already working since the nineteenth century. Vigorous activity followed, particularly after 1945. While most denominations in Latin America are the outgrowth of European and North American mission efforts, they are now almost totally autonomous in structure, institutions, theology and finances.

Yet all of these denominations have been surpassed in vigor by the Pentecostal groups, who constitute a new "third force" beside Roman Catholics and Protestants.[2] Numerically they add up to more members than all other Protestant groups together with a mid-1985 total of nearly 23 million and growing rapidly. Of these 6.5 million are in Brazil, 1.3 million in Chile, 200,000 in Colombia, 300,000 in Argentina and 300,000 in the rest of South America, plus at least seven million in Mexico, and an equal number in Central America and the Caribbean.[3] Some Pentecostals have also become advocates of social justice and human rights.

Mennonites Move to Latin America

An interesting account written in Spanish by a traveler in Argentina in 1877 reports the existence of three thriving Mennonite villages on the banks of Nievas Creek and in the Olavarria Valley. They had apparently arrived from Russia recently and harvested two excellent crops of wheat. They were part of a larger settlement of Germans from Russia. Unfortunately, this is the only knowledge we have of such a group. The story of their migration and what eventually became of them awaits further research. In a kind of sequal to this, some 1,000 Old Colony Mennonites from Mexico and Bolivia began the Remeco-Guatrache Colony some 435 miles west of Buenos Aires on 25,000 acres of land in 1986. Others will likely follow. (See ME 5:764.)

Apart from the mystery of the 1877 report, the first Mennonite settlers to come to Latin America, as far as we know, were Old Colony and Sommerfelder groups from Manitoba and Saskatchewan. Both groups felt threatened by a new law passed by the Manitoba legislature in 1915 providing for provincial control of education and the use of the English language in all schools. They considered this law to be a violation of the promises given to their fathers when they first came from Russia in 1874.[4] The loss of German meant to them the gradual loss of their Mennonite faith and culture through assimilation into the Canadian environment. The Manitoba government had no desire to undermine the faith of any of her settlers but, in contrast to the multiculturalism now being promoted, desired to create greater national unity through standardization of education and less emphasis on the ethnic uniqueness of minority groups.

Mexico. With this apparent threat before them, the Mennonites sent out commissions to find a new land of greater freedom. Numerous locations were considered, including North Africa and Australia. A team of six explored settlement possibilities in several of the South American countries including Paraguay, but finally returned with the recommendation to settle in Mexico. Mexico could be reached with little difficulty from Canada. Even more important was the fact that its president Alvaro Obregon had personally guaranteed to them all the rights and privileges they requested, including freedom of religion and full control of their own school program.

From 1922 to 1926 several thousand Old Colony and Sommerfelder Mennonites left Canada for Mexico, most of them settling in the state of Chihuahua. Others followed in a continuing stream, some settling south of the earlier colonies in the state of Durango. In 1948 a major movement, including 100 families of the *Kleine Gemeinde* (Evangelical Mennonite Conference) who were troubled by the progressive thinking of some of their leaders, likewise left for Mexico. All of these migrations, together with the high birth rate since the settlements began, brought the total number of Mennonites in Mexico to approximately 16,000 by 1950 and to 45-50,000 persons by the late 1980s despite the many migrations from there to other lands. Of these some 16,500 were baptized church members.

Most of these settlers are farmers. Members who leave the colonies for the cities are not in good standing with the church. The

MEXICO

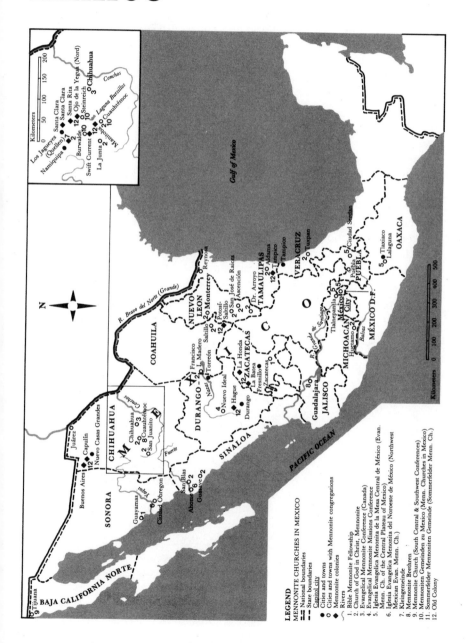

LEGEND

MENNONITE CHURCHES IN MEXICO

━ ━ National boundaries
─ ─ State boundaries
      Capitol city
● ○ Cities and towns
● ○ ◆ Cities and towns with Mennonite congregations
      Mennonite colonies
      Rivers

1. Bible Mennonite Fellowship
2. Church of God in Christ, Mennonite
3. Evangelical Mennonite Conference (Canada)
4. Evangelical Mennonite Missions Conference
5. Iglesia Evangelica Menonita de la Mesa Central de México (Evan. Menn. Ch. of the Central Plateau of Mexico)
6. Iglesia Evangelica Menonita del Noroeste de México (Northwest Mexican Evan. Menn. Ch.)
7. Kleingemeinde
8. Mennonite Brethren
9. Mennonite Church (South Central & Southwest Conferences)
10. Mennonite Gemeinden zu Mexico (Menn. Churches in Mexico)
11. Sommerfelder Mennoniten Gemeinde (Sommerfelder Menn. Ch.)
12. Old Colony

village pattern of settlement which had prevailed in Russia and Canada was also followed in Mexico. Each village consists of from ten to thirty farms of approximately 160 acres and sufficient grazing lands for the village cattle. Corn, beans, and a variety of other crops are grown, but the climate is not suited to wheat production. Some modern machinery is used. The buildings are usually of adobe brick with a tin roof. Particular attention is given to the raising of cattle and horses. Cheese factories are scattered throughout the colonies.

All colony life is under the control of the church. Because of the geographical and cultural isolation, the ban is a much feared form of discipline since the delinquent has nowhere to go when he is excommunicated except into the strange and unknown outside world. Each village has its own school, but the teacher is selected at random and has little special training. A simple reader, the Bible, catechism, and hymnary are the basic study materials. Emphasis is placed upon memorization rather than upon independent thought. Sunday morning worship services are usually two or more hours long with silent prayer, the reading of an old sermon, and exhortation to obedience by the ministers and elder.

A General Conference Mennonite fellowship was organized in the city of Cuauhtemoc by Mennonites from Russia who were unable to go to Canada and came to Mexico in 1929-30. Some of the persons who felt uncomfortable in the colonies have moved to the city and joined this fellowship. Membership of the group was 400 in 1990. A *Kleinegemeinde* (called the Evangelical Mennonite Conference in Canada) congregation of some 960 members in 1990 had grown up in Cuauhtemoc, while several congregations with a total of 400 members of Mexican origin had also been established.

Five families of the Church of God in Christ, Mennonite (Holdeman) moved to Mexico from Oklahoma in 1927 to witness to the Mennonite settlers but soon shifted their attention to work with the native Mexican population. Other Mennonite and non-Mennonite groups have made similar efforts and have found that tradition is a hard frontier. Extensive medical, educational, and agricultural assistance programs have been carried on by MCC for many years. In 1957 this work was transferred to the General Conference Mennonite Church.

Many of the settlers do not believe Mexico to be their permanent home. A pilgrim motif? There is constant migration from Mexico to Paraguay, Bolivia, Argentina and Texas. During a prolonged drought in 1954 several hundred returned to Canada, and many since. Others began to settle in *Belize* in 1958 until more than 3,000 persons had moved there from Mexico, settling at Spanish Lookout, Orange Walk Colony, and the Blue Creek Colony. While Orange Walk was the largest settlement and prospered, as Spanish Lookout also did, the future of Blue Creek Colony remained uncertain with many of the Old Colony families moving to Bolivia. The Eastern Board of Missions (Salunga) began relating to the Belize settlements in place of MCC in 1963.

Paraguay. In contrast to the negative report which a delegation had brought back from Paraguay in 1920, six delegates who left Manitoba on February 11, 1921, brought back a very favorable description of Paraguay and many became eager to leave. Through the help of a New York banker, Samuel McRoberts, the Paraguayan government was asked to provide guarantees of full religious and educational freedom to the Mennonites if they should settle in Paraguay. This request was generously met by the Paraguayan Congress in its passing of Law No. 514 on July 26, 1921, the provisions of which are referred to as the *Privilegium* (privilege) by the Mennonites of Paraguay. With the passing of this legislation came a most cordial invitation to the Mennonites to make Paraguay their home. Economic conditions in Canada, however, delayed emigration until 1926, though large numbers did go to Mexico.

In the meantime McRoberts formed two land-holding companies, the *Inter-Continental Company* in Winnipeg to buy the land of the emigrants in Canada, and the *Corporacion Paraguaya* in Paraguay to sell them lands there in return. The first land purchased by the Mennonites consisted of 137,920 acres in the Chaco, approximately 155 miles west of the river landing at Puerto Casado, which in turn lay some two days and two nights by boat up the Paraguay River from Asunción, the capital city.

The first group of fifty-one families (309 persons) left Altona, Manitoba, on November 23, 1926, followed by other groups totaling 279 families, 1,767 persons, by 1930. Though they received a cordial presidential welcome in Asunción, the immigrants were soon to experience great suffering. Upon arrival at Puerto Casado they discovered that few preparations had been made for their coming. Worst of all, their land had not been surveyed by the *Corporación Paraguaya*. Sixteen weary months were to elapse before they could move to their farm locations in April 1928. During this

PARAGUAY

LEGEND

MENNONITE CHURCHES IN PARAGUAY
=== International boundary
O Towns & cities with Mennonite congregations
● Other towns & cities
   Capitol city
◆ Mennonite colonies
-- Colony boundaries
▼ Indian settlements with Mennonite congregations
— Selected roads
╫╫╫ Selected railroads
? Indicates the location is only approximate
   (Not all colonies, towns, & settlements with congregations are shown.)

difficult period many became discouraged and returned to Canada, while 147 died of a typhoid epidemic. The majority remained, however, to establish *Menno Colony* with thirteen villages and learned to wrest a simple living from the region which was known as the "Green Hell."

Despite numerous group migrations to Bolivia and other lands over the years, the colony grew to 6,600 inhabitants in eighty villages by 1986, comprising a land area of 2,700 square miles, used in agriculture and ranching. Eleven schools were in operation with 1,100 students at both the elementary and secondary levels. In 1990 there were some 3,000 church members in the total colony. A missionary program among Indians and native Paraguayans is maintained, including a variety of voluntary service and emergency relief activities.

A second colony known as *Fernheim* was established in the Chaco in 1930 by Mennonites from Russia. They had fled to Germany from their lands in 1929 in the hope of finding a new home in North America, but neither Canada nor the United States was willing to receive them at that time and they could not remain in Germany. Through MCC arrangements were finally made to have them settle in the Paraguayan Chaco. The government was willing to include this group also under the privileges of Law No. 514, and *Corporación Paraguaya* had sufficient land available. Consequently a total of 1,853 persons in 374 families made their new home in the Chaco in 1930.

Though they were aided by the Menno Colony people pioneering hardships again took their toll, including sixty-five persons who died of a typhoid epidemic. Drinking water was so scarce from their only good well during the early months that a boy was at times stationed at the bottom of the well to dip the trickling water with a cup and gradually fill the bucket. Many of the immigrants were extremely frustrated with their location and economic potential, but few had sufficient resources to leave. In 1937 a group of 140 families relocated in East Paraguay in the hope of achieving greater economic success, founding what became known as colony *Friesland*. Through great sacrifice and unrelenting toil both colonies gradually became moderately well established. In 1986 Fernheim counted 3,300 persons and Friesland 725.

A third group of immigrants came to Paraguay from Russia after World War II, establishing colony *Neuland* in the Chaco and colony *Volendam* near Friesland in East Paraguay. Having fled west-

ward before the advancing Russian armies, thousands of Mennonites from Russia had been crowded into Berlin and West German
refugee camps awaiting resettlement. When emigration to North
America seemed impossible, large numbers of them decided to go
to Latin America. Consequently 2,314 persons in 641 family units,
of which 253 were without father or husband, came to establish
Neuland Colony between 1947 and 1950. During the same period
1,810 persons in 441 families founded the *Volendam* Colony, so
named after the Dutch ship which brought them to the New
World.[5] Though the help of the previous immigrants made life
much more bearable for the later groups than they themselves had
experienced, many of the *Neuland* and *Volendam* settlers left at the
first opportunity, some going to Canada and others returning to
Germany. Consequently the number of persons in *Neuland* was
1,325 in 1987 while *Volendam* counted 676 in twelve villages.

There was a fourth group of Mennonite immigrants to
Paraguay. Like the first settlers, these came from Manitoba and Saskatchewan for the same reason as in 1926—to preserve their spiritual heritage through isolation from the corrosive influence of
modern society and its effects upon their children. Nearly 1,700
persons left the prairie provinces in 1948 to settle on 27,500 acres
of virgin forest land in Eastern Paraguay some 65 miles east of Vil-
larica. They came with substantial financial resources which made
possible the purchase of modern farming equipment, but the agricultural patterns as well as the climate were so different from what
they had been accustomed to that approximately one-third of the
immigrants returned to Canada. The remainder were able to establish themselves in two colonies, *Bergthal* and *Sommerfeld*, some 15
miles from each other. Further immigrants from Canada later established additional settlements.

All of these colonies—*Menno, Fernheim, Friesland, Neuland,
Volendam, Bergthal,* and *Sommerfeld*—are primarily agricultural communities with only sufficient industrial equipment to meet their
own agricultural needs. With hard work and frugal living most of
the colonists can claim to have their daily bread and modest com-
forts. In an attempt to help meet their economic needs North
American Mennonite businessmen formed a Mennonite Economic
Development Association (MEDA) and have achieved significant
results in partnership with the settlers.

In the Chaco the primary cash crops are cotton, peanuts (oil),
and kafir corn. In East Paraguay the acreage is much smaller but

Since the late 1920s successive waves of Mennonite immigrants from Russia and Germany have moved to Paraguay to establish **colonies in the Chaco** and in the forests of Eastern Paraguay. Mennonite Economic Development Associates (MEDA), now an organization with a worldwide mission, was originally set up to improve the economic situation of the **Paraguayan Mennonite farmers** through loans, donated equipment, and professional counsel.

peanuts, sugarcane, and other crops provide some cash income, as does the sale of timber. In recent years the experimental farm has successfully developed a strain of wheat suited to the climate of East Paraguay to the great joy of the people who had not forgotten the white loaves of bread they took for granted on the steppes of Russia. This has led to a significant strengthening of the economic base in both Volendam and Friesland. Manioc has replaced the potatoes of Europe and Canada. Fresh vegetables are strictly seasonal in the Chaco, but citrus fruits are available in abundance. Meat is the staple food of most major meals.

The educational program of all classes is completely under the control of the colonies themselves and is conducted in both the Spanish and German languages by their own teachers. As with the Mennonites in Mexico, only a few years of schooling are offered in the *Bergthal* and *Sommerfeld* colonies. A more adequate basic education is being achieved in *Menno* Colony, though trained teachers are limited. In the other colonies the European system of six years' elementary and four years' secondary training is followed by a two-year teacher-training course available to those who desire it. Resources and financial help for education have been received from Germany. A cooperative Bible school is conducted in Filadelfia, the center of Chaco activities. Together with Mennonites in other lands in Latin America, a Bible Institute is operated in Brazil and a seminary (CEMTA)[6] and Bible school in Asunción. For advanced studies students travel to Europe or North America, though several Mennonite medical doctors have received their degrees from the University of Paraguay.

Church activities continue to remain central to the social and community life in the colonies, with regular worship services held in many places. With the exception of Bergthal and Sommerfeld, an active Sunday school, prayer meeting, and mid-week Bible studies program is carried on. The Bergthal and Sommerfeld communities have not formed an official conference, but work together among themselves and maintain close relationships with their co-religionists in Canada. In 1986 Bergthal counted 1,478 settlers, of whom 495 were church members, while Sommerfeld counted 1,750 settlers, of whom 586 were church members.

From the time of their arrival in the Chaco in 1930, the Fernheim group, and those who came later, as well as the Menno Colony churches more recently, have been keenly aware of their mission responsibility, and numerous programs have been undertaken. Little did the early pioneers envision the scope these early beginnings would lead to by 1990. After years of work with the Lengua tribe people, it seemed best to locate them away from the colony center in Filadelfia and a separate settlement was formed at Yalve Sanga. The first congregation was founded in 1946, after many years of loving, but seemingly fruitless ministry. By 1987, however, there were six places of worship with 1,400 baptized members. Similarly the witness to the Chulupi tribe people, which had begun in 1958, led to seven places of worship and 1,500 members by 1987. Guarani congregations had a membership of 300 in 1987. The total Indian population in the Chaco colony area at this time was about 7,000 persons. A joint inter-church agency *Licht den Indianern* (Light to the Indians) had been founded early to carry this work.

In 1958 Cornelius Isaak was speared to death as he attempted contact with the fierce Ayoreo (Moro) tribe people, but many of them have now also been won to Christ. Major attempts were being made by the Mennonite colonies, together with the MCC, to settle into self-supporting agricultural communities these thousands of people who streamed to the Mennonite communities in search of work. Health services were established, as also a cooperative store, schools, crafts and light industry in a total missionary effort probably exceeding in scope that of any other effort by Mennonite missions anywhere.[7]

A unique situation arose when the Chaco Indian young men were called up in the military draft and claimed exemption as Mennonites under the *Privilegium*. The predictable reply of the authorities was, "You're not a Mennonite, you're an Indian." But with the help of the "real" Mennonites an excellent solution was found whereby Mennonite farmers would take these young men as apprentices to teach them how to farm and then help them get started on farms of their own.

The Mennonite settlers also reached out to the national population of Paraguay, at first through two city missionaries in Asunción and a Bible school program. In 1959 the first congregation was formed in Asunción, but by 1962 active work was also being carried on in the Chaco and numerous other locations. By 1990 there were many meeting places where ethnic distinctions had almost disappeared. The work at Kilometer 81 (Itacurubi) with persons suffering from Hansen's disease (leprosy), begun together with MCC in 1951, was also having a profound Christian witness impact upon many across the nation, including state and Catholic church officials, but also upon the Mennonites themselves, who supported it with gifts and a voluntary service program.[8]

All baptized Mennonite groups in Paraguay, including those of ethnic German, Paraguayan and Indian background totaled 16,602 members in 1986.[9] A strong spirit of fellowship among the churches has strengthened their ministry and witness. Coordinating committees serve to unite church and mission activities. The biweekly paper *Menno Blatt* keeps the scattered settlers in touch with each other as does a radio station (ZP-30), established in Filadelfia in the 1970s.

Brazil. Among the Mennonites who left Russia for Germany in 1929 were about 280 families totaling 1,300 persons who chose to settle in Brazil instead of Fernheim in the Chaco of Paraguay. This became possible for them through the efforts of the German government and substantial help from the Dutch Mennonites. Land was secured for them in Santa Catarina, a state with a large German population in Southern Brazil, and the first Mennonites arrived there on February 10, 1930. Two settlements were laid out: Witmarsum in the Krauel River Valley and Auhagen on Stoltz Plateau, but neither seemed to prosper economically, though the forests, hills, and valleys afforded very beautiful scenery.

The Auhagen settlers soon moved to the outskirts of Curitiba city and took up dairying on such a large scale that they eventually supplied over half of the milk required by the one quarter million inhabitants of that city. The Witmarsum Colony also relocated, some establishing themselves 60 miles northwest of Curitiba in New Witmarsum and some near the Uruguayan border in Colonia Nova at Bagé. Some also found employment in the cities, particularly in São Paulo. Through these relocation efforts most of the immigrants were soon able to achieve economic independence. In 1986 the total baptized Mennonite community in Brazil numbered 6,000 persons, including those in Portuguese-speaking congregations, scattered over much of the nation with concentrations in Curitiba, Bagé, and New Witmarsum. A biweekly paper *Bibel und Pflug* kept the German-speaking members in touch with each other and served to strengthen their spiritual life.

As in Paraguay, church and school activities are patterned after the traditional forms developed in the Mennonite settlements in Russia. Since all education is state controlled, however, the Mennonites have sought to preserve their values by having their teachers receive state training and certification and by having their own schools meet certification requirements. In this way several excellent schools have been developed, including the elementary and high school *Erasto Gaertner* in Curitiba, where many non-Mennonites are being taught also. A Bible Institute has been established in Curitiba by the Mennonite Brethren churches of South America.[10]

Church activities are carried on in both the German and Portuguese languages. The pressures to acculturation are much greater than in Paraguay and young Mennonites consider themselves more Brazilian than German. Fortunately, there is growing cooperation with the larger evangelical Protestant community in Brazil, which helps to make their faith indigenous rather than extraneous to their culture. Earlier difficulties in securing conscientious objector classification for Mennonite men of draft age have been eliminated by the 1991 constitution which provides for this possibility, together with alternative service.

In a potentially rich country of 150,000,000 people (1990), with huge areas of urban poverty, human suffering and need is endless. To facilitate witness and service on a national level the *Associacao Menonita de Assistencia Social* (AMAS—Mennonite Association for Social Assistance) agency, was founded in 1972. At any given time dozens of volunteers can be found at work in city slums and other areas of poverty, including northeast Brazil. In some locations volunteers work together with MCC and IMO (European) workers. Day-care centers for children are an important part of their program. A strong evangelical concern combining word and deed is evident among the congregations.

Uruguay. The settlement of Mennonites in Uruguay began in 1948 with the coming of 750 immigrants from the Vistula Delta. Together with all of their coreligionists they had been forced to leave these homelands in the closing days of World War II in 1945. Upon arriving in Uruguay they immediately found employment and by 1950 were able to purchase *El Ombu,* a 2,900-acre ranch northwest of Montevideo, with the help of MCC. In October 1951, a second group of 431 came to join them, locating on an even larger ranch near Tres Bocas, which they named *Gartental.* A third colony was established in 1955 on 3,600 acres 55 miles northwest of Montevideo and named *Delta* after their Vistula Delta homeland in Prussia. All three of the colonies are primarily agricultural, growing wheat, peanuts, corn, potatoes, and other crops, as well as raising cattle

Thirty-three Mennonite families from Russia settled in Brazil in 1930, followed short-ly by numerous additional arrivals including a group of thirty-four families from Har-bin, China. All of them located in Santa Catarina state where they established the vil-lages of Witmarsum and Auhagen. Because of economic hardships and adverse cli-mate these villages were later abandoned. The majority of the settlers moved on to **Curitiba,** capital of Parana State. The Mennonites in and around Curitiba are en-gaged in dairying and in the plywood and furniture industries. The ninth Mennonite World Conference was held in Curitiba in 1972.

and operating a successful dairy industry. Except for help in purchasing land, most of the settlers were self-supporting from the beginning due to their energetic spirit and the rich economy of the country. Later national economic and political difficulties led many to return to Germany. In 1986 the total census of all baptized Mennonites, including Spanish-speaking congregations, was 877.

As in Brazil the schools are subject to state supervision and must meet national certification requirements. In 1956 Montevideo was chosen as the location for a seminary sponsored by the Mennonite Church and General Conference Mennonite churches of North and South America. It was known as the *Seminario Evangélico Menonita de Teología* and offered a three-year course of instruction to some thirty-five to forty students annually. Theological, economic, and other factors led to its closing early in the 1970s and reopening on a small scale in Asunción, Paraguay, several years later (CEMTA), where workers were once again being trained for congregational and missionary tasks.

This, then, is the picture of the ethnic German-Dutch Mennonite groups in Latin America, *and* of indigenous national and Indian groups. The amalgam of immigrant and national groups has, by now, become such a given that earlier separate treatment of these groups is no longer possible. This is surely a sign of progress in the church. This picture is not complete, but a survey. For example, Mennonites have long worked successfully among the Toba Indians of the Argentinian (and Paraguayan) Chaco and continue to relate cordially to them, even though they have formed the independent, non-Mennonite Evangelical United Church.

Reliable statistics about total Mennonite population figures and baptized membership are difficult to obtain. Some groups are reluctant to provide statistics. The constant migration of some groups also makes a census difficult. While there have been many migrations from Mexico, the figure of 45,000-50,000 persons, indicated above, may be inflated. Baptized members have been estimated to be 16,500 of this total. Paraguay would number 16,600 church members in 1987, including the large Old Colony settlements in East Paraguay. The census in Bolivia is too transient at this point to count, but a 1986 estimate lists 15,000 persons, of whom one-third might be church members. The total number of baptized persons in Belize in 1987 was listed at 2,236. Brazil may be listed with 6,000 and Uruguay with 877 baptized members. Membership was listed at 2,000 in Argentina in 1988, and perhaps 500 members in the new colony. This would place the total of baptized members in the "Southern Cone," plus Mexico and Belize, somewhere near 50,000 (49,713).[11]

Northern Latin America, Including the Caribbean

With a task force of this size it might be assumed that a great believers church witness is spreading across Latin America. This is indeed true in many areas. Ethnic Latin Mennonites are now the primary agents of witness. Still, in some areas North American mission boards are in the first stages of church planting. Increasingly mission boards and national groups of believers combine in a joint program. There seems to be hardly a country in Latin America where Mennonites are not actively witnessing, with the possible exception of Guyana, Surinam, and French Guiana.

Long before the first immigrants came to Paraguay, North American Mennonites were interested in Latin America as a mission field. One of the first missionaries described this interest as follows:

> During the 13 years, 1904 to 1917, the movement developed that gave birth to the Argentine Mennonite Mission. Mennonite youth in Goshen College studied about the neglected South American continent. Churches and wide-awake individuals contributed to a fund for South American missions. The Mennonite Board of Missions and Charities in 1911 sent J. W. Shank as its representative on a six months' tour of investigation in Peru, Bolivia, Chile, Argentina, and Uruguay. Then followed a general solicitation campaign that brought over $20,000 for the new mission. By the late summer of 1917 the four missionaries under appointment, the T. K. Hersheys and J. W. Shanks, sailed to Buenos Aires, arriving on September 11.[12]

Argentina. The first work was begun in a semi-rural town called Pehuajó, some 200 miles west of Buenos Aires, in 1919. After ten years seven growing young churches, with outstations and Sunday schools, were in existence. In 1942 work was begun among the Toba Indians of the Argentine Chaco, and later in Buenos Aires itself. By 1988 these efforts had led to a membership of 2,000 and attendance of over 3,000 in what is known as the Argentine Evangelical Mennonite Church. North American mission personnel relate to them as needed in Bible translation, literature production, and other ways as fraternal Christians. The official periodical of the

In the mid-1950s Old Colony Mennonites from northern Mexico began to settle in Belize. At the same time MCC, the Eastern Mennonite Board of Missions, MEDA, and our colleges established mission, medical, and economic assistance programs in the country. Today Mennonites produce most of the food needed in the country. The **papaya processing plant** operates in Shipyard Colony. The Virginia Conference began mission work in Jamaica in 1954. In 1990 there were 422 Mennonite church members on the island, including the **Calvary Mennonite Church** near Retreat on the north coast.

conference is *Perspectiva*. In 1990 one of their leaders, Raul O. Garcia, was elected president of Mennonite World Conference (MWC).

Colombia. An equally dynamic program was launched in *Colombia* by the General Conference Mennonites in 1943 and the Mennonite Brethren Church in 1946. Both groups established schools and orphanages, the former giving particular attention to the care of children of parents suffering from Hansen's disease (leprosy) near Cachipay. A second and third school were added later as were medical clinics. A Bible school is operated by the Mennonite Brethren Church.

Almost from the beginning all missionary groups experienced strong opposition from authorities and the Roman Catholic Church, at times even persecution. The spirit and decrees of Vatican Council II (1962-65) marked a turning point in Roman Catholic-Protestant relationships. Tolerance and cooperation became increasingly common and with it mutual benefits. Four Anabaptist groups are at work, growing out of General Conference, Mennonite Brethren, the Ashland (Ohio) Brethren, and the Brethren in Christ missions. A seminary program was begun in 1989. Membership in 1990 is approximately 2,300 in 40 congregations. Colombian Christians are the primary channels of reaching out to their neighbors, including a social service agency (MENCOLDES) since 1977, schools, peace education, retirement homes, children's homes, a rice-processing plant (with the help of MEDA), and in many other ways.

Puerto Rico. Different circumstances led to the beginning of Mennonite work in *Puerto Rico* in 1943. Mennonite conscientious objectors from the United States were invited to do their service in Puerto Rico. Initially their program included medical, recreational, educational, and agricultural services at La Plata and surrounding regions. Two years later the Mennonite Board of Missions began work on the island, establishing a church at La Plata in 1947. In 1958 both the service and evangelism programs were united under this board, including the administration of a 32-bed hospital in Aibonito. Meanwhile the Conference of Mennonite Evangelical Churches had been established in 1955 and by the 1970s took full responsibility for its own life and work. In 1986 there were 893 members in 16 congregations.

A veritable explosion of Mennonite missionary activity began in Latin America about 1950. Mennonite Brethren witness led to a membership of 150 in Peru in 1990. In *Ecuador* several congregations have formed in the coastal area since the 1980s through the work of the Conservative Mennonite Conference (Rosedale Mennonite Mission). In Central America the Eastern Board of Missions began work in *Honduras* in 1950 and by 1990 an independent Honduran Mennonite church, in four branches, reported a membership of 8,000 with a total community of 12,600. The Eastern Board took over work from MCC in *Belize* in 1961, forming the first Spanish-speaking congregation in 1965, and reaching a membership of 247 by 1990 within a community of 669. In 1971 the same board began work in *Guatemala*, reaching a membership of 4,000 in two branches by 1990, and a community of 5,750. In 1961 the Mennonite Brethren Board of Missions began work in *Panama*, reaching a membership of 700 by 1990.

The first Brethren in Christ congregation was organized in *Nicaragua* in 1965, reaching a membership of 1,794 by 1990, and in 1970 the *Fraternity* formed its first congregation, growing to a membership of 300 by 1990, autonomous, but with fraternal help from the Evangelical Mennonite Conference. Meanwhile the Nicaragua Mennonite Conference, with help from the Conservative Mennonite Conference, had been formed with a membership of 780. The Eastern Board began work in *Venezuela* in 1978, in Caracas, and in July of 1979 the Evangelical Mennonite Church of Venezuela was formed with the baptism of the first five believers. In 1990 they reported 120 members, including the Brethren in Christ. Work was begun in *Costa Rica* by the Conservative Mennonite Conference in 1961, leading to a membership of 1,050 by 1990. Three Mennonite groups began work in *El Salvador* since 1968, including MCC as a relief agency. Church membership is over 100 and, with the end of the civil war in 1992, came hope for new beginnings.

The rise of these congregations has been marked by a great interest in the life, thought, *and modern relevance,* of sixteenth-century Anabaptism. The result was the forming of the *Central American Mennonite Conference (Consulta Anabautista Menonita de Centroamericana* (CAMCA) which first met in Honduras in 1974. The conference is active in literature production and the training of leaders through its seminary program *Seminario Ministerial de Liderazgo Anabautista* (SEMILLA). As a term, *Anabaptism* seems to have appeal as more universal, less sectarian, than Mennonitism. This interest in Anabaptism has gone far beyond Mennonite circles in the region. It represents, in that context, a synthesis of biblical and liberation theology motifs.

The same intense activity was also being pursued in the area we identified as the West Indies. The Brethren in Christ and the Mennonite Church both began work in *Cuba* but were forced to leave after the revolution. The church of Christ did not leave, however, nor did the Mennonite and Brethren in Christ congregations fade away. In 1990 some 45 members were listed in a community of 150. The Virginia Board of Missions began work in *Jamaica* in 1954 and by 1990 the Jamaica Mennonite Church counted 422 members. The Church of God in Christ, Mennonite reported a membership of 354 in *Haiti*, and the Evangelical Mennonite Church began work in the *Dominican Republic* in 1949, reaching a membership of 1,400 by 1990. The Virginia board was also at work in *Trinidad* and *Tobago*, reporting 110 members in 1990.

The ethnic German Mennonite settlers in *Bolivia* have, thus far, not shown much concern for evangelism, but a small beginning has been made by workers from Argentina and North America. In Uruguay both the Mennonite Church and General Conference Mennonite Church mission boards facilitated the forming of the Uruguayan Mennonite Conference in 1956. A Spanish-speaking Mennonite Brethren church was formed in Uruguay in 1948. In both of the latter groups, as in the congregations in Brazil, immigrant Mennonites (and their descendants) worship together with nationals in the same congregations, though the strictly German-language congregations are also continuing.

Finally, with reference to *Mexico*, we remember that both the General Conference and Mennonite Brethren mission boards began work there in 1950. While the former concentrated their primary efforts, though not exclusively, on the Mennonite settlements, the latter established four areas of evangelistic outreach, combining education, medical, and gospel ministries. Major attention was given to literature distribution. The Franconia Conference began work in Mexico City in 1958 and in 1990 reported 200 baptized members with a total community of 300 in ten locations. The group became known as the Evangelical Mennonite Church of the Central Plateau of Mexico. The Pacific Coast Mission Board began work in Mexico in 1959, working in three locations with Sunday and Bible school programs and community service activities.

Some of these pages can be read as little more than dates and statistics, but they can also be read as individual biographies of persons coming to faith in Christ and into fellowship with other believers in the church of Christ. The number of those who are sometimes called "New Mennonites" may be between 30,000-35,000 members in 1990, including Indian believers mentioned earlier, but it is no longer possible to count them, or Mennonites of ethnic German background, accurately because so many congregations worship together with nationals and do not count separately (cf.: Gal. 3:28). It is clear that the so-called "New Mennonites" are persons who made a deliberate choice, often with dire social consequences, and are in the forefront of witness and service in every land in Latin America. Their influence on Latin American and global Anabaptists-Mennonites cannot help but be significant for the 1990s and beyond.

If we add to these 30,000-35,000 members the 50,000 mostly ethnic German-Dutch Mennonites reported above as members, we have an approximate total of 80,000-85,000 members in the believers church (Anabaptists), or Evangelical Church (Evangélicos), within a much larger total community, living and speaking for their faith.

The significance of these developments lies not only in the statistics, but much more in the spirit which prevails in the churches, in the quick maturity and autonomy new congregations and conferences have developed—and mission boards have been willing to let happen—and in the usually strong partnership between North and South in carrying on the missionary task. Also significant is the fact that in many instances these witnesses have been able to work not only with Protestant denominations but with Roman Catholics in a common front against the forces of social evil and spiritual darkness. In this struggle the believers church conviction that *word and deed must be kept together* is often sorely tried.

Endnotes

1. David B. Barrett, *World Christian Encyclopedia*. New York, N. Y.: Oxford University Press, 1982., p. 780.

2. For a parallel analysis see Carter Lindberg, *The Third Reformation?* Macon, Georgia: Mercer University Press, 1983.

3. Barrett, op. cit., p. 783. See also Walter J. Hollenweger, *The Pentecostals*. Minneapolis, Minn.: Augsburg Publishing House, 1972.

4. For discussion of these issues see Adolf Ens, "A Second Look at the Rejected Conservatives," *Mennonite Reporter*. Centennial of Russian Mennonite Immigration. Vol. 4, no. 24 (November 25, 1974) pp. 36-37, and Ens, "The Conspiracy That Never Was," *Mennonite Historian*. Vol. XI, no. 3 (September, 1985), pp. 1-2.

5. Read Peter J. and Elfrieda Dyck, *Up from the Rubble*. Scottdale, Pa.: Herald Press, 1991.

6. Centro Evangelico Menonita de Teologia Asunción (CEMTA).

7. For a comprehensive description of Mennonite and Indian relationships in the Chaco see Calvin W. Redekop, *Strangers Become Neighbors*. Scottdale, Pa.: Herald Press, 1980.

8. See *Im Dienste der Liebe* (In the Service of Love), a periodical begun in 1951.

9. MWC *Handbook* (1990) pp. 380-385.

10. Centro Evangelico Menonita de Teologia por Extensao (CEMTE), which also cooperates with the theological school CEMTA in Paraguay.

11. See the relevant ME 5 articles for groups and countries. Also check the cross-references listed with the articles. The statistics for Mennonites are derived from ME 5, and *Mennonite World Handbook*, edited by Diether Götz Lichdi. Carol Stream, Ill.: Mennonite World Conference, 1990., pp. 356-391, and other sources. It will have been noted that some are estimates and most have been rounded out. For information about individual conferences in a given land see the respective Mennonite yearbooks.

12. J. W. Shank, "Argentine Mennonite Mission," ME 3:154-56.

Other Resources: ME 5. MWC *Handbook* (1990). Daniel S. Schipani, ed., *Freedom and Discipleship: Liberation Theology in Anabaptist Perspective*. Maryknoll, N.Y.: Orbis, 1989. LaVerne Rutschman, "Anabaptism and Liberation Theology," MQR (July 1981), 55:255-270. Thomas P. Fenton & Mary J. Heffron. *Latin America and Caribbean: A Directory of Resources*, Maryknoll, N.Y.: Orbis, 1986. *Mission Focus* (March 1989), 17:1. Contact any MCC or conference office, Mennonite museum or information office for audiovisual resources.

18

Mennonite Churches in Asia

THE PEOPLE of Asia are justifiably proud of their ancient cultural heritage. Thousands of years before the American continents were known, great civilizations flourished in India, China, and the large peninsula between them. Any good museum with an Oriental section will quickly convince one of this. India's literary tradition goes back at least 500 years before the Old Testament. The Chinese were using movable type in printing books about 700 years before printing was invented in Europe. The architectural wonders of Burma, Thailand, and Indonesia are accessible to us through art books, encyclopedias and travel.

Moreover the people of Asia have been as religious as any people in the world. Hinduism and Buddhism, the main religions, are both older than Christianity and have much in them that is worthy. With the emergence of national independence for most of the Asian countries since 1945, the ancient religions are experiencing a revival. Today Buddhists in Asia are sending missionaries to North America. Islam, the youngest of the great world religions, is also experiencing world-wide resurgence and growth.

The change of the Asian nations from colonialism to political independence hastened the process of change from mission to church in the whole of the Christian missionary enterprise. While there was some sentiment in the 1960s and 1970s for the withdrawal of Western missionaries from Asia, the wiser course has been recognized to be a partnership relationship, missionaries and national leaders working together as equals. In some cases, the organizational structure of the newer churches in Asia had become Western-oriented, with schools, hospitals and other institutions, making it impossible now for the younger churches to carry the costs of these structures alone. Throughout Asia today Mennonite churches are independent, assuming responsibility for mission work in their own countries, and gradually developing structures suited to their needs and tasks.

Indonesia. When and where can we find the first non-white Mennonites? Did early eighteenth-century colonial Mennonites win any Native Americans to their faith, or later, any slaves from Africa, though most Mennonites did not own slaves? We do not know. However, we do know that on March 16, 1854, Pieter Jansz, a Dutch Mennonite missionary, baptized five persons near Japara on the Indonesian island of Java. Soon there were to be others in India, Africa, and elsewhere for a total of over fifty nations outside of Europe and North America but using 78 languages, if the latter are included, in 1990.[1]

In July 1851, Pieter Jansz and his young wife sailed quietly from Holland without a farewell. Although they knew they were going to Java, they had no idea where they would settle down. After traveling about the island, Jansz decided on the Muria Mountain area in the north-central part as a suitable place for his work. Progress was difficult and slow. Gradually Jansz developed a novel strategy which was put into practice about 1890 by his son. The Javanese who became Christians were settled in a colony because, argued missionary Jansz, it was difficult for new Christians to live in a hostile Muslim environment. They could grow better as Christians if they lived and worked together. Actually anyone was free to join but all had to adhere to the Christian rules of the colony. The church developed slowly with help from Mennonites in Holland, Germany, Switzerland, and Russia both in missionaries and in money. By 1940, nearly a century after the beginning of the church, there were twelve congregations and about 1,200 members.

In addition to the Javanese Mennonite Church, a church developed among the Chinese in the neighborhood as well, primarily through the vision of a layman, Tee Siem Tat, who was a printer by

Dutch Mennonites started mission work on the island of Java in 1851. By 1990 the two conferences of Indonesian Mennonites totaled 83,492 members. **An informal gathering of students** turns into a sing-along on the porch of the seminary at Pati. Recently the Java Mennonites began a relocation and mission program resulting in the construction of **new Mennonite meetinghouses** in the fishing villages of Sumatra. The smaller of the two Indonesian conferences was once known as the Chinese church because of the ethnic origin of the majority of its members. The **church at Jepara** belongs to this conference.

profession. He began his work in 1918 and in 1927 a separate Chinese conference was organized. Except that Tee and others were baptized by a white missionary, this Chinese Mennonite Church was begun and is being continued without any missionary help.

The Javanese Mennonite Church became completely independent from the European church in 1940, although developments toward independence began in 1928. Almost immediately the new church faced severe tests. The Japanese invaded Java in 1942 and in the attending unrest Christians were cruelly persecuted by Muslims and much church property was destroyed. Japanese, Muslims, and Dutch all suspected the Christians of collaborating with the enemy. But the time of testing strengthened the church, and after peace finally came to Indonesia in 1949, a period of growth and expansion set in. Schools and churches were built, and medical service was again established with the help of MCC.

In 1965 a communist attempt to win control of the nation failed. An estimated 500,000 people were killed in the coup and its violent aftermath. The army issued a decree that anyone not belonging to an approved religious group would be considered a communist and either jailed or executed. This both helped the church and became a problem for it because people came to join, Mennonite churches also, with very mixed motives. The need for teachers and other church workers for these new converts became great. But many new converts also came from Islam, which was an approved religion, partly because they could not understand the *Koran*, which must always be in Arabic, and partly because they sensed among the Mennonites a spiritual depth and caring for which they longed.

Two experiences have forced the Indonesian Mennonites to clarify for themselves their identity and their mission. First, the difficulties of independence as a church and the strain of the war years raised seriously the question about the justification for continued existence as a Mennonite church. The Reformed Church in Java invited the Mennonites to join them, but at a conference in 1942 they overwhelmingly decided to remain Mennonites. A statement of faith drawn up at that time said: "We believe that God has helped us during all these difficulties, and that our church will now be used by God to do the part of the task He has given to the church in Indonesia." [2]

The second experience was that of living and working as the church of Jesus Christ in the new Republic of Indonesia. One of the

JAPAN

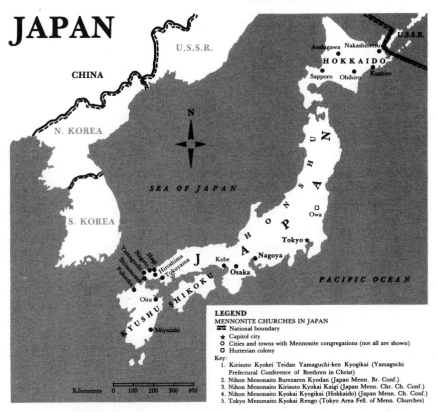

LEGEND
MENNONITE CHURCHES IN JAPAN
═══ National boundary
★ Capitol city
○ Cities and towns with Mennonite congregations (not all are shown)
❑ Hutterian colony
Key:
1. Kirisuto Kyokei Teidan Yamaguchi-ken Kyogikai (Yamaguchi Prefectural Conference of Brethren in Christ)
2. Nihon Menonaito Burezaren Kyodan (Japan Menn. Br. Conf.)
3. Nihon Menonaito Kirisuto Kyokai Kaigi (Japan Menn. Chr. Ch. Conf.)
4. Nihon Menonaito Kyokai Kyogikai (Hokkaido) (Japan Menn. Ch. Conf.)
5. Tokyo Menonaito Kyokai Rengo (Tokyo Area Fell. of Menn. Churches)

five principles of Indonesia's *Democracy of Pancasila* government is belief in one God. All religious groups are called upon to participate actively in the construction of Indonesia, especially in the intellectual and religious area. The churches, including the Mennonite Church, are given certain privileges by the government in return, as it were, for their contribution to the life of Indonesia. The Mennonites share in the excitement of playing a meaningful part in the building of the nation. This represents both an unparalleled opportunity and a subtle danger. It can mean the increased possibility of rendering the educational and humanitarian services so much needed today. It can also mean an identification with Indonesian nationalism which can prevent them from being truly the church which knows no national boundaries.

The Mennonite churches of Indonesia have worked closely with the government in relocating landless families from overcrowded Java to the island of Sumatra. Although Java is a small island over one-half of the population of Indonesia, which is about 170,000,000 (1990) people, live there while many islands lie idle. By 1978 some 645 Mennonite families had been relocated in South Sumatra on land of their own. The relocation project continues. The Indonesian Mennonite church, with some help from the MCC, supplemented government aid as possible, including pastors and teachers. In a new region different agricultural practices needed to be developed. The families are happy and the church is growing there too. One man, who had been a Muslim, was asked why he was happy and he replied: "Because I know Jesus. Because I and my family are healthy. Because I can be a part of the church. Because I own all this land [five acres]. Because I have a draft ox [a gift from MCC]. Because my house keeps the rain out even though it is a poor man's house."[3]

There are two Mennonite conferences in Indonesia, the Evangelical Church of Java (GITJ) with a membership of 67,332 in 59 congregations in 1989, and the United Muria Indonesia Christian Church (GKMI) with 16,160 members in 106 congregations.[4] The latter have sometimes been known as the "Chinese" church because of their ethnic origin but they are now as Indonesian as the others. Neither of the groups use the term Mennonite. Elementary and secondary schools are maintained and particular attention is given to leadership training at a seminary in Pati, sponsored by both conferences. Women play a significant role in the churches, including some who are ordained. Clinics, a hospital, and an orphanage are being supported. The conferences are also constituent members of a Christian university in Salatiga. (See also ME 5, pp. 436-438.)

Japan. The growth of the Christian church in Japan has been slow. The Jesuit mission of the sixteenth century won many converts, but the young church was soon destroyed by persecution. When Protestant mission work began in Japan in the 1860s, becoming a Christian was a crime punishable by death. This law seems not to have been enforced, however, and was soon removed. In 1986 about 1.1 percent of the estimated 121 million population of Japan were Christian. With a land mass approximately the size of California, but of which only about 20 percent is arable, Japan ranks among the most densely populated areas of the world.[5]

Mennonite missionaries followed close on the heels of the conquering American army, and reconciliation was indeed needed

An **Indonesian Mennonite teacher** instructs children from the village of Jemeluk in reading and arithmetic. **Young people from West Kalimantan** travel by canoe to share the gospel.

after the war ended with the atomic destruction of Hiroshima and Nagasaki. A specific peace and reconciliation ministry was begun in Hiroshima by Mennonites in the late 1970s. In 1949 the Mennonite Church began work on Hokkaido Island. In 1950 the General Conference Mennonite Church began on Kyushu Island and the Mennonite Brethren on Honshu Island. In 1953 the Brethren in Christ likewise located on Honshu. From the beginning the Mennonite Church, General Conference Mennonite Church, and the Brethren in Christ have worked together in Tokyo in evangelism, peace witness, literature production, and young people's work. In the 1970s an Anabaptist study center was developed in the city.

Though the Mennonite missionaries wished to work also in rural areas, their success has been limited. This is due, in part, to the drift of young people to urban centers, and in part to the strong social ties of the rural *buraku* (a group of households or families). The *buraku* is a voluntary association for dealing with common concerns like festivals, road repair, seeding and harvesting, funerals, but it is also concerned for religious affairs. Disagreement with a decision within the group can lead to social ostracism. The *buraku* is said to be collapsing due to rapid changes in agricultural techniques and family structure, but it still remains a major obstacle to the personal acceptance of the Christian faith in rural areas.

The high literacy and advanced technology of Japan also help to determine the manner of church growth. Missionaries do not normally engage in medical and education work as in Africa and other parts of Asia, these services being adequately provided for by the government. Consequently there is a strong emphasis on personal evangelism along with radio evangelism and literature distribution on a personal basis, through the mails, and by operating bookstores. During the early years effective work was done through kindergartens operated by missionaries, frequently leading to the formation of Sunday schools and contacts with the whole family. Work among high school and university students, often through the medium of English instruction offered by the missionaries, has shown itself to be both rewarding and challenging.

The Mennonite church in Japan will continue to be a cooperative work, with Japanese and North American Christians working side by side for some time to come. Though it is an independent church, it receives some support from North America, primarily to uphold the unique roles of missionaries and their expense. If, however, it should become necessary for the missionaries to leave, the

Mennonite missionaries arrived in Japan in 1949. By 1990 there were fifty-eight congregations with a combined membership of nearly 3000. The **congregation at Obihiro** on the island of Hokkaido is one of the older ones. Visiting professor **C. Norman Kraus and native pastor Takoi Tanase** conduct a seminar with the Kushiro churches on the theme "What Is Church?"

work of the Mennonite churches would continue, for they are fortunate to have the leadership of trained and dedicated young men and women.

In 1990 the Japan Mennonite Church Conference had a membership of 410, the Japan Mennonite Christian Church Conference numbered 763 members, the Japan Mennonite Brethren Conference listed 1,619 members, the Yamnaguchi Prefectural Conference of Brethren in Christ had 97 members, and the Tokyo Area Evangelical Mennonite Cooperative Conference had 73 members for a total of about 3,000 members. The Japan Mennonite Fellowship, an inter-Mennonite successor to the MCC, is alert to needs in and beyond Japan.

China. Although it was almost completely cut off from its sister churches elsewhere in the world for many years, a Mennonite fellowship continues to exist in the land. That fellowship began in 1905 when H. C. Bartel, a member of the Krimmer Mennonite Brethren Church, began independent work in Ts'aohuen, Shantung province, in the hope of attracting Mennonite support. This work was adopted and supported by the China Mennonite Mission Society, an organization in which several Mennonite bodies participated. In 1909 and 1912 the General Conference and Mennonite Brethren began work with J. J. Brown and F. J. Wiens in Hopei and Fukien provinces respectively.

In all areas of Mennonite work, expansion was rapid during the first few decades, with considerable numbers of believers being baptized. The main methods of church extension were evangelism, medical work, distribution of literature, and education work at the primary and secondary levels. Immediate assumption of missionary responsibility by the Chinese themselves characterized the Chinese Mennonite Church, and the move to independence began early.

All of this subsequently proved to be of great importance, since China has had a troubled history in this century. Serious political unrest disturbed China in 1926 and 1927. In the early 1930s civil war involving communism ravaged a number of provinces. Added to this was the undeclared war between China and Japan which began in 1931, and by 1937 became a war of Japanese conquest. Then came World War II. In 1940 a number of missionaries were evacuated only to be interned by the Japanese. Others remained and moved into western China where Chiang Kai-shek ruled over what was called Free China.

During this time the Chinese Mennonite churches continued their work of preaching and living the gospel under very difficult conditions. When World War II ended in 1945, many of the missionaries returned to their old places of work. But the trouble was not yet over, for throughout the years of unrest since the early 1930s the communists had been establishing inreasing control over large areas of China. The civil war continued until Mao Tse-tung proclaimed the birth of the *People's Republic of China* on October 1, 1949.

In 1948 the Mennonite Church had entered China with a mission at Hochwan in Sichuan province. But the days of the missionaries in China were numbered. Conditions became more and more difficult and missionaries began to go home or to other fields, leaving the Chinese Mennonite churches to carry on in a war-weary and exhausted land. The last Mennonite missionary to leave was H. C. Bartel, the founder of Mennonite work in China. That was in 1952. There were at that time over 5,000 Mennonite Christians in China.

One missionary, Loyal Bartel, remained in China. In more recent years word of his death in 1971 from natural causes was given to his brother who had twice traveled to China. (See ME 5:690-691.) In the spring of 1979 MCC and several former missionaries received letters from friends in China expressing joy and confidence: "We are living a happy life. . . . The Hengyang and Puyang Mennonites are all fine." The former location had been the site of an MCC orphanage, the latter of a high school operated by the General Conference. News of strong small Christian fellowships was also being received.

In 1980-81 a teacher-student exchange program became possible between China and Goshen College, Goshen, Indiana. This program grew with the forming of the *China Educational Exchange* (CEE) in 1982, involving an exchange of teachers between Chinese universities and North American Mennonite colleges. A growing stream of North American Mennonite tourists also found their way to China. In 1982 Stephen Wang, an early Mennonite leader in China, was able to visit North America and, in 1985, James Liu (d. 1991) and his son Timothy were also able to come.[6] It has been estimated that there were at least 50 million Christians in the *People's Republic of China* in the late 1980s, of whom an uncounted number were Mennonites.

Taiwan. When the communist regime consolidated its control over mainland China in 1948 and 1949, the nationalists fled to Taiwan under the leadership of Chiang Kai-shek, and soon established control of the island. Christianity had been brought to the island by the Dutch early in the seventeenth century, but they were driven out in 1661. It remained for British and Canadian Presbyterians to begin work there in 1865. Mennonite work in Taiwan began in 1948 when MCC workers were forced to leave mainland China. Many mission agencies did the same.

Political and cultural tensions exist in Taiwan over its history, identity, and future. Mainland China considers it as one of its provinces. The population of Taiwan was 19.5 million in 1986 of whom 83 percent are descendants of immigrants from the mainland in the seventeenth century. They consider themselves a separate nation, at present under the occupation of some three to four million mainland nationalist Chinese. Ten aboriginal tribes and other smaller groups are also on the island.

MCC work concentrated first on mobile clinics and a small hospital at Hualien on the east coast. In 1954 this work was transferred to the General Conference Mennonite Church. A new hospital was built during the 1980s, and a strong evangelism program

MCC workers forced to leave mainland China in 1948 relocated on Taiwan. By 1990 there were 1,500 Taiwanese Mennonites. Members of **the Po-Ai Mennonite Church** are seen here enjoying an outdoor service.

The eleven-story **Lin Shen Road Mennonite Church** in Taichung, Taiwan. Floors one, three and five are classrooms, senior citizens' center fourth floor, guest rooms and senior citizens' rooms on sixth floor, two apartments for pastors on eighth floor, church activity center, fellowship hall and kitchen on the ninth floor, the sanctuary on the tenth and eleventh floors. Three underground levels provide parking and recreational facilities, including an Olympic-size heated swimming pool. Courtesy Verney Unruh.

has been undertaken mostly by Taiwanese Mennonites. In 1990 the *Fellowship of Mennonite Churches in Taiwan* (FOMCIT) listed a membership of 1,493, with a total community of 4,500. All congregations are fully independent churches carrying on a variety of ministries in cooperation with each other and North American workers. Particular attention was being given to the training of theological leadership by sending students to schools in Taiwan and in North America. A newspaper called *Manna* served as an important communication link between the widely scattered congregations.

Vietnam. Christianity first came to Vietnam in 1533 with the Portuguese. The Jesuits opened a mission in Danang in 1615. In due time Roman Catholicism became a dominant Christian faith, competing with Buddhism, as well as ancestor worship, Caodaism, and other forms of religion. The first Protestant missionaries seemed to have been sent by the newly founded (1887) Christian and Missionary Alliance Church in North America in 1893, but their work really began only in 1911. Numerous other missions followed during the French colonial occupation until 1954, and after.

The Evangelical Mennonite Church of Vietnam began with the coming of MCC in 1954. Three years later the Eastern Board of the Mennonite Church initiated work in Saigon. Because of the ravages of war and political unrest, progress in building Christian fellowships was slow, but relief and educational services were given, including help with the leprosarium at Banmethuot. By 1961 the building of a hospital in Nhatrang had been completed with the help of MCC. Later MCC also gave leadership to Vietnam Christian Service, which included Church World Service and Lutheran World Relief.

By the end of the war in 1975 most North Americans, including Mennonites, had left the country. MCC had given heroic service during the long and tragic years of the war. Daniel Gerber, a Mennonite, was one of a number of relief workers who perished there in 1962. (See ME 5:912-913.) Several MCC workers continued their work for a time after 1975. Mennonites from two former congregations have become part of the *Evangelical Church of Vietnam.* Hope continued for the return of fraternal relations with North American Mennonites.

Philippines. The Mennonite congregations of the Philippines had their origin in the vision and commitment of Felonito A. Sacapaño (d. 1987), an executive of International Nutrition Products, Inc. Together with another Christian they used their available time and resources to initiate weekend Bible studies among the mountain tribes of Abra, near Luzon, beginning in 1950. A unique part of their ministry was a deep concern for the economic and social problems of the people they were teaching. Small cottage industries were started; carpentry was encouraged; fishing, rice processing, and other income-producing activities soon flourished. This gave necessary income to impoverished families and from their tithe they helped to begin similar projects in other areas.

Nine churches had been started in this way by the time Eastern Board representatives of the Mennonite Church came in contact with them in 1972. With their help and some small loans from MEDA these efforts could be extended to the lowlands and markets could be developed for their products, both at home and abroad. A strong mutual concern permeates the congregations in which helping each other with difficult or unexpected problems is taken for granted, whether the needed help is economic, spiritual, or social in nature.

During the 1980s differences between the Eastern Board of Missions and *Missions Now, Inc.*, in the understanding of mission approach led to a new agreement between them, but also to the loss of numerous congregations. By 1990 there were 431 believers in what is still known as *Missions Now, Inc. (Mennonite)*, headquartered in Manila, and 235 members in the more recent Church of God in Christ, Mennonite congregations.

Central to the work of all of these congregations is the task of evangelism. Sessions on how to win people to Christ are a regular part of worship experience. It appears to take about three years for a new congregation to be founded in a new area. Particular emphasis is placed upon using the skills (gifts) of lay people. In all activities the early church of the book of Acts is taken as a model. The unique blending of message and method has shown evangelistic power which is attracting the attention of other mission and church groups.

Australia. In 1952 Foppe Brouwer, a young Mennonite from the Netherlands, arrived in Australia as an immigrant. He knew of no Mennonites in the country and occasionally attended a Presbyterian church because the preaching was in Dutch. Four years later he met and married Alice, an immigrant from Friesland. While visiting their families in the Netherlands in 1964 they received catechism instruction and were baptized in their home church in Friesland.

For the past two decades **Foppe Brouwer** of Fennell Bay, New South Wales, Australia, has attempted to forge a tie between the widely scattered Mennonites of Australia and New Zealand through personal correspondence, lending of books by mail, and publication of a Dutch/English periodical called **De Mennist.**

On their return to "down under," as Australia is sometimes referred to, they placed a notice in the Dutch Sydney paper inviting other Mennonites to write to them. When nine persons responded the Brouwers mimeographed a news sheet and called it *De Mennist.* The mailing list soon exceeded 200 names. They estimate that there may be from 2,000-5,000 ethnic Dutch Mennonites in the land, of which no fewer than 500 might be baptized members of some Mennonite church in the Netherlands or elsewhere. A few families also live in New Zealand.

A turning point to the Brouwers' life came in 1975, beginning with Alice's involvement in a small charismatic group in a Methodist church. Before long Foppe too had experienced new Holy Spirit power at a conference in Brisbane and later their children and relatives. Neighbors were won to Christ through their new life and witness. The Brouwers do not consider themselves charismatic but simply new, joyful disciples of Jesus. They were ordained in their home congregation in the Netherlands in 1978.

In 1977 Ian Duckham of Australia, who had studied at the Eastern Mennonite Seminary, Harrisonburg, Virginia, was ordained and, with his wife, commissioned to work in Australia. They located in Perth on the west coast. Meanwhile, Foppe Brouwer continued his planning for a Mennonite church. He hoped this might include a retreat center where Mennonites could vacation, meet, and fellowship together. "The Mennonite Church in Australia has a future," he wrote. "The peace doctrine, believers baptism, and the separation of church and state appeal to the youth. The time has come for Mennonites to plant a church in Australia." [7] In July 1979 the first congregation was indeed organized at Fennel-Bay, New South Wales, and Ian Duckham installed Foppe Brouwer as pastor of the *Mennonite Church of Hope*. While most immigrant Mennonites in Australia live in the Melbourne, Sydney, and Brisbane areas, the initial 33 members of the church come from all walks of life and mostly not of Mennonite background.

It may be noted that a group of Mennonites from Russia settled in Palestine about 1870, expecting the imminent return of Christ. They became known as the *Templers*. During World War II many of them and their descendants were deported to Australia by the British as German aliens. Others followed later. Considerable growth in membership has been reported. The number of "Templer-Mennonites" of Russian Mennonite background in the Victoria and New South Wales states is unknown.[8]

India. When we speak of the Mennonite church in India we also include the United Missionary Church and the Brethren in Christ Church, all of whom together numbered approximately 76,670 members in 1990. Together with the four Mennonite groups they share a commitment to the Anabaptist vision of faith and church life, and all six groups are members of the MCSFI family (Mennonite Christian Service Fellowship of India), a service agency created by them in 1964.

The first Mennonites to come to India as missionaries were the Abraham Friesens from the Mennonite Brethren Church in Russia, who came in 1889 and worked with the American Baptists. Two years later the Mennonite Brethren Church was officially organized in India. The first Mennonites from North America came in response to the famine of 1898-1900, bringing wheat and other relief supplies sent by the Mennonite Brethren, Mennonite Church, Gen-

INDIA

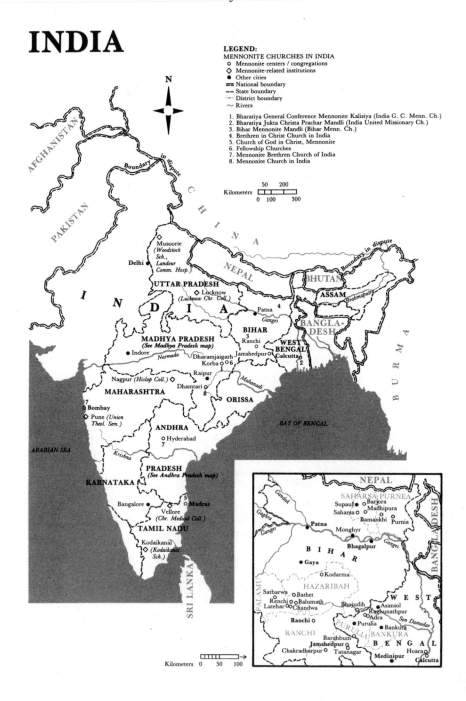

LEGEND:
MENNONITE CHURCHES IN INDIA
○ Mennonite centers / congregations
◇ Mennonite-related institutions
● Other cities
══ National boundary
―― State boundary
―·― District boundary
～ Rivers

1. Bharatiya General Conference Mennonite Kalisiya (India G. C. Menn. Ch.)
2. Bharatiya Jukta Christa Prachar Mandli (India United Missionary Ch.)
3. Bihar Mennonite Mandli (Bihar Menn. Ch.)
4. Brethren in Christ Church in India
5. Church of God in Christ, Mennonite
6. Fellowship Churches
7. Mennonite Brethren Church of India
8. Mennonite Church in India

eral Conference Mennonite Church, and others. They spent the first few years in the physically and spiritually exhausting work of trying to feed too many people with not enough food. Many children orphaned by the famine became their responsibility. A number of these eventually became strong leaders in the churches.

The Mennonite Brethren churches are located in Andhra Pradesh, and have been unusually effective in winning others to Christ, totaling 63,250 members in 1990. In identifying the methods used intensive evangelism is listed first, followed by mass movements including sociological or other factors, and third, the transfer of members from missions terminating their work in a given area. With this "automatically came hundreds and thousands of baptized believers. Suddenly, they were all Mennonite Brethren." [9] The Mennonite Church work centered in Madhya Pradesh (2,060 members), and later on a second field in Bihar (700 members), while the General Conference workers also located in Madhya Pradesh (6,000 members). The India United Missionary Church located first in West Bengal (2,500 members) and the Brethren in Christ in Bihar (1,920 members), plus 240 in Orissa. In each case work began at one initial station and then branched out in all directions into the many villages of India.[10]

The primary methods of church extension in India have been personal and preaching evangelism, medical work, and education. Medical work soon occupied a central place, with hospitals and clinics being built, and mobile clinics put into operation. Nursing schools were begun to provide the necessary help for these institutions, and to bring health care into the villages. Special efforts were made early to help those suffering from Hansen's disease (leprosy). At first it was simply a matter of providing food and shelter, but treatment programs soon followed. With the advance of modern medicine, many could experience the arresting of their disease and return to meaningful living. Several Mennonite missionaries received the Kaisar-i-Hind medal from the Viceroy of India for distinguished service to patients.

It is no accident that literacy is high among Indian Christians since the church in India has always considered education to be one of its first responsibilities. Primary and secondary schools came into existence in large numbers on the mission stations, as well as in the villages. Industrial schools were also begun to teach agriculture to the boys, and homemaking to the girls. All six groups support and send students to the inter-denominational Union Biblical

North American Mennonites arrived in India just before the turn of the century in response to the spiritual and physical needs of the subcontinent. As a result, practical programs have always occupied a central part in the work of the church in India. **Lab technicians** received their training and employment in Mennonite hospitals, and **nurses** graduated from Mennonite schools of nursing.

Seminary at Pune. The production of literature for use in school and church programs has also been carried on jointly by these groups. They likewise cooperated in sponsoring the first Asia Mennonite Conference at Dhamtari in 1971, and later in refugee and relief aid to Bangladesh.

Because of the devoted work of missionaries and national leaders, and because of the strong educational program, responsibility for the gospel ministry has been assumed fully by the churches in India. Today we can truly speak of these churches as independent in every way. Mennonite missions in India continue, but as the joint work of foreign and national missionaries. Occasional governmental pressure upon foreigners in the 1970s made their continuing stay tenuous, but this was not much different from other times and places of mission.

The 1960s and 1970s brought significant changes in the areas of the Mennonite churches in Madhya Pradesh. Dhamtari, the first station of Mennonite Church activity, was suddenly near a center of steel production because of the presence of iron ore. Korba, the location of one of the first General Conference stations, became an electric power center because of large deposits of high-quality coal in the area. It attracted a large fertilizer plant and a technical institute. Suddenly a quiet rural area became an industrial center. This created new opportunities, as well as new problems for the church.

A large number of technicians and workers from all over India came to Korba. They spoke different languages. Among them were Christians from various denominations. The language used in the Mennonite church is Hindi which many of the newcomers did not know. How was the church to minister to these people? These new situations demanded the development of new methods. In 1958 a "church-in-the-house" program was begun partly to deal with the language barrier, partly to overcome transportation difficulties. Soon numerous house churches employing different languages were meeting regularly for worship and study. Each one had a leader but members participated freely. Because of the high literacy rate of the newcomers, the Dhamtari and Korba churches have established reading rooms and bookstores to provide Christian literature. Graduates of the seminary are in charge of this work, seeking to meet the educated on their own level.

The Christian church in India is not keeping up with the population growth numerically (685 million in 1981) but its witness is creative and effective: evangelism, relief ministry to the poor,

A group of Mennonite young people meet for **an evening of music**. The educational program of the church in India includes secondary schools, reading rooms, adult literacy projects, and Bible correspondence courses. **Teacher Kehso Rao** checks on the work of one of his high school students.

schools including a seminary and Bible schools, a Bible correspondence school with offices in Calcutta, radio broadcasts even in Sri Lanka and Manila, clinics and hospitals which also practice preventive medicine and train nurses and midwives, youth work and voluntary service programs, prayer fellowships and many other forms of witness. The burden of supporting all of these institutions weighs heavily upon the mostly poor churches of India. P. J. Malagar, a leader in the Mennonite Church has written:

> Our opportunities are great in this day and age. For a numerically small church, the area is too big; the opportunities are too many for planting churches and gathering in the harvest. "Laborers are few." Our stewardship of the gospel and means are inadequate.

> But our hopes and challenges for the future are thrilling and exciting. By the grace of God the roots of the church are firmly set. We are true both to the gospel and to our Anabaptist-Mennonite heritage in this land.[11]

Nepal. Mennonites have been in Nepal since 1954, working in cooperation with the United Mission to Nepal, an interdenominational agency, in clinics and other health services, in education, and agricultural and technical development projects. These are being carried on jointly by the Mennonite Board of Missions, the Mennonite Brethren, working with the TEAM mission, and MCC. By 1987 some 400 missionaries from over 20 countries were at work there. Christians were estimated to number 20,000, but there has also been suffering and persecution.

Other areas. There continues to be a Mennonite presence in other areas of Asia—in Bangladesh through the work of MCC, in Hong Kong through mission agencies, and in South Korea and Laos through MCC. The *Conference of Mennonite Churches in Hong Kong* listed a membership of 59 in 1990. We have seen that Asian Mennonite Christians, numbering at least 170,205 members in 1990, are reaching out in constantly new forms of witness and service in partnership with each other and other Mennonites. In 1974 Asia Mennonite Services was established to coordinate and pioneer in ministry to the needy in word and deed. Takashi Yamada, a Japanese Mennonite leader, has said: "The world of Asians is still largely an unsecularized one, and the people keep a sense of respect for the holy." This respect for the holy is generally rooted in one of the ancient Asian religions, which are experiencing new vitality. The opportunities for Christians in Asia to share and live their faith continue to be enormous on every hand.

Endnotes

1. MWC *Handbook* 1990, pp. 323, 326-327.
2. C. J. Dyck ed., *The Lordship of Christ.* Scottdale, Pa.: Herald Press, 1962, p. 273.
3. Jim Bowman in *The Mennonite Reporter.* Waterloo, Ont.: vol. 9, no. 2, January 22, 1979.
4. From the *Almanac of the Communion Churches of Indonesia (1989).*
5. Hiroshi Yanada in Kraybill, *Mennonite World Handbook* (1978), p. 169. ME 5, p. 464.
6. James Liu and Stephen Wang, *Christians True in China.* Robert Kreider, ed. Newton, Kan.: Faith and Life Press, 1988.
7. Foppe Brouwer, "Australia" in Kraybill, *Mennonite World Handbook* (1978), pp. 43-44. See also the article by La Verna Klippenstein, "A Church Is Being Born in Australia," *The Mennonite*, 94:06, 6 February, 1979, pp. 84-85. ME 5, p. 44.
8. ME 4:693-694; ME 5:878.
9. P. B. Arnold in Kraybill, *Handbook* (1978), p. 140. ME 5:422-427.
10. *MWC Handbook*, (1990), pp. 346-349.
11. Cited in ibid., p. 144.

Other Resources: For each area see ME 5, including the bibliography. Kraybill, *MWC Handbook* 1978 and 1984; MWC *Handbook*, 1990.

Contact any MCC or conference office for audiovisual resources.

19

Mennonite Churches in Africa

FROM ASIA we move across the Indian Ocean to the continent of Africa. Christianity is old in Africa, having existed there in some form since apostolic times. Four of the greatest church leaders after the apostles, Tertullian, Origen, Cyprian, and Augustine, were all North Africans. Much of our theology today is indebted to their work. However, Christianity was limited to the area bordering the Mediterranean and Red seas and did not penetrate into the interior of the continent until David Livingstone took it there between 1850 and 1870. Since then, it has been as busy a place for Christian witness as any in the world.

Africa, too, has a rich cultural history. The great civilization of ancient Egypt is well known to most people, but beyond that Africa was often called the "Dark Continent" by whites who saw black as bad and knew little about African history. Artifacts from Ethiopia and the Sudan indicate an early and dynamic culture. Tirhakah, the king of Ethiopia (2 Kings 19:9), called himself "the Emperor of the world." North Africa, the Nile Valley, and West Africa all developed together before climatic changes displaced fertile land with the Sahara Desert.

West Africa became particularly noted for its culture, centering in the kingdom of Ghana, Mali, and Songhay in the areas of the Senegal and Niger rivers. By A.D. 800 Ghana was a powerful trading state, succeeded eventually by Mali. Under King Mansa Musa (d. 1332) the Egyptian scholar As-Saheli became the master architect for the city of Timbuktu which by late fifteenth century had a population of about 100,000, a banking and credit (card?) system, poetry and chess clubs, and a good medical school at Sankore University, which reportedly even performed cornea transplants. Islam, luxury, and European penetration led to the disintegration of the Songhay dynasty, which was overthrown by the Sultan of Morocco, who had guns, in 1585. Gradually Africa came under European domination, beginning with King John II of Portugal, who settled the Gold Coast region in 1482. In most areas of Africa colonialism only began to disappear in mid-twentieth century.

The Republic of Zaire. The Mennonite church began in what was then known as the Belgian Congo in 1911 when a missionary couple was sent to find a suitable site for a mission location. The area chosen is located west of the Kasai River, a large tributary of the Congo, and about 400 kilometers southeast of Kinshasa. It was chosen, in part, because of the influence of Alma Doering, who was not a Mennonite, but who had spent a mission term in the Congo and who played a major role in bringing Mennonites to this undertaking.[1] Mennonites had been in the Congo since 1890. In the year 1912, the Congo Inland Mission (since 1972 the Africa Inter-Mennonite Mission, AIMM), was organized as the joint enterprise of the Defenseless Mennonite Conference (now the Evangelical Mennonite Church) and the Central Illinois Mennonite Conference (now part of the General Conference).

Initial progress was slow, with only twelve converts by 1916, but soon membership increases exceeded all expectations. By 1990 membership stood at about 66,000 with a total community double that number. In the course of time other Mennonite groups became involved in the work, either through the sending of workers or through membership in AIMM, including the Mennonite Church, the Evangelical Mennonite Conference, and others. This has been one of the best examples of inter-Mennonite cooperation, including a fruitful relationship with MCC. Since 1943 independent work has been carried on by the Mennonite Brethren Church to the west of AIMM related congregations. Their membership was 46,906.[2] The total membership in Zaire in 1990 thus was about 113,000.

The twentieth century saw many denominational missions in

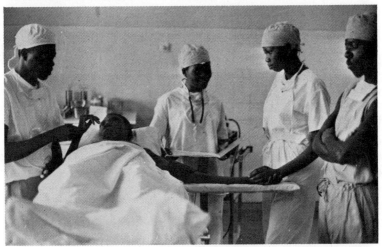

Mennonite mission work in Zaire started in 1911. By 1990, with a combined membership of 113,000 the Zairian Mennonites form the largest groups in any country outside North America. A Mennonite village parsonage serves as the backdrop for this pose of **Zairian sisters and their children**. At the medical center in Tshikaji **student nurses** learn operating room procedures.

Zaire, including particularly Roman Catholicism. In 1921 a renewal movement began under the leadership of Simon Kimbangu. Known as *The Church of Jesus Christ by Simon Kimbangu* or *Kimbanguism* it grew rapidly to a membership of three million by the early 1980s, making it in effect *the* non-Catholic national church. It is in every sense an African church, having arisen without the help of a single missionary dollar. Much of its early dynamic has been lost, however, as it settled into a pattern of denominationalism. As a quasi-nonresistant church, potentially the largest in the world, North American Mennonites have had a particular interest in Kimbanguism.

The move to political independence of Zaire in 1960 brought serious problems to all the churches. For some years prior to that time there had been progress among the Mennonites toward an independent, self-supporting, self-governing church. In February of 1960 a meeting took place in Charlesville at which the national Mennonite leaders were invited by the mission to assume full leadership responsibility, with the missionaries remaining as counselors. The invitation was accepted with the knowledge of its importance and awareness of the weight of responsibility involved, and *The Mennonite Community of Zaire* came into existence. (See also ME 5:953-956.)

When the Belgians left, law and order crumbled rapidly, and missionaries were forced to leave also. Responsibility for the church in Zaire had been accepted by the Africans in February. In July it was forced on them in extremely dangerous and uncertain circumstances. But the responsibility was shouldered; the work of the church continued, and when the missionaries returned later in the year they found the church of Christ a living, active reality. This was followed by a determined attempt at a communist take-over; missionaries left and returned a second time.

The missionaries survived the revolution following independence, but many members of the church did not. Their suffering was accentuated by tribal rivalry between the Luluas and the Balubas, both of which had Mennonite members. Eventually the Balubas were forced to flee eastward to their early tribal homeland, including some of the most capable leaders in the church. There they organized a new conference in their ancestral location, *The Mennonite Evangelical Community of Zaire*. Deep gratitude was felt some years later when reconciliation took place between the divided groups, but the conferences remained separate.

The Mennonites had long been known in Zaire for their extensive literature program, including a large printing press at Kinshasa, as well as for their educational, medical, and evangelistic programs. Since 1970 they have cooperated with other Protestants in supporting and staffing a theological school in Kinshasa. Perhaps their most innovative program, however, was the combining of all of these concerns, together with the economic, into the Service for Development of Agriculture (SEDA) in the mid-sixties. Teams of two young men, one from North America and one from Zaire, worked from village to village in teaching agricultural techniques, with significant success. Out of these developed New Life for All weekend seminars conducted in village after village, with the team including an agriculturist, evangelist, public health nurse, bookseller, woman's worker, and a youth folk-singing group.[3] Never had word and deed been combined more effectively.

Before 1960 the Mennonite churches in Zaire were a rapidly growing fellowship, working with the missionaries but also heavily dependent on them. During the revolution they truly became the suffering church, but then also the victorious church with faith and optimism. They have become fully autonomous, working in close partnership with the missionaries who continued to serve in Zaire. Meanwhile AIMM also sent workers into Lesotho, Botswana, and Burkina Faso.

Eastern Africa. Mennonite churches have also emerged in eastern Africa: in Tanzania, 1934; Ethiopia, 1948; Somalia, 1953; and Kenya in 1965. Events have moved fast, for in only thirty years the church in *Tanzania* is a free, self-governing sister church of other Mennonite churches throughout the world. Perhaps this particular Mennonite church stands out as one that has grown rapidly through the impetus of a revival which began in those regions in 1942. Through confession of sin and the resulting establishment of mutual trust, confidence, and love, the maturity and strength of the church was greatly increased. Its transnational and transcultural concern could put to shame many churches of the traditionally Christian West. The rapid growth of this church has brought with it the need for a sufficient number of qualified teachers. Yet this has not kept the church from healthy growth to 13,078 members in 1990.

The Mennonite church in *Ethiopia* faces a different situation altogether. The Ethiopian Orthodox Church, which is a daughter church of the Coptic Church of Egypt, has existed there in unbro-

The **Bukiroba Mennonite Church**, Musoma, Tanzania, is considered the center of the 13,000-member Tanzania Mennonite Church. A group of **Tanzanian church leaders' wives** exchange ideas after a church fellowship meal.

ken succession since the fourth century. This gives it a Christian background which no other country in Africa, except Egypt, can claim. In 1948 Emperor Haile Selassie made a special concession to the Mennonites to begin missionary work because he had been impressed with the work of MCC, but on condition that they not interfere with the Orthodox Church. By 1950 Eastern Board representatives had begun to operate a number of schools and clinics. The *Meserete Kristos Church* was founded in 1959 and early distinguished itself with the maturity of relationships to the missionaries, working autonomously yet cooperatively. The church was not granted formal government recognition.

In 1974 a revolution replaced the traditional monarchy with a socialist government. Together with the continuing civil war against the Eritrean guerrillas in the north, this became a time of troubles for the nation and the church, including the Mennonite Church though few of its members advocate nonresistance. Since the new regime assumed responsibility for education and welfare, most of the Mennonite institutions ceased to be the responsibility of the church.

At the same time an awakening spread among its ranks. Members began giving time and funds in totally new proportions with the result that membership increased rapidly to about 10,000 by 1990. Since membership had been around 500 when the missionaries left, "more than 4,500 come from other evangelical groups having been attracted through the efforts of our own evangelists." Many of these evangelists are young people. Freedom of religion returned with the overthrow of Marxism in 1991. A new and vigorous chapter began in the church.

Somalia. Somalia is a Muslim country. It is also one of the poorest and driest countries in the world. Missions to Muslims have usually been difficult because of the nature of Islam and its hostility to Christianity. A border war with its long-standing enemy, Ethiopia, and inter-tribal strife has left the country devastated in 1992.

In 1950 two Mennonite Church missionaries from Tanzania entered Somalia, then under Italian-UN trusteeship, to investigate the possibility of establishing a Christian witness. They recommended to the Mennonite Board of Missions that work be started. The recommendation was accepted and the Mennonite Church became the first Protestant body to establish work in that land. Two groups had begun earlier but had withdrawn. Work began in 1953

The twenty-year-old Meserete Kristos Church grew eightfold after the missionaries were forced to leave Ethiopia in 1974. To accommodate all the worshipers, several services are conducted each Sunday in **the meetinghouse at Addis Ababa**, capital of Ethiopia.

and slowly expanded into six stations, including, primarily, educational and medical services.

The warnings of the dangers involved became tragically real in 1962, when a fanatical Muslim attacked missionaries Merlin and Dorothy Grove, killing the former and seriously wounding the latter.[4] Despite this setback and a government curb on evangelism, work continued and a handful of committed believers began meeting regularly and unobtrusively for fellowship and prayer. The educational opportunities provided by the schools were appreciated by many students. Nevertheless, all missionaries were ordered to leave in 1976. Some contact with the believers, of which there may be as many as 100, continues through congregations in Kenya and other channels, though the civil war of the early 1990s has devastated the country.

Kenya. The *Tanzania Mennonite Church* is the parent body of the congregations in Kenya. Its origin seems to have been with the Luo people of Kenya who settled in Tanzania in the 1930s and were won to the faith, but returned to Kenya again in the 1960s. Congregations including 4,900 members in 1990 are located in South and Central Nyanza, along the Tanzania-Kenya route, as well as in

Nairobi.[5] Some of the workers formerly in Somalia have given particular attention to work with Muslims. Nairobi has also served as an administrative center for East African Mennonite missions.

The first congregation was organized in 1963 and a national conference in 1977. In 1990 there were over 70 regular places of worship and some believed that the church would continue to grow at the rate of 20 percent annually. Methods of witness centered primarily around personal evangelism and small-group Bible studies rather than an institutional approach through schools and hospitals. The need for Bible training schools was being met through leadership and district Bible training classes.[6]

Ghana and Nigeria. The Mennonite church in Ghana was in existence before American missionaries came there. It began through the work of a Mennonite layman, T. George Thompson, whose home was in Ghana, and who gathered a Christian fellowship in his home. In 1957 the first congregation was founded and a conference formed in 1964. Opportunities for mission work were plentiful, and within three years forty-five missionaries were working in the Accra area. Emphasis was placed on medical and educational work, but since the government was taking over these areas the emphasis of the work changed in the direction of thorough training of persons for local leadership.

The *Ghana Mennonite Church,* which had a membership of 1,200 in seventeen congregations in 1990, seemed unique in its teaching emphasis. The Ramseyer Training Center prepares teachers and catechists, in-service training is practiced regularly for church workers, the New Life for All program has itinerated through congregations, a Home Bible Studies (HBS) program is carried on, and students are encouraged to attend both Ghana Christian College and the theological Trinity College. Several leaders have also studied in North America. Close ecumenical relations are maintained with the Bible Society and the Christian Council of Churches in Ghana. In the late 1970s the Mennonite Church was also involved with a number of churches in union negotiations through the Ghana Christian Union Committee.

In addition to these activities MEDA has helped fund farmers, traders, and other small businesses. A bookstore ministry is maintained. Every other year fraternal delegates are sent to visit sister churches in Nigeria.

In 1958 a call for help came to the Mennonite Church in Ghana from *Nigeria.* A considerable number of Christian congregations

The Ghana Mennonite Church represents a partnership with the Mennonite Board of Missions, and maintains a close relationship with the Mennonites of Nigeria, their closest neighbors. **Teacher Erma Grove** at work in Ghana. In 1958 some fifty native churches around Uyo, Nigeria, declared themselves to be "Mennonite" before any Mennonite mission worker ever set foot in the country. These **three Nigerian church leaders** are among those who serve congregations which remain in the fellowship.

in Calibar Province asked for leadership and for medical and educational help. Church members from Ghana responded to the call, investigated, and proposed that help be sent. The story of this help is eloquently told by Irene and Ed Weaver in *The Uyo Story*. As they neared Uyo, which was to be the center of their work, they saw a roadside sign which read *Mennonite Church, Nigeria, Inc.* What a story! Some forty to fifty congregations of Christians already awaiting the first missionary! What a change from the early days of missionary work in Nigeria!

But if a church was already there, the first missionaries wondered if it was a blessing or a burden. These were congregations that had broken away from the older Presbyterian and Methodist churches for various reasons. They were in the care of leaders who were poorly trained; their religion was a mixture of Christian faith and animism. And yet they wanted to be Christians; they wanted Bible schools so that they could know more about what it means to be a Christian.

On the other hand, the older missions did not welcome the Mennonite intention of starting work there. It would merely increase Christian fragmentation further, they said. Other denominations had come and gone; these churches had been known by various names. Now they would be called Mennonite for a while and a few years later something else. What these churches needed to do was to repent and return to the established churches. A lot of heart-searching, conversation with older missionaries, praying, and agonizing took place. The people clearly needed help, but there was the bitterness of long division. They also seemed to be more eager for the benefits of Western civilization than being disciples of Christ. And yet there was that longing for schools so that they might know.

It was finally decided that the Mennonites would stay and begin work in this complicated situation. A real ministry of reconciliation began to unfold between these believers and the older missions. Medical work was begun in cooperation with the Presbyterians and leadership training began immediately. By 1990 the Nigeria Mennonite Church counted 6,634 members in 57 congregations. A new seminary had begun the task of leadership training. Mennonite Board of Missions workers served as needed and requested by the Nigerian Church and under their direction.[7]

The Church of God in Christ, Mennonite also began mission work in Nigeria in 1963. Literature distribution has been emphasized particularly, together with an attempt to direct all teaching and training of new Christians in such a manner as to make them ready, in their turn, to work effectively in evangelism. Membership in 1990 was 239.

Zimbabwe and Zambia. The Brethren in Christ Church began mission work in Zimbabwe, then known as Rhodesia, in 1898. Zambia was part of Northern Rhodesia at that time and included in the same field of work. By 1924 the mission had expanded to include three stations, Matopo, Mtshabezi, and Wanezi, and which has remained the general field to the present, except for the Gwaai area in the northwest, where work began in 1954. Particular attention was given to educational institutions and medical work.

From the present perspective the missionary approach has been criticized as having been too institutional and too legalistic in its regulations, but leaders who have themselves arisen in the church under this system defend it as the only way whereby the present healthy state of spiritual life and numerical growth could have been reached. The approach has changed as a mature and autonomous church reaches out to new areas in Salisbury, Victoria Falls, and in the area north of Bulawayo. All foreign missionaries were withdrawn in 1977, but some financial support from North America continues.

The internal political tensions in Zimbabwe made church work extremely difficult during the 1970s. Independence came to Zimbabwe in 1980. Nevertheless, evangelism continued, supported by the Bible Institute and a Theological Education by Extension (TEE) program which is a traveling Bible school moving through the districts. The departure of missionary personnel, while prepared for and anticipated, accented the need for leadership training at all levels of church work, including Sunday schools, youth activities, and counseling. Since the school programs have continued there is also constant need for Christian teachers in science, math, history, and all subjects. Though Zambia has enjoyed political stability these same needs are also underscored there. During the 1960s and 1970s MCC was of significant aid in meeting this need through its Teachers Abroad Program (TAP), and during the 1980s through help in agricultural development.

In 1990 church membership of Zimbabwe was listed at 12,039, and 6,632 members in Zambia. While there are no Mennonite missionaries in either of these nations, expatriates are made available as resource persons under the direction of the Brethren in Christ

Church in Zambia. A report from Zambia summarizes many of the concerns in this crucial area of Africa, concerns not too different even from those in North America, when it states:

> Economic prosperity, promotion, materialism, tribal and ideological clashes, culture, tradition, modernism and industrialization, poverty, corruption and injustice, liberation, freedoms, education and international travel, and self-reliance all bear heavily upon the lives and emotions of our people.[8]

Yet the church was continuing actively in the midst of these pressures. New congregations were being founded, a witness was given through Trans World Radio in Swaziland, the Ekuphileni Bible Institute was playing an increasing role in preparing leaders, patience was being exercised in the face of crucial political issues. Clearly the Spirit of God was at work. (See also ME V:957-960.)

The African Independent Churches (AICs). Perhaps the most powerful Christian movement in Africa since the 1960s was not related to any denomination or any unique new strategy for mission strategy. They were the AICs which were rising across the land by the hundreds, even thousands. Sometimes they were schisms from established congregations, sometimes described best by the woman who said, "I go to worship in the big church on the corner over there. But when I have sickness I go to a spiritual church; they know how to pray."[9] Sometimes they arise where there is no church at all, but where a prophet arises to prophesy and heal and pray. In some ways it is more correct to refer to them as *spiritual churches* rather than as independent churches, but the latter term stresses their autonomy and uniquely African nature.

For a time missions from the West, and churches established by them, saw the AICs as a threat because of their strong appeal to the people, their uncontrollable dynamics and power in the lives of people, their seeming lack of concern about "right" theology, the selfish objectives of some of the prophets, and other reasons. Most have come to see, however, that many of the AICs are profoundly Christian in their reliance upon the Holy Spirit, in the simplicity of their faith, in their commitment to Christ, and in their daily living. One of the groups, which is well known because it has been so thoroughly analyzed by sociologists, anthropologists, and theologians of the West, is the *Church of the Lord (Aladura)*, but there are hundreds, likely thousands of others. Over 6,000 new religious movements have been documented in Africa, but not nearly all of them are AICs.

At the center of an AIC stands the prophet, called only by God. Some may be imposters, but they soon lose their following because they lack spiritual power to have visions, to heal, to "bring God close." One of the well-known prophets of Ghana, F. A. Mills, who has also traveled in North America, once told his story as follows:

> In the year 1965, on September 14, I went to Mount Gemi at Amedzofe for fasting and prayer. I arrived at 4:30 in the afternoon and went first to greet the chief. That evening I started my fasting of seven days without food or water. I stayed at the foot of the cross day and night, through sunshine and rain, fasting and praying. In the presence of God, one is not conscious of cold or wet or hunger.

> On the third day a woman brought her mad child and by the grace of God he was healed. This wonder brought the whole village trooping up the mountain for healing and messages. To my surprise other surrounding villages were informed and they also came up to the mountain to test the power of God.

> I wish you had been there to see things for yourself. They brought the blind and crippled children and in the name of the Lord Jesus they were healed. The chief of the village also came with some problems and those were solved.

> I left there on the eighth day and returned to Accra with joy and happiness. May the name of God be praised.[10]

Mennonites are relating to the AICs as Bible teachers—when and where they are asked. There is a great longing for more biblical knowledge, and many more teachers are needed, though some prophets have been known to leave Bible study groups because they felt study diluted their spiritual power. Some AICs have been drawn close to Mennonites, but it has not been the intention of Mennonite Bible teachers to make Mennonite churches out of the AICs. Instead of establishing institutions of learning the itinerant Bible teacher is free to meet a given need when and where it arises. He or she is available as the Spirit leads. Hundreds of lay teachers have been and are being trained, particularly in West Africa but also across the length and breadth of the continent. Western Bible teachers invariably report that they learn at least as much as they are able to teach about the faith and power of God.

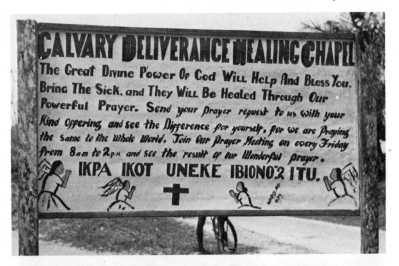

Some of the **African Independent Churches** (AICs) are closely associated with the Mennonites although they have not officially become part of the denomination. Mennonite Bible teachers serve the movement when and where they are asked. A **special prayer session** is held in behalf of a witch doctor who accepted Christianity and destroyed his juju.

There are other significant Mennonite involvements in Africa, from MCC volunteers in nearly every country in Africa at some time since the 1960s to the July 1979 meeting of over 6,000 Christians of all persuasions in Pretoria, at the South Africa Christian Leadership Assembly (SACLA), where two Mennonites and a Brethren in Christ person addressed the meetings. One person continued a witness in *Algeria* begun by the Mennonite Board of Missions in 1956. The same board began new work in the *Ivory Coast* in 1978. The Eastern Board and MCC have together been involved in both *Swaziland* and the *Sudan* in relief and witness ministries since 1978, and MCC continues to be involved in *Lesotho* and the *Transkei*. AIMM and MCC continue involvement in *Botswana, Lesotho,* and *Burkina Faso.* The French Mennonites are working in *Chad* together with the Sudan United Mission. And we might add *Morocco* and *Burundi* for MCC work as well as *Uganda* and other areas in a constantly changing, dynamic attempt to show compassion, to break down the barriers of racial prejudice, of economic injustice "to preach good news to the poor . . . to set at liberty those who are oppressed" (Luke 4:18).

All of these developments and concerns were already anticipated and, in a sense, climaxed long ago at Limuru, Kenya, in 1962 when representatives from all Mennonite and Brethren in Christ groups in Africa met together for the first time. While the conference had been convened primarily to discuss the peace testimony Mennonites could give in volatile Africa, it soon became apparent that the representatives had many other problems they wished to share with each other. A second conference was therefore convened at Bulawayo, Rhodesia, in 1965, under African leadership, to provide opportunity for discussion on some of the critical issues facing the church in Africa. The following five problems emerged as common to all nations and groups present at the conference:

1. There is a growing awareness of the fact that Christianity must speak to all of life and must be relevant to everyday needs and problems.

2. The church is stretched far beyond its means and so has great difficulty expanding. It takes the full tithe of many, many members to support one highly trained pastor. Yet there is a reluctance to ask Western churches for large subsidies, and Western churches are honestly asking whether this is the way.

3. There is growing unrest on the part of the masses because, even after independence, they see their conditions as wretched as compared to industrialized nations, and things are not improving. They wonder why. Can the rich Christian brother turn his back on the poor ones, even though separated by an ocean?

4. Since independence the new nations find themselves in the East-West struggle. This arises out of their need for foreign capital. Also some non-African nations are still in Africa, speaking from a lofty position of power, and showing that power when necessary.

5. The problem of race relations is far from settled in Africa, and the rest of the world, for that matter. Africa is disturbed by what she sees in the world. How long are her children destined to be second-class citizens, at home and abroad?[11]

It was a *landmark* conference. Most of the issues are still real, except that the East-West struggle (item 4) might now be identified as a North-South economic struggle. The conference decided also to continue to meet in the future and organized the African Mennonite and Brethren in Christ Fellowship (AMBCF) to aid in coordinating interchurch activities and to serve the churches when unified action is required.

It has become clear from our discussion of Latin America, Asia, and now Africa, that the fellowship of Mennonite and Brethren in Christ churches circles the globe. Its members belong to many nations and races. In Asia and Africa alone there are 147,600 and 176,500 church members respectively, for a total of 324,100 mostly *nonwhite* members in the Mennonite family, in a total Christian community of 586,495 persons in 1990, not counting an undetermined number in North and South America.[12]

This has had its effect on the church. Today it is no longer a matter of home churches—European and North American—and foreign missions. The fact is that Mennonites throughout the world are working at witnessing as partners, sharing the resources, and bringing to the one task the special gifts given to each by Christ, the Head of the church. The question of whether affluent North American and European Christians could still be heard by the millions of poor around the world became increasingly acute. While workers were continuing to go to Africa and Asia and Latin America, it has become clear that North America and Europe too need to hear the good news in a new, prophetic way from believers in the so-called third world.

Endnotes

1. James C. Juhnke, *A People of Mission*. Newton, Kan.: Faith and Life Press, 1979, pp. 67f.

2. *MWC Handbook* 1990, pp. 342-343.

3. Ibid, pp. 180-182.

4. Omar Eby, *A Whisper in a Dry Land*. Scottdale, Pa.: Herald Press, 1968.

5. *MWC Handbook* 1990, p. 337.

6. ME 5:476-479; 488-489. Mahlon M. Hess, *The Pilgrimage of Faith of Tanzania Mennonite Church*. Salunga, Pa.: EMBMC, 1985.

7. Edwin and Irene Weaver, *From Kuku Hill Among Indigenous Churches in West Africa*. Elkhart, Ind.: Institute of Mennonite Studies, 1975.

8. Helen Amolo and Meshack Osiro, in *Mennonite World Handbook*, 1978, pp. 85-90.

9. Weaver, op. cit., p. 121.

10. Ibid., pp. 53-54.

11. *Messages and Reports, Africa Mennonite Fellowship*. Bulawayo, March 3-10, 1965, pp. i, ii.

12. *MWC Handbook* 1990, p. 328.

Other Resources: ME 5 articles, cross-references and bibliographies. *MWC Handbook* 1978, 1984 and 1990. Samuel Escobar and John Driver, *Christian Mission and Social Justice*, Scottdale, Pa.: Herald Press, 1978. James C. Juhnke, *A People of Mission*, Newton, Kan.: Faith and Life Press, 1979. Theron F. Schlabach, *Gospel Versus Gospel*: Mission and the Mennonite Church, 1863-1944, Scottdale, Pa.: Herald Press, 1980. Wilbert R. Shenk, Editor, *Mission Focus: Current Issues*, Scottdale, Pa.: Herald Press, 1980. Idem, ed., *Exploring Church Growth*, Grand Rapids, Mich.: Wm. B. Eerdmans, 1983. Contact any MCC or conference-related mission office for audiovisual resources.

AFRICA

ATLANTIC
OCEAN

MEDITERRANEAN SEA

N

MOROCCO

TUNISIA

WESTERN
SAHARA
(Morocco)

ALGERIA
□

LIBYA

EGYPT
★

MAURITANIA

MALI

NIGER

A   F   R   I   C   A

SENEGAL

DJIBOUTI

GAMBIA

GUINEA-BISSAU

GUINEA

BURKINA
FASO

CHAD
★

SUDAN
★

SIERRA LEONE

LIBERIA

IVORY
COAST
□

GHANA

BENIN

NIGERIA
■□□□★

CAMEROON

CENTRAL
AFRICAN REPUBLIC

ETHIOPIA
■★

SOMALIA ■★

TOGO

EQUATORIAL GUINEA
SAOTOME & PRINCIPE

GABON

CONGO

ZAIRE
■■■□★

UGANDA

KENYA
■★

INDIAN
OCEAN

Kilometers   0   500   1000   1500

RWANDA
BURUNDI

TANZANIA
■■★

SEYCHELLES

ANGOLA
■

ZAMBIA
■★

MALAWI

ZIMBABWE

MOZAMBIQUE □★

COMOROS

MADAGASCAR

NAMIBIA
(S. Africa)

BOTSWANA
□★

VENDA

SWAZILAND □★

BOPHUTHATSWANA

SOUTH
AFRICA

LESOTHO □★

TRANSKEI □★

CISKEI

LEGEND
MENNONITE CHURCHES IN AFRICA
■ Organized bodies
★ Countries with MCC involvement
□ Other programs and missions (not incl. missions relating
   to organized bodies)
● 500 members (approx. locations)

TABLE

Organized Bodies	Membership (1986 unless noted)
ANGOLA	
Igreja Evangélica dos Irmãos Menonitas em Angola (Ev. Menn. Br. Ch. of Ang.)	1250 (1987)
BURKINA FASO	
La Mission et l'Eglise Mennonite en Burkina Faso (Menn. Miss. and Ch. in Burkina Faso)	34
ETHIOPIA	
Mennonites in Ethiopia	700
GHANA	
Ghana Mennonite Church	854
KENYA	
Kenya Mennonite Church	2700
NIGERIA	
Mennonite Church	5000
SOMALIA	
Somalia Mennonite Believers Fellowship	ca. 100
TANZANIA	
Kanisa la Mennonite Tanzania (Tanzania Menn. Ch.)—North Mara Diocese	4183
South Mara Diocese	10258
ZAIRE	
Communauté des Eglises de Frères Mennonites au Zaïre (Menn. Br. Community of Zaire)	35000 + (1987)
Communauté Evangélique Mennonite (Menn. Evan. Community)	7583
Communauté Mennonite au Zaïre (Menn. Community of Zaire)	ca. 50000
ZAMBIA	
Mbungano Yabunyina Muli Kristo (Br. in Christ Ch.)	6000
ZIMBABWE	
Ibandla Labazalwane e-Zimbabwe (Br. in Christ Ch. in Zimbabwe)	7718

Other missions and programs (not incl.
missions relating to organized bodies):
ALGERIA: MBM
BOTSWANA: AIMM
CHAD: EMEK
IVORY COAST: MBM
LESOTHO: AIMM
MOZAMBIQUE: EMBMC
NIGERIA: Ch. of God in Christ,
   Menn.; Fell. Churches
ZAIRE: MBM

Notes
No country except S. Africa has recognized the independence of
the "homelands" of Bophuthatswana, Ciskei, Transkei, and
Venda.

20

Mennonites in Europe Since 1815

When the Thirty Years' War ended with the Treaty of Westphalia in 1648, the age of nationalism in politics and denominationalism in religion had arrived in Europe. The meaning of these new forces for the states and churches became clearer by the nineteenth century, particularly also through the French Revolution, which was both a sign and a product of the new age.

The French Revolution (1789-99) was initially a struggle between the French people on the one hand and the king with his nobles on the other. The ideals of the Revolution had strong appeal to the masses and were embodied in the slogan *Liberty, Equality, Fraternity*. They seemed to agree with Christian teaching, but in the French context came more from social and political reformers who based their theory on natural law which said that since people are born equal, no one has the right to make them unequal or enslave them.

When these ideals were combined with Napoleon's military and political plans, they brought both hope and new problems for the Mennonites. Persecution by death or imprisonment had ended, but the Mennonites were still second-class citizens whose privileges were restricted beyond those of others in most of Europe. Because of this they had withdrawn to isolated rural areas, where they remained unmolested as "the quiet in the land."

The ideal of equality brought full citizenship to most people, but the granting of equal rights also meant accepting equal responsibilities, and among the latter military service was a primary duty. Mennonites had always faced this requirement in some form, and had tried to meet it—sometimes by working out special exemptions, sometimes by cash payments, sometimes by hiring substitutes, sometimes by emigration, sometimes by dying for their faith. By the time Napoleon introduced universal military service, however, the first three options were becoming almost impossible to obtain. Some forms of alternative service were available in several countries, but they were related to the military and therefore usually unacceptable to the Mennonites. As defined in the nineteenth century, equality did not include freedom of conscience when it conflicted with the demands of the majority, and liberty was more national than personal.

In 1803, and again in 1805, the South German Mennonites decided, after much prayer and fasting, to ask Napoleon for some acceptable form of alternative service. Pastor Möllinger of the Ruchheim congregation was sent to begin negotiations with him to that end but was unable to even get to see him. The French Mennonites made five appeals to secure acceptable alternatives, in 1809, 1811, 1812, 1814, and 1829, but without any success. A regulation made in 1793 would actually have given them relief, but it was not observed by the authorities. Some Mennonites were still able to hire substitutes, but conscription left few available men at large, and the cost of paying a substitute soon became a heavy burden also. Some Mennonites doubted the virtue of the practice as well.

A course still open to many was the fourth option listed above—emigration, but many had come to love their home and found it difficult to leave. We have seen from chapters 10 and 11, however, that large numbers chose the fourth option. Only one group left from the Netherlands; in 1854, most of the members of the Balk, Friesland, congregation, consisting of fifty-two persons, settled near New Paris, Indiana, not far from Goshen. The large Amish migration and the Swiss migration described in chapter 11 were motivated primarily by these military pressures. The migrations of large numbers of Mennonites from Prussia after 1789 and from Russia after 1870 were also caused in large measure by this problem, though other social and economic factors were involved as well.

There were other Mennonite beliefs, in addition to nonresistance, which came to be seen differently by others because of the ideals of the French Revolution. Equality tended to mean uniformity; why should Mennonites be different from others and refuse to swear an oath, or believe in the lay ministry? On the other hand, however, the lay ministry appealed to those who had imbibed something of the Revolution's anticlericalism, and to many equality also meant trusting each other—so why swear an oath at all? Most countries were still willing to make exceptions to the swearing of the oath, Switzerland by substituting a handclasp for it, France by requiring only the simple statement that one would tell the truth.

Migration siphoned off those who held most strictly to traditional Mennonite beliefs. The constant demands for conscription and for conformity in other ways nibbled away at the identity of many until few Mennonites living in Western Europe in late nineteenth century were willing to make an issue of military service any longer. In Switzerland noncombatant service became the rule for Mennonites, which had been provided in the constitution of 1848, and which Mennonites felt to be a recognition of their principles. The fact that Switzerland did not take part in either World War I or II helped support the idea that military service does not involve them in any real conflict.

In Germany and the Netherlands, where Mennonites were more fully accepted in industry, politics, and culture, more young men have willingly accepted military service as a duty. In 1848, a Mennonite deputy from Krefeld opposed in Parliament a request for special exemption from military service for the Mennonites, when it was introduced by a non-Mennonite from Danzig. The congregation at Emden had among its members Isaac Brons, president of the East Friesland Navy League in 1861, a major general in the army, and an admiral in the navy during World War I. By 1914 nonresistance was largely a historical memory for the Mennonite churches in Western Europe.

The Netherlands

The Dutch Mennonites had suffered a steady drop in membership during the eighteenth century. From an approximate high of 160,000 members in 1700, they dropped to less than 27,000 by 1808, on average closing one congregation annually. The Haarlem congregation, for example, had about 3,000 members in 1708, but only 488 in 1834. Even in rural Friesland membership dropped from 20,000 in 1666 to 13,000 in 1796. It was not until after 1830 that the decline was stopped. Beginning in 1855, but especially after 1880, the direction changed to where they again increased to 39,000 by 1960 but declined to 18,000 members in 1990.[1]

Much of this loss must be attributed to the impact of the Enlightenment on all of Europe, including the Mennonites. The Enlightenment was an eighteenth-century movement characterized by love for the scientific method and a consequent questioning of anything which seemed irrational, including the authority of the Bible, the church, and tradition. The movement was strongest among the educated classes, and this included the Mennonite seminary in Amsterdam which had been established in 1735. Soon a reaction against traditional Anabaptist-Mennonite ideas and practices as old-fashioned set in among the congregations. Particularly noticeable among the Mennonites was also the individualism which the Enlightenment brought; people were free to do their own believing, to write their own confession of faith, and to interpret the Bible for themselves and by themselves.

There were, nevertheless, those among the Mennonites who were not swept away by the flood of Enlightenment thought, though they could not stop its eroding effects in the church. A leader among these was Samuel Muller (d. 1875), a professor at the Mennonite Seminary and an able preacher. D. S. Gorter, another minister, wrote in 1856: "I do not want to be either liberal or orthodox . . . but only biblical." A movement called the *Reveil* found support among some intellectuals concerned for more traditional values. Unfortunately the so-called orthodox were at odds among themselves over the kind of orthodoxy they felt ought to prevail. Some of these later organized an Association for the Maintenance of God's Word in the Mennonite Congregations. Seeing this confusion, the enlightened rationalists were confirmed in the wisdom they believed they had shown in rejecting the church.

A prophet arose in Jan de Liefde (d. 1869), but his voice went unheard—perhaps because it was too true. He charged that the Mennonites tolerated every heresy except infant baptism. In graphic language he wrote of a fishing boat driven before a storm and in danger of sinking, while some on board saw no danger, and the others could not agree on how to save themselves. He entitled the 110-page pamphlet *Danger, Danger, and No Peace*, with the subtitle "A Word to Those Sleeping and Lulled to Sleep," but it went almost

The historic Singel Mennonite church of 1608 is considered the symbolic center of Dutch Anabaptism. Here the congregation gathers around a half circle of **baptismal candidates.** The long-standing Mennonite concern for the welfare of the elderly and the needy—their own and others—find modern-day expression in the **Menno Simonzhuis** in Amsterdam.

unnoticed. In desperation de Liefde left the Mennonites, and nobody responded to that protest either, but recent scholarship has finally recognized what it was that de Liefde tried to do.[2] There were others like Assuerus Doyer of Zwolle, Taco Kuiper of Amsterdam, and Jan Hartog of Utrecht, who tried to maintain a more authentic Mennonite position.

Interestingly enough, it was the Enlightenment spirit itself which helped to bring unity and recovery to the Mennonites in due time. Some of the increase in membership came from the Reformed Church, whose members were restive under an increasing stress upon confessions as tests of orthodoxy; but it was the tolerance of liberalism which finally brought the Dutch Mennonites together for the first time, ending divisions which had begun in the time of Menno Simons. This new unity marked a turning point in their life, leading to the organization of the ADS (*Algemeene Doopsgezinde Societeit*), a general conference of all congregations, in 1811. The growing unity and the financial needs of the seminary and small congregations were the reasons for its founding. The ADS immediately set about strengthening the training of ministers, giving financial support to small congregations, and in other ways working for the health of the membership.

Although many Dutch Mennonites had no interest in missions because of their liberalism, a small group was interested enough to organize the Mennonite Missionary Association in 1847. Many of these had already been instrumental in founding the Dutch section of the interdenominational London Missionary Society in 1821 and now decided to transfer the assets to the Mennonites and to change the name, since they were almost the only supporters. They soon gained support from other European Mennonites, especially those in Germany and Russia. In 1851 Pieter Jansz was sent to Java to open the first field. The mission soon encountered difficulty because converts found it too difficult to live as Christians in a society run by Muslims. The mission continued, but new methods of approach were used after 1879, as discussed earlier in connection with Indonesia.

The Dutch opened a second field in Sumatra in 1871. It had only moderate success, and when financial difficulties came after World War I, it was turned over to a German mission society in 1928. The General Conference in America contacted the Dutch Mennonite Missionary Association when it first became interested in foreign missions. Some contributions were sent to that work by the General Conference and for a time the first American Mennonite missionary, S. S. Haury, considered going to Java under the Dutch Association.

The Mennonites in Holland have a long history of charity and service. During the nineteenth century they were in the forefront of a number of welfare activities. An Association for the General Welfare (*Maatschappij tot Nut van't Algemeen*), organized by a Mennonite, worked for improvement of the school system, as well as for a system of savings banks. Special efforts were being made to care for the elderly, the sick, and others in need, with some congregations adding social workers to their staff as these became available.

The Dutch story takes a new turn with the coming of World War I, though not directly related to it. During the war three young Mennonite ministers went to a Quaker center in England. The Quakers had experienced a spiritual decline in the nineteenth century and had established the center as a source of renewal among them. Though at least one of the Dutch ministers did not really expect much to happen, they all came back fired with a new vision for awakening in the church. Their work led to the *Gemeentedagbeweging*, a Church Day Movement. On August 2, 1917, a conference in Utrecht launched the effort, with far-reaching results. A series of retreat houses have been built. Conferences, meetings, and vacations together have afforded new fellowship and the opportunity to work in bringing new life to the churches. An active program for youth grew out of a youth day held in 1922, leading also to renewed interest in the peace witness, in missions, in student work, and in other avenues of service and witness.

During the years between World War I (1914-18) and World War II (1939-45), new direction was given to European theology. Older beliefs were reexamined and put in terms understandable to twentieth-century people. The Dutch Mennonites have had leaders who shared in these efforts and agreed with many of them. They have helped to check the movement that led many out of the church. Mission work has become a part of the work of the entire conference since World War II. A relief organization for special needs collects money and goods and supports a variety of projects. A Fellowship for Mennonite Brotherhood Work acts as a clearinghouse for much lay activity sparked by the Church Day Movement. A weekly paper, the *Algemeen Doopsgezind Weekblad*, serves a variety of needs, carrying special inserts from the different groups such as missions and peace work, as well as church news and announcements.

In 1922 the Dutch Mennonites organized a Work Group of Mennonites Against Military Service and reorganized its work after 1945. They hold regular conferences, orientation meetings for prospective conscientious objectors, camps for young people, and service projects. In 1963-64 they built their own camp on the island of Texel. A strong testimony was given against the Vietnam War, against placing American missles in Europe, and against the continuing arms race. The work of the peace group extends far beyond the Mennonites only and is related to the most important peace movements in the Netherlands. Meanwhile a Concern Group for Development Cooperation has been organized to help developing nations and sensitize Western Christians to world need in the areas of economics, justice, and social growth.

A director and regional consultants work with the Central Organization for Mennonite Youth, serving as consultants for church programs, service opportunities of relief and mutual aid, and helping in strengthening a sense of their identity and heritage. One of the strongest groups in the ADS is the Federation of Mennonite Sisters Circles, organized in 1952. This organization not only works with traditional women's programs in congregations, but stimulates many of the developments occurring in other areas of ADS. Women have served as pastors since the first decade of the twentieth century. A *Historische Kring* (Historical Society) was organized in 1975, after a lapse of sixty years, and in 1975 resumed publication of the *Doopsegezinde Bijdragen*, a historical journal which had been published from 1861-1919. The society also undertook sponsorship of a major sixteenth-century sources publication project. The Dutch Mennonites carry a great concern for Christian unity and continue vigorous support of MWC. They are also members of the World Council of Churches.

In the late 1970s an experiment in lay education for ministry was begun as a pilot program and held good promise for the future. During the 1980s it became a regular part of ministerial training. As the largest group of Mennonites continuing in one geographical location in Europe since the sixteenth century, their life and thought and history was being studied with particular interest by other Mennonites, especially in North America, for whatever lessons it might hold for them also. [3]

Germany

The Mennonite churches in Northern Germany had much in common with the Dutch and differed very little from them in their activities and spiritual direction. They maintained close contact with the Dutch congregations and reflected the same influences which had shaped their co-religionists in the Netherlands. In Southern Germany, on the other hand, Mennonites continued to be a rural people with quite different attitudes and values. The nineteenth century brought more toleration for them, but migrations continued because of military conscription and because of economic needs. In addition to the steady flow to North America, some moved to the east along the Danube, settling as far away as Galicia in Poland.

In addition to the long-standing influence of pietism among the southern congregations, the Baptists also began to influence the Mennonites. They appealed to them because of their warm personal religious life and their stress upon the Scriptures. Adult baptism, and the belief that the church is composed only of believers, also agreed with Mennonite views. On the other hand, the Baptists did not stress discipleship in the way Mennonites had been taught, nor did they believe in nonresistance. By mid-nineteenth century congregations in the Palatinate were employing salaried ministers, but in other parts of south Germany many congregations continued to use the lay ministry pattern for a time. By 1990 this pattern was reinforced by the immigrants from Russia, but they mostly formed their own congregations.

During this entire period the *Weierhof* came to be a significant center of south German Mennonite life. Michael Löwenberg (d. 1874) was minister and teacher on this estate, also establishing a training course for ministers. He had a vision for the founding of a secondary school and seminary and became a pioneer in Mennonite education in South Germany. After 1884, Ernst and Gustav Göbel carried on the work with such success that the *Weierhof* became the largest private school in the Palatinate—a boarding school which also accepted non-Mennonite students. From it came many church leaders, and the school itself provided a center for congregational renewal activities.

One of the outstanding leaders who worked from this center was Christian Neff (d. 1946). Neff was ordained at the *Weierhof* in 1887 and soon became known for the depth of his spiritual concern

GERMANY

Prior to unification

Kilometers 0   50   100   200

and his vision for the Mennonites in Germany. In addition to his pastoral and conference duties, he was an earnest and able scholar. It was he who first envisioned the compilation of an encyclopedia about the Mennonites, beginning the *Mennonitisches Lexicon* in 1913.[4] It was Neff also who convened the first meeting of the Mennonite World Conference in Switzerland in 1925.[5] He was active in historical writing and research, in editing journals, hymnbooks, and other literature for the needs of his people, while at the same time teaching in the *Weierhof* school and serving as pastor of the *Weierhof* congregation for nearly fifty-five years.

Under his influence, and together with others of like mind, the German Mennonites also showed signs of renewal, even as the Dutch. In 1924 a relief agency called *Christenpflicht* (Christian duty) was organized by them to help the Mennonites in Russia. A Mennonite historical society was founded, which began publishing a periodical in 1936. A retreat and Bible study center called the *Thomashof* was founded near Karlsruhe in 1920. The *Gemeindeblatt der Mennoniten,* a church paper founded in 1870, continued to serve the congregations, and a youth paper called *Junge Gemeinde* was founded in 1948. Support was given regularly to the German missions committee, and through it to the international Mennonite missions committee (EMEK). Mennonite students from Germany regularly found their way to the Bienenberg Bible School in Switzerland, an international school which the German Mennonites helped to support.

World War II took a heavy toll of the German Mennonites. All of those living east of the Oder-Neisse rivers were driven west into what became West Germany or emigrated to Uruguay and Canada. Their own poverty, however, did not keep the German Mennonites from helping refugees from Russia and other eastern areas, together with MCC. Beginning in the 1960s some 50,000 immigrants (*Umsiedler*) from Russia and South America have been helped in resettling in Germany particularly in Espelkamp, Bechterdissen, and Neuwied, but also Backnang, Enkenbach, Torney, and Wedel. For this purpose an International Mennonite Organization (IMO) was established in cooperation with the Swiss, French, and Dutch Mennonites and MCC. Material and spiritual aid was given to the immigrants as needed. New interest has been taken in youth work, Bible study retreats, and dialogue with non-Mennonite Christians through local and regional organizations. The historical society continues to publish the *Mennonitische Geschichtsblätter* and encourages studies in Mennonite history and identity. Nonresistance has again become a live option for some young people, as has service in under-developed countries.

The traditional north-south separation of conferences has given way to a *Union of German Mennonites* organization to carry on joint work in mission, relief, youth activities and other concerns. However, the earlier conferences still continue. In the north the *Vereinigung* (United German Mennonite Congregations) lists 34 congregations with a membership of 7,034 while in the south the *Verband* (Union of Mennonite Churches in Germany) lists 1,610 members in 22 congregations in 1990, but these figures do not include the immigrant groups. The official publication of the *Vereinigung* is *Menonitische Blätter*, and of the *Verband* the *Gemeinde Unterwegs*. An annual yearbook is published jointly.

There were also an unknown number of Mennonites scattered throughout what was formerly East Germany, with a congregation of some 300 members meeting in (East) Berlin. Two or three times a year services are also held in cities scattered throughout the area. Whatever movement has taken place from East to West in Germany and vice versa since unification is not known statistically. Mennonite Brethren congregations would include about 5,000 members. The combined membership in Germany would thus be about 14,000, plus the approximately 50,000 *Umsiedler*, with the latter figure including children and persons who had not joined any congregation by 1992.

France

The French Mennonites had a troubled history in the nineteenth century. Most of them had come from the Bern district of Switzerland, settling in the more isolated areas of the Vosges Mountains in the province of Alsace, although some moved on northwest to Lorraine, and some later moved to the interior of France. Montbeliard became an early refuge. Since 1912 it has been the largest and most compact Mennonite settlement in France.

Being few in number, and scattered over these regions, the French Mennonites were hard put to retain their faith. They were often surrounded by French Catholics who envied their prosperity and took numerous occasions to molest them. They also suffered because of the wars which swept over their area. While they were not heavily affected by the Napoleonic wars except through the

Following World War II North American MCC workers, Pax men, and European volunteers cooperated in the construction of refugee settlements at Enkenbach, Espelkamp, Backnang, Neuwied, and elsewhere. **The Mennonitenstrasse** in Neuwied-Torney is typical of the new towns.

conflict over military service, the wars of 1870, 1914, and 1939 all ravaged their lands. Most difficult of all was the changing political status of Alsace and Lorraine, whereby its ownership was thrown back and forth between France and Germany, accompanied by all the hatred engendered by the wars.

By the end of the nineteenth century French Mennonitism was at a low ebb. Available statistics place the number of French Mennonites at 4,450 in 1810. An official government source listed them as numbering 5,044 in 1850, undoubtedly including children. A German source gives their numbers as 3,143 in 1892. Intermarriage with non-Mennonites, French nationalism, and continuing migrations added to the problems already mentioned. The Mennonites in German-speaking France tried to retain the German language. Those among them who felt more French than German, as well as their non-Mennonite neighbors, resented the German invasions of 1870, 1914, and 1940. This expedited the transition from German to French.

By the turn of the century several factors and the work of two men began to lead to a strengthening of spiritual life among the French Mennonites. There was, first of all, the influence of other groups such as the Salvation Army and the Baptists, to which the Mennonites had always been open. The immigration of a number of Swiss Mennonite families into Alsace also brought fresh life among them. It ended those distinctions in dress which had still prevailed, and with it the external evidences of the Amish background of the group.

To these influences must be added the work of Valentin Pelsy (d. 1925) and Pierre Sommer (d. 1952). Sommer had been influenced by Christian Neff at the Weierhof. In an effort to unite the scattered groups these two men initiated the organization of the French Mennonite conference in 1901. In the same year Sommer founded a paper first called *Bulletin de la Conference* and *Christ Seul* (Christ Alone) since 1907, promoting Christian living and meaningful congregational activity. Though its publication was interrupted several times, it became a major organ of renewal with Sommer editing it until 1941.

Other activities followed the work of these two men. First one and then a second minister was employed to visit the scattered families and congregations, a mission committee was formed, a youth committee and a relief organization were set up. Two orphanages were operated together with MCC but without outside help since 1959. A retirement center and care for persons who are mentally ill have been added. A mission committee was formed in 1951, which supports EMEK, work in Chad, and other efforts. Home mission work is also carried on, in some locations in cooperation with American Mennonites. Conscientious objector status is now legal in France, and some young people are choosing civilian work as an alternative to military service. A historical society was formally established in 1979.

For many years the French Mennonites were organized into two conferences, the *Association* or primarily German-speaking conference, and the *Groupe* or French-speaking one. In 1980 these two conferences merged to form the *Association des Eglises Evangeliques Mennonites de France* with a membership of approximately 2,000 in 16 congregations in 1990. By 1979 a French Mennonite teacher, a woman, was also on the faculty of the Bienenberg Bible School in Switzerland. Jean Séguy, not a Mennonite, had published a rather definitive 904-page study of the French Mennonites—*Les assemblées anabaptistes-mennonites de France.*[6]

Switzerland

The story of the Swiss Mennonites from the time of Napoleon to the present has already been told, in part; the effects of toleration on the practice of nonresistance and their emigration to France and America. Those who did not emigrate had withdrawn to remote mountain regions, where they developed thriving farming communities. Except for nonresistance, they were able to preserve much of the heritage of their Anabaptist ancestors, which continued to make them suspect in the eyes of their neighbors. A number were able to keep a kind of nonresistance through accepting medical corps service. At times their relative prosperity also caused them to be envied and discriminated against even in the twentieth century. By the 1970s urbanization had led to the establishing of numerous congregations in cities also. Officially they were not known as Mennonites until the 1980s, but as *Die Altevangelische taufgesinnte Gemeinden der Schweiz* (the old evangelical, baptism-minded congregations of Switzerland). All of the congregations are united in a conference organized in 1780, which had a total membership of 3,000 in 15 congregations in 1990.

From 1946 to 1952 the Swiss Mennonites had much contact with the North American Mennonites through MCC which had located its European headquarters in Basel. In 1951 Basel became the location of a European Mennonite Bible school, which relocated to the *Bienenberg*, a huge building at Liestal, near Basel, in 1957. The fifth meeting of the MWC was held at St. Chrischona, near Basel, in 1952. The conference also held a memorial service for Felix Mantz, who became one of the first known Anabaptist martyrs at the hands of the Reformed when he was drowned in Zurich in 1527.

The Swiss Mennonites participate in EMEK with other European Mennonites and have founded their own relief agency, the Swiss Mennonite Organization for Relief Work (SMO), which cooperates with IMO and MCC as necessary. A youth retreat center in Les Mottes serves as activities center, with non-Mennonite youth also participating. Sunday schools are operated in all congregations. Most Swiss Mennonite congregations are rural and are served by lay ministers, but there are also some urban churches. The greatest loss of membership seems to be due to upward social mobility coming with success and affluence. Nevertheless, the Swiss Mennonites are conscious of the fact that many European and North American Mennonites trace their roots back to their own land. A Swiss Association for Anabaptist History was founded in 1974 and by 1978 had a membership of 200. Its expressed intention was not only to recover an almost lost heritage, but to transmit it to the coming generation.

Between 1832 and 1835 Samuel Fröhlich (d. 1857), a Reformed minister, organized a new group called the NeuTaüfer (New Baptists) or Fröhlichianer. About half of his initial membership came from Mennonites in the Emmental region who were dissatisfied with the low spiritual life in their congregations. Emigration soon scattered the new group, however, many moving to Hungary and Yugoslavia, while others moved to Ohio, New York, and Illinois, from where they scattered to other states and Canada. The groups in Hungary, Czechoslovakia, and the areas formerly comprising Yugoslavia have grown to several thousand in number and manage to retain many of the early Anabaptist emphases in a remarkable way. They are called *Nazarenes*. They are the only Slavic people knowing Anabaptist doctrine and seeking to follow it, except for the Baptists in Czechoslovakia and Russia, who are also quite interested in and informed about Anabaptism.

The groups which came to America in 1846 and later have been known as "New Amish" or *Apostolic Christians*. Two or three families also came from the German-speaking area of Lorraine and settled in Canada. They have no direct connection with the Amish but in their attempt to reform the church on the apostolic pattern have many practices which Jacob Ammann and his followers brought from the same area of Switzerland.

Luxembourg

There were about 100 baptized members in the Mennonite church in Luxembourg in 1990, in two congregations, most of whom were descendants of three families which had come there in the nineteenth century. Several meeting places have been established, including a small stone chapel built on a farm with the help of a voluntary service camp in 1953-54. In 1946 these groups started an annual Bible conference, which helped to keep the faith alive among them and served as outreach center to others. In most of their activities they worked closely with the Association Mennonites in France.

Other Developments

Mennonite life in Russia has been discussed in chapter 10, and in this chapter reference has been made to those who are settling in Germany. They are commonly referred to as *Umsiedler* (repatriates) and have received major financial help from the German government. In church and spiritual affairs they have been helped by IMO, MCC, and Canadian Mennonite conferences. The *Umsiedler* find it difficult to adjust to the church in the West. After expressing his appreciation for all the help received, one *Umsiedler* said, "But spiritually speaking, God has now led us into a desert."

North American Mennonites have been active in mission work also in Europe after 1945. The Mennonite Brethren have been particularly active in ministering to the *Umsiedler* and had established at least 22 congregations with a membership of 5,000 in Germany in 1990 and 300 members in seven congregations in Austria. These congregations include many new members from the national communities in which they live. In 1976 some of these joined the Mennonite Brethren of North America in beginning work in Spain. Twenty-four members were reported there in 1990, in addition to 200 in an autonomous community in Burgos.

Through several of its mission boards the Mennonite Church began work in *Sicily* in 1949, *Belgium* in 1950, *Luxembourg* in 1951, *England* in 1952, and *France* in 1953. Most of the work in these countries grew out of the relief activities of MCC. The work of Luxembourg and France has already been mentioned. The membership of about 40 in Belgium is similarly related to the *Groupe* conference in France and included in its work. The work in Italy has grown to include Florence, with membership in *Italy* being 129 in 1990. There was little communication, however, with the 20,000-member Waldensian Church in Italy, though historically and theologically the Anabaptists had much in common with them. A growing witness was being felt in England through the work of the London Centre, with 27 members in 1990, and plans were progressing for a peace witness ministry in *Ireland*, where 10 members were reported.

European Mennonite Evangelism Committee: Known from its German title as EMEK, this committee was set up in 1952 to coordinate the mission work of the churches in the Netherlands, Germany, France, and Switzerland. It continued the mission cooperation begun among the Mennonites in the nineteenth century. Particular support has been given to the Dutch work in Indonesia and New Guinea. The French have worked in Chad in Africa. The Dutch sent workers Roelf and Juliette Kuitse to Ghana in the Islam project, a joint undertaking of many mission groups. References have been made in preceding pages to other EMEK activities. It is also serving increasingly as liaison office with North American and other Mennonite mission agencies in promoting a unified worldwide believers church witness.

International Mennonite Peace Committee: The IMPC was organized in 1936 in the Netherlands, immediately following the third MWC. In 1949 representatives of most of the European and American Mennonite groups met in the Netherlands to reorganize this committee, in order that the cause of peace might be promoted more effectively. Annual meetings were projected and have been held since 1961, an information bulletin was begun, and aid was given to conscientious objectors having difficulty with their respective governments.

Relatively few Mennonites in Europe had chosen nonresistance in the twentieth century. In World War I Pierre Kennel, a French Mennonite, refused the call to army service and was dismissed from his teaching position at the University of Geneva as a result. His own congregation did not support him in his stand. There were a handful of conscientious objectors in World War II, several of whom were executed for their stand, but these were led more by individual conviction than historic roots. Active peace groups have now arisen, as indicated, and local provision has been made for conscientious objectors in the Netherlands, France, and Germany.

The IMPC is not active now, but on a standby basis. The annual meetings have been discontinued. Meanwhile a worldwide peace committee has been formed under MWC with representation from each continent. The Peace Section of MCC has been providing staff services for this committee.

In review it may be said that persecution had driven most of the Mennonites in Western Europe to the farms and mountains. Except for the Mennonites in the Netherlands and Northern Germany, they had been isolated from the main stream of history. Persecution and isolation led them to a formalism which centered primarily in the attempt to preserve the faith among themselves. The greater freedom of the nineteenth century exposed them to other influences around them. In the south and east, pietistic influences were strong, while the theological liberalism of the Enlightenment made its inroads in the north and west. Nationalism and cultural influences also had a bearing on their development.

Despite these tensions, Mennonites in the isolated byways of Europe did preserve a memory that might otherwise have been lost. When they were either isolated, or too much a part of a nation, they tended to decline in numbers and lost their vitality. Meetings with other Mennonites and a study of the past stimulated new life among them all. The disappearance of divisions was sometimes simply the result of a lack of conviction, and such unity did not greatly help the church, but when differences were overcome to achieve a larger goal, the unity became fruitful. Similarly, contact with other Christian groups stimulated the Mennonites, but sometimes it led to divisions, sometimes to the loss of their heritage.

In 1990, the total number of baptized Mennonites in Western Europe was approximately 42,332.[7] The estimated 50,000 *Umsiedler* in Germany included children, young people and other non-members, as did the estimated 10,000 remaining in Russia. They are not included in this total. There was growth numerically in some areas but loss in others. EMEK, IMO, the Bienenberg Bible School, and other developments were solid reminders of increasing unity and cooperation. New interest was apparent in their Anabaptist origins and Mennonite identity. New centers and methods of witness were developing. They were entering the decade of the 1990s with significant opportunities and challenges. Only time would tell what the response would be.

Endnotes

1. A 1992 government report lists 43,000 members, but Mennonites explain that 25,000 simply left the church without registering it with government statisticians. Some also cherish their Mennonite (*Doopsgezinde*) lineage and basically hold many of the traditional values, but have not joined a Mennonite congregation.

2. Frits Kuiper, "The Discordant Voice of Jan de Liefde," in C. J. Dyck, ed., *A Legacy of Faith*. Newton, Kan.: Faith and Life Press, 1962, pp. 159-168.

3. See also articles in ME 5 and MQR 62 (July 1988), a special Menno Simons issue on the occasion of his becoming an Anabaptist in 1536.

4. Nearly one-sixth of the material in *The Mennonite Encyclopedia*, 1-4 is translated from the *Lexicon*. See ME 5:571.

5. The idea for a MWC grew out of the All-Mennonite Conventions held from

1913-1936 in the United States and discussed with Heinrich Pauls in Lemberg, Poland, by H. H. Regier of Mountain Lake, Minnesota in 1912. Cornelius J. Dyck, "The History of the Mennonite World Conference." *Mennonite World Handbook* 1978, pp. 1-9. An earlier version can be found in MQR (July 1967) 41:277-287.

    6. Paris: Mouton, 1977.

    7. For statistics on all groups see MWC *Handbook* 1990, pp. 392-402.

Other Resources: See relevant articles, bibliographies and cross-references in ME 5. Also MWC *Handbook* 1978, 1984 and 1990. Gerald R. Brunk, ed., *Menno Simons: A Reappraisal*, Harrisonburg, Va., Eastern Mennonite College, 1992. Contact any MCC office for audiovisual resources.

21

Mennonites in the North American Environment

SINCE MENNONITES came to North America from many different regions of Europe and over a period of more than 250 years, from 1683 to the 1960s, as we have seen in earlier chapters, they naturally brought with them a variety of cultural forms and religious concerns. Their subsequent choice of location in the vast lands of the United States and Canada further determined their development and added to the variety among them. Yet in spite of these historical and geographical differences Mennonites have much in common because of their faith and because they have been a cohesive and homogeneous ethnic group throughout much of their history. The following description of their life in the North American environment, therefore, deals briefly with some of their common experiences and concerns in an attempt to see them in their present context from the perspective of their Anabaptist heritage.[1]

The North American Way of Life

Most Mennonites came to the United States and Canada to escape European intolerance and persecution. It was difficult for them to leave their homes in Germany, Switzerland, France, Prussia, and Russia, but force of circumstances *pushed* them into the New World to preserve their faith. Yet there were also *pulling* forces which attracted them—economic opportunity, relatives, and most of all the prospect of establishing the ideal Mennonite community on the frontiers of civilization. They yearned for freedom without having the vision of a democratic society, desiring only to be left alone to worship God according to their conscience and their tradition, which they assumed to be biblical.

For most of them being a Mennonite was something they inherited, rather than being a deliberate choice made by each individual between several religious options. Until late twentieth century most members of a Mennonite community were considered either actual or potential members of the church. For many of them non-Mennonites were a threat to the faith, necessitating withdrawal from the "world" with its temptations. Marriage with non-Mennonites, for example, was opposed until mid-century, and sometimes led to excommunication because the new partner was an "outsider." By the 1950s the primary marriage criteria increasingly became "only in the Lord," (1 Cor. 7:39).

Vocational Life. From an earlier perspective the agricultural economy was long considered ideal by Mennonites. For 300 years farming was thought to be *the* Mennonite way of life and the rural community the indispensable form of organizing their common life. Initially, to be sure, Anabaptism had been an urban movement but under the pressure of persecution it quickly became rural, surviving best in small, isolated, ethnic communities. Throughout most of the seventeenth, eighteenth, and nineteenth centuries to be a Mennonite almost invariably meant to grow up in an agricultural community. So strong was this heritage that many believed Mennonites could not survive in the cities; they would either be lost to the church, or compromise the essentials of Mennonite doctrine.[2]

All this began to change in the twentieth century. Following World War II, urbanization took place on an unprecedented scale in North America. As farms became more difficult to acquire and to operate profitably, Mennonites too found their way to the cities, serving in the professions, in business, or attending schools of higher learning. While the degree of urbanization varied from group to group, the phenomenon itself was common to all but the most conservative groups and the Amish. By 1989 about one-half of Mennonites in the four largest groups and the Brethren in Christ (BIC) were classified as urban, with only fifteen percent of the

Winnipeg, Manitoba, has the largest urban Mennonite population in the world. Mennonites minister through **forty-three congregations in Winnipeg**, as well as three colleges, two collegiate institutes, a hospital, retirement centers, a credit union, the offices of MCC Canada, two archives and heritage centers, two conference headquarters, and the Christian Press.

males engaged in farming.[3] An illustration of this movement was the city of Winnipeg which, by 1990, had a population of just under 20,000 Mennonites, worshiping in forty-three congregations (ME 5:533).

This movement to the cities and consequent shift in the vocations of many Mennonites tested their faith and moral values in a new way.[4] As tensions increased between inherited values and the common social values of their environment, some gave up any pretensions of having a unique faith and left the Mennonite church. Others became what might be called *marginal* Mennonites, retaining a certain nostalgic love for the tradition which nurtured them but discarding most of its claims upon them as outdated. Many, however, took up the challenge of relating their heritage in a meaningful way to their late twentieth-century culture. Some of the most penetrating critics of Mennonitism were among this last group, appealing to the biblical and early sixteenth-century Anabaptist models in their call for renewal.

It may, therefore, be said that the history of North American Mennonitism in the twentieth century was in part a history of their gradual accommodation to the North American environment. Sometimes this accommodation was an accepting of some of the values of others around them, sometimes it led to full assimilation or even secularization with a rejection of the heritage of faith. But for some this heritage was also one of spiritual renewal which made them conscious of the unlimited opportunities for witness and service in the cities and everywhere.[5]

Language. Initially many of the Mennonite immigrants to North America believed the preservation of the German language to be necessary for their survival as a church. This was particularly true of the Mennonites from Russia, where they had become accustomed to including instruction in the Bible and in the German language under the term *religion*. One of the primary reasons for the establishing of their own schools was, in fact, the need to preserve the faith in and through the language. Nevertheless, the language transition from German to English had been largely completed by 1990. The German language continued to be promoted as a cultural asset, particularly in Canada, and as the international Mennonite "Latin" or universal language, but it was no longer seen as inseparable from historic faith.

With the change to the English language came an increasing desire to see other than ethnic Mennonite names on church registers. New efforts in evangelism and church extension were common. Membership in the church came to be more in terms of a voluntary decision as in early Anabaptism, rather than as a birthright, ("birthright Mennonites"?) but American evangelicalism may have been more responsible for this than the influence of Anabaptism. New methods of church planting also led to the welcome, if unexpected, adding of other languages as Native North American, Chinese, Vietnamese, Laotian, Hmong, French, and Hispanic people have formed congregations in our conferences.[6] Still, in 1982 only 7 percent of the Mennonite population in North America were members of minority groups.[7]

Nonresistance

The wars of North America naturally also involved the Mennonites in one way or another. In the United States this included particularly the War of Independence (1775-83) and the Civil War (1861-65), World Wars I (1914-18) and II (1939-45), in which Canada was also involved, as well as the Korean War (1950-53) and the Vietnam War which ended in 1975. Other overt conflicts included the Granada and Panama interventions and the Gulf War of early 1991. Covert operations were global, but especially in Central America and the Middle East.

During the War of Independence the Colonial Assembly was most cordial in its treatment of Mennonites and Quakers, warning zealots against violating the rights of the conscience of others, while at the same time encouraging nonresistant people to "cheerfully assist in proportion to their abilities" those who were suffering from the war. The same year, on July 18, 1775, the Continental Congress passed the following resolution:

> As there are some people who from religious principles can not bear arms in any case, this Congress intend no violence to their consciences, but earnestly, recommend it to them to *Contribute Liberally*, in this time of universal calamity, to the relief of their distressed brethren in the several colonies, and to do all other services to their oppressed country which they can, consistently with their religious principles.[8]

Beginning in November 1775, a special fee was imposed on those not in the military services. In addition to this all people had to pay a war tax, but many Mennonites refused and it was consequently collected by confiscating their goods. Some Mennonites believed that Jesus would have paid the tax, and a schism came to the church over this issue (ME 2:421.1).

The Mennonites were also often accused of being Tories or Loyalists, and some did leave for Ontario in order to remain true to the British crown. Their motivation, however, was usually not political but stemmed from their being asked to renounce the British government to which they had given their pledge of obedience, which they did not wish to break. Some, perhaps, may have felt more comfortable under a monarchy than under a democratic form of government, but most of them soon were giving full obedience to the new American government.

During the Civil War (1861-65) a system of hiring substitutes

Inter-Mennonite cooperation has been most visible in response to man-made and natural calamities around the world. All groups have donated generously to **Heifer Project**, the braindchild of Dan West of the Church of the Brethren. Since 1920 **Mennonite Central Committee** has distributed food, clothing, and services around the world "In the Name of Christ."

was available to the Mennonites both in the Union (North) and in the Confederacy (South). Most Quakers and some Mennonites objected to hiring others to do what they would not do themselves, but the majority of the Mennonites were content with the arrangement. Some opportunity for hospital service was also provided in the North, but very few took advantage of it. Because of a decline in the teaching on nonresistance in the churches, Mennonite young people were poorly prepared for the war and its demands, and "to judge from the records, many men from Mennonite and Amish homes must have entered the ranks of the Union Armies."[9]

In the South the Mennonites had a rather difficult time since they were not only nonresistant but also opposed to slavery. Some fled to the free Northern states; others hid in the mountains of Virginia. Some were drafted under protest and decided among themselves, together with other peace church men, that they would not shoot. This became enough of a problem for General T. F. (Stonewall) Jackson to say:

> There lives a people in the Valley of Virginia, that are not hard to bring to the army. While there they are obedient to their officers. Nor is it difficult to have them take aim, but it is impossible to get them to take correct aim. I, therefore, think it better to leave them at their homes that they may produce supplies for the army.[10]

Some served as teamsters and cooks for the army. Many suffered hardships, as did the Mennonite communities of Virginia, where many of the battles of the war were fought. It was a very difficult time for the church, and there were many failings, but the church itself never sanctioned participation in the military either in the Union or in the Confederacy.

World War I found the church better prepared and more creative in thinking through the issues involved. Conscientious objectors were legally exempt from military service, but they were subject to the draft and being taken to military camps. There some of the men were abused, and a few died of injuries inflicted on them by antagonistic officers and enlisted men.[11] Misunderstandings also occurred in the home communities; some church buildings were painted yellow, and several ministers were tarred and feathered and abused in other ways. One was hanged from a telephone pole by a mob but rescued before he died. But the war forced the Mennonites to clarify their stand on several issues, including noncombatant service and the purchase of war bonds, both of which were rejected.

In place of the bonds a new zeal for relief ministries gripped the Mennonite churches, which led to real sacrifices on the part of many. While the motive of compassion was clear, there may well also have been a hidden desire to prove that Mennonites were good citizens, but motives are usually hard to identify. In 1920, two years after the war, MCC was formed to serve as their relief agency. During the war most of the eligible Mennonite men were assigned to significant farm projects, which marked the beginning of the full-scale alternative service program of World War II.

As World War II approached, leaders of the Historic Peace Churches (HPC) (Mennonites, Brethren, and Friends) approached the United States government with the plea that no law establishing universal military training be adopted, but if it was, that provision be made for those conscientiously opposed to all forms of military service. The Selective Training and Service Act of 1940 granted this request, assigning conscientious objectors to work of national importance under civilian direction. This led to the setting up of Civilian Public Service (CPS) camps where such men did work in soil conservation, dam building, and other projects. A similar program was provided by the Canadian government. The cost to the churches of supporting the CPS camps in the United States amounted to over three million dollars.[12]

Overseas relief ministries were proposed for draft-age men, some actually leaving for the Far East, but they were recalled to service in the United States, including Puerto Rico. Eventually many men volunteered to serve as attendants in mental hospitals, where they gave distinguished service and helped to bring about major changes in the treatment of the mentally ill. The regional psychiatric centers established by the Mennonite churches during World War II were a direct outgrowth of this earlier involvement.

By the end of World War II in 1945, the Mennonite churches were more than ever convinced that the doctrine of love and non-resistance meant for them a continuing relief and service ministry around the world. These continuing services included emergency food, clothing, and medical aid, as well as agricultural development programs, work in the field of education, and a host of other areas of human need. It was almost taken for granted that all Mennonite and BIC young people would include voluntary service of some kind in their life plans. In 1991, a total of 986 persons were serving

In addition to food and clothing distribution, MCC has been involved in refugee resettlement, village reconstruction, **youth and adult literacy programs**, agricultural
education, vocational schools, medical services, drug and alcohol abuse counsels,
native ministries, and similar programs designed to move persons from dependency
to self-sufficiency.

through MCC with a budget of 31,526,907 dollars. Of these workers 149 were in Africa, 96 in Asia, 28 in the Middle East, 23 in Europe, 143 in Latin America, and 547 in North America. A unique
program known as the Exchange Visitor or Trainee Program providing for one year of work in another country, was begun in 1950.
These statistics do not include programs operated by the conferences themselves, nor mission board programs.

These ministries were made possible through new life in the
congregations, a new sense of social responsibility, more inter-
Mennonite cooperation, and increasing economic abundance.
While some continued simply to enjoy what they had, many others
were becoming increasingly concerned with what they saw as they
looked around their own communities and tried to envision the
year 2000. There was the continuing massive arms buildup and
trade, even though East-West tensions had abated by 1992. How
could nonresistant Christians witness to this madness? Should they
allow their taxes to be used for war purposes, or was the use of tax

funds the sole responsibility of government? How could Mennonites work to relieve racism in their own communities and in the nation? Were the churches doing all they could to help minorities overcome personal and systemic, institutional injustice? Could they become agents of social change in offender ministries, in drug and family abuse rehabilitation, and increased community violence, like they had in mental health after 1945?

There were other deep social problems. What about world hunger and overpopulation and the socio-economic needs of the developing nations? What about issues like abortion (ME 5:1), AIDS, human sexuality (ME 5:814-817), changing gender roles, the decline of family stability and values? What about North Americans' exploitation of global natural resources? The Mennonite response in the face of these issues tended to be increased agency cooperation and networking, legal counsel and advocacy. Justice and love were no longer seen as contradictory. But there was also much work at local levels, in small ways, through personal witness and sacrifice rather than through formal pronouncements or political processes. Yet so much more needed doing. An increasing number of North American Mennonites were also politically involved, at local, regional and national levels, particularly in Canada, to change things from the top down while others worked from the bottom up.

Movements of Spiritual Renewal

For about 150 years the Mennonites in North America remained largely isolated from each other and from other churches by a strong sense of loyalty to their heritage and by their use of the German language, but the protective walls were crumbling and new life did come. The spiritual renewal which came in mid-nineteenth century was initiated and promoted in large part by John F. Funk (1835-1930), who as a young man worked with evangelist Dwight L. Moody in Chicago. Soon after his conversion in the winter of 1857-58 Funk found his way to Elkhart in Indiana, from where he began to wield great influence for good among the Mennonites for many years, particularly through his publishing of a paper—the *Herald of Truth*—beginning in 1864.

This does not mean that Mennonitism in the Colonial Period had been without spiritual life. As early as 1690 the Germantown Mennonites had chosen William Rittenhouse as minister. Other leaders continued to be called in increasing numbers until a report written to Holland in 1773 said the ministers were too many to count. Some, like Hans Herr in 1710, came to America with many years of experience in church work.

The pioneers were also not without literature. In 1712 the Dutch Mennonites translated into English and printed the 1632 Dordrecht Confession of Faith for the colonies. By 1749 the *Martyrs Mirror* had been translated from the original Dutch into German and printed at Ephrata, Pennsylvania. Devotional writings like J. P. Schabaelje's *The Wandering Soul*, Gerrit Roosen's *Spiritual Dialog*, and others were in circulation, including particularly the *Ausbund* hymnal. By early nineteenth century more literature began to be published in the English language.

One of the major movements for renewal among Mennonites was the Sunday school, but it also helped to dilute Mennonite identity and uniqueness. The Sunday school had come to America from England during the era of the Second Great Awakening late in the eighteenth century, together with numerous other innovations like the Bible, tract and temperance societies and the new interest in missions. Mennonites resisted Sunday schools from coming into their churches until it became obvious that they were losing hundreds of their own young people who attended the schools of other denominations. Frequently the schools were union efforts of many denominations in a given community and Mennonite leaders soon found their lay members active in teaching and leadership.

The first Mennonite Sunday school was probably held at the Wanner and Bechtel meetinghouse in Waterloo County, Ontario, in 1840. In the United States it may have been the school at the Masontown (Pa.) church in 1842. John H. Oberholtzer, who broke with the main body of Mennonites in 1847, was convinced of the importance of the schools for the future of the church. Many arguments were brought against the schools by their opponents and some schisms resulted because of them. They did, in fact, promote a piety foreign to Mennonites and, in the absence of Mennonite materials, introduced literature not in harmony with Mennonite doctrines of nonconformity, nonresistance, the meaning of conversion, church membership, and other basic issues. The Sunday schools became one of the major avenues through which Mennonites were drawn into the main stream of American evangelicalism.

Revivalism was another renewal movement which affected the Mennonites both negatively and positively. It was a uniquely North American way of winning new church members in contrast to the

European state church system with automatic membership and state financial support. The first Great Awakening, approximately 1725-50, had come quite unexpectedly, leading the Puritan Jonathan Edwards to write about it as a "surprizing work of God" (1737), but by the time of the second Great Awakening, approximately 1790-1830, the leaders were learning to program their approach to increase effectiveness. By the time of Charles Finney (d. 1875) and Dwight L. Moody (d. 1899), revivalism had become a highly specialized evangelistic method with predictable results in terms of souls saved, and specific styles of preaching and doing theology. Unfortunately, it also became a highly divisive issue within most denominations and congregations.

It also became a divisive issue among Mennonites. The period of 1800-1860 has sometimes been described as one of "stress and strain" among them, but we might well include the entire nineteenth century under this theme. Until the twentieth century Mennonites in North America were largely a rural people, conservative in both their theology and social views, suspicious of the urban methods for spiritual renewal. Revivalism was suspect for its enthusiasm, for its stress upon one specific form of conversion, for its prayer meetings, frequent theological oversimplification, and the close contact it gave Mennonites with all kinds of persons of unknown values and theology.

While Mennonites had not worked this way before, they were actually not strangers to revivalism. Many of the immigrants of the 1870s from Russia had become familiar with this method through the work of Eduard Wuest in mid-century, which had led to the founding of the Mennonite Brethren Church in 1860. American Mennonites also knew about it through John F. Funk, who had greatly appreciated the work of Moody, and had held some revival meetings among Mennonites. But Funk's work was not encouraged by the church leadership, nor were the responses of the people encouraging.

It remained for John S. Coffman to make the long meetings for decision, the altar call, the appropriate hymns of invitation, acceptable to Mennonites. His gentle and irenic spirit overcame most opposition and the results were encouraging. Consequently, he worked effectively as evangelist from 1881 until his death in 1899. By then revivalism had been legitimized as a method Mennonites could use. His work led to new life in many places, to new interest in missions and even in education, but through the literature it in-

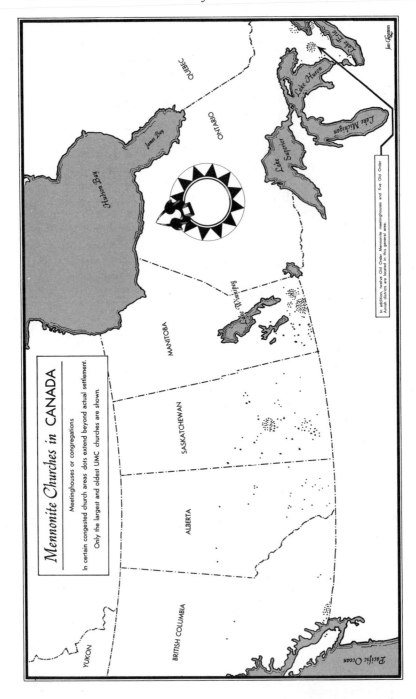

Mennonite Churches in CANADA

• Meetinghouses or congregations

In certain congested church areas, dots extend beyond actual settlement.
Only the largest and oldest UMC churches are shown.

In addition, twelve Old Order Mennonite meetinghouses and five Old Order Amish districts are located in this general area.

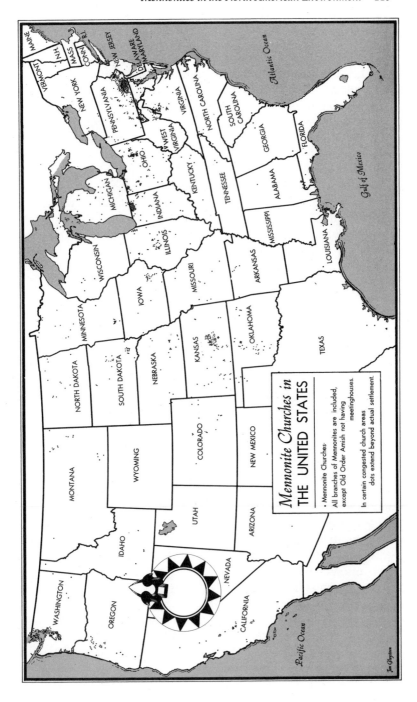

Mennonite Churches in
THE UNITED STATES

• Mennonite Churches:
All branches of Mennonites are included,
except Old Order Amish not having
meetinghouses.

In certain congested church areas
dots extend beyond actual settlement.

troduced and the association it provided with other revivalists, it opened the Mennonite door wider to the impact of alien theologies, particularly Fundamentalism.[13] It was to take to mid-twentieth century before Mennonites would overcome these influences, partly through the work of Harold S. Bender, who saw Anabaptism as a third way between Liberalism and Fundamentalism.

There were other sources of renewal. The coming of the Russian Mennonites to the Canadian and American Midwest in the 1870s brought new life to mission interests and to education, as well as simply numerically. Bethel College, North Newton, Kansas, was founded in 1887; Bluffton (Ohio) College in 1889; Goshen (Ind.) College in 1903 as an outgrowth of the Elkhart Institute; and Tabor College, Hillsboro, Kansas, in 1908. Winter Bible schools were popular both among the "American" Mennonites and the immigrants. Mennonite high schools proliferated. Other colleges emerged. In the twentieth century education seemed to be a very major thrust among Mennonites in North America.

Other Twentieth-Century Developments

One of the significant developments of the twentieth century has been the growth of Mennonitism in Canada, numerically as the statistics in this volume indicate, but also in their strength and influence in church and society. In the field of education, for example, the number of high schools is significant as is the establishment of three colleges in Winnipeg, and a college of arts in Waterloo, Ontario. Numerous Mennonites can be found on the faculties of most of the major universities across the land and in responsible administrative positions in public education.

Equally significant has been the phenomenal growth of MCC activities in Canada on both the provincial and national levels, and the way different conference bodies have been able to join forces in MCC for the achieving of common goals. So also the Canadian government has found it expedient to use MCC channels for some of its overseas development programs. Mennonites in Canada seem to have been able to identify more closely with their government than have Mennonites in the USA with theirs.

Through historical development many of the schools, administrative offices, and other centers of Mennonite denominational life are located south of the forty-ninth parallel. These situations have led to questions of nationalism and its meaning on both sides

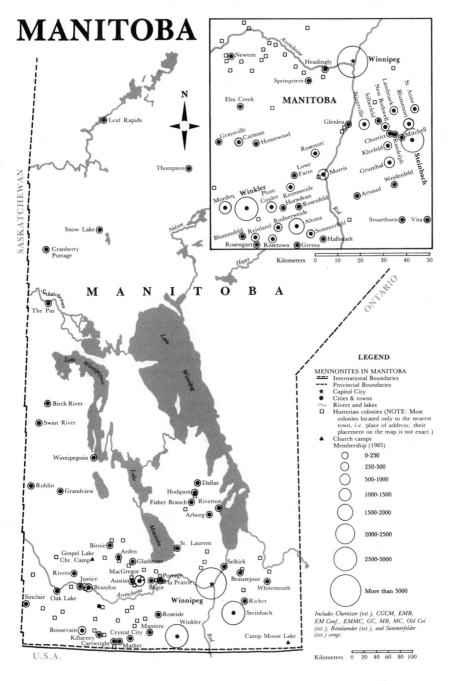

MANITOBA

MANITOBA

Newton
Headingly
Winnipeg
Springstein
Elm Creek
Leaf Rapids
Graysville
Carman
Homewood
Glenlea
Niverville
Silberfeld
New Bothwell
Landmark
Blumenort
St. Anne
Chortitz
Randolph
Mitchell
Kleefeld
Rosenort
Thompson
Lowe
Farm
Morris
Grunthal
Randolph
Steinbach
Weidenfeld
Morden Winkler
Plum
Coulee
Kronsweide
Horndean
Rosenfeld
Arnaud
Snow Lake
Blumenfeld Reinland Rudnerweide
Altona
Stuartburn
Vita
Sommerfeld
Cranberry
Portage
Rosengart Rosetown Gretna
Halbstadt
Kilometers 0   10   20   30   40   50

M A N I T O B A

The Pas
ONTARIO

Lake
Lake Winnipegosis
Lake Winnipeg

LEGEND

MENNONITES IN MANITOBA
- ≡≡≡ International Boundaries
- ‑‑‑ Provincial Boundaries
- ★ Capitol City
- ● Cities & towns
- ～ Rivers and lakes
- □ Hutterian colonies (NOTE: Most colonies located only to the nearest town, i.e. place of address; their placement on the map is not exact.)
- ▲ Church camps

Membership (1985)

○ 0-250

○ 250-500

○ 500-1000

○ 1000-1500

○ 1500-2000

○ 2000-2500

○ 2500-5000

○ More than 5000

Birch River
Swan River
Winnipegosis
Roblin Grandview
Dallas
Hodgson
Fisher Branch Riverton
Arborg
Birnie
St. Laurent
Gospel Lake
Chr. Camp
Arden
Gladstone
Selkirk
Rivers
MacGregor
Justice
Austin
Portage
la Prairie
Beausejour
Brandon Bagot
Whitemouth
Sinclair Oak Lake
Assiniboine
Winnipeg
Richer
Roseisle
Steinbach
Boissevain
Manitou
Winkler
Killarney Crystal City
Cartwright Mather
Camp Moose Lake

Includes Chortitzer (est.), CGCM, EMB, EM Conf., EMMC, GC, MB, MC, Old Col. (est.), Reinlaender (est.), and Sommerfelder (est.) congs.

Kilometers 0   20   40   60   80 100

U.S.A.

of the border, resulting in the implied need for a realignment of denominational structures along national lines. The need for a change in structures is shared by many, as is the conviction that nationalism has no place in the church of Christ. The merging of the Mennonite Conference of Ontario and Quebec, the Western Ontario Mennonite Conference, and the Conference of United Mennonite Churches in Ontario in 1988, to form the Mennonite Conference of Eastern Canada illustrates the changing patterns.

In sharp protest against the rapid acculturation of Canadian Mennonitism have been small groups of emigrants who, beginning in the 1920s, migrated to Mexico, Paraguay, Bolivia, Central America, and other places in an attempt to preserve their religious identity. These movements can be interpreted as genuine attempts at counter-culture faithfulness, but the question of their deeper spiritual significance remains. The departing groups seemed to have a clearer vision of who they were, or wanted to be, than those who remained, both in Canada and the USA.

Mennonite Identity. In 1975 a book appeared under the title *Anabaptists Four Centuries Later*, reporting the findings of a study of four Mennonite conferences and the BIC, in both Canada and the United States, on issues of piety, beliefs, and practices. The study was carried out by J. Howard Kauffman and Leland Harder and represents a profile of who the Mennonites and BIC were in faith and life at that time.[14]

This study both symbolized and stimulated the increasing Mennonite and BIC search for a usable (acceptable?) profile of their identity. It seemed to be axiomatic that Mennonites and the BIC were experiencing an identity crisis that was, somehow, related to modernity. By 1992 at least seven other identity studies followed, four of them in 1988 alone, as well as at least three study conferences and numerous journal articles.[15] Still not clear, however, was whether the identity problem was more a concern of scholars, or whether the people in the pew were also struggling with these questions.

The 1991 *Mosaic* report by Kauffman and Driedger, based on late 1980s research, provided important answers to this question. To begin with, the study found that about one half of the Mennonites in North America were urban, as mentioned above. However, the study also showed that while urbanization fostered secularization to some degree, this effect was countered by increased education: "More education is associated with somewhat less materialism, individualism, and secularism," leads to some decline in religious orthodoxy and support of conservative moral standards, but increased church participation, devotional practices, evangelism, and support for social and ethical issues. Church attendance was shown to be highest among the college educated. Those with college or higher degrees increased from 19 percent in 1972 to 31 percent in 1989.[16]

As in the previous study, *Mosaic* reports wide divergence on some religious issues, but also correlations between socioeconomic levels and religious attitudes. Increased education led to increased opposition to the death penalty. Similarly, higher education led to favoring expanded leadership roles for women in the church, 52 percent compared to 32 percent in 1972. More men than women favored the ordination of women (47 vs. 42 percent). An increased resistance to abortion was observed since the earlier study, with 15 percent opposed even if the mother's life was at risk, 41 percent opposed to it in case of rape, and about one half if there was the chance of a serious defect in the fetus. Nine out of ten opposed it for any other reasons.[17]

One of the issues in the previous study was the influence of Fundamentalism on Mennonite ethics. Most Mennonites would measure as conservatives on basic issues of orthodoxy like biblical inspiration, Christology, belief in the resurrection—as well as on issues of morality like drinking, gambling, use of illicit drugs. Here they would make common cause with most Evangelicals, even moderate Fundamentalists. However, in their view of the state and military or other force, the heart of discipleship, i.e., love, Mennonites would vary widely among themselves as well as in relation to the other groups mentioned. Here 73 percent of the Mennonite Church said they would do alternative service, while only 17 percent of EMC respondents gave that answer. The 1989 study concludes, "It is clearly the Mennonites in the larger denominations who are continuing to spearhead nonresistance and peacemaking."[18]

The study did not find that urbanization seriously undermined the Anabaptist heritage, but age was a significant factor in how modernization was shaping identity. That is, while Anabaptism was found to be the strongest faith profile shaping late twentieth-century in-group identity, teenagers scored highest among the age groups on the un-Anabaptist mores of secularism, individualism and materialism (p. 250, chapter 11). Whether this was a trend or

For a relatively small denomination, Mennonites have an unusually ambitious publishing program of books and periodicals. Some Mennonite authors such as Barbara Claassen Smucker, Rudy Wiebe, and the late **Doris Janzen Longacre** (*More-with-Less Cookbook* and *Living More with Less*) have won national and international acclaim.

due primarily to peer pressure, for example, was not clear. Youth conferences, the Great Trek, and other youth activities were well attended. Attendance at Mennonite colleges was increasing in the late 1980s. Membership in a congregation, however, was often deferred.

Anabaptist values like community, love, peacemaking and service continued strong, also attracting many not formerly in this faith tradition. While clearly conservative on most doctrinal issues, Anabaptist-Mennonites continued to be truly progressive in their broad social service ministries through MCC, voluntary service, victim-offender (VORP) programs, concern for the poor, for justice, the environment, all of life. Traditional Mennonite activism continued strong, but the building of new institutions, except retirement centers and centers of worship, had definitely crested.

The 1990 MWC sessions in Winnipeg strengthened its potential for the future as North American Mennonites, already globally conscious through the work of MCC, established new relationships with their often very different sisters and brothers worldwide. Mennonites totaled 856,600 baptized members globally in 1990, of whom 114,400 were in Canada and 266,100 in the United States. A total of seventy-eight languages were being spoken in the global Mennonite family and English, rather than German, had become the new "Latin."[19] While MCC was clearly the strongest unifying agency, other alliances were being explored. Discussions between the Mennonite Church and the General Conference Mennonite Church continued about ways of further cooperation, including questions about the advantages and disadvantages of possible integration.

Spiritual Roots. Coupled with the activism described above, or perhaps in counterpoint to it, was a new search for meaningful relationships and deeper spiritual roots. There was manifest a strong new interest in Bible study, in marriage and family enrichment retreats, in Christology, in seminars on discipleship and the broader, life-encompassing meanings implicit in Anabaptism. Most congregations have small groups meeting for Bible study, prayer, and mutual support. The charismatic movement has helped to bring new freedom and joy to many congregations without, for the most part, causing serious division. The term *Anabaptist*, rather than Mennonite, seemed to be becoming the preferred term for more than a few, including especially believers churches in Latin America. A prominent Canadian leader proposed this change in a special publication.[20]

During the 1980s a new form of combining the active and reflective life emerged in what came to be called *spirituality* or the discipline of *spiritual formation*. Borrowing extensively from past and present practices in Roman Catholicism, but also integrating it with Anabaptist understandings of Scripture, writings, and tradition, it sought to promote prayer, meditation, solitude, spiritual guidance, and especially meaningful worship. As one spiritual director put it,

> Mennonite spirituality must have God as its source, the Holy Spirit and the church as its means, and the world as its concern; it must be a missionary spirituality. . . . (it means) following Jesus by taking time to be "with" Jesus. . . . It is impossible to be truly with God and not to be sent out with authority to "cast out demons" in the world.[21]

This was not a retreat from the *real* world but preparation for engaging it in the power of the Spirit. While many Catholic retreat centers were being used, Mennonites were also developing their own, together with programs to train persons as spiritual directors.

The Hermitage, a Mennonite retreat Center run by **Gene and Mary Herr,** at Three Rivers, Michigan. Settings like this provide time for the renewal of the soul, reflection on personal growth, spiritual maturity, and call.

Amid all of these activities and movements, were Canadian and U.S. Mennonites becoming more aware of the factors shaping their identity and, therefore, their mission? The answer was not clear. What was clear was general economic prosperity as in society as a whole, but also significant economic and social differences which, in turn, helped shape differing theological understandings and biblical norms. While many held to the vision of an ideal Anabaptist type congregation, the cultural milieu was diluting this with its individualism and materialism. It would be a statement of faith to say that most seemed seriously to want to "grow up in every way into him who is the head, into Christ" (Eph. 4:15).

Endnotes

1. For comprehensive treatment consult the *Mennonite Experience in America* (Herald Press) MEA series: Richard K. MacMaster, *Land, Piety, Peoplehood. The Establishment of Mennonite Communities in America, 1683-1790* (1985); Theron F. Schlabach, *Peace, Faith, Nation. Mennonites and Amish in Nineteenth-Century America* (1988); James C. Juhnke, *Vision, Doctrine, War. Mennonite Identity and Organization in America, 1890-1930* (1989); Paul Toews, volume 4 in process. Beulah Stauffer Hostetler, *American Mennonites and Protestant Movements*. Scottdale, Pa.: Herald Press, 1987. For Canada consult Frank H. Epp, *Mennonites in Canada, 1786-1920*. Toronto, Ont.: Macmillan of Canada, 1974 and idem, *Mennonites in Canada, 1920-1940*. Toronto, Ont.: Macmillan of Canada, 1982. Volume 3 in preparation by Theodore Regehr.

2. The J. Howard Kauffman and Leo Driedger, *The Mennonite Mosaic*. Scottdale, Pa.: Herald Press, 1991, volume is an excellent resource to study this thesis.

3. Ibid., pp. 36-38.

4. Ibid., pp. 38ff.

5. Ibid., pp. 65-85.

6. See conference yearbooks/directories for congregational listings.

7. Kauffman and Driedger, op. cit., p. 232, based on MQR (October 1985), 59:307-349.

8. MQR (October 1927), I:23.

9. Quoted in Guy F. Hershberger, *War, Peace, and Nonresistance*. Scottdale, Pa.: Herald Press, 1946, p. 101.

10. Ibid., pp. 107-108.

11. Ibid., pp. 121-122.

12. Albert N. Keim, *The CPS Story*. Intercourse, Pa.: Good Books, 1990.

13. Theron F. Schlabach, *Gospel Versus Gospel*. Scottdale, Pa.: Herald Press, 1980, esp. chapter 4, pp. 109ff.

14. Scottdale, Pa.: Herald Press, 1975.

15. Rodney J. Sawatsky, *Authority and Identity*. North Newton, Kan.: Bethel College, 1987; Leo Driedger, *Mennonite Identity in Conflict*. Lewiston, N.Y.: Edwin Mellon Press, 1988; Calvin Wall Redekop and Samuel J. Steiner, *Mennonite Identity*. New York, N.Y. University of America Press, 1988; Harry Loewen, ed. *Why I Am A Mennonite. Essays on Mennonite Identity*. Scottdale, Pa.: Herald Press, 1988; Calvin Redekop, *Mennonite Identity*. Baltimore, Md.: The Johns Hopkins University Press, 1989; Leo Driedger and Leland Harder, eds. *Anabaptist-Mennonite Identities in Ferment*. Elkhart, Ind.: IMS, 1990 *(Occasional Papers No. 14)*; J. Howard Kauffman and Leo Driedger, *The Mennonite Mosaic. Identity and Modernization*. Scottdale, Pa.: Herald Press, 1991. See also "Acculturation," and "Modernity," in ME 5:1-5; 598-60l, especially the bibliography in the latter article as also the MQR index and other relevant indices.

16. Kauffman and Driedger, op. cit., pp. 240-241, all of chapter 11.

17. Ibid., pp. 205-206, 195-196.

18. Ibid., pp. 172-176.

19. Lichdi, *Handbook* (1990), pp. 323-327.

20. John H. Redekop, *A People Apart*. Winnipeg, Man.: Kindred Press, 1987.

21. Marcus Smucker, "Mennonite Spirituality," in the *AMBS Bulletin*, 50:2 Winter 1986. The entire issue is given to this subject. See also ME 5:850-853 and the literature cited.

Other Resources: Beulah Stauffer Hostetler, *American Mennonites and Protestant Movements*, Scottdale, Pa.: Herald Press, 1987. Frank H. Epp, *Mennonites in Canada, 1920-1940*, Toronto, Ont.: Macmillan, 1982 (volume 3 in process). David A. Haury, *Prairie People: A History of the Western District Conference*, Newton, Kan.: Faith and Life Press, 1981. Carlton O. Wittlinger, *Quest for Piety and Obedience: The Story of the Brethren in*

Christ, Nappanee, Ind.: Evangel Press, 1978. John A. Toews, *A History of the Mennonite Brethren Church,* Fresno, Calif.: Board of Christian Literature, 1975. J. R. Burkholder and Calvin Redekop, eds., *Kingdom, Cross, and Community,* Scottdale, Pa.: Herald Press, 1976. Contact any MCC or conference office, Mennonite museum or information office for audiovisual resources.

22

The Continuing Vision

IN THE PRECEDING CHAPTERS the history of the Anabaptists and the
Mennonites has been told from earliest beginnings to the present.
It is a history of obedience and disobedience, of human strength
and weakness, and of the grace of God. It is human history, in
which by faith we see the hand of God.

Having studied this history, it is in order to ask questions
about its meaning for the individual, the church, and the world today. Does the Anabaptist-Mennonite faith have a contribution to
make to our own day which would not be made without it and, if
so, what is it? If it has vital significance for people today, why is it
that the Mennonites have remained a small denomination of just
under 900,000 members in a Christian community of about 1.5 million persons worldwide in 1992? We know that statistics are not a
measure of faithfulness, but the question is still there: have Mennonites "kept the faith," is it only a history or also a heritage, and how
is it being expressed? In an article entitled "Influenced but Not Imprisoned by Our Heritage" Robert S. Kreider writes:

> A few months ago a middle-aged Mennonite university professor
> commented to me: "I am working on the spiritual capital of my par-
> ents. They gave me a powerful heritage—a memory of suffering in
> Russia, exodus, tragedy and deliverance, and then an ethnic thing
> (German language and all) to rebel against; what spiritual capital am I

building into my kids? . . . We can't live for long on the heritage of the early 1920s."

Nor, we might add, on the heritage of the sixteenth century, unless we reinterpret it and find fresh applications for it in our own experience. Kreider goes on to say:

> I am of the conviction that our Mennonite heritage speaks to the sickness of our society. Here are people who take seriously the biblical record and their dramatic Anabaptist-Mennonite heritage. This heritage expressed in the language of family, smallness, neighborliness might offer answers to the ills of our society with its vacuum of the soul, its value-free chatter, its rootlessness, its restless movement, its mindless conformity, its buy-use-and-throw-away approach to things and people, its dreary sameness, its temporariness, its bondage to public opinion, its pressures "to be with it," its manipulation of images.[1]

In an article on "Mennonite" in ME 5:555-557, Rodney J. Sawatsky writes a final sentence as follows: "To be a Mennonite then means to identify with a particular Christian community with a particular story, remembering what has been in the beginning and over time, and shaping what might yet be to the glory of God."

With these comments in mind let us return once more to the Anabaptists, with whom we are now familiar, to see how they fitted into their time and served the people of their day. In so doing we may see more clearly the issues and possibilities facing Mennonites and all believers church people as we near the year 2000. Let us do this by seeing the Anabaptists both as others saw them and as they saw themselves as individuals and as a people. Let us place these images into the context of our contemporary life to see if they belong and how these images might be applied. Times have changed, but in doing this we should be alert to (a) the unchanging nature of the good news of Jesus Christ, (b) the human inclination to sin which has not changed with increased knowledge, and (c) the continuing tension between the church as the people of God and society as our human context.

Revolutionaries

In turning to the sixteenth century we are struck by the extremely harsh names with which the Anabaptists were identified by some of their contemporaries, who honestly considered them to be tools of the devil. Surely such hatred must have shriveled the souls of those who felt it and closed their eyes to new truth. For the most part, however, these were persons in authority in Catholic or Protestant churches, or in the state. The common people were not unfriendly to the Anabaptists, unless they were aroused by the authorities. The hatred of officials was, in fact, poured out upon the Anabaptists precisely because they were so popular with the people.

When we search for the reasons for this popularity, we soon discover that the clean living and simple faith of the Anabaptists met a deep longing in the hearts of the people who were disgusted with the corruption of the church and the oppression of the state. In redefining the nature of the church to consist of believers only, the Anabaptists were also redefining the nature of the state, since church and state were one society which all were expected to enter through infant baptism. As heretics they were thus also considered to be revolutionaries, people intent on undermining the state. The charge of sedition, of revolution, is very common in the records of the court hearings available to us.

There were other reasons for this charge in addition to their rejection of infant baptism as the rite of passage into the church. They refused to swear an oath of any kind, including the required annual oath of loyalty to the state;[2] they would not serve as soldiers and most believed a Christian should not be in government; because of persecution they frequently met at unusual times and places, giving the further impression of secrecy and subversion. Besides this, they were extremely zealous promoters of their cause, ignoring all risks for the sake of spreading their faith. Felix Mantz was one of the first of many who died because they would not promise to keep quiet about their faith. When they were caught and tortured and burned, they died as victors, not as victims of a cruel age, confident to the end that their cause would ultimately triumph. All of these signs convinced the authorities that they were dealing with dangerous revolutionaries for whom the only answer was death.

There was a final major reason for calling the Anabaptists revolutionaries. Revolution meant violence to the authorities. The tragic events of the Peasants' Revolt under the leadership of Thomas Müntzer (chapter 1) and the equally tragic Münster episode a few years later (chapter 6) convinced them that all Anabaptists were revolutionary at heart. Even the most peaceful, they said, were no more than wolves in sheep's clothing waiting for the right moment to overthrow all government and order: "For although Müntzer is thrown down, yet his spirit is not; it lives even yet, indeed rules in many corners—especially in the Anabaptist sect which was planted by Müntzer in this part of the land—and it has been impossible up to now to root it out."[3]

This interpretation of Anabaptism as being related to the revolutionary violence of Müntzer and Münster was more polemical than historical, though there was a relationship. Chapters 2 and 6 have traced the connections as understood now. In their legitimate attempts to show the peaceful nonrevolutionary nature of Anabaptism, Mennonite and other scholars have over time obscured the truly radical nature of the first generation of the movement. They have emerged as unfortunate victims who were born before the world was ready for them, as quiet and timid people who wanted only to be left alone. But this is not a faithful reading of the sources and was not the image most of the early Anabaptists had of themselves. They did not want pity; they were out to change the lives and destinies of people at any cost. In a way they were indeed revolutionaries, and history has shown that they did succeed in changing both church and society at numerous points.

We have shown that most Anabaptists were peaceful. Instead of violence their approach to change was love, witness, and faithful discipleship; but this method was already so revolutionary that it threatened the foundation of church and state enough for the authorities to execute all the Anabaptists they could find as a measure of self-defense. The Anabaptists did not have a revolutionary program for society; their message was a call to repentance and obedience, but they knew that those who responded would need to make a radical break with the old church and with society. With the apostle Paul they were announcing a new order (2 Corinthians 5:17) and like him, were accused of turning the world upside down (Acts 17:6). It was revolutionary to propose the complete separation of church and state as they did, together with freedom of religion, and a church composed of adults who would freely decide whether to join it or not. It was revolutionary to reject the sacramental system, to say that people are not saved by works, but neither are they saved without them. Both Catholics and Protestants condemned them on this last point.

In human history the nonviolent revolutions promoted by people like the Anabaptists have usually been more effective and have changed the course of society more permanently than violent political or other revolutions. We are not used to a pacifist reading of history. The means used to achieve a given end cannot be separated from the end itself. We think of the deep changes over the centuries in the history of ideas, of science and its Copernican Revolution, of the Industrial Revolution and the revolutionary developments in contemporary technology. Revolution in itself is not a bad word but has come to be so interpreted because it is associated with violence and brings rapid changes which threaten the established order.

To accept the label of *revolutionaries* for the sixteenth-century Anabaptists, therefore, means to associate with them a great vision and courageous witness in the face of severe resistance from church and state. It means a willingness to pay the highest price anyone can pay, life itself, to see the vision realized. Normally people resist change today as much as they did nearly 500 years ago. They still confuse the church with their cultural environment and are often unable to distinguish between church and society. It is truly difficult to be counter-culture meaningfully. People will go to great lengths to defend themselves against those who threaten the established order. Whether the heirs of the Anabaptists can in their turn be revolutionaries in the highest sense of the word also, speaking and acting on the many social and spiritual problems of our day depends on the extent of their "owning" of the biblical witness and identity in our day as the Anabaptists did.

Socialists

Related to the charge of being revolutionaries was the interpretation of the Anabaptists as socialists or even communists. It was believed that they came from the lower classes of society, and that all of them practiced community of goods, even of wives, a system which they hoped to impose on everyone eventually. Court hearings and inquisitions in torture chambers, often centered around economic issues, showing how afraid the privileged classes were of losing their wealth and status. That the Anabaptists were pioneers of economic and social justice is amply verified by the sources. Their economic practices need further study.

Many of the charges, however, were not true as stated. We know now that Anabaptism did have a particular appeal among the poor, but we know also that they counted persons from all classes of society among their members—laborers, nobles, priests, artisans, fishermen, theologians, and others. It is also well known that only one group of Anabaptists, the Hutterian Brethren, practiced complete community of goods, and that none of them ever believed it could or should be practiced among any except believers who agreed to do so voluntarily. But all Anabaptists believed that the Christian has no moral right to a selfish enjoyment of goods while others suffer want. While being severely tortured one Anabaptist said:

> And as to community of goods, no one is forced among us to put his property in a common treasury and we have no intention of making it common by force. But he who possesses and then sees his brother or sister in need, he is duty bound in love and without constraint to help and to succor.[4]

But they refused to believe him as they refused to believe the others, and suspected him of communism. Under further torture they told him, "Though you say that this community of goods is meant for you and your people only, yet your heart and ambition are far different, in actuality to have the goods of all men [people] in common."

As with the former charge of being violent revolutionaries, so here the charge of communism against them was false, but underlying it was a deep insight into the nature of Anabaptism nevertheless—that Christians must not attach themselves to things in this world, but use them only as instruments in the service of God for the welfare of others. Their persecutors were suspicious of Anabaptist indifference to material possessions, an attitude which struck them as unnatural, crazy, and demonic.

In a time when the majority of the people of the world are poor and suffer malnutrition, and when an underlying factor in many revolutions of our day is a struggle between those who have and those who do not have food, clothing, and shelter, it goes without saying that the Anabaptist concern for sharing with the less fortunate is a vital part of Christian obedience. Modern Mennonites have a good record of global relief and service ministries, but even that is no more than a fraction of what they could do if an Anabaptist sense of responsibility for their neighbor really gripped them as a people. With the Anabaptists this sense of responsibility arose out of their great joy over what God had done for them in Jesus Christ. To help the needy physically as well as spiritually was an integral part of the good news of salvation. "First they gave themselves (2 Cor. 8:5).

Salvation-by-Works Christians

The Anabaptists were also often accused of trying to earn their own salvation instead of relying on the free grace of God because they stressed the importance of obedience and moral purity. Luther and the other Reformers also wanted clean living and church discipline, but they wanted even more to have everyone in the church in order to be saved. To them the church was like the ark of Noah, a place of refuge and salvation, while the Anabaptists saw the calling of the church to be a city set on a hill as an example for all to see. To the former grace was first and last, and while good works would hopefully grow out of faith, it was grace that really mattered. To the Anabaptists faith without works was dead, meaning that the way people lived showed how and what they believed.

Because of this, unfortunately, almost anyone living a clean life was suspected of being an Anabaptist. It was reported at the trial of Hans Jeger, for example, that "because he does not swear and because he leads an unoffensive life, therefore men suspect him of Anabaptism. . . . He has for a long time passed for such, because he did not swear, nor quarrel, nor did other such-like things." [5] Some even considered good works a hindrance to salvation and pointed to the disciplined life of the Anabaptists as a further sign of the work of the devil. So Bullinger wrote about good works that "this is an old trick of the devil, with which he has in all churches, from the days of the Apostle Paul, sought to catch his fish."

Historians today are quite protective of the late medieval period. Nevertheless, it must have been a wicked age if anyone who lived a clean moral life was suspected of being a heretic, an Anabaptist, because of it. For them, however, it was not work-righteousness, but holiness brought about through faith, by the power of the Holy Spirit. The first article of the Schleitheim Confession of 1527 speaks of the candidate for baptism as one who "desires to walk in the resurrection of Jesus Christ." Menno Simons wrote much about the relationship between grace and good works, including the following:

> The regenerate, therefore, lead a penitent and new life, for they are renewed in Christ and have received a new heart and Spirit. . . . And

they live no longer after the old corrupted nature of the first earthly Adam, but after the new upright nature of the new and heavenly Adam, Christ Jesus. . . . Their poor weak life they daily renew more and more, and that after the image of Him who created them. Their minds are like the mind of Christ: they gladly walk as He walked; they crucify and tame their flesh with all its evil lusts. . . . They put on Christ and manifest His Spirit, nature, and power in all their conduct.[6]

This emphasis on obedience has been described by the word *discipleship*. The Anabaptists were convinced that Christians need not lightly resign themselves to the necessity of sinning; sin could be overcome by the grace of God. Thus their refusal to baptize infants was not because they believed that little children were not sinners. They were assured of the salvation of infants because in Jesus Christ, the second Adam, the sin of the first Adam had been overcome. Sin was primarily disobedience before God arising out of an act of the will. It has been suggested that they were able to achieve holiness in living because (1) they insisted on conversion and personal commitment of every member of the church, (2) they worshiped in small groups where everyone knew each other and could admonish and help each other, (3) they had high standards for the Christian life, (4) they practiced church discipline, and (5) they were able to keep themselves separated from the evil influences of society around them.[7]

If this witness is to continue among the Mennonites, this description of the church and discipleship might well serve as a model for today. Words are easily spoken, but often mean little. People need to see and experience the love of God in human relationships in order to believe. Christ was the Word of God made flesh, setting the pattern for his disciples to follow with his help. If the Mennonite faith can produce such disciples, then it has an urgent and continuing calling indeed.[8]

Bible Christians of the Reformation

Historians have identified two images of Anabaptism which may help us in understanding them. The first is that they were the Bible Christians of the Reformation. In 1931 Walther Koehler (d. 1948), a church historian of Heidelberg, wrote that "The Anabaptists are the Bible Christians of Reformation history . . . seeking to restore the Early Church of Jerusalem as a holy people, strictly separated from the world."[9] Before him an Old Catholic historian

C. A. Cornelius had called them *eine Kirche der Radikalen Bibel-leser*—a church radically committed to the reading of the Bible. More recently it has been said that the rediscovery of the Bible was *the* great and all-inclusive contribution of the Anabaptists, as seen in their attitude to the Scriptures:

> Thus, the inspiration, infallibility, unity, and authority of the Bible was fervently affirmed. Yet, they maintained the basic distinction between the old and new covenants; and they did this without denying the inspiration of the Old Testament.[10]

There is no doubt that Anabaptism arose because there were those who believed that the Scriptures meant what they said, and ought to be obeyed. Some of the early Anabaptist leaders had received a university education and had come under the influence of humanism. One of the major contributions of humanism to the Reformation, including the Anabaptists, was its stress upon the importance of studying the sources. Its slogan *ad fontes* (to the sources) led to a new interest in and recovery of the Scriptures, which in turn led to the Reformation. All of the major Reformers had been deeply influenced by humanist biblical studies in their earlier years, but where they insisted that only a trained minister could really interpret Scripture, the Anabaptists believed with Menno Simons that "the Word is plain; there are no glosses." David Joris (d. 1556) rejoiced that the Holy Spirit no longer spoke only in Hebrew, Greek, and Latin but now, finally, also in Dutch. Not that they understood it all, but they were troubled at how the learned were able to twist Scripture to suit their own purposes. So they became convinced that what was needed was not more knowledge but more obedience.

It was from the Scriptures that they also received their model of what the church should be like. Instead of a reformation they wanted *restitution*—to restore the New Testament church. The church had fallen by becoming a state church under Constantine in the fourth century and could be restored only by returning to a point before the fall. It was with the fall, they believed, that infant baptism, militarism, clericalism, and all the ungodly practices and doctrines had come into the church. The true church, according to Menno Simons, should have (1) pure doctrine, (2) scriptural use of the Lord's Supper and baptism, (3) obedience to the Word, (4) love, (5) a willingness to witness, and (6) a willingness to suffer. This was a desire to return to the first or primary model.

Originally founded to help Paraguayan Mennonite pioneers become better established economically, Mennonite Economic Development Associates (MEDA) has grown into a worldwide organization. Their projects include a credit union in Colombia, well drilling in Haiti and the Central American nations, encouraging **home industries** in the less developed countries, a shoe factory in Paraguay, a public transit system in Indonesia, and land development in Belize and Bolivia.

It is this faithfulness to the Scriptures, seeking to apply its message to the needs of our time, which makes the church more than just another organization set up by people to serve their own interests. Often the Scriptures are used by the Holy Spirit to bring under judgment the things people do and fail to do. Because of this no great renewal has ever occurred in the history of the church without a recovery of the Scriptures and a willingness to listen to what God is saying through them. The Bible is not God; it points to God and his saving work in the lives of those who follow him.

Mennonites are not the only people who love the Bible and seek to follow its teaching, of course, but many Christians still do not read it as seriously as the Anabaptists did who believed it meant what it said about love, peace, swearing of oaths, and other emphases which are contrary to human nature, and therefore, unpopular in any society. But if, as the Anabaptists believed, God is in control of the destinies of persons and nations, then those who know and do the divine will also serve the best interests of all as they serve God. The calling to be Bible Christians of the twentieth century in the full sense of the term as the Anabaptists understood it is a major challenge and holds great promise. The call for Mennonites to become this more fully, and witness to its power, remains an ongoing challenge.

People Ahead of Their Time

The second image historians have identified has been that the Anabaptists were far ahead of their time, advocating principles which it was to take further centuries to make acceptable, and some principles which still seem to be unacceptable to society. One of the men saying this was the German sociologist and historian Ernst Troeltsch (d. 1923), who ended his discussion of Anabaptism with the words, "The whole movement was an early premature triumph of the sectarian principles of the Free Churches." Among those who agreed with this view was the Quaker Rufus Jones, who wrote:

> And yet, as has happened many times before and since, with movements that have been showered with scorn and opprobrium, the conquered and defeated became in the end the conqueror . . . when nearly every one of the constructive principles of the Anabaptists got written into the Constitution of the United States, or got expressed in some important branch of American Christianity.[11]

By the "sectarian principles of the Free Churches" Troeltsch meant what Jones also implied, the separation of church and state, freedom of religion, and voluntary church membership. In contrast to these principles, much of the history of Europe has been characterized by a power struggle between church and state and the domination of one or the other; church membership has not been voluntary, and consequently there has been little freedom of religion, but many wars of religion. The Anabaptist hope for a church composed only of believers, free from interference by the state, was completely opposed to the idea of a state or people's church which included everyone from birth to death.

While these tributes are indeed encouraging, the Anabaptists do not deserve all the credit. Historian Roland H. Bainton has suggested that the principles of the voluntary church, the separation of church and state, and religious liberty came into North American life and thought more through the Puritans and the influence of the

French Revolution than through the Anabaptists, though the latter were the first to hold them in the Western world. Bainton does not deny the influence of Anabaptism in these areas, but limits it.[12]

Though these three principles are now generally accepted in the Western world, they are often misunderstood. The right of a person to believe or not to believe in Christ, as the principle of freedom of religion affirms, is often taken by believers to claim "what I believe is my business" which, in a believers church, is not adequate. Many Mennonite young people do not really make a free and independent, voluntary decision to be baptized and join the church; they do this because they are "old enough," or because their friends do, or their parents wish them to, or for other reasons. These reasons are important, but not primary. Similarly it is difficult to keep the demands of the state separate from the claims of Christ and his church, as indicated in the taxes for war issue, in business, in teaching in public school systems, and like situations.

A great contribution can be made to church and society by Christians who seriously hold these principles to be true and put them into practice. To believe in the separation of church and state then, for example, means to let word and deed speak to vital issues, to turn back nationalism in the church; to believe in freedom of religion then means to love those who believe differently and those who do not believe, while at the same time witnessing to the power of God in history and in one's own life; to believe in voluntary church membership then is the end of traditionalism, practicing believers baptism rather than adult baptism, and restoring the meaning of covenant in the congregation.

What Shall We Do With It?

Now that we have considered some of the possibilities of recapturing in a new way the biblical heritage as the Anabaptists did in the sixteenth century, what shall we do with it? There seem to be at least five choices before us, in addition to a variety of combinations of several of them:

First, we can choose to do nothing with it if we are Mennonites. Since a Mennonite has traditionally been defined as one who is born into a Mennonite family, there is really nothing those who are so born can or ought to do about it. Being a traditional Mennonite has become quite respectable by now—Mennonites have the reputation of being

Following British Quaker example, the Dutch Mennonites established their church camps and retreat centers during the 1920s. The first Mennonite camp in North America, Men-O-Lan, was established in 1938. Several of these "summer only" camps have evolved into year-round church centers. For a number of years Laurelville Mennonite Church Center hosted a **Christmas International** for the foreign students of various large university campuses.

good farmers and honest businessmen. If difficult questions are asked about the faith, we can always quote a text, or say that this is what our church teaches, without really knowing much about it ourselves.

Second, we have the choice of rejecting the claims of this history upon us as meaningless and irrelevant to our day and age. While the accounts of faith and martyrdom inspire us, these are all history. As a faith Mennonitism is then considered unrealistic and outdated in a time in which people struggle with poverty, justice, nationalism, drugs, racism, ecology, and population growth. But since it takes a good deal of courage to announce publicly that one is rejecting the faith, and raises a lot of fuss, a simpler way is to limit and finally neglect participation in the life of the church, drifting away little by little.

Third we can acknowledge the great contribution of the Anabaptist-Mennonite tradition to church and society, but also feel that the time has come to let Mennonitism die—either by changing the name and theological accent to something more acceptable in our culture, or by becoming nondenominational Christians, or by merging with other Christians. Such choices might be motivated by a feeling of sacrifice, or inferiority, or simply frustration with the organized church and a desire to get rid of all the traditionalism by starting over. If such a new beginning is made in small groups, discipline could become possible, and one might hope to prevent the old hardening of the arteries from repeating itself.

Fourth, in frustration over the sad state of the church as we may know it, we can select some period of the past, either in Anabaptist or earlier history, as the *Golden Age* and spend our time talking about how wonderful it would be if everyone would catch that vision of the church. All the while, however, we would continue to be conscious of the humanness of people even in the church of Christ, and we would recall the impossibility of turning back the pages of history to reproduce the past. Positively, the holding up of such a model for the church to imitate would remind Christians of their high calling in Christ; negatively, it could become an excuse for not becoming involved in the life and work of the church.

Fifth, we can choose Anabaptist-Mennonite history as the heritage of faith which seems to us to be a most faithful interpretation of the biblical message and by "owning" it—making it truly our own, testify to its truth and power in word and deed. The glory and obedience of our ancestors then becomes our history also, as does their stumbling and disobedience. In studying them we learn to understand ourselves better and become more able to discern where we are going, both as individuals and as a church. Instead of seeking to start over with the church we begin where we are. By accepting our past we become free to change, adapt, and relate in new ways to the needs of our time without being bound by traditionalism or by the emotional effects of rejecting the heritage. This choice means we then have nothing to defend—neither ourselves nor the church, nor a rejection of the church nor even the gospel; we have then only to testify to the power of Jesus Christ in the past and in our own living experience.

In July of 1990 some 25,000 Mennonites gathered together in Winnipeg, Manitoba, for the twelfth Mennonite World Conference (MWC). Nowhere has the life of Mennonitism around the world become more visible in a single event than in those sessions. Here was a sign of what the Anabaptist-Mennonites, a small part of the people of God, may yet become.

MWC had a small beginning in Switzerland in 1925 when approximately 100 Mennonites, including one North American, met to remember the 400th anniversary of the founding of the Swiss Brethren (Anabaptist) movement. It was a gathering of Germanic-Dutch Mennonites expressing gratitude for a rich heritage. Later conferences continued in this tradition, but gradually the meetings began to mirror the rising up of a believers church people around the world, sometimes called Mennonites, sometimes not, but always standing in the biblical stream of faith pioneered by the Anabaptists. More and more non-Western participants became involved until the ninth conference was held in Brazil in 1972, the first meeting away from Europe and North America.

And then came Winnipeg. Mennonites were still ethnic, of course, but now ethnic Africans, ethnic Asians, ethnic Cheyennes, ethnic Latin Americans, and yes, ethnic Germanic-Dutch Mennonites too, but all together a new family in Christ which the Spirit had raised up in the East and West and North and South. There was Bible study, and lectures, and preaching, and prayer, and carefully rehearsed drama, but the biggest drama was the unity of minds and hearts, and love expressed across national, racial, and cultural boundaries as participants discovered who they really were all together.

From this large new family a new identity emerged for each individual. They came from over sixty countries, speaking seventy-eight languages, but were one family in Christ. Mennonites a family church? Yes indeed, but with global dimensions vastly extending the experience of the early church recorded in Acts 2. In the sixteenth century there had been suffering and persecution of the Anabaptists in Europe, now it was happening in other places too. There had been faithfulness then and there was now, worldwide.

And so to the question of "What shall we do with it?" we need to add "What is the Spirit doing with it—with the Mennonites as part of God's people?" The future seemed to be as bright as the divine promises if, as Paul Peachey reminds us, we look for the "tender shoots," and discover that "many tender shoots of new growth are evident," in and far beyond Mennonitism, and we learn to nurture, cherish, and embrace this new growth.[13]

The **First Mennonite World Conference**, suggested by Christian Neff, was held in Basel, Switzerland, in 1925 to commemorate the 400th anniversary of the Anabaptist-Mennonite tradition. Attendance at the first conference was small, with only one delegate from America. By contrast, the **Tenth Mennonite World Conference** in Wichita, Kansas, in 1978 brought together 16,000 Mennonites from around the world (shown above). The **Eleventh Mennonite World Conference** was held in Strasbourg, France, in 1984, the **Twelfth** in Winnipeg, Manitoba, in July 1990, and the **Thirteenth** in Calcutta, India, in January 1997.

Endnotes

1. *The Mennonite*. 88:34 September 25, 1973, pp. 539-540.

2. Edmund Pries, "Oath Refusal in Zurich from 1525 to 1527: The Erratic Emergence of Anabaptist Practice," in Walter Klaassen, ed. *Anabaptism Revisited*. Scottdale, Pa.: Herald Press, 1992, pp. 65-84.

3. Justus Menius, *Von dem Geist der Wiederteuffer* (1544), quoted in Franklin H. Littell, *The Anabaptist View of the Church*. Second edition. Boston, Mass.: Starr King Press, 1958, p. 145.

4. *Quellen II*, p. 238, quoted in Leonard Verduin, *The Reformers and Their Stepchildren*. Grand Rapids, Mich.: Wm. B. Eerdmans Publishing Co., 1964, p. 235.

5. Ibid., pp. 108-109.

6. *Menno Simons, Complete Works* (1956), quoted in Harold S. Bender, MQR (April 1961), 35:100.

7. Ibid., pp. 108-109.

8. Alan Kreider, *Journey Towards Holiness*. Scottdale, Pa.: Herald Press, 1987.

9. *Die Religion in Geschichte und Gegenwart* (1931), 5:1916-1917.

10. Donovan E. Smucker, MQR (January 1945), 19:10.

11. *Mysticism and Democracy in the English Commonwealth*. Cambridge, Mass.: Harvard University Press, 1932, pp. 32, 33.

12. "The Anabaptist Contribution to History," in *The Recovery of the Anabaptist Vision*, Guy F. Hershberger, ed. Scottdale, Pa.: Herald Press, 1957, pp. 317-326.

13. Walter Klaassen, ed. *Anabaptism Revisited*. Scottdale, Pa.: Herald Press, 1992, p. 184. MWC *Handbook* (1990), pp. 15-17, 167-170. In the latter article Rodney J. Sawatsky asserts that Mennonite identity is: Located in community . . . shaped by history . . . defined by the incarnation . . . inspired by the kingdom . . . expressed in service . . . empowered by the Spirit . . . and rooted in God, who was, and is, and ever shall be (p. 170).

Other Resources: "Anabaptism," ME 5:23-26; "Mennonite," ME 5:555-557; "Historiography, Anabaptist," ME 5:378-382; "History, Theology of," ME 5:382-384. Walter Klaassen, ed. *Anabaptism Revisited*, Scottdale, Pa.: Herald Press, 1992. Idem, "The Relevance of Menno Simons; Past and Present," in George R. Brunk, ed., *Menno Simons: A Reappraisal*, Scottdale, Pa.: Herald Press, 1992, pp. 17-35. Idem, "Menno Simons: Molder of a Tradition," MQR (July 1988) 62:368-386. Timothy George, *Theology of the Reformers*, Nashville, Tenn.: Broadman Press, 1988, chapters 6 and 7. Werner O. Packull, "Some Reflections on the State of Anabaptist History: The Demise of a Normative Vision," *Studies in Religion*, 8 (1979), 313-323. Calvin W. Redekop and Samuel J. Steiner, eds., *Mennonite Identity*, New York, N.Y.: University Press of America, 1988. Calvin W. Redekop, *The Free Church and Seductive Culture*, Scottdale, Pa.: Herald Press, 1970.

Index

The Author

CORNELIUS J. DYCK comes to the writing of
this history from a wide background of
service in the church. Born in Russia, he
grew up in Canada, but later made his
home in the United States. From 1945-
1951 he served with the Mennonite Central Committee (MCC) in Europe and
South America and later as a member of
the MCC Executive Committee.

From 1951-1955 he pastored a Mennonite church in Kansas. In addition to
membership on numerous conference
and community boards and committees over the years, he served
as executive secretary of Mennonite World Conference from 1962-
1973.

Dyck received his Ph.D. degree from the University of Chicago
and has served as visiting fellow at other centers and universities in
North America and Europe. In addition to teaching at the Associated Mennonite Biblical Seminaries from 1959, Dyck was for two decades director of the Institute of Mennonite Studies, a research
agency of the seminaries.

He is the author and editor of numerous books, chapters of
books, and articles in professional journals. Biographical vignettes
and a bibliography of his major writings may be found in Walter
Klaassen, editor, *Anabaptism Revisited* (Scottdale, Pa.: Herald Press,
1992, pp. 189-209).

Dyck is married to Wilma L. Regier of Laird, Saskatchewan,
and they have three grown children. He is a member of the Hively
Avenue Mennonite Church in Elkhart, Indiana.